BRITAIN'S ECONOMIC PERFORMANCE

Despite more than a decade of major supply-side reform, serious doubts remain about the performance of Britain's economy. Will it be competitive enough to generate the extra jobs so urgently needed, or will inflation, capacity problems, technological shortcomings, and skill shortages once again prove the decisive factor?

At this critical juncture Britain needs to consider the factors which might underpin industrial success more than ever. Yet the Chancellor of the Exchequer made the astonishing decision to abolish the National Economic Development Council (NEDC). In this volume economists who have worked for the NEDC over the last ten years bring experience from the public and private sectors to bear in an authoratitive, hard-hitting and wide-ranging study.

What are the roots of Britain's lack of competitiveness?

- Investment and innovation: how innovative is Britain? Is it investing enough in fixed capital? Or in research and development or training?
- The City and industry: what has been the impact for industry for deregulation of the financial markets? Can we lift the curse of 'short termism'?
- The labour market: is pay still a problem in Britain? Why is unemployment so persistent? Will new training structures help?
- The structure of the UK economy: what are the implications of the decline of manufacturing and the rise of the service sector?

Britain's Economic Performance provides a clear and challenging account of how fifteen years of economic policy have led to such an impasse. It shows that a naive belief in the efficacy of the market has provided an inadequate platform for meeting the challenges facing a modern economy, and illustrates how industrial policy and corporate strategy can help Britain take a place in the first tier of a modern Europe.

D1365213

BRITAIN'S ECONOMIC PERFORMANCE

Edited by
Tony Buxton, Paul Chapman and
Paul Temple

London and New York

First published 1994
by Routledge
11 New Fetter Lane, London EC4P 4EE

Simultaneously published in the USA and Canada
by Routledge
29 West 35th Street, New York, NY 10001

Typeset in Garamond by
Mathematical Composition Setters Ltd, Salisbury, Wiltshire

Printed and bound in Great Britain by
Mackays of Chatham PLC, Chatham, Kent.

British Library Cataloguing in Publication Data
A catalogue record for this book is available from the British Library

Library of Congress Cataloging in Publication Data
Britain's economic performance / edited by Tony Buxton, Paul Chapman,
and Paul Temple.
    p. cm.
Includes bibliographical references and index.
ISBN 0-415-10872-1. — ISBN 0-415-10873-X (pbk.)
    1. Great Britain—Economic conditions—1945–   2. Great Britain–
–Economic policy—1945–   I. Buxton, Tony, 1946– . II. Chapman,
Paul G., 1952– . III. Temple, Paul, 1952– .
HC256.6.B7298   1994
338.941—dc20   93–45694
                                                              CIP

ISBN 0-415-10872-1   0-415-10873-X (pbk)

CONTENTS

CONTENTS

LIST OF FIGURES AND TABLES

FIGURES

Chapter 3

Chapter 4

Chapter 5

Chapter 6

Chapter 7

Chapter 9

Chapter 10

Chapter 11

Chapter 13

Chapter 14

Chapter 15

Chapter 16

Chapter 17

Chapter 18

TABLES

Chapter 3

Chapter 4

Chapter 5

Chapter 6

Chapter 7

Chapter 8

Chapter 9

Chapter 10

Chapter 11

Chapter 18

NOTES ON THE CONTRIBUTORS

Tony Buxton was an economics lecturer at Salford and Sheffield Universities before spending nine years at NEDO as an Economic Adviser. He is now a Principal Lecturer in Economics at London Guildhall University. His writings include published articles on industrial economics and two editions of NEDO's *British Industrial Peformance*.

Sir Geoffrey Chandler CBE, began his career as a journalist on the BBC and *Financial Times*, subsequently spending twenty-two years with the Royal Dutch/Shell Group in a variety of posts at home and abroad. He was Director General of NEDO between 1978 and 1983, Director of Industry Year 1986, and Industry Adviser to the Royal Society for the Encouragement of Arts, Manufactures and Commerce (RSA) until the end of 1992.

Dr Paul Chapman BSc, MA, PhD, is a lecturer in economics at the University of Dundee who also worked as an Economic Adviser at NEDO during 1991 and 1992. His publications have covered a wide variety of economic policy issues, including training, unemployment and regional labour markets. He is the author and co-author of two books on training policy.

Ciaran Driver has lectured in Economics and Statistics at a number of London universities. He was at NEDO for three years until 1986, and is now a Senior Lecturer in the Management School at the Imperial College of Science and Technology. He has written books on employment and investment, and has published numerous journal articles.

Dr Ewart Keep is a Senior Research Fellow in the Industrial Relations Research Unit, in Warwick Business School. He graduated from Royal Holloway College, University of London, in modern history and politics in 1979, and was subsequently employed in the CBI's Education and Training Division, before moving to Warwick University to undertake a PhD on industry-level collective bargaining. Since 1985 he has undertaken research within the IRRU on British training policy, and personnel policies for the education system's workforce.

David Mayes is Senior Research Fellow at the National Institute of Economic and Social Research and Honorary Professor at the University of St Andrews. He is also Co-ordinator of the ESRC's Single European Market Research Programme. He has published widely on economics and related disciplines, and his recent books include *Public Interest and Market Pressures: Problems Posed by Europe 1992*, *The External Implications of European Integration* and *Achieving Monetary Union*. He is an editor of the *Economic Journal* and a former Director of the New Zealand Institute of Economic Research.

Ken Mayhew has been a Fellow of Pembroke College, Oxford since 1976. From 1989 to 1990 he was Economic Director at NEDO. After reading Modern History at Worcester College, Oxford, and obtaining an MSc(Econ) from the LSE in 1970, he worked as an economic assistant at HM Treasury (1970–2), and as an Assistant Research Officer and Research Officer at the Oxford Institute of Economics and Statistics from 1972–81. From 1986 to 1988 he was Chairman of the Oxford University Social Studies Board. He is an Associate Editor of the *Oxford Review of Economic Policy* and former editor of the *Oxford Bulletin of Economics and Statistics*. He has worked as a consultant for various private and public sector organizations at home and abroad. His research interests include labour markets, organizational theory and design, macroeconomics, and his publications include: *Pay Policies for the Future* (edited with D. Robinson), 1983; *Trade Unions and the Labour Market*, 1983; *Providing Health Care* (edited with P. Fenn and A. McGuire), 1990; *Improving Incentives for the Low Paid* (edited with A. Bowen), 1990; *Reducing Regional Inequalities* (edited with A. Bowen), 1991.

Dr Derek J. Morris MA, DPhil, has been a Fellow and Tutor in Economics, Oriel College Oxford since 1970 and is currently Chairman of the Social Studies Board, Oxford University. From 1981 to 1984 he was Economic Director at NEDO. He has been a Director and Chairman of Oxford Economic Forecasting since 1984 and is an associate editor of the *Oxford Review of Economic Policy* and on the Editorial Board of *Oxford Economic Papers*. Author of numerous books and articles, primarily in the field of Industrial Economics; these include *Industrial Economics and Organisation* (with D. Hay) in 1991; *Unquoted Companies* (with D. Hay) in 1984; *Industrial Enterprises and Economic Reform in China, 1980–89* (with D. Hay) in 1993; *The Economic System in the UK*, 3rd edition 1984.

Andy Murfin has been at the Henley Centre for Economic Forecasting, the Centre for Labour Economics at the LSE, and at NEDO. He is currently an Adviser at the Bank of England. His publications include articles on industrial entry, price–quality and market share relationships, and on pricing behaviour.

Martin Ricketts DPhil, Professor of Economic Organization, took up the position of Dean of the School of Accounting, Business, and Economics and Pro Vice-Chancellor of the University of Buckingham on 1 January 1993. From

1991 he was Economic Director of NEDO. His main research interests are in the area of public choice, public finance, housing and economic organization. He is author of the *Economics of Business Enterprise: New Approaches to the Firm* (Harvester Wheatsheaf, 1987), and numerous other books and academic papers.

Dr Martha Prevezer is a Research Fellow at the Centre for Business Strategy, London Business School. She has worked as an economist with the Bank of England and as an Economic Adviser at NEDO from 1988 to 1992. Her research interests include the economics of both technology and capital markets. Her publications include *Capital Markets and Corporate Governance* (edited with Nicholas Dimsdale) for Oxford University Press (1994).

Soterios Soteri is a Research Officer at the National Institute of Economic and Social Research. He has been working on the National Institute's Econometric model of the UK economy. He has recently joined the team researching European integration and is working on the relative costs of redundancy across the EC.

Margaret Sharp is Senior Fellow and Director of Research at the Science Policy Research Unit (SPRU). Her interest in industrial policy stems from the time she spent at NEDO at the end of the 1970s and early 1980s, and she has written extensively in the area including *Europe and the New Technologies* (Pinter, 1985) and in Freeman, Sharp and Walker (eds), *Technology, and the Future of Europe* (Pinter, 1991).

Paul Temple is currently a Research Fellow at the Centre for Business Strategy, London Business School. He has lectured at universities in Britain and the United States and has also worked in television. Between 1989 and 1992 he was an Economic Adviser at NEDO, working on issues related to pay and productivity and international competitiveness. His publications include *The Business Game* (1985).

William Walker is Senior Fellow and Director of Research at the Science Policy Research Unit (SPRU). He has written widely on industrial innovation, military industries and the control of military technology, particularly in the nuclear field. In 1993, his publications have included the case-study of Britain in the book on *National Innovation Systems*, edited by Richard Nelson; *Nationalism, Internationalism and the European Defence Market* (with Philip Gummett) and the *World Inventory of Plutonium and Highly Enriched Uranium* (with David Albright and Frans Berkhout), published by Oxford University Press on behalf of the Stockholm International Peace Research Institute (SIPRI).

ACKNOWLEDGEMENTS

This book arose from work begun at the National Economic Development Office (NEDO) prior to its closure in 1992 and from discussions held at a conference at the London Business School in March 1993. We would like to thank all those members of the Office who contributed advice and suggestions, and for the input of the Economics Division 'Statistics Room' and especially that of Leslie-Anne O'Donnell, Marco Pianelli, Currim Oozer, Jane Powell and Jim Tricker. Geraldine Cooke provided invaluable advice and support throughout the project, and Will Hutton offered encouragement at an early and critical stage. We would also like to thank all those others whose help and forbearance made the book possible, in particular members of the Centre for Business Strategy at the London Business School.

The Editors

1

INTRODUCTION

Tony Buxton, Paul Chapman and Paul Temple

For longer than most people can remember, the question of Britain's economic performance has been close to the surface of political and economic debate. Within a few short years the brief flirtation with notions of a resurgence of economic strength has collapsed amidst feelings of disillusion, confusion and concern. This book has been written to provide a record of economic development in Britain over the recent past, as well as to provide a framework within which that record can be interpreted and discussed.

In a small way, the book's genesis forms a part of the economic record itself, since its origins can be traced to a brief statement by the then Chancellor of the Exchequer to the House of Commons, announcing the closure of the National Economic Development Council and Office (NEDC and NEDO). The date was 16 June 1992, almost midway between a General Election victory and the events of Black Wednesday. As examples of the maligned concept of 'corporatism', Mr Lamont said that their time was 'long passed' in a world now pursuing 'more market-oriented policies, the promotion of competition and the smooth functioning of market mechanisms'. But the pro-market sentiment was less strident than that of some of his predecessors, for the statement concluded that 'a close relationship between government and industry remains as essential as ever if we are to develop our policies to create in Britain a strong, dynamic and competitive economy. But the age of corporatism must be put firmly behind us'.

Most of the work programme of NEDO was thereby terminated. One part of the work-in-progress was a study by the Economics Division – British Industrial Performance – the latest in a series which over the years had provided authoritative accounts of economic progress across a broad front. The present study arises out of the ashes of that work, but enriched in at least two respects. First, it will not be vetted by the 'social partners' – or more especially the Treasury, which over the last decade has reasserted itself as a particularly zealous guardian of economic 'truth'. The result, we hope, is something considerably more challenging. Second, a number of economists have been invited to contribute their own views. They, like the editors, have worked at NEDO at some stage over the last decade and therefore have first-hand

1

knowledge of the role of the economist in policy-making. They also have collective experience of the problems of working for an allegedly independent organization charged with enhancing the competitiveness of British industry. The need neither to offend the government, nor the employers, nor the unions, frequently encouraged a blandness which had little hope of stimulating purposeful debate. Some of the frustrations are described in Chapter 2 by Sir Geoffrey Chandler, who served as Director General of NEDO during the crucial sea changes between 1978 and 1983, and who therefore witnessed both the dismantling of the 'Industrial Strategy' of the 1970s, as well as the early impact of an administration bent on the idea of 'disengaging' the government from industry.

The task of 'setting the record straight' is not as straightforward as it sounds. Two aspects of the nature of current economic debate in the UK stand out. One key obstacle to rational assessment is the way in which discussion has become so narrowly circumscribed. Thinking about economic policy has increasingly become confused about the difference between the *tools* of policy and the actual *objectives*, i.e. between means and ends. Basically this has meant the government is no longer seen as (at least partly) responsible for the economic health of the nation – for jobs, for job security and for longer-term prosperity – but is seen as responsible for the economic backcloth which it believes will achieve those things – removal of all obstacles to the functioning of the market, restoration of economic incentives, the 'creation of level playing fields' and so on. It is surprising how often it is simply accepted that 'government borrowing must come down' or that lower inflation, regardless of how it is achieved, is necessarily a good thing. Ultimately these and other statements are dependent upon a theory (or perhaps just a prejudice) about how the world behaves. Part of Mr Lamont's strictures against a corporatist society were aimed at those who would like to reintroduce more meaningful targets for economic policy; in effect, an unqualified belief in the market conveniently absolves government from responsibility for those ends that really matter to people. It seems astonishing that the decision by a political party, in September 1993, to put the creation of full employment back at the top of the political agenda could be treated with derision in some circles. Yet in 1945, at a time when many were predicting a rapid peace-time return to pre-war slump conditions, the idea of a goal of full employment was simply a starting point for a consensual view of the functioning of a decent, progressive and modern society. Quite why the situation is so different in the 1990s certainly requires some explanation.

A more specific example of the widespread confusion between targets and instruments and of direct relevance for the record of the last decade has been the question of manufacturing productivity which, at least in the contention of many, has been one of the recent successes. Equity considerations aside, productivity performance at the level of the entire economy has great consequences for living standards. But today, manufacturing industry employs only a little more than one-fifth of those in work, so that even a substantial improvement in manufacturing productivity growth could contribute only a little to the rate of advance in the economy as a whole. It is perhaps better to see the productivity record in manufacturing as a tool (and by no means the only one) by which industrial competitiveness can be enhanced and consequently output and employment increased. Yet the presumption of many commentators is that manufacturing industry is today 'leaner and fitter' as a result of the 1980s' spurt in productivity growth; having retrenched to a more appropriate base, capacity can confidently be expected to expand in future on a secure footing. Unfortunately a more complete picture would not be so sanguine. Contributions below provide a number of reasons for supposing that investment decisions may be systematically biased towards forms emphasizing a cost-cutting and employment-reducing route to productivity growth. If this is indeed the case, then redundancy may be the inevitable (if undesirable) sidekick of productivity advance.

The second aspect of contemporary economic debate which is pertinent is the way in which it so neatly follows the economic cycle. Most obvious in the case of inflation, many of the supply-side problems exposed in the boom conditions of the 1980s – skills shortages, demographic dips in numbers of school-leavers, the volatility of the housing market and its impact on worker mobility, the capacity and quality of transport infrastructure, and the relationship between industry and the City – have all receded into the background. It is absolutely essential that policy should transcend the stop–go cycle and not simply follow it.

A simple statement of the UK's record over a decade or more would be a laudable achievement in itself, but mere fact without interpretation is an impossibility. Accordingly, we have explicitly developed the various contributions around a framework suggested by the idea of 'competitiveness' at the international level. Appropriately, this is precisely the notion that has taxed the imagination of economists at NEDO since its inception in 1962. Even at that early stage the balance of payments was seen as an obstacle (or 'constraint') to the achievement of the faster rates of economic growth seen in France, Germany and elsewhere.

THE FACTORS BEHIND COMPETITIVENESS

At the level of the individual firm success or failure is based on the notion of competitiveness – its ability to compete and as a consequence to be successful and grow. The translation of the concept to the national level is more problematic. Perhaps more than anywhere those involved with the work of NEDO developed an increasingly sophisticated view of the basis of the UK's international competitiveness. Originally this was seen in very conventional terms – a problem of costs and prices – soluble, within a regime of fixed exchange rates, by a period of more rapid productivity growth (as, for example, envisaged in the National Plan of 1965), slower wage growth or, as events turned out, by the 'one-off' devaluation of sterling in 1967. By the early 1970s persistently faster rates of inflation in the UK than in many of her trading partners convinced many that a freely floating exchange rate might be the answer. But by the middle of the decade, and with the rapid acceleration of inflation in a devastating wage–price–devaluation spiral, it was increasingly asserted that the principal problem of competitiveness faced by the economy was one of 'non-price competitiveness' – that British producers could not get delivery right, or their marketing, or the specification that consumers increasingly desired. Moreover, rising exchange rates in Germany or Japan did not seem unduly to harm their competitive position in world markets. Meanwhile devaluation and depreciation of the pound may actually be making matters worse by encouraging producers to concentrate on price-sensitive sectors of the market rather than on more sophisticated sectors where longer-term growth might be quicker.

The issue of non-price or quality competitiveness is nowhere better illustrated than by the fact that today, hourly labour costs in UK manufacturing are only a little more than half those in Germany. Even allowing for productivity differences it is clear that unit labour costs are significantly lower in the UK; German success (and that of other economies such as Japan) can only be comprehended if the importance of *quality* competition is added to that of *price* competition. Over the recent past, productivity growth in UK manufacturing has indeed exceeded that in Germany, yet export performance has been inferior. As a result, between 1979 and 1990, UK manufacturing employment fell by over 25 per cent, in Germany by less than 1 per cent. The consequent strain on services to provide additional jobs to compensate has been far higher in the UK, as has the resulting level of unemployment.

Beyond all that was a deeper question, related not so much to the individual producers themselves, but to the *structural* aspects of the economy in which decisions are made. After all, can it be true that British management was *consistently* underperforming? The notion of *structural competitiveness*, as recently noted by the OECD (1992), refers to the fact that national institutions (especially in training, education, labour markets, capital markets and infrastructure) have consistent effects on individual firm performance. The UK, for example, has very distinctive patterns in the organization and financing of industry, in the provision of education and training, in the support by government of R&D and in the way in which many institutions combine to effect the operation of the labour market. These factors and many others help to condition the *strategic* behaviour of firms in the UK. Structural competitiveness is fundamental in explaining why the national economy continues, despite the importance of the processes of globalization and economic integration, as an essential unit of analysis. Differences between nations in their relative economic performance display remarkable persistence over time, and it is highly improbable that the discovery of the causes of this can ignore differences in national institutions. It is important in this respect that several of the contributors to this volume point to the fact that UK institutions are closer to, or are increasingly being modelled on, those observed in the US rather than those of our European partners. These differences may increasingly become serious sources of friction within Europe.

The explanation of differences in economic growth rates underpinning our approach can be contrasted with some alternatives. The textbook neoclassical approach emphasizes two fundamental forces in the growth process – population growth and technological change – which are themselves unexplained. The investments required to adapt to these opportunities are signalled by prices and coordinated by markets. Differences in national performance reflect the flexibility of producers to the signals thrown up, as well as to the inherent potential of economies – their 'endowments' in terms of the supplies of various factors of production. As expressed in the statement by Norman Lamont, the problem for policy is one of allowing markets to operate better, correcting where necessary for clearly defined 'market failure'. Even here, however, the case for intervention is not necessarily strong, and the idea of 'government failure' is pervasive in some influential circles – i.e. the view that even if markets are not working as well as they might in theory, there is no necessary reason why intervention should improve matters – politicians, regulators and others charged with the public interest are more likely to act either incompetently or simply in their own self-interest.

In the British case, thinking about policy has also been influenced by the Austrian School, who adopt a slightly more dynamic view of economic growth, emphasizing the role of the entrepreneur in spotting and acting upon favourable profit opportunities. In the 1980s much was heard about the creation of an 'enterprise culture', although what this meant in practice was rather more obscure, except that it appeared to involve small business – a sector which, despite its undoubted growth, does not appear to have performed as well as some of its European counterparts.

A rather different school of economists (based mainly in the US) emphasizes the institutional framework of the economy and its relationship to the competitive process. Institutions are no mere reflection of market forces but are shaped in specific periods and may function rather better in some contexts than others. Compared to the pace of developments in technology, institutional change can be very slow, and 'mis-match' or 'institutional failure' a real possibility. In the UK, for example, the centralization of political authority and the adversarial nature of political debate may be exactly opposed to the smooth functioning of more liberalized markets. In Germany the more decentralized power structure, combined with a similar market-oriented culture, may have operated more effectively in promoting competitiveness.

The framework we have adopted in this study owes something to all these approaches; it has also been informed by other developments in economic thinking, some of which are worth spelling out.

Some orthodox economists appear to have taken a major leap forward by placing much greater emphasis upon the role of investment processes, not simply in tangible forms of plant, equipment, building and so on, but also in intangible forms – education, training, research and development, marketing, etc. The key point in this literature is that investment processes are also essentially learning processes, both on the part of individuals and organizations. Significantly, the owners of private firms cannot therefore capture all the benefits from investment in the form of higher profits, and hence the social returns from investment will exceed private returns. Clearly, this provides considerable scope for policy intervention, but its effectiveness will depend upon the agents or institutions mobilized for that purpose.

At the same time, views of the nature of technology have been changing rapidly, away from the idea that technology can best be thought of in terms of 'codified' information (e.g., sets of blueprints) which can readily be transferred from one location to another, to a view of technology which is substantially more 'tacit' in nature – consisting of the skills of both individuals and teams and the specific competencies of firms. These factors in turn depend upon the *prior investment record* of the firm – in R&D, training and so on. In short, technology is much more costly to transfer than was commonly supposed, and depends upon the past history of firms and institutions. It follows that recessions may do much more damage to an economy's technology base than is apparent from the current loss of output. Certain types of company acquisition may have a similar effect. The importance of continuity within firms is well illustrated in the case of Japan, where management seems to realize more acutely that valuable *assets* are disappearing along with the current *cost* of a worker made redundant. The problem is partly that the value of such assets is very difficult to assess from the outside, and the governance structures of economies such as the UK and the US may be inimical to these kinds of investment.

In short, the view of economic performance that we are putting forward can be thought of as a synthesis of a number of perspectives. The key role played by external trade in determining the relative performance of regions or nations owes much to the extensions to Keynesianism suggested by the late Lord Kaldor, who argued that Keynes had overemphasized domestic saving and investment compared to exports and imports in an open economy. But this was also a persistent theme in the institutional history of NEDO. The question of competitiveness cannot, however, be reduced to one of either the effectiveness of markets or the behaviour of firms alone; institutions and infrastructure, both conceived in the broadest terms, really do matter. The contributors to this book may not themselves subscribe to all (if any) of these views; nevertheless we have placed their efforts within a framework suggested by the idea of structural competitiveness.

PLAN OF BOOK: SUPPLY-SIDE THEMES

Unravelling the elements of structural competitiveness is the task of interpretation we have set ourselves in this study. Apart from the chapter by Sir
Geoffrey Chandler, the book is grouped into five parts, corresponding to
themes reflecting major supply-side debates. If not all of them appear
immediately topical, then the reader should recall the way in which economic
discussion follows the real contours of the economy.

Each part has its own 'overview', intended to draw the reader's attention to
the main issues and present a judicious mix of fact and relevant theory.

Part I looks specifically at the UK's trading performance. The overview charts
the general parameters of Britain's overall performance in relation to other
major economies, its growth record and its susceptibility to recession. It is
argued that the balance of payments is fundamental to understanding the UK's
relative growth performance. The remaining chapters first examine the factors
immediately underpinning trading success – price versus non-price factors –
before taking a rather more detailed look at the trade performance of UK
manufacturing industry.

Part II examines investment (in a broad sense) and innovation as the foundations for competitiveness. The overview tracks the comparative record of the
UK over the past decade or more for a number of indicators. Subsequent
chapters discuss the roles of fixed investment and training, as well as the
relationship between profitability, investment and economic performance.

Part III turns to the perennial controversy about the relationship between the
City and industry. The overview shows to what extent Britain really does differ
from Germany and Japan in its forms of corporate control, and how this fits
in with conventional measures of corporate financing. The performance of the
financial sector is reviewed. The role of the Stock Exchange then comes under
scrutiny. Can the idea of short-termism be given a precise interpretation or is
it simply inconsistent with rational economic behaviour? Strong reasons emerge
for doubting the efficacy of 'outsider control' of management, however
efficient the institutions of the City. The impact on investment may be
considerable.

The labour market forms the basis for investigation in Part IV. The overview
challenges the relevance of the simple model of how labour markets work. The
thorny problem of pay is re-examined as well as the idiosyncratic 'voluntaristic'
approach to training. In both, decentralization has been a key issue. In the case
of pay determination it is arguable that the problem of inflation may have been
exacerbated by the growing number of bargaining units, while the increased
'flexibility' and responsiveness to local labour market conditions may not have
been realized. Rapidly-changing training policy has been a theme of the past
decade where the rhetoric of a highly skilled, highly trained workforce
responding rapidly to the challenges of a technically-oriented economy,

contrasts ill with the claimed need for lower labour costs and Britain's unwillingness to participate in the social aspects of the Maastricht Treaty.

Part V examines issues relating to the rapidly changing economic world in which Britain exists – globalization, technological change, European economic integration, the increasing importance of services and the role of manufacturing have all changed both the nature of, and the scope for, economic policy. Old-fashioned industrial policy aimed at lame ducks and the efficient run-down of ailing industries is being replaced increasingly by technology policy.

The book contains many chapters and yet there are clearly many omissions. Many familiar themes such as monetary and fiscal policy were long ago deemed to be outside the remit of NEDO, and they do not feature here, despite their undoubted relevance to tripartite debate. In addition, the very important work done at the individual industrial level, for the NEDO sector groups and working parties, has been omitted for lack of space. What remains is an exploration of the supply-side of the British economy using the tools of the applied economist. We hope that it will be of considerable interest to a wide spectrum of readers – the target for most of the output of NEDO's Economics Division over its thirty-year life.

REFERENCE

Organization for Economic Co-operation and Development (1992), *Technology and the Economy: The Key Relationships*, Paris: OECD.

2

THE POLITICAL HANDICAP

Sir Geoffrey Chandler

THE POLITICAL ROLLER COASTER

For some forty-five years party politics have imposed their own particular burden on a British industry already suffering from the self-inflicted wounds of low skills, poor training and inadequate investment. The political process has been wholly inimical to industrial success. The Labour Party's exaggerated belief in the efficacy of the state has vied with the Conservative Party's exaggerated belief in the efficacy of the market to bring damaging fluctuations of policy towards industry. In its crudest and most visible form the impact was manifested in the obsession with ownership rather than efficiency. It was visible not only in the fluctuations *between* rival administrations, but also *within* administrations as the ideological rigidities with which each government entered office were tempered by industrial imperatives.

There is growing understanding today of the complexity of causes which have brought the United Kingdom to the bottom of the major industrial league by almost every relevant measure. It is increasingly clear that we need to reject any theory of single scapegoats, whether in management, the City, the trade union movement or government. None the less, while industrialists must ultimately solve the problems of industry, the role of politics and the political process requires special attention.

This is not only because in a mixed economy (whatever the changes to the boundaries of ownership) government will remain a huge investor, supplier to and purchaser from industry, significantly influencing the private as well as the public sector; nor simply because as legislator and tax gatherer government has immense impact on industrial competitiveness. It is also because the adversarial nature of British politics, exaggerated by an inequitable electoral process, has damagingly infected the two chief institutions of industry and the whole of national debate. This has not only prevented what should be an attainable consensus within industry itself, but stifled debate altogether. There is the further reason that government, as the elected leadership of the country, has an inalienable responsibility for telling the facts in perspective and pointing the direction ahead.

9

Britain's growth rate in the post-war period, fast by our own standards, helped to disguise the decline relative to our competitors. The creation of the National Economic Development Council[1] in 1962 by a Conservative government reflected some recognition of the problem and of the need for joint solutions; but while its roots were embedded deeply enough in principle to enable it to survive through subsequent changes of government for the next thirty years, its influence in practice remained less than its potential.

From 1962 the trend of relative failure continued inexorably regardless of the complexion of government. In terms of conventionally measured gross domestic product per head – a crude approximation for standard of living – Germany and France surpassed us in the 1960s, Japan in the 1980s and Italy by 1990. No government gave uniform support to the competitiveness of industry in all its policies, even where it declared the intention of doing so. Each chose initially to pursue those aspects of policy which were ideologically attractive to it and which, even if relevant to the problem, could only make a partial impact if other policies had a contrary effect. We witnessed not only sharp reversals of policy as governments changed, but also reversals of policy within the lifetime of governments.

Most economic policies affect industry, but government attitudes to industry are chiefly manifested in those policies whose primary aim is to influence industrial structure and performance, and it is these which can be collectively described as 'industrial policy'. In May 1979, with the change from Labour to Conservative, there were few points at which the contrast between governments was more sharply focused than here. For some three-and-a-half years the Labour government's *Approach to Industrial Strategy* had provided a framework for its industrial policy, using the NEDC mechanism – in particular the tripartite sectoral committees and the NED Office – as an integral part of that approach. This was a 'supply-side' policy in which priority was explicitly given to industrial development 'over consumption or even our social objectives'[2] although in practice many government actions and attitudes remained inconsistent with this priority.

The 'industrial strategy' (the modesty of the White Paper's title was soon omitted in the over-politicizing of the exercise) made considerable sense so long as its limitations were recognized. Tangible results undoubtedly appeared inadequate in relation to the effort put in, but the achievement of joint understanding at sectoral level of the nature of the problems – their complexity and the need for joint solutions – meant that there were few managers, trade unionists or civil servants involved who did not learn from the exercise, even if that knowledge went little further. And the growing understanding at national level that our fundamental problem was one of competitiveness, insoluble through demand management alone, was assisted both by the committees' and the NED Office's analytical work.

The NED Council itself became chiefly the coordinator of the committees, giving them weight and authority, while broader policy discussion was emasculated, a process accentuated by the close bilateral relationship between the TUC and the Labour Government. Certain subjects, for example pay, were by common consent – including that of the CBI – explicitly taboo. While this avoided potentially disruptive subjects, it was clearly not fulfilling the potential of the Council and this period remained the source of much ex-ministerial disillusion on the Labour benches about the function and capabilities of the Council, although it was the government representatives, as was to be the case with most of their Conservative successors, who contributed to its impotence until an impatient Chancellor finally dealt a mortal blow to the whole organization.

The Conservative victory of May 1979 brought radical change. Over the next thirteen years there were to be ten Secretaries of State for Industry,[3] a rapid succession which if it happened in industry itself would be accounted indifference or incompetence. They differed in temperament, philosophy, approach and understanding, although all shared the new Government's objective of 'rolling back the frontiers of the State and improving the functioning of the market economy'.[4] The first, Sir Keith Joseph, doubted whether there should be a Department of Industry at all. The second, Patrick Jenkin, undertook to be 'the voice of industry in Cabinet', a concept anathema to his predecessor, extolling what government was doing for industry rather than minimizing it as undesirable. Paul Channon, number six, in 1987 presented a view of government policy as being 'designed to establish a framework for enterprise within which industry and commerce can thrive and therefore maximize the production of wealth in this country'.[5] He believed that 'the surest – indeed the only – route to this is through a properly functioning free market'. No phrase has proved more debilitating to constructive thought than the 'free market'. The market as we know it in practice is constrained by health and safety, environmental and employment regulations reflecting the views of society at a particular point in history, posing no pragmatic or ideological obstacles to further limits to its freedom. But the phrase was used to caricature – with Manichean distinction – any suggested alternative as an East European style of command economy.

Lord Young, Channon's successor and one of the longer-serving incumbents with just over two years in the post, brought all the aids – and costs – of modern image-making into play to implement his 'Enterprise Initiative'. This initiative, with its implicit recognition that the market needed prodding and did not work successfully on its own, had more in common with Labour's 'industrial strategy' than with prevailing doctrines. Nicholas Ridley, following Lord Young and closer to Joseph in approach, reportedly believed that the DTI should be left to wither on the vine. Others lacked either the time, capability or inclination to make a mark beyond dogged adherence to the policies of increasing competition, 'levelling playing fields' and supporting small businesses.

No-one exemplified the change of attitude more strikingly than the first. As an individual, Sir Keith Joseph brought a breath of fresh air to political life and

11

thought. A capacity for listening, an intellectual honesty and a rigorous logic, allied to a limited understanding of people or of the realities of industrial life, made a remarkable combination. Joseph inexorably pursued the logic of his beliefs in small things – the change of name of the Social Science Research Council to the Economic and Social Research Council (sociology not being accepted as a science) – as he did in big. When he was right – as in his later identification of the 40 per cent of children effectively excluded from education by a narrowly academic curriculum – he was very right; when wrong – as in his understanding of the industrial market – he was very wrong. His beliefs appeared to postulate a market of theory, rather than the international market in which the governments of our main competitive countries worked fruitfully with industry, or at least did it no harm. Their provenance could in great degree be derived from the reading list which, uniquely among ministers, he gave to his officials on taking office.[6]

He regarded NEDC meetings as 'a dialogue of the deaf'; would emerge from them murmuring 'railway arches', implying – with some justification – that small businesses would burgeon given appropriate locations; and believed that government's industrial policy should be to have no policy. The Taoist apophthegm 'Do nothing, and nothing will not be done' could well have been his motto: providing a 'framework' and leaving everything else to the market would resolve matters satisfactorily without intervention from government. The trouble was that doing nothing meant that nothing, or too little, would be done. Underlying the new policies appeared to be a widespread ignorance of the nature and extent of the problems of industry. Manufacturing was no Frog-Prince to be awakened by the kiss of monetary policy or fiercer competition, but a Rip Van Winkle, which, with notable exceptions of excellence to be found in individual companies in almost every sector, had slept for a century while its competitors moved ahead in the development of human resources and application of technology.

A new paradigm emerged: of a country whose wealth would henceforth be dependent on services, on profits remitted from overseas investment, and on North Sea oil. Manufacturing was seen as a balancing item, which, if temporarily eclipsed by the impact of oil, would automatically revive as oil declined. That the reverse was true – that manufactures would need to continue to be the most significant element in our international trade, that traded services, while growing fast and enjoying a positive balance of payments, were losing market share as had manufacturing earlier, that the nature and time-scale of manufacturing did not allow it to be switched on and off – was then an unfamiliar thought.

The British problem was that individual examples of excellence remained individual and did not spread to other parts of their sectors. This was not lack of knowledge: each NEDC sectoral committee could point clearly to the elements required for higher productivity for each part of industry they dealt with. The resistance to change of the industrial environment as a whole stemmed from other factors: from the failure of the conventional stimuli to better management – shareholders, non-executive directors, an involved workforce, the trade unions – and from the deep-seated handicap of an unsuitable education, inadequate training and anti-industrial attitudes. It was astonishing that in a political atmosphere where sporting metaphors abounded – the creation of level playing fields (that is, the equalizing of competitive conditions) and getting our competitors to play cricket – little thought was given to the quality and training of the players themselves which most of the electorate would know were fundamental whatever the state of the pitch. It naively postulated an industrial competence which, once the fetters were removed, would take its rightful place in the world.

In addition, as the trade unions were put on the defensive and their influence modified by legislation long overdue and welcomed both by the country and majority of trade unionists, a new and corrupting concept entered the scene. This was 'the right to manage'. 'I have given you back the right to manage', said the Prime Minister, Margaret Thatcher, at a CBI annual dinner. It was a 'right' frequently invoked by the Coal Board in the 1984–5 dispute, by ministers,[7] and even used, so pervasive did the concept become, by the former official conciliator, Sir Pat Lowry of the Advisory Conciliation and Arbitration Service.[8] It was a concept which ignored the experience and example of successful managers; it implied wholesale ignorance of the work of behavioural scientists and pioneering employers who over the years had demonstrated that effective management is by consent not authority, requiring all the human and intellectual skills a manager can summon; it ran counter to the recognition, to which at least lip-service was paid by successive presidents of the CBI, of the need for the better involvement of the workforce. It assisted a management style characterized as 'macho' which might be briefly successful in financial terms, but would lay no foundations for a long-term future.

Discussion of policy was hampered by a dogmatism of approach seen as necessary to the implementation of that policy. Joseph claimed that the only alternative offered was a 'siege economy'. While it was true that successive TUC conferences and many beleaguered industrialists called for protection, if only on a transitional basis, most realized that protection would only deal with the symptoms of relative decline while leaving the causes untouched.

The NEDC sat only on the periphery of the power centres of Westminster and Whitehall. But because it was the only regular forum for national economic debate, other than Parliament; because the sectoral committees and the Office were the only entities voicing an unpoliticized view of the needs and problems of industry; and because Sir Geoffrey Howe, the new Chancellor in 1979, with a considerable degree of courage and optimism, initiated a series of macroeconomic discussions in which all aspects of government policy were for the first time for many years put on the table, NEDC reflected with remarkable clarity the conflicts and contradictions of the time. Furthermore, for much of the 1980s, the Council was the only forum for government and trade union dialogue and indeed for CBI and TUC dialogue.

Given this climate, if any discussion of industrial policy was to be continued at national level in the NEDC it had to be done in a fashion which did not offend too obviously against prevailing beliefs. In a paper for the October 1981 NEDC,[9] widely accepted by the CBI, TUC and also Government, the Office approached the issue by examining the industrial policies pursued by our Continental competitors. It noted that the wide spectrum of policy measures operated on the Continent since the war had almost all been pursued by the United Kingdom at some time over the same period. But UK performance had been signally worse than our competitors. While recognizing that the factors determining industrial success were complex and varied, precluding the selection of any single policy, institutional framework, or type of expenditure, certain characteristics appeared to be common and to have played a contributory role in success.

These characteristics were continuity and stability of policy; concentration of effort with mutually reinforcing packages of measures; a realistic view of long-term priorities, considering systematically how the structure of industry might look in the longer term; an element of choice or selectivity; massive investment in human resources; and, finally, consensus (whether explicit or implicit) and commitment, both at national and company level.

None of these characteristics was dependent on a particular political or economic philosophy; they were common to countries which adhered strongly to market principles, such as West Germany, as well as to those with more dirigiste philosophies, such as France. None appeared beyond our own capabilities.

A second paper in April 1982 examined the record of the UK over the preceding twenty years in terms of the characteristics identified in the first. The central phenomenon emerging from this[10] was an underlying continuity and stability in the elements of UK industrial policy obscured by significant discontinuities at a general level. While capital incentives, regional and competition policy, support for research and development, trade policy, public purchasing, and standard setting were free from major fluctuations over a long period, this apparent continuity was overlain – and therefore destroyed in practice – by significant political change. This included the experiment with national planning in the mid-1960s; the move towards disengagement in 1970; its reversal in 1972; attempts to introduce a more central role for government in industrial performance in the mid-1970s; its abandonment and replacement by the 'industrial strategy'; and a renewed focus on disengagement from 1979. A further phenomenon was that these major changes were generally short-lived and were succeeded by convergence back to an identifiably more continuous progression of policy development.

It was probably naive to expect such a paper to find the same universal welcome from Council as its predecessor. The Secretary of State for Industry,

Patrick Jenkin, characterized it as 'cotton wool', providing him with no prescriptions. This should perhaps have been expected in that the analysis was a considerable indictment of the adverse impact of the political process on industrial performance from which the new administration could not be excepted.

THE STIFLING OF DEBATE

The inexorable conclusion was that ideology, however relevant to the distribution of income and wealth, was inimical to its creation. But the damage had been not only in the uncertainties added to those already inherent in industry, but also in the distortion or discrediting of ideas which would have been valuable in themselves had they been presented with a greater sense of the realities and needs of industry. There is logic in a disengagement which puts decisions nearer to the marketplace and further from politicians and civil servants: but disengagement needs to be qualified in a world where the market is comprised of governments which play a significant role in industry: it must be matched to our competitors' actions.

The 1977 Bullock Report[11] damaged sensible national discussion about participation and involvement within companies – a human and industrial necessity – by a political rather than pragmatic point of departure. A narrowly doctrinaire conclusion was allowed to set back progress on an aspect of human relations in industry in which we continue to lag woefully behind our competitors, and possibly in some cases was used as an excuse to do so. Sir Terence Beckett, Director-General of the CBI from 1980, repeatedly said that Bullock had 'poisoned the well'. But he never proposed digging another. And while the need for employee involvement was frequently urged at CBI conferences, it was never effectively followed up.

Disengagement made sense for Mrs Thatcher, pushing back responsibilities to where they should lie and seeking to make the market operate more effectively as a stimulus to industrial performance. But most thinking industrialists would argue that government policies remained inadequate for the real challenges they faced in a world where many other governments played a more perceptive and constructive role in relation to industry's complex problems. Moreover, the coining of the ironic phrase 'picking winners' – in other words politicians and civil servants attempting to second-guess the market and failing – contributed nothing to the argument when used to caricature all government intervention.

The NEDC potentially provided a forum for debate of these issues; but even with a chairman such as Sir Geoffrey Howe, who from his appointment as Chancellor in 1979 saw a use for the Council, many significant issues were proscribed, sometimes by one, sometimes by all three parties. The problem of pay settlements unrelated to productivity and greater than country or company might be able to afford has emerged in every economic downturn and was particularly acute in 1979. Incomes policies were deemed to have failed, although it was more accurate to say that their aftermath was considered worse than the success they temporarily enjoyed in restraining increases. But as a low-wage, though high labour-cost, economy it has never proved enough to attempt simply to preach wages down. There were a number of ways in which the subject could have been approached: the potential trade-offs within companies between training and investment on the one hand and pay restraint on the other; the better involvement of company employees enabling them to understand their mutuality of interest; or some form of incomes determination – a phrase devised to meet the TUC's legitimate objection that 'pay' did not relate to all types of income.

We had the spectacle of trade unionists advocating settlements they must have known to be destructive to competitiveness and therefore ultimately jobs; of managements doing nothing to inform or involve their workforce. None the less all proved undiscussable subjects, even if pay itself became an element in some macroeconomic discussions and the parties eventually agreed to the creation of a small tripartite working group on involvement (the Steering Group on Joint Arrangements at Company Level) under the chairmanship of the Director General. The government meanwhile resorted to exhortation on pay restraint for the private and cash limits for the public sector.

The ill-conceived and discredited national economic planning of the 1960s had left planning too as a non-discussable subject ever since – the British tradition of throwing out the baby with the bathwater. Any Council discussion which appeared to touch in any way on a government role in planning or strategy provoked caricature and trivialization from the government team. But it was precisely because we did not know the answer to these problems, or because past attempts at solving them had failed, that rational discussion of the limits and possibilities was necessary.

THE POLITICIZING OF INSTITUTIONS

The policy-swings from government to government were increased rather than diminished by industry's chief institutions, the CBI and TUC. Each lent weight to party political views rather than slowing the pendulum by using its unrivalled experience of industry as a counterweight to dogma. Under Labour governments the trade union movement sought legislation to strengthen its own position regardless of the impact on industrial success and regardless of management response. Under Conservative governments the CBI acted similarly. Politics predominated over industrial interest.

The CBI had forged close links with the Conservative Party during its years in opposition. At its first annual conference under the new regime, in November 1979, the closing address of the Director-General, Sir John Methven, contained the striking image that Britain was 'drinking at the Last Chance saloon'.[12] Methven was by temperament a diplomat and politician who had done much to put the CBI on the map by the initiation of its annual conference. While in no way matching the TUC annual conference as a serious policy-making occasion, it provided a media-opportunity compelling the presence of journalists and obtaining wide coverage. Its debates were stilted and any resolutions unpalatable to the leadership quietly ignored. But at least it acted as a sounding-board for some of the views of this vastly heterogeneous organization.

The metaphor of 'the Last Chance saloon' could well have implied the belief that business and industry could only flourish under a Conservative government. But Methven also called on business leaders to go out on the shop floor and in the schools and in the pubs to present the true economic position. Some companies, he said, had communications procedures that would 'make a quiet night in a Trappist monastery sound like the last night of the Proms'. The nation had to find a way to talk, to argue and work together like reasonable and responsible people in the search for common ground. 'The unions have tried it their way. Now let's try it our way.' Methven's premature death the following year left unknown the manner in which he might thereafter have led the CBI. But an extraordinary private discussion published posthumously (the journalist concerned asserting that death should put on the record what in life had been off)[13] suggested an antipathy to the trade union leadership which would have done little for a reasonable search for common ground.

His successor, Sir Terence Beckett, previously chairman and managing director of Ford, was a very different character – a straightforward industrial manager plunged into an unfamiliar political world. His first annual conference in November 1980 was to prove a watershed both for him and for the CBI. Spurred by the protests of some of his members to call for an easing of the current recession, Beckett spoke out. 'You had better face the brutal fact that the Conservative Party is in some ways a rather narrow alliance. How many of them in Parliament or the Cabinet have actually run a business? This matters. They do not all understand you. They think they do, but they do not.' Those in industry, he said, had 'to take the gloves off for a bare-knuckle fight', because effective and prosperous industry was vital.[14]

Beckett was right on most counts, but fighting the battle at the wrong time. He directed his criticism not only at the Government's monetary policies, but also at industry's own inadequacies, including the failure to involve and motivate employees. But only the first was heard. Keith Wickenden of European Ferries and Jeffrey Sterling, chairman of Town and City Properties, immediately resigned; and from a meeting with the Prime Minister the following day, unpropitiously planned before his speech, Beckett emerged expressing enthusiasm for Mrs Thatcher and calling it 'a very encouraging meeting'.[15] From then on the CBI was effectively muzzled, not by government, but by itself. Its diverse membership, the contribution of some member companies to Conservative Party funds, the seduction and flattery of senior industrialists by private meetings with ministers, and, for some, the hope of honours, all helped to neuter the CBI as an independent industrial voice.

Criticism of the Government was only permitted in the context of the Government's own monetary policies. The fundamental relationship between government and industry was not a discussable subject, although at the 1986 annual conference members present voted overwhelmingly for a 'coherent industrial strategy' for which James McFarlane, Director-General of the Engineering Employers' Federation, had skillfully argued, calling not for a return to the past, but for an intelligent synergy between government and industry which matched that of our competitors. The vote, carried in the teeth of opposition from the leadership, was thereafter ignored. If the sobriquet 'the Tory Party at work' was unfair to the CBI as a permanent appellation, there were occasions, not least during the election campaigns of 1987 and 1992, when public support for that party was voiced by leading CBI members, which fully merited the description.

The trade unions, 'their' party defeated, could expect to exercise little or no influence. The first TUC congress after the election called for the reversal of government measures, import controls and the abolition of cuts, with no discussion of how such measures might be resourced – themes which would be repeated annually. Abuse of a 'reactionary' government characterized most contributions, and the President, Tom Jackson, emphasized the need to plan relationships with a future Labour government.

Alienated by legislation they regarded as anti-union, and also, with greater justification, by the social insult some ministers heaped upon them, union leaders none the less for most of the period successfully fought off calls to leave the NEDC and continued to play their part both in Council and on the sectoral committees in some of which they made a real contribution. But the unions' inadequate research and analytical capability – disproportionately small in relation to their role and membership – made them the weakest members of NEDC.

Moreover, with the Labour Party in opposition, the tendency to regard the TUC as a surrogate for it made its representatives in NEDC acutely conscious of their constituency outside. It is conventional wisdom that the trade unions constitute an albatross round the Labour Party's neck: it is too little recognized that the reverse is also true and that the relationship hampers the contribution to industrial effectiveness that the unions might otherwise make in the interests of their members.

It might rationally be expected that the TUC and CBI could find some agreement at least on fundamentals. But the absence of any formal contact for many years, other than through the NEDC, meant that mutual ignorance was reinforced by mutual suspicion and hostility at both institutional and, in some cases, personal level.

THE SELECTIVITY OF DATA

If reasonable discussion was inhibited by unwillingness to tackle certain subjects, it was also hampered both by inadequacy and selectivity of data. There has been little indication that any government in the post-war period – or for that matter the City or industry – has fully understood the extent and nature of Britain's lack of industrial competitiveness or, what is crucially important for devising prescriptions, the length of our relative decline now measurable over a hundred years or more. Little in their actions demonstrated a long-term commitment to tackle so deep-seated a problem. Low inflation, competitive interest and exchange rates are necessary, but insufficient, conditions of success – 'hygiene factors' which, if wrong, will prevent growth, but if right will not transform performance or touch the fundamental causes of relative decline.

Statistics comparing British performance with that of our main industrial rivals were – and are – neither readily available nor popular. Comparisons unfavourable to the United Kingdom were condemned as 'gloom and doom' or as 'knocking Britain' rather than as a challenge and spur to action. The charge of 'moaning minnies' and of 'whingeing', while hardly contributing to intellectual debate, managed to suppress protest on the part of otherwise robust industrialists. Forecasts of domestic performance were more plentiful – and more prominent in the media – than analysis and fact. Government statistics charted domestic performance which might show improvement against an inadequate past, but told nothing of our standing in the market in which we operated.

The independence of the NED Office, together with its economic and statistical capability, gave it its one weapon in a world where power lay elsewhere. Both at micro- and macro-level its comparative analyses could illuminate problems and even stimulate action. Both were evident in 1981.

The growing dismay of significant industrial consumers of energy at what they saw as the disparity between British and Continental prices, in particular for electricity and gas, led to the Office submitting a paper to the Council illustrating the situation. Forewarned of this, the Secretary of State for Energy, David Howell, threatened that it would 'get a bloody nose' if it did so. The figures none the less provided sufficient grounds for the Council unprecedentedly to set up an Energy Task Force under the independent chairmanship of the Director General to analyse the situation and report back.

Such was government sensitivity to what might be interpreted as a retreat, the terms of reference were to contain nothing which suggested that the task force might make recommendations, although the CBI and industry – quite apart from the logic of the exercise – clearly expected this. The word 'conclusions' was therefore proscribed, as indeed was the word 'problems' lest this implied solutions were required. After marathon discussions, doggedly fought by the fuel suppliers, the case for the consumers was clearly demonstrated and, as a result, two successive budgets, in 1981 and 1982, gave £320 million relief in energy charges to industry. It was perhaps a pyrrhic victory: despite the acknowledged success of the exercise, the Office was never to be allowed such scope again.

At the macro-level the Office in July 1980 produced its first edition of *British Industrial Performance*,[16] a booklet intended to illustrate the underlying historical trends of British industry compared to our competitors over the preceding twenty years and the interdependence between broad economic policies and specific industrial performance. The data were purely historical, but the parties to Council, in particular the Government and TUC, argued over what should be included, the first anxious to illustrate any signs of upturn since they took office and to reveal the imperfections of the labour market, the second to minimize these imperfections and show the pain that industry was suffering. The booklet was indeed intended not as an academic economic record, but as a challenging backdrop to NEDC discussions illustrating the seriousness of the task we faced. More ambitiously, it was hoped that it could have a widely educational impact in a country ignorant of where it stood.

The draft of a second, more detailed, edition was put to the Council in March 1983, having been agreed with the Office by the staffs of the three parties. The historical comparisons, even though it was possible to illustrate some stabilizing of the UK share of international trade, remained sombre. Electioneering was already in the air and the Council was at its most sensitive. The president of the CBI, Sir Campbell Fraser, chairman of the failing Dunlop company, damned the document as being so gloomy that people would want 'to get the first boat out of the country' and moved for its rejection. Beckett did not believe publication would be productive because there was not a single item of cheer in it. The government, surprised, acceded. So too reluctantly did the TUC, agreeing to a postponement of two months. This was later to become the basis of a bizarre election canard when the minutes of the meeting were leaked to the press and the paper described as 'a secret report highlighting the grim prospects for jobs and industry in Britain ... deliberately held back'.[17] After the Conservative victory of 9 June this innocent historical document, whose statistics deliberately covered a period of time to show the continuity of relative decline under both Labour and Conservative governments, was duly published without demur and without a figure changed.

The Office suffered further in the 1983 pre-electoral period in presenting a paper summarizing a group of sectoral committee reports which took the view that there would be no employment increases in manufacturing in the coming decade. These were the views of senior managers, as well as trade unionists who might be expected to be pessimistic, and with knowledge of what has subsequently happened the paper was moderate in its prognoses. An advance leak in the *Financial Times* soured the meeting. (All the parties to Council leaked periodically if they saw it to be in their interest; *cui bono* was the surest test of who was responsible.) Beckett characterized the paper as depressing,

saying that he would sack anyone in his company who gave depressing forecasts, although privately, at a meeting a few weeks earlier of the Group of Four
(an informal gathering of the Permanent Secretary to the Treasury, the TUC
General Secretary, the CBI Director General and the NEDO Director General)
he had complained that great holes were being shot through British manufacturing capability which would be very damaging in the upturn. Bare
knuckles had become thickly gloved and the public voice of industry silenced.
Had the paper not been leaked it would probably have been suppressed. There
was no room for objective comment at times of political sensitivity.

Discussion also requires the availability of data on a consistent and agreed
basis. A memorable example of the frustration of discussion by the absence of
such data occurred at the February 1983 meeting of the NEDC. A paper
submitted by the Office analysing United Kingdom trading patterns indicated
UK strength in the slower growing world export markets and weakness in the
faster growing, with a similar mismatch in the supporting research and
development and investment back-up.[18] The Secretary of State for Trade,
Lord Cockfield, using a shorter time series as evidence, presented an optimistic
picture of UK trade and characterized the Office paper as 'muddled,
inaccurate, prejudicial and ill-informed', epithets duly reported in the press.
Yet only a few months later a trading deficit in manufactured goods was
recorded for the first time in history and economic recovery had begun to show
the familiar and ominous symptom of imports rising faster than exports. The
Secretary of State's attack may have been no more than a premature and
idiosyncratic shot in an electoral battle still to come, but its effect was to
preclude rational discussion and, by the provision of competitive data, to
obscure a central problem of industrial performance.

A third issue of *British Industrial Performance* was published in 1985; a
fourth, and last, in 1987. Today the UK's position in the world is obscured by
the predominance of purely domestic data. Indeed, from the more than a
thousand pages, numerous graphs and tables of Nigel Lawson's memoirs[19] it
is impossible to tell how the UK fared competitively over the period of which
he writes in terms of most major economic or industrial yardsticks.

THE DEEPER CAUSES

The mid-1980s presented the paradox of a flourishing City and cash-rich
country accompanied by growing awareness of the basic flaws in our industrial
capability. A series of seminal reports quantified the UK's deficiencies in
vocational education and training, shop floor skills and management qualifications and training.[20] A number of initiatives were started in response to
their recommendations, but all were based on the Government's principle of
voluntaryism, rather than seeking pragmatically the most effective way in which
we might match our competitors. The Management Charter Initiative would
embrace those companies which traditionally gave thought to the development

of managers; it would not transform a climate where amateurism was still too common. The Training and Enterprise Councils were saddled not only with the responsibility of encouraging training – the most fundamental need – but of tackling unemployment and promoting enterprise. Underfunded and with diverse objectives, they would not touch the anti-training ethos prevalent in industry. There was not even any attempt by government to use market forces to encourage the spread of good practice by requiring the publication of training plans in annual reports. Concentration on financial measurements built in short-termism both for companies and investors.

There was in addition a growing realization that attitudes towards industry played a role in our performance – that we were an industrial country with an anti-industrial culture. The timing and nature of the Industrial Revolution and a narrowly academic education still rooted in a nineteenth-century ethos had contributed to shaping the views of a society which, although ultimately dependent on industry, regarded participation in it as intellectually and morally inferior to the professions.[21] Some might cavil at this analysis, but it was sufficiently compelling to obtain support across the political and institutional spectrum for the designation of 1986 as Industry Year by the Royal Society for the Encouragement of Arts Manufactures and Commerce (RSA). This campaign, targeted towards practical action through local working groups across the country and continued for a further three years under the banner of Industry Matters, had significant results in helping to transform awareness in primary and secondary schools and teacher-training institutions of the nature of industry and of its potential as a partner in delivering the curriculum. It was fortunate in coinciding with changes in education that brought a wider range of human capabilities into formal teaching and examination, many of these being particularly apposite to the needs of industry, though their greater importance was that they began for the first time to touch the previously ignored potential of Sir Keith Joseph's excluded 40 per cent. That education itself was to undergo a series of upheavals, from the necessary and fundamental to the purely gimmicky, prompted by the government's political philosophy and frequently changing Secretaries of State, is another story. It is none the less relevant to industrial performance since until our education matches our competitors' at all levels we start from a disadvantaged position.

The sustained Industry Year campaign inevitably triggered institutional jealousy and political ambition. The CBI leadership (though not its members, whose efforts were to intensify) as early as September 1986 declined to support the continuation of the campaign beyond the end of the year.[22] The Department of Trade and Industry introduced its own scheme for industry–education links in December 1987, its civil servants emphasizing that the credit would need to redound to the Secretary of State and his Enterprise Initiative, with a resultant fragmentation of what was becoming a nation-wide effort with its own momentum.

At least by the 1990s all the elements – education, training and attitudes – were for the first time on the national agenda, even if they had been identified in principle more than a hundred years before.[23] Some progress was being made in all: the question remained whether it was fast enough to keep up with the pace of change in competitor countries, let alone catch up with their level of achievement, or whether a narrow political philosophy and lack of national consensus about ends and means would condemn us to remain in our bottom place in the industrial league.

THE RECKONING

In July 1987 the Chancellor, Nigel Lawson, drastically reduced the NEDC mechanism, having first secured the connivance of the CBI President, David Nickson, whom he praised for his understanding of the climate needed for business success.[24] The CBI had not effectively barked, let alone bitten, for many years: it was safe to pat its titular leader on the head. By contrast the NEDC committees and the Office, with their sectoral analyses and international comparisons of performance, could still discomfort. Their final silencing, from which Lawson according to his memoirs had been dissuaded by Margaret Thatcher, was effected at the end of 1992 by the new Chancellor, Norman Lamont.

Lawson's criticism of the Council as a waste of ministerial time was no more than a self-fulfilling prophecy; his view of the organization as part of 'the corporate state' simply reflected the shallowness of debate which had characterized the previous years. The Council had in practice long ceased to fulfil the function for which it had been created. Its chief value now was to provide a higher media profile for the work of the committees and of the Office. The sensitivity of politicians to unpalatable analysis and the reluctance of the parties to NEDC to engage in debate meant that the disappearance of the Council itself was a small loss, even if it removed the last non-parliamentary forum for discussion and mutual education about industry and the economy. The extinction of the sectoral committees and the Office, however, meant that there would now be no comparable body, accepted as independent and free of any political slant, arguing the corner for industry on the basis of collective experience and statistical analysis.

What we had seen had been no consistent 'supply-side' policy. It had been shaped by what was politically acceptable, rather than what was industrially necessary. Government policies had shown themselves capable of controlling inflation, also of creating it and generating recession and boom, not of significantly influencing the foundations of competitiveness across the broad spectrum of industry. There had been genuine gains: the reform of the trade unions; the encouragement of self-employment and indeed of 'enterprise' until political overuse devalued the word. The diminution of government intervention in industrial disputes was also welcome, though the ending of

23

'beer and sandwiches' in No. 10 Downing Street was replaced by ministerial appearances on television when they felt their appointed managers were inadequately equipped for the task. The encouragement of a customer orientation, whether in the remaining public sector or the newly privatized monopolies, helped to make those entities more responsive to the consumer. But these reforms, important though they were, simply removed some of the archaic institutional and attitudinal clutter which hindered effective management. The fundamental changes required in the training of management and workforce continued to be left to the principle of voluntaryism which had long shown itself inadequate except for a minority of companies which in this, as in other requirements for market success, adapted to match their competition. Ministers simply continued to assert that government was impotent to play a role in these matters.

As the 1992 election approached it remained doubtful if much had been learnt from the preceding thirteen years. In the depths of the longest post-war recession, with unemployment again rising towards three million, a significant balance of payments deficit and a level of poverty wholly unacceptable in an advanced nation, there was little sign of new thinking. The Foreign Secretary, Douglas Hurd, asked in the pre-electoral period why government rejected intervention in industry, could only respond 'It's this business of "picking winners". It hasn't worked in the past'.[25] Even if the economy might be considered outside a Foreign Secretary's domain, nothing could better illustrate the shallowness of debate and staleness of prevailing shibboleths. In the economic policy debate of 24 September the Prime Minister, John Major, declared 'The essential conditions for Britain's economic success are low inflation, low taxes, free trade and freedom from excessive state interference. I am happy to re-affirm those principles today. The Government stand for a low inflation, low tax economy – and so, I believe, do the British people.'[26] There was nothing new here: only the familiar 'hygiene factors'. That nearly 60 per cent of the British electorate had voted for something else was ignored.

The requirements for industrial success do not sit happily with the time-span or ambition of politicians. They are complex, inter-related and long term, not susceptible of quick fixes. Whitehall and Westminster remain remote from industry in their training and experience. Government, of whatever complexion, needs a coherent 'industrial opposition' – a clearly articulated input into the formulation of policy affecting industry and clear signals about the effect of all government policies which have an impact on industry. But this input had been muddied by a *trahison des clercs* – a professional betrayal by both sides of industry, seeking political goals and the pursuit of external political leverage to achieve a changed balance of power.

The conduct of economic argument by rhetoric, slogan and reflex action has barred from intelligent public debate many matters crucial to industrial performance. 'Planning' and 'strategy' are discredited words at national level, though the commonplace of corporate terminology. 'Incomes policy' or 'pay determination' produce Pavlovian reactions from government, CBI and TUC; but the issue of pay is central to industrial relations. The Maastricht Social Chapter, like the earlier draft EC 'Vredeling Directive' on employee rights to information and consultation and the EC Fifth Directive on company practices, is a part of demonology or hagiology according to where one sits. Yet all – regardless of merit – touch in principle upon important aspects of relationships within industry: in the absence of any real debate we are left with a series of separate ritual responses, untempered by rational discussion.

Unwillingness to agree on any accepted set of statistics as a point of departure for national debate on the economy and industrial performance vitiates much discussion. Failure or success are suggested (by the opposition and government of the day respectively) as emerging fully-fledged from the actions of individual governments like Athena from the head of Zeus, whereas a set of statistics over time would show how widely spread is the responsibility for the poverty of our performance compared to our competitors. Elected British governments are not 'wicked': nor are they infallible. For the government of the day to claim the second and the opposition the first debases the stature of politics and of political debate.

The concept of a government of industrialists or businessmen is a nonsense. It is therefore essential to seek to bring industrial experience to bear in other ways so that there will be better understanding of the impact of policies directly or indirectly affecting the productive capabilities of the country.

If absence of industrial experience at the parliamentary level is to be compensated for, then it can most readily be done within the governmental system by broadening the input into the civil service. Secondment of civil servants to merchant banks, non-executive directorships, or to temporary staff jobs in industrial companies is no substitute for the experience of line management in industry. The opening of middle-ranking and senior civil service posts to such industrial experience would encourage stronger internal debate about policies from people conditioned by a generally more pragmatic and target-oriented world and so likely to be usefully impatient of the conventions of Whitehall.

In 1983 Sir John Hoskyns, former head of the Prime Minister's Policy Unit, made a radical analysis of the existing political establishment.[27] Included in the objectives he set out were the organization of Whitehall for strategy and innovation and the introduction of high-quality outsiders into the civil service. He also recommended a deepening of the shallow pool of talent from which any prime minister has to choose a government by bringing in wider experience than is available through the present system. Beckett was right: Parliament and Cabinet are indeed ignorant of the nature of industry. But it is unlikely that the character of Parliament, and therefore of governments, will be influenced by a greater measure of industrial experience through the normal process of election. An electoral system which gave results more representative of the pattern of voting would undoubtedly help to diminish the adversarial nature of politics and policy formation and would in this way assist industry. It would also loosen the political ties of the TUC and CBI. But while electoral reform remains a necessary condition of industrial success, it would not of itself offset the industrial inexperience of Parliament.

Forecasts have continued to prevail over facts. In place of competing forecasts, whose quantitative differences reflect qualitatively different economic and political assumptions, which tell us little about real changes in the economy and divert attention from the basic factors determining our performance, we need different indicators. Statistics should exist to keep politicians – and indeed all of us – honest, not to assist a battle for short-term debating advantage. The 'lap-markers' proposed by the NED Office as long ago as 1981,[28] as indicators that the underlying conditions for sustained growth without inflation are being achieved, would be much more valuable than any judgement of the plausibility of competing forecasts.

The NEDO paper suggested that these should include real changes in long-term productivity growth; a substantially improved share of profits in income, allowing and encouraging higher levels of investment, research and development, and ultimately employment; continuing decline in the average level of nominal wage settlements; and indications of a marked change in the basic ability of industry to meet competition successfully, for example by a better trend of exports and investment, increased acquisition and utilization of new skills, and signs of greater adaptability in both product and labour markets. Such markers, moreover, unlike forecasts, would indicate areas for action for both institutions and individuals.

There may today be the beginnings of realization that we cannot conduct industrial affairs on the time-scale of politics or within the framework of political as opposed to industrial perceptions. 'Consensus' is a word which has been proscribed for the past thirteen years and it is of course expedient for governments elected on a minority vote to discredit it. Indeed, if it is interpreted as a muddy compromise it merits rejection. But a consensus which harnesses the understanding and commitment of people in a task which requires both practical and attitudinal change, and in which virtually all have a part to play, is the necessary foundation for tackling the task we face. Relative decline might well be acceptable if the country's absolute growth were sufficient to meet the needs of all its citizens. It clearly is not. But relative decline is invisible to those in work, who will in general have enjoyed a rising standard of living. It is therefore difficult to summon the national effort required.

A new note was sounded towards the end of 1992. At the Conservative Party Conference the President of the Board of Trade, Michael Heseltine, indicated his readiness to ˙ntervene in industry. More specifically, after thirteen years in which the phrase had been taboo or rubbished, he stated his unequivocal belief in the need for an 'industrial strategy', emphasizing that government was 'not powerless' to help to do things overdue by a hundred years in the interests of competitiveness.[29] Any impact this might have had was overwhelmed by the fiasco of the pit closure announcement. But other voices were also speaking up. At its November 1992 annual conference the CBI appeared to be rejecting its past and calling for a fresh partnership between business, government and the City to prevent further erosion of the manufacturing base. The chairman of the National Training Task Force, Sir Brian Wolfson, called on the Cabinet to abandon its philosophy of 'voluntaryism' and introduce a compulsory levy on company payrolls to ensure that money was spent on training.[30]

Whether the CBI targets for investment, trade share, import substitution and productivity would be pursued with more effective action than in the past remained to be seen, as did Sir Brian's ability to raise a following behind his banner. If they are to succeed, political reform will need to be one of the foundations on which they build.

NOTES

Some of the material for this chapter appeared in the *RSA Journal*, vol. CXXXI, no. 5319, February 1983 and *The Three Banks Review*, no. 141, March 1984.

1 The NEDC comprised three parts – the Council itself, the sectoral committees and the Office. Where the context is clear they are referred to in this fashion; where there may be doubt they are prefaced by NED.

2 An Approach to Industrial Strategy, Cmnd 6315.

3 Secretaries of State for Trade and Industry since 1979: Sir Keith Joseph, Industry, May 1979–September 1981; John Nott, Trade and President Board of Trade, May 1979–January 1981; John Biffen, Trade and President of the Board of Trade, January 1981–April 1982; Patrick Jenkin, Industry, September 1981–June 1983; Lord Cockfield, Trade and President of the Board of Trade, April 1982–June 1983; Cecil Parkinson, Trade and Industry, June 1983–October 1983; Norman Tebbit, Trade and Industry, October 1983–September 1985; Leon Brittan, Trade and Industry, September 1985–25 January 1986; Paul Channon, Trade and Industry, 25 January 1986–13 June 1987; Lord Young, Trade and Industry, 13 June 1987–24 July 1989; Nicholas Ridley, Trade and Industry, 24 July 1989–14 July 1990; Peter Lilley, Trade and Industry, 14 July 1990–11 April 1992; Michael Heseltine, President of the Board of Trade, 11 April 1992–. Source: Department of Trade and Industry.

4 Nigel Lawson, *The View from No. 11. Memoirs of a Tory Radical*, 1992, p. 52.

5 'Why is there a DTI?' *RSA Journal*, Vol. CXXXV, No. 5375, October 1987.

6 Of the twenty-nine books listed, twelve were imprints of Sir Keith Joseph's Centre for Policy Studies; seven of the Institute of Economic Affairs. He was himself author, or joint author, of eight.

7 For example, Lord Glenarthur, Parliamentary Under-Secretary of State in the Home Office, spoke of the 'absolute right to manage' in the context of the prison officers' dispute. BBC *Today* programme, 24 April 1986.

8 'The industrial relations outlook: confrontation or cooperation?' *RSA Journal*, Vol. CXXXVI, No. 5383 June 1988. The reference is omitted in the published text, but its use in the lecture is revealed in a published question and answer.

9 Industrial Policies in Europe, NEDC (81) 51, October 1981.

10 Industrial Policy in the UK, NEDC (82) 25.

11 Report of the Committee of Inquiry on Industrial Democracy, January 1977, HMSO, Cmnd 6706.
12 *Daily Telegraph*, 12 November 1979.
13 *The Guardian*, 1 May 1980. Article by John Torode based on a discussion with Methven which had taken place three months earlier. The story was repudiated by the president of the CBI, Sir John Greenborough (*Guardian*, 8 May 1980), but, whatever the journalistic impropriety of revealing what was said in confidence, the presumption must be that Torode did not fabricate his story.
14 *The Times*, 12 November 1980.
15 *The Times*, 13 November 1980.
16 *British Industrial Performance*, NEDC, July 1980. Revised March 1981.
17 *Daily Mirror*, 23 May 1983.
18 The International Context of the UK, NEDC (83) 7, February 1983.
19 Lawson, op. cit.
20 *Competence and Competition*. Training and education in the Federal Republic of Germany, the United States and Japan. NEDC, Manpower Services Commission, 1984. *The Making of Managers*. A report on management education, training and development in the USA, West Germany, France, Japan and the UK. Manpower Services Commission, NEDC, British Institute of Management 1987 (the Handy report).
21 Key sources for this are: Correlli Barnett, *The Collapse of British Power*, 1972; and *The Audit of War*, 1986; and Martin Wiener, *English Culture and the Decline of the Industrial Spirit 1850–1980*, 1981.
22 The president of the CBI, David Nickson, pleading other priorities for the organization, said that the continuation of the campaign would have the CBI's 'passive acceptance rather than whole-hearted or enthusiastic support'. Meeting with RSA representatives, 3 September 1986.
23 See, for example, *Report of the Endowed Schools (Schools Enquiry) Royal Commission*, 1867–68; and Lyon Playfair, *Industrial Instruction on the Continent*, 1852, both cited by Barnett.
24 Lawson, op. cit., p. 717.
25 BBC *World at One*, 12 February 1992.
26 Hansard, Vol. 212, No. 52.
27 *The Times*, 22 November 1983.
28 NEDC (81) 45, July 1981.
29 BBC *Today* programme, 15 October 1992.
30 *The Independent*, 14 December 1992.

Part I

INTERNATIONAL TRADING PERFORMANCE

3

OVERVIEW:
UNDERSTANDING BRITAIN'S
ECONOMIC PERFORMANCE
The role of international trade

Paul Temple

It is the great multiplication of the production of all the different arts, in consequence upon the division of labour, which occasions, in a well-governed society, that universal opulence which extends itself to the lowest ranks of the people.

(Adam Smith, *The Wealth of Nations*, Book I, chapter 1)

As it is the power of exchanging, that gives occasion to the division of labour, so the extent of this division must always be limited by the extent of the market.

(Adam Smith, *The Wealth of Nations*, Book I, chapter 3)

INTRODUCTION – THE PROSPERITY OF THE NATION

Concern with Britain's economy is today more or less endemic. The idea that economic performance was converging with that of its closest European partners was shattered in the brief period of membership of the Exchange Rate Mechanism which ended with the devaluation of the pound in September 1992. The rapid declines in inflation over the recent past were only made possible by a huge surge in rates of unemployment and business closures. Even with the achievement of low rates of inflation, the emergence of the 'twin deficits' – in both the balance of payments *and* in the government's own budget – reveals a basic weakness in performance that may yet prevent recovery proceeding briskly enough for unemployment to fall significantly before the new millennium. In this overview we shall be reviewing some of the evidence regarding Britain's economic strength – viewed (in some ways rather narrowly) in terms of the ability of the system to deliver economic goods and services. We shall also be advancing the hypothesis that any improvement will require as a necessary condition an improvement in international competitiveness – the aspect of performance that has repeatedly been the economy's Achilles' heel in the many disappointments of the post-war period.

But where exactly do we stand today? Perhaps the broadest measure of the economic strength of a nation is that provided by gross domestic product (GDP), which is an estimate of the value of all goods and services produced within a given period. Its use in a variety of contexts is open to all manner of grave objections. As a measure of relative living standards, which of course is the ultimate aim of all economic activity, then these objections are even fiercer: much valuable human effort is not counted at all, such as the services of those working in the home, whilst other activities which exist simply to clear up pollution, or combat a crime wave, count positively.[1] Perhaps more importantly, no account is taken of the distribution of living standards amongst the population.[2] Nevertheless, levels of GDP per head of population give some idea as to average standards of living across countries,[3] and large differences are certainly informative. Figure 1 shows a comparison of GDP per head in 1990 for the six leading economies of the developed world, the so-called 'G6'. Rather than actual exchange rates, the values of GDP are converted at more appropriate purchasing power parity (PPP) rates of exchange.[4]

Evidently, GDP per capita in the UK stands below that of the other members of the G6 and the average for the OECD as a whole, and is only slightly higher than the average for the European Community. In relative terms, the UK is

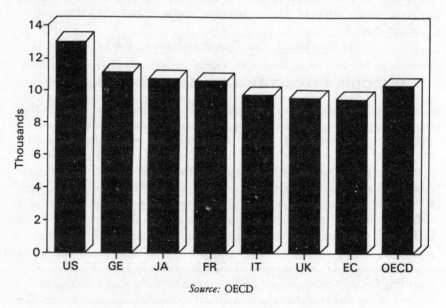

Source: OECD

Figure 3.1 GDP per head in 1990 (£ at PPP exchange rates).

36 per cent below the US, 16 per cent behind (West) Germany and 11 per cent behind France.

BRITAIN'S RELATIVE ECONOMIC DECLINE

The relative position of the UK in 1990 is the outcome, over a long period of time, of a process of economic growth; Table 1 compares the performance of the UK at a variety of dates starting in 1950. It indicates a number of important features in the post-war period. Of obvious significance is the continuing strength of the US, whose leadership reflects a generally superior productivity performance. In the words of some economists, it has acted as a 'technological leader', much as the UK did at the time of the Industrial Revolution. This leadership role provides a potential source of 'catch-up' for the other economies – and the table shows how Germany, France and most spectacularly Japan, have experienced sufficient economic expansion to close the gap on the US. In the UK too the gap has closed somewhat since 1950, but most of the improvement seems to have occurred in the period between 1950 and 1960: indeed, relative to the US, the UK is no better off today than it was in 1960, with little exploitation of catch-up potential.

The long-term relative decline of the UK is well attested by its levels of per capita GDP compared to those in Germany and France. The clear advantages enjoyed by the UK in 1950 had been overturned by the time of the great 'watershed' of post-war growth in 1973. However, the most recent complete economic cycle in the UK, from 1979–90, reveals that this long process may have begun to arrest itself and possibly have gone into reverse, certainly as far as the comparison with France and Germany is concerned.

How sanguine can we be that performance has actually improved between 1979 and 1990 relative to France, Germany and the US? A number of questions have to be addressed, the most important of which is whether the growth of the UK economy in this period was actually sustainable. Much of the remainder of this chapter is devoted to an examination of this issue.

Table 1 Comparative levels of GDP per head (UK = 100)

	1950	1960	1973	1979	1990
US	148	135	139	141	136
Germany	65	98	110	119	116
France	74	84	106	114	111
Japan	27	44	91	95	112
UK	100	100	100	100	100

Source: Maddison (1987) for 1950–73; OECD National Accounts, Vol. I, for 1979, 1990

Table 2 The growth of real GDP and real GDP per capita (average annual percentage growth)

	1950–73		1973–79		1979–90	
	GDP	GDP per capita	GDP	GDP per capita	GDP	GDP per capita
US	3.7	2.3	2.4	1.4	2.6	1.6
Japan	9.4	8.2	3.6	2.5	4.1	3.5
Germany	5.9	5.0	2.3	2.5	2.0	1.7
France	5.1	4.2	2.8	2.3	2.1	1.7
UK	3.0	2.5	1.5	1.5	2.1	1.9
Italy	5.5	4.8	3.7	3.2	2.4	2.2
Total EC	NA	NA	2.5	2.1	2.2	1.9
Total OECD	NA	NA	2.7	1.9	2.7	1.9

Source: Maddison (1982, 1987); OECD Historical Statistics, 1960–90

The years chosen for comparison in Table 1 are not arbitrary, but correspond to cyclical peaks in economic activity. It is important that comparisons are made between peaks in the cycle in order that we are measuring genuine changes in economic *capacity* rather than merely *the extent to which capacity is utilized*.[5] Even between peaks, we cannot be certain that capacity utilization is similar, and indeed evidence suggests that for the UK it was far higher in both 1973 and 1990, than in 1979.[6] If 1979 were not a comparable peak, then this would have the effect of exaggerating growth in the period 1979–90 compared to the period 1973–9. On the other hand, growth in the economy as a whole owed much to the build-up of North Sea oil production in the earlier period. Indeed the non-oil economy has been estimated to have grown by only 0.9 per cent between 1973 and 1979, whereas in the later period it grew just as fast as the whole economy (Her Majesty's Treasury, 1992).

Table 2 shows some comparative growth rates, between peaks, for the G6 economies. It clearly shows that the convergence in growth rates between the UK and the other economies has been achieved by a slowdown of growth post-1973 in the other economies rather than any acceleration of UK growth.

GROWTH AND RECESSION

There is one important respect in which the comparison of growth rates between cyclical peaks can be highly misleading. If output is particularly volatile, then the actual path of GDP may be inferior from the point of view of economic welfare than a steady rate of expansion which none the less exhibits a similar growth rate. In view of the well-known characterization of the UK as a 'stop–go' economy, this point warrants further investigation.

Figure 2 confirms the extent of the problem and suggests that the susceptibility of the UK to serious economic recession may be worsening. After 1973
the typical 'growth cycle' was replaced in the UK with recessions in which
output actually declined. In fact, prior to 1973, this had happened only once
(on an annual basis) since the Second World War – in 1958. As the figure
shows, in comparison with both the OECD economies and the European
Community as a whole, the decline in output between 1973 and 1975 was of
a similar order of magnitude; subsequent recessions have, however, been much
more severe in the UK both in relation to other developed economies and to
its own experience. It is important that the assessment of overall performance
takes this into account; neither the rate of growth over the cycle nor the
comparison of levels in 1990 do so.

Some of the effect of the loss of output in recession years can be estimated
by looking at *cumulative* levels of GDP over the entire period. Strictly,
however, the total should include a discount factor r, which reflects the greater
value attached to GDP at an earlier date. In this way GDP in, say, 1980 is given
a value in 1990 equal to $GDP_{80}(1 + r)^{10}$. Table 3 repeats the simple comparisons of Table 1, but also includes a comparison of the cumulative totals of
GDP using a variety of discount rates. The effect of discounting is evidently
small, but that of looking at performance over the entire period worsens the
comparison between the UK and France, Germany and the US by about 2 to
4 per cent – in effect removing the apparent improvement in relative standing
of the UK since 1979. It is worth stressing that whatever recovery is achieved

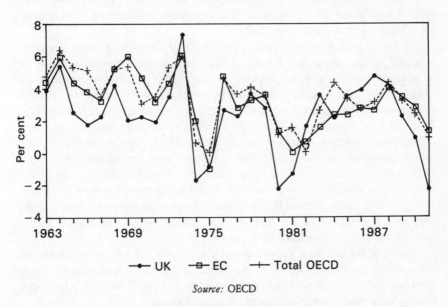

Source: OECD

Figure 3.2 Growth in GDP, 1963–91 (percentage growth over previous year).

Table 3 Relative levels of GDP per capita (UK = 100)

	Comparison based on single years		Comparisons based on 1979–90 period as a whole		
	1979	*1990*	*r = 0*	*r = 2.5%*	*r = 10%*
US	141	136	140	140	141
Germany	119	116	118	119	119
Japan	95	112	104	104	103
France	114	111	114	114	114
Italy	99	102	102	103	103
UK	100	100	100	100	100

Source: OECD National Accounts, Vol. I, own estimates

over the next few years, the years of recession represent periods of *permanently* lost output.

Such estimates only begin to scratch at the surface of the real costs of recession, the key feature of which is the destruction in capacity that occurs and which cannot be reversed. The most visible signs are, of course, the rise in unemployment and the loss of physical capacity as factories are closed down and investment spending plummets. Less visible but just as important is the destruction of 'intangible assets' – the skills of a team, a firm's reputation for reliability, the acquired knowledge of a particular market or a brand name. All these things which are of course vital to the competitiveness of an economy, are all destroyed as businesses close.

The volatility of economic activity in the UK is obviously a cause of serious concern. Just as important for the longer term is the economy's ability to increase its capacity at a rate capable not only of preventing unemployment from rising, but actually of reducing unemployment below its current unacceptable level, a problem that emerged with such force only after 1979. This will be the continuing challenge for the UK economy well into the new millennium. A key question is the extent to which the sort of growth rate actually achieved over the last complete economic cycle is sustainable and likely to be achievable in the coming years. Note that even the achieved rate of 2.1 per cent was unable to lower the rate of unemployment between 1979 and 1990. On the standardized OECD measure, unemployment rose from 5.0 per cent to 6.8 per cent of the labour force, and it was much higher in the intervening years – touching 11.8 per cent in 1986.

Given the far-reaching importance of the growth process, we must extend the analysis at this point to a consideration of the circumstances which underpin differences in national growth records. First of all we shall take a brief look at what may loosely be described as orthodoxy.

ACCOUNTING FOR GROWTH

Any answer to the question of sustainability of growth requires some under-standing of what is the most complex economic, social and political process. The standard economic approach tends to rely on the measurement of the contribution of the various inputs into the production process (primarily labour and capital), ascribing any 'residual' element to 'technological progress'. This exercise is known as 'growth accounting'.

In Table 4, estimates of the growth in output for the period 1979–89 are supplemented by estimates of the growth in both employment and in the gross capital stock, i.e. of the major inputs into the production process. In fact, both the measures deployed here are extremely rough and ready; employment is estimated by a simple head count and the capital stock by cumulating the gross investment occurring in each of the economies and deducting the value of assets which are scrapped. Techniques used for determining the scrapping of capital equipment are extremely rudimentary and in any event vary between countries. For this reason, a comparison of *levels* of the capital stock between economies is rarely attempted. Nevertheless, a comparison of the growth of gross capital stocks may give some idea of the relative speed at which an economy is adding to its capital assets.

The growth in labour productivity can be found by subtracting the growth rate of employment from that of output as a whole.[7] It is the most frequently discussed measure of the efficiency with which resources are utilized and of vital importance in assessing the progress of welfare and technology, not least because the rate of labour productivity advance can be quite stable over long periods of time. It can be seen that labour input in the UK grew somewhat over the decade, but this did not represent any steady rate of expansion; rather a falling away of employment until 1983, with very rapid growth between 1987

Table 4 A simple growth accounting exercise for five major OECD economies, 1979–89 (average annual rates of growth (%))

	US	Japan	France	Germany	UK
(1) Output	2.8	4.1	2.1	1.8	2.3
(2) Employment	1.7	1.1	0.1	0.4	0.5
(3) Gross capital stock	2.9	6.9	2.8	2.8	2.3
(4) Capital per unit of labour	1.2	5.8	2.7	2.4	1.8
(5) = (1)–(2) Labour productivity	1.1	3.0	2.0	1.4	1.8
(5) = (1)–(3) Capital productivity	– 0.1	– 2.8	– 0.7	– 1.0	0.0
(6) Capital share* (%)	34.0	33.0	37.0	37.0	29.7
(7) Total factor productivity	0.7	1.1	1.0	0.5	1.3

*Business sector only for 1989
Source: OECD, Flows and Stocks of Fixed Capital, 1964–89; Economic Outlook, June 1992; Historical Statistics, 1960–89

and 1989. The results show the UK experiencing very similar rates of labour productivity growth to France, and a little ahead of Germany. In each of these economies, labour productivity contributes more to output growth than increased employment. But in the US, labour productivity growth has been decidedly modest, and was less important than employment in explaining output growth.

The notion of capital productivity (line 5) is less well known and almost certainly more prone to measurement error. Unlike labour productivity, which declines only rarely on an annual basis (and usually for reasons of sharp reductions of capacity utilization in a recession), capital productivity can fall over quite long historical time periods. In fact, declining capital productivity is a distinguishing feature of the period after the 1973 watershed in many of the leading economies. Of the five economies examined, only the UK does not seem to have experienced any decline in capital productivity. On the basis of the data, however, neither the US nor the UK have been undergoing a major process of 'capital deepening' (equipping the workforce with more capital) as shown by the growth of capital per unit of labour (row 4).

It is impossible to estimate, from the evidence so far, how much capital and labour independently contribute to the growth of output. Some economists have attempted to do just this by making assumptions about the nature of technology (constant returns to scale) and the existence of a state of 'perfect competition' in product and input markets.[8] If these assumptions were to be true, then the contribution of each factor could be measured by the share of labour and capital in GDP. Some estimates for capital's share is given in line 6. If the shares of capital and labour sum to unity, then these can be used as weights to obtain 'total factor productivity' (line 7): this can be thought of as the 'residual' after accounting for the impact on output of increases in factor inputs:

$$Y = aL + (1 - a)K + \text{TFP}$$

where

$$Y, L, K = \text{proportionate growth rates in output, labour input and capital input, respectively}$$

$$a, (1 - a) = \text{labour and capital shares, respectively}$$

$$\text{TFP} = \text{growth rate of total factor productivity}$$

From this perspective, the 'residual factor' (TFP) is clearly a very significant contributor to growth. Although some economists have attempted to define it as 'the rate of technological progress' it is in reality a catch-all term that captures the other influences on economic growth. Maddison (1987) has, however, surveyed attempts to improve the idea of growth accounting and provides a list of factors that a comprehensive exercise should include, and which helps to diminish the power of the residual. He mentions:

1 The increasing quality of inputs, through the education and training of labour and the 'embodiment' of technical progress in additions to the capital stock.
2 Economies of scale both at the national level and through increasing specialization in international trade.
3 Structural change, especially the impact of declining employment in agriculture and rising employment in services; for many of the OECD economies, manufacture is now also in decline. Structural effects occur because different sectors have different levels and growth rates of labour productivity. It is now believed that the benefits of movements away from agriculture into higher productivity sectors have all but exhausted themselves in the leading economies, and that there is increasing 'drag' on economic growth as resources move into slower-growing service industries. Maddison marks 1973 as the turning point in this regard.
4 'Catch-up' bonuses based on higher levels of labour productivity in the US than elsewhere. Catch-up was much stronger prior to 1973 everywhere except the UK, which is now, according to Maddison, able to benefit as a result of poor growth performance between 1950 and 1973.
5 A miscellany of other factors including the impact of higher energy costs, environmental regulations and capacity utilization.

Making allowances for these factors does not entirely remove the 'residual', and indeed a decline in the residual accounts for a substantial part of the fall in economic growth rates after 1973. More significantly, many of the assumptions required become increasingly vague and arbitrary as the exercise progresses. Problems over input measurement abound. Indeed, even the apparently simple task of measuring labour input can be fraught with difficulty, and the use of a headcount, as in the illustration above, can be far from satisfactory.

If we take the UK as an example, we find that the growth of the labour input is the outcome of a number of different factors: changes in the numbers employed and changes in the numbers of hours actually worked per person. Precise estimates of hours worked in the UK are complicated by the growing importance of both part-time and self-employment. If part-time working substantially reduces labour input compared to the simple headcount, self-employment tends to raise it. Surveys carried out for the EC found that self-employed males tend to work a 52-hour week and females 34 hours. In a study covering the years 1979–88, Feinstein and Matthews (1990) estimated that labour input actually declined by 0.6 per cent per annum, rather than the slight rise indicated by the headcount measure.

INTERNATIONAL TRADE AND THE GROWTH PROCESS

In contrast to the growth accounting framework and the disembodied approach to technological change, Adam Smith's vision of the growth process placed great emphasis on 'the division of labour', i.e. increasing specialization made possible by a growing market. On this basis, the large gap in levels of GDP per head that the US opened up should be explained by the access of its businesses to a large national market as much as it should to any advantage in terms of natural resources. International trade modifies this somewhat: exports allow an individual nation to overcome some of the deficiencies of possessing too narrow a domestic market, permitting an increasing division of labour – although this is limited by barriers to trade, which even in the European Community after several decades, can remain substantial.

A key feature of Smith's vision of economic growth is therefore the idea that as markets expand, production becomes more efficient – in other words we expect 'increasing returns'. When these are important in a branch of industry, cumulative processes begin to dominate progress. However accidental, an early lead can be critical in establishing more than a temporary advantage for individual industries and economies, as learning and other effects begin to take hold.

This gives great strategic importance to the export sector in economic development. Figure 3 shows how close the association is between an economy's export performance in goods and services and its achieved rate of growth over long periods of time. The diagram plots annual export growth and GDP growth for each of the twenty-three members of the OECD between 1960 and 1990.[9] An important feature of the scatter is the extent to which export growth exceeds GDP growth; this reflects the fact that the export sector of the economy is highly dynamic. The more that an industry relies on export demand, the greater its growth rate will tend to be relative to the rest of the economy; investment will be higher and output concentrated in more modern plant and equipment. Even more important is the fact that modern patterns of trade and specialization tend to be dictated by technological progress, particularly in the development of trade between the advanced economies. The export sector therefore becomes a major vehicle for the transmission and diffusion of technological change, partly through the introduction of new products and processes to other sectors of the economy.

Within the export sector itself, pride of place must certainly go to manufacturing industry, where it is widely recognized that the potential for technological and productivity advance is greatest. In the UK today, despite the clear importance of services to overall trade, the pre-eminence of exports of manufactures is clear. In 1991, total exports of goods (visibles) were some £103 billion; of these manufacturing exports were f85 billion, with oil exports only £7 billion. By contrast, service sector exports totalled about £32 billion. Moreover as Greenhalgh (1989) makes clear, the manufacturing demand for

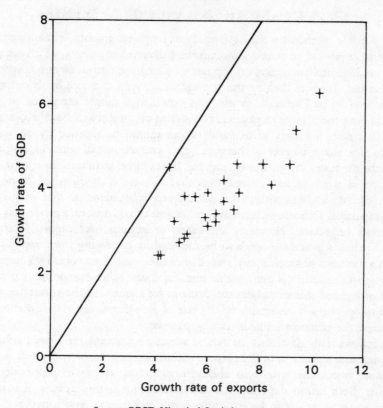

Source: OECD Historical Statistics, 1960–90

Figure 3.3 Export performance and economic growth, 1960–90 (per cent per annum).

services is greater than the other way around, implying that increases in demand for manufactured products create more output and employment elsewhere in the economy than do services. This means that the traditional conception of services being labour intensive and manufacturing capital intensive is slightly misleading once inter-industry linkages are explored. Moreover, the demands made by manufacturing on the service sector are increasing.[10] The technological dynamism of the manufacturing sector is clear from the fact it carries out the major portion of industry-financed research and development activity. This means that the demands placed by manufacturing on other sectors of the economy are likely to be particularly progressive ones – design, marketing, finance and so forth. With these features in mind, it seems clear that trading performance, or 'international competitiveness', particularly but not exclusively in manufacturing, are key ingredients of economic prosperity. The special role of manufacturing in the economy is discussed further by Mayes in Chapter 17 (this volume).

GROWTH AND THE BALANCE OF PAYMENTS

One possible mechanism through which trading performance is connected to sustainable rates of economic growth is the balance of payments, which can act as a fundamental constraint on the rate at which the output of any economy can expand. The ideas behind this approach have been advanced by Kaldor and more recently by Thirlwall, Godley and others.[11] A simple exposition of the idea behind the balance of payments constraint might run as follows: economic growth creates a variety of demands which cannot be satisfied by domestic production alone; in general therefore, the faster the rate of demand (output) growth, the faster the growth of imports. It would be natural to think of these imports in terms of natural resources that cannot be produced at home – especially fuel and raw materials – but the idea is broader than that and today the import of 'technology intensive' or sophisticated consumer goods may be far more important. However, any excess of imports over exports (a trade deficit) that is generated needs to be financed by borrowing from overseas or from a rundown of an economy's stock of overseas assets, and over long periods of time this situation is not a viable one. Of course other economies may also be growing and this stimulates the demand for exports, so the constraint will tend to operate as a constraint on the rate of growth *relative* to that occurring amongst the economy's major trading partners.

It follows from all of this the rate at which an economy can grow (without running into a problem of debt accumulation) *depends essentially on its international competitiveness* – its ability to export as well as its propensity to import. Both factors depend upon similar elements – the capacity of manufacturers in particular to be responsive and innovative in world markets.[12]

In fact, limitations to economic growth created via the balance of payments can be thought of as an example of a resource constraint in much the same way that labour or capital might limit growth when the growth of demand begins to outstrip supply in a closed economy. In an open economy it might be said that growth outstrips the capacity of the supply-side. Inflationary symptoms may therefore also appear at a similar point in time, and in the case of the UK, frequently do. Moreover, the idea of balance of payments constraint reverses the growth accounting picture at least in as far as the latter provides a story of causation: the accumulation of capital and the absorption by the economy of technological change, the foundations of growth in the orthodox story outlined above, become the effects of competitiveness itself: trading success stimulates both capital accumulation and technical progress.

There can be little doubt that the balance of payments acted as the key feature in the 'stop–go' economic cycle of the 1950s and 1960s. Figure 4 charts the current account of the balance of payments[13] (movements in which are dominated by the net trade balance on goods and services) and compares it with the deviation of actual GDP from trend – this gives a fair indication of the output cycle.

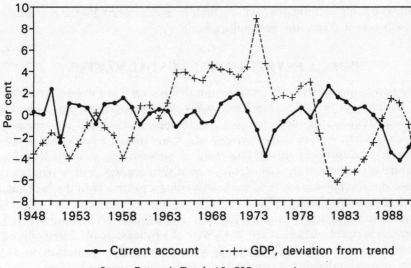

Source: Economic Trends AS; CSO; own estimates

Figure 3.4 UK current account as a percentage of GDP, 1948–91.

The regular cyclical pattern of the current account in the early post-war years charts the progress of the stop–go cycle with almost uncanny precision. For example, 1955, 1960, 1964 and 1968 were all cyclical peaks in GDP as well as troughs in the balance of payments cycle; 1973 was also a year of a major deficit and the clearest output peak of all. In fact the deficit reaches a post-war record only in 1974, exacerbated by the quadrupling of oil prices at a time when the UK was still a large net energy importer.

The economic cycle 1973–9 differed from earlier ones in key respects. We have seen that output growth was significantly slower than in previous periods; in addition both the nominal and real exchange rate declined in the middle of the decade and, significantly, North Sea oil began to make an important contribution towards the balance of payments. Together, these factors actually began to break some of the ingredients of stop–go. By 1979, the output peak, the current account was actually in reasonable shape.

Against this background the serious recession of the early 1980s saw the current account return into surplus despite the huge rise in the real exchange rate that was occurring. After 1981, when the surplus peaked, the drift into deficit was prolonged and substantial; 1983 was a clear marker, as the balance on manufacturing trade moved into deficit (it was believed) for the first time in centuries. By 1988, the current deficit reached over 4 per cent of GDP, which amounted to a post-war record. Sluggish growth in 1990, and the subsequent recession have caused some improvement, but the absence of any surplus by 1992, the second full year of declining output, provided ample evidence of a

43

parlous trading performance, and a serious long-term worry for the economy's growth potential into the new millennium.

DOES A PAYMENTS DEFICIT STILL MATTER?

The significance of recent current account deficits, even at the levels recorded at the end of the 1980s, has been highly contentious, especially with the growing importance and freedom of international capital movements, which in practice mean that 'shortages' of foreign exchange and a 'run on the reserves', hallmarks of the sterling crises of earlier times, were no longer a feature at the close of the last decade, even if they returned with a vengeance when the attempt was made to maintain sterling's parity within the Exchange Rate Mechanism during 1992.

Many commentators (including the then Chancellor, Nigel Lawson) believed that the payments deficits of the 1980s were of a fundamentally different kind from those of the 'bad old days'. As we have seen, the counterpart to the current account deficit is a transfer of assets between home and overseas. This amounts to a net change in domestic borrowing. In the 1960s and 1970s, it was argued that the increase in borrowing was largely a question of government, i.e. fiscal imprudence resulting from misguided 'Keynesian' demand management policies. However, the new economic regime of the Conservative government was based on 'orthodox' financial strategies – a balanced budget, reflecting the belief that the authorities should 'neither a lender nor a borrower be'. And indeed, in the later years of Lawson's chancellorship, the government was able to create a budget surplus, and was thereby able to repay outstanding debts. It follows that the counterpart to the current account deficit was an increase in the borrowing of the private sector. This, so the argument went, was a matter for private individuals alone, and no real occasion for public concern, still less for public policy. In the context of the deep and prolonged recession that emerged after 1989, however (and admittedly with the benefit of hindsight), the shallowness of the thinking here is remarkable. As the real burden of debts incurred by the private sector rose with the sharp and considerable tightening of monetary policy, private expenditure was reined in and public borrowing rapidly replaced private borrowing: the new problem of the 'twin deficits' emerged with considerable speed and vigour.

Even if the counterpart to a payments deficit is private borrowing, the validity of the argument that it is not a matter of policy concern depends critically upon the underlying explanation of the increased borrowing from overseas. A number of possibilities casting doubt on the significance of the deficit can usefully be listed:[14]

Proposition 1 That the counterpart to the deficit was an increase in foreign investment in the UK. Rates of return on longer-term UK assets had become attractive enough to justify net inward foreign investment. The much publicized Japanese direct investment in automotives and consumer electronics was regarded as an example of the attractiveness of the UK as a location.

Proposition 2 That the counterpart to the deficit was an increase in domestic investment. In this case an increase in the UK's stock of domestic assets was at the expense of its foreign assets. Here, arguably, the capacity of the economy to produce and export in the future will be enhanced, and the deficit will eventually be corrected.

Proposition 3 Finally, the counterpart to the deficit may be in terms of higher private consumption. A temporary increase in consumer expenditure may be perfectly rational if, for example, a permanent reduction in taxes is expected or if consumers correctly anticipate higher incomes in the future. Alternatively, the deregulation of financial markets may have released constraints on consumers and enabled them to borrow more, if so desired, for immediate spending. Many commentators stressed the positive wealth effects stemming from the property boom and the marked increase in house prices in real terms. Although this factor may have contributed, it should be noted that rising house prices imply a rise in the price of housing services, so that the wealth effect only operates for those planning to exchange some of their housing assets for goods and services. For others wishing to become home owners, the effect is to reduce wealth and this may actually restrain consumption. It is of course quite possible that some illusion is attached to an increase in house prices.

If any of these propositions were borne out in fact, then the huge deficits built up during the 1980s should be regarded as a temporary phenomenon, with no need for a policy response from the authorities.

In fact, as far as the first proposition is concerned, there has been no net inflow of long-term capital to sustain the deficit, and the idea that profitability in the UK has generally risen sufficiently to attract large-scale net inflows of long-term capital has little to commend it (see Martin Ricketts, Chapter 10, this volume). Figure 5 shows how, if anything, the addition of the balance on portfolio and direct investment to the current balance (to create what is known as the 'basic balance') exacerbates the situation.

The growing importance of these capital flows in the 1980s is readily apparent. Nevertheless, with the exception of 1987, the net flow has been negative, implying that the overall need for short-term borrowing is even greater than that for the current account alone. Two possible mitigating circumstances must however be considered.

Overall, the 'balance of payments must balance' – at least if all transactions and sources of finance are recorded correctly. In fact, the practicalities mean that not all transactions are faithfully recorded and so there is a large 'balancing item' which is needed to ensure that all items sum to zero. For many of the years in the 1980s, this item has been quite large and frequently positive. Most likely perhaps, these flows involve unrecorded short-term borrowing. But if they were actually current account receipts, then it is possible that they might

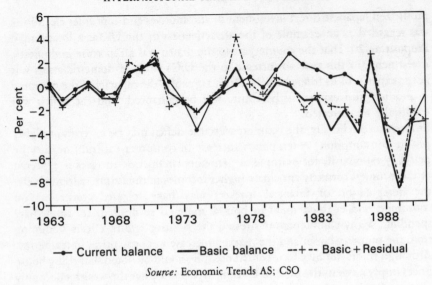

Source: Economic Trends AS; CSO

Figure 3.5 UK current account and basic balance as a percentage of GDP, 1963–91.

alter our picture of the decade somewhat. Figure 5 shows, however, that if the residual item were included in the basic balance, no major revision of interpretation is required.

The other factor that needs to be considered is the real capital gains accruing on the stock of overseas assets held by UK citizens, which are not recorded in the statistics, but may actually offset some of the deficit. Estimates by Coutts and Godley (1990), however, suggest that real capital gains, although of importance, may be small in relation to the size of the deficit.

It seems certain then that a net inflow of long-term capital is not the counterpart to the payments deficit and that UK borrowing has been increasingly short term, a factor which will not have escaped the notice of the authorities when they battled to stem the tide of speculation against sterling on the so-called 'Black Wednesday' in September 1992.

In order to consider the second and third propositions further we need to consider the *domestic* use to which this short-term borrowing was put. In particular, was it for domestic consumption or investment? One way of identifying at least the proximate cause of the increased deficit can be found by the use of the well-known national income identity:

$$Y \equiv C + I + G + X - M$$

where

Y = output (GDP)
C = consumers' expenditure

46

I = investment expenditure
G = government consumption
X = exports
M = imports

It follows that the net trade deficit B ($= M - X$) can be written as:

$$B \equiv D - Y$$

where D is 'domestic demand' $(C + I + G)$, so that the deficit, B, can be thought of as the excess of domestic demand over domestic output.

The change in B as a proportion of output can now be expressed as:

$$\Delta(B/Y) \equiv \Delta(C/Y) + \Delta(I/Y) + \Delta(G/Y)$$

In other words, the deterioration in the UK's net trade balance in relation to GDP is identically equal to the sum of increases in the ratio of the components of domestic demand in relation to output, and it is useful to consider it in this light. Application of the identity to the UK reveals the results contained in Table 5.

Over the period being considered, the table suggests that the proximate cause of the deterioration in the balance of payments was the increasing claim of consumption on the nation's production. The share of investment actually fell between 1979 and 1990. The story, however, is really one of two parts since the trade position actually improves somewhat between 1979 and 1985. In this early period it is the claim of government consumption which is increasing, and made possible by a large, and undoubtedly damaging, fall in the investment claim. After the middle of the decade, consumption and investment both contributed to the deterioration, although it was the consumer boom which played the lion's role, and the surge in investment spending was only sufficient to return it to something like the (proportionate) levels witnessed in 1979. That the counterpart to the deficit was an increase in domestic investment with favourable repercussions on the nation's capacity to export is not consistent

Table 5 The causes of the deterioration in UK net trade, 1979–90

	C/Y (%)	I/Y (%)	G/Y (%)	B/Y (%)
1979	59.1	21.1	20.8	− 1.0
1985	58.7	18.4	22.6	0.3
1990	61.8	20.3	21.4	− 3.5
Changes				
1979–90	+ 2.7	− 0.8	+ 0.6	− 2.5
1979–85	− 0.4	− 2.7	+1.7	+1.4
1985–90	+ 3.1	+1.9	−1.2	− 3.8

Source: CSO, National Income and Expenditure, various issues

with the known facts; so proposition 2 can also be rejected. We are left with an increase in consumer spending financed by international borrowing. This would be fine if the expectations on which such expenditure is based prove to be correct. In the event, however, with rising unemployment, falling house prices, combined with increasing question marks against the government's ability to hold taxes down and the economy's ability to deliver productivity growth, the basis of the 1980s boom has proved to be an illusion.

A comparison of the first half of the 1980s with the latter half is also illuminating. The growth in GDP over the early period, which of course encompassed the recession years, was insufficient to jeopardize the external payments position; it averaged a mere 0.7 per cent per annum. Between 1985 and 1990, the economy expanded at 3.2 per cent per annum, a rate apparently quite unsustainable. On the basis of performance over the entire period, it is also questionable whether the 2.1 per cent achieved could be maintained through the 1990s, unless trading performance improves dramatically.

It is important to realize that attributing the deterioration in Britain's trade position to the increasing claims of consumption is not really a theory of causation, and should not be taken to imply that the economy's problems were simply ones of 'excess demand'. The essential point is that domestic demand was excessive in relation to output, and this may stem just as much from problems on the supply side as from the demand side. This is considered further below.

It is also instructive to compare the UK with the rest of the G6. This is done in Table 6. A slowing down of the growth in international trade is apparent for all the economies except the US. From the UK's point of view the important thing to note is that it has the slowest growth of total exports of goods and

Table 6 The growth of volumes of international trade, 1960-90 (average annual percentage growth rates)

	Exports of goods and services		Imports of goods and services		Differences	
	1960-90	1979-90	1960-90	1979-90	1960-90	1979-90
US	6.3	6.6	6.1	5.8	0.2	0.8
Japan	10.2	6.5	8.4	4.3	1.8	2.2
Germany	6.0	5.0	6.1	3.8	− 0.1	1.2
France	6.6	3.7	6.6	3.9	0	− 0.2
UK	4.1	3.1	4.3	4.7	− 0.2	−1.6
Italy	7.2	3.4	6.8	4.7	0.4	−1.3
EC	6.0	4.2	6.1	4.3	− 0.1	− 0.1
Total OECD	6.3	5.0	6.2	4.8	0.1	0.2

Source: OECD Historical Statistics, 1960-1990

services of any of the G6 economies and, with the singular exception of the US, the fastest growth of imports. The tendency for the 1980s to produce growing payments imbalances is illustrated by the increasing differences between import and export growth permitted by the enhanced mobility of international capital. The weak position of both the UK and Italy in regard to their balance of payments position is highlighted.

SO WHAT ABOUT INFLATION?

Placing so much stress on the relationship between the tradeable sector of the British economy and its overall growth performance begs the inevitable question, given its primary focus in 1980s macroeconomic strategy: what about inflation? After all, it was the re-emergence of inflationary pressure that, ostensibly at any rate, forced the damaging interest rate hikes after 1988.

Somewhat tongue in cheek, it is interesting to compare the relationship between an economy's inflation record and its growth outcome within the OECD and compare it with Figure 3 above. The resultant scatter in Figure 6 is more or less a random one, although Japan features (yet again) as an outlier. In contrast with Figure 3, however, Japan's experience appears to be qualitatively as well as quantitatively different. In no other economy is comparatively low inflation combined with a rate of growth above 4 per cent per annum. If Japan were removed, then the relationship would be (weakly) positive. It is also worth noting that Japan itself achieved a truly miraculous rate of economic expansion in the 1950s and 1960s with a reasonably high rate of inflation – averaging some 4 per cent per annum in the 1950s and nearly 6 per cent per annum in the 1960s.

On closer reflection, it is not surprising that the diagram reveals little connection between inflation and economic performance. Export growth is of course a real variable and since it is a component of GDP, it is naturally at least partially correlated with it. The impact of inflation on economic growth must occur (if at all), indirectly, through other real variables. Moreover, the period covered, 1960–90, spans a whole plethora of exchange rate regimes both over time and between economies. For example, there is little doubt that the UK had a tendency to inflate faster than many competitor economies during the Bretton Woods period and that this was inimical to export growth and hence to overall performance.

In fact it is not very difficult to concoct completely plausible stories about the connection between inflation and economic performance. First, it has to be recognized that inflation is at least believed to be politically very unpopular. Not only can inflation redistribute income between groups and individuals, but everybody's *general* experience is of falling living standards, as the price rises of goods and services occur in a seemingly continuous way throughout the year, while adjustments to money wages or salaries are an intermittent and, quite possibly, a fraught affair. At the same time it must be recognized that many

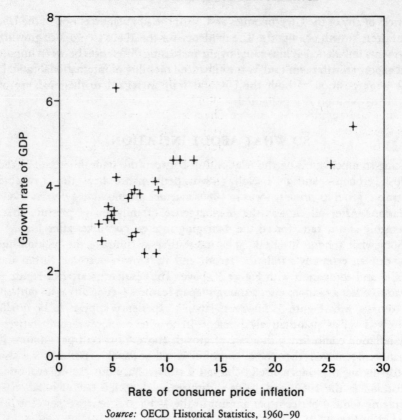

Source: OECD Historical Statistics, 1960–90

Figure 3.6 Inflation and economic growth, 1960–90 (per cent per annum).

groups in the UK, not least those experiencing the problem of 'negative equity', whose mortgages are worth more than their homes, are actually praying for a bout of inflation to reduce the real value of their debts. The very inconsistency of UK attitudes to inflation forms a part of the economic problem. In any event, the need to maintain international competitiveness at a time when the virtues of floating exchange rates have increasingly been called into question puts limits on the tolerance of inflation on the part of government at least. Correctives to an excessive rate of inflation involve, in the main, real deflationary measures (i.e. employment reducing – the taxonomy of economists is curiously obfuscatory in this regard) so that inflation can certainly contribute to a destabilizing stop–go cycle with damaging effects on saving and investment. More subtly, higher nominal interest rates, typically associated with higher rates of inflation, imply large negative cash flows in the early years of an investment and this may deter the riskier kind of investment.

The interaction between inflation and the real side of an economy is therefore likely to be extremely important, but the link between inflation and performance is a highly mediated one. In addition, the role of inflation depends upon its underlying causes, and it is important to examine the question of the re-emergence of inflation in the latter half of the 1980s in light of the rather old-fashioned view of supply-side or demand-side inflation. This is done in more detail below (see Chapter 14). It is shown there that as with the emergence of the balance of payments deficit, the rising levels of inflation and the sharp increases in real interest rates that were considered to be a necessary antidote, had their roots in supply-side difficulties and a distinct slowdown in economy-wide productivity growth.

THE ESSENTIAL PROBLEM

In this chapter we have considered the relative performance of the UK in terms of broad measures of economic activity. From the point of view of levels of GDP per capita, a considerable gap exists between the UK and other comparable countries. However, in terms of growth rates, the performance seems to have improved somewhat over the period 1979–90 relative to the same set of economies. In the longer sweep of history, this seems to be more the result of a slowdown of growth in those economies, than to any acceleration in UK growth rates. Growth rates, however, ignore the particular and undoubted susceptibility of the UK to recession; if this were included, then there is little evidence of 'catch up'. Moreover, the overall economic situation of 1990 suggested that even the growth achieved over the whole period 1979–90 may be unsustainable in the future, at least without a substantial improvement in supply-side performance.

Whether one analyses the problem of the balance of payments or the problem of inflation, the evidence of a supply-side failure is overwhelming. There may well be structural problems on the demand side, as suggested for example by Muellbauer and Murphy (1990), in relation to the housing market, but it is the inability of the supply-side to respond effectively to changes in effective demand that appears to create the major problem. Poor productivity performance remains inextricably linked to this, by continuing to pose a problem of international competitiveness, and by failing to grow fast enough to satisfy the aspirations of the populace.

Further insight into the balance of payments dilemma can be gleaned from Figure 7, which shows balances in terms of commodity composition, and Figure 8, illustrating visible balances in terms of geographical composition, with all balances as a proportion of GDP.

While balances tend to display cyclical patterns, some major trends are apparent. The deterioration in terms of commodity composition has mainly been in finished manufactures (Figure 7). Comparing the 1973 cyclical peak with 1989, we can see that the deterioration has been of the order of 4 per cent

51

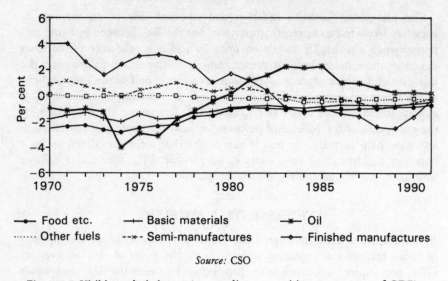

Figure 3.7 Visible trade balances (commodity composition; percentage of GDP).

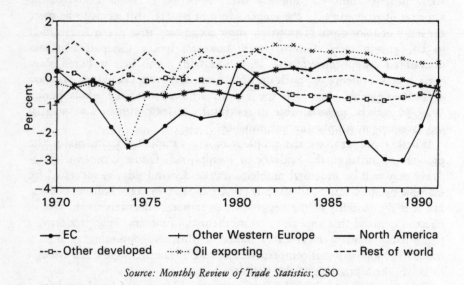

Source: Monthly Review of Trade Statistics; CSO

Figure 3.8 Visible trade balances (geographical composition; percentage of GDP).

of GDP, with the long-lived (probably over several centuries) surplus disappearing between 1982 and 1983. The bulk of the deterioration occurs over the later cycle, 1979–89. Semi-manufactures show a similar, if less pronounced, declining trend.

The dynamic impact of North Sea oil is reflected in the oil balance, which deteriorated rapidly under the impact of the price rises between 1973 and 1974, but then improved steadily until 1983, when the surplus was worth over 2 per cent of GDP – an overall improvement of around 6 per cent of GDP. Although some commentators were fond at the time of attributing the worsening manufacturing balance to North Sea oil (e.g. Forsyth and Kay (1980)), it is clear from Figure 7 that the deterioration of the overall manufacturing balance has not been stemmed by the apogee of the dynamic contribution of North Sea oil. Although indigenous oil supplies remain extremely important for the economy, it is now a largely negative factor, in that the fuel balance is tending to deteriorate. The steady and at times dramatic erosion of coal-producing capacity will tend to exacerbate this trend.

Of course, many have contended that the invisible balance is a likely saviour for the external position, but no obvious compensating trend for manufacturing is discernible. Fluctuations occur within the range 0 to 1.5 per cent of GDP. The invisible balance is made up primarily of the balance on services and on property income (interest, profit and dividends). The latter is vulnerable in the wake of several years of cumulating current account deficits in the early 1980s, which were largely financed by short-term borrowing and which of course necessitates increasing outward flows of interest payments. Nor does the position on services allow greater optimism. Here, import volumes have been rising faster than export volumes. Between 1979 and 1990, the volume of services exported expanded by only 0.7 per cent per annum, against 3.4 per cent for imports. That this has not yet affected the balance reflects the fact that the value of exports was much higher than imports in 1979, and that the terms of trade in services have shifted somewhat towards the UK. Obviously, if these trends continue, Britain's trade surplus in services is under threat.

The geographical composition of trade is also of interest, one reason being that the impact on the structure of UK trade because of entry into the EC in 1973 has been vast. Table 7 shows that visible imports from the EC increased

Table 7 Geographical structure of UK visible trade (percentages of total)

	1973		1979		1991	
	Exp.	Imp.	Exp.	Imp.	Exp.	Imp.
European Community	35	38	45	48	57	52
Other Western Europe	13	14	11	13	8	12
North America	16	15	12	13	13	13
Other developed	7	7	4	5	4	7
Oil exporting	7	8	9	7	6	2
Rest of the world	22	18	19	14	13	13

Source: CSO, Monthly Review of External Trade Statistics (various issues)

from 38 per cent to well over half the total between 1973 and 1991. The increasing importance of the EC as an export market is even more marked, since today it accounts for nearly three-fifths of total exports. North America has declined a little in importance, but it is with the rest of the world where the decline in share has been most dramatic, especially in terms of exports. Partly this reflects the declining importance of the Commonwealth in UK trade, but also the increasing competitiveness of the new industrializing countries (NICs) in many markets.

The dominance of the EC for British trade is readily visible in the geographical distribution of the visible trade balance, and Figure 8 shows that, relative to GDP, the movement in the EC balance swamps all the others. It is remarkable that the 1974–9 payments cycle saw a large improvement in our trading balance with the EC, which was more than unwound by the performance between 1979 and 1989.

If the analysis contained in the preceding pages is correct, then Britain's growth performance in the coming decade will depend critically on its ability to increase its exports of goods and services at a faster rate than it managed in the past decade. Essentially this creates a two-fold problem for the UK: one of export capacity and one of competitiveness. But these are inter-related problems: two major recessions have severely curtailed Britain's capacity in those industries which must respond if a faster rate of export growth is to be achieved. But here the economy finds itself in a classic double bind for which there is no quick fix. Investment-led growth, given the high import content of fixed investment, will only further tighten the balance of payments constraint. Logically, export growth needs to precede any strategy based on investment, and this means a strategy directly geared towards the competitiveness problem. Obviously, the recent devaluation of the pound helps in this regard. But this is only of short-term assistance, since most analyses point to inadequacies in the labour market preventing any longer-term gain in price competitiveness. Ultimately, it is the non-price competitiveness of British industry which is paramount in improving performance, and if industrial strategy is to be implemented, it needs to consider the factors underlying competitiveness. In essence, this is the problem facing the UK, and the focus of attention throughout this book.

NOTES

1 Alternative approaches to GDP/GNP abound; for a recent survey see Anderton (1992). The United Nations Development Programme (1992) has also recently been developing a human development index (HDI), which tends to show the UK in a slightly better light than the GDP indicator.
2 The subject of the distribution of income, which has become significantly less equal in the UK in the recent past, is discussed in Chapter 14 by Chapman and Temple (this volume).

3 Strictly, gross national product (GNP) (rather than GDP), should be used for comparisons of living standards for the inhabitants of nations. In practice, the levels of GDP are close to levels of GNP for all members of the G6. This is not necessarily the case, and in small economies there is often a considerable divergence.

4 Purchasing power parity exchange rates convert currencies at rates that make price levels between economies appear equal. Thus the PPP rate between the pound and the mark measures the number of marks required to purchase a pound's worth of goods and services in the UK. The composition of the basket of goods and services is determined by the composition of GDP.

5 In the 1992 General Election campaign, some politicians were fond of making a comparison, not between peaks in the business cycle, but between troughs (in this case 1981 and 1992). As a procedure this is highly misleading, since we are in large part simply measuring the extent of recession in both years.

6 The CBI index of capacity utilization, which of course covers only manufacturing industry, shows that the average percentage of firms operating at full capacity was 53.5 in 1973, 42.25 in 1979 and 51.5 in 1990.

7 Strictly, a simple subtraction of growth rates is an approximation, valid only when the rate of growth is small.

8 The classic references are Solow (1957) and Abramovitz (1956).

9 The relationship is not quite as close (although it still exists) in the more recent period 1979–90. Partly this is because the period is not really long enough for the effects we are talking about to dominate, although it also reflects the growing importance of international capital flows. On the other hand, the close relationship of export success in some countries not in the OECD, such as South Korea, and the extraordinary progress achieved tends to confirm the relationship.

10 For further discussion of this point in relation to the service sector, see Chapters 16 and 17 below.

11 The idea behind the balance of payments constraint can be traced back to Harrod's 'foreign trade multiplier'. Kaldor however stressed the importance of 'outside' demand in determining the growth of a national or regional economy (Kaldor 1971, 1977); for recent applications see Thirlwall (1980), McCombie (1992), Coutts and Godley (1990, 1992), McCombie and Thirlwall (1992). The basic idea behind the constraint can be explained more formally as follows: if movements in the price levels prevailing in different economies are, over time, counterbalanced by movements in the exchange rate, then the growth rate of an economy consistent with balance of payments equilibrium, G_b, can be expressed as $\varepsilon W/\pi$, where W is the rate of growth of income in the 'rest of the world', ε is the world income elasticity of demand for exports, and π is the domestic income elasticity of demand for imports. Thirlwall (1979), shows that G_b predicts actual rates of growth around the world with reasonable accuracy.

12 In fact, it seems as if the ability to export is probably the more important factor in explaining differences in national growth rates. It is interesting to note that, in general, policies aimed at stimulating exports have generally been more successful as part of industrialization strategies than policies aimed at restricting imports. The difference between the two may be thought of as being between the cultivation of strengths and the defence of weaknesses.

13 The current account consists of all those transactions between the domestic residents of an economy and foreigners which constitute income, i.e. all trade in goods and services, including non-labour factor services (interest, profit and dividends).

14 For further discussion of whether the balance of payments matters, see Coutts and Godley (1992).

REFERENCES

Abramovitz, M. (1956) 'Resource and output trends in the United States since 1970', *American Economic Review*, Papers and Proceedings, May, pp. 5–23.

Anderson, V. (1991) *Alternative Economic Indicators*, London: Routledge.

Coutts, K. and Godley, W. (1990) 'Prosperity and foreign trade in the 1990s: Britain's strategic problem', *Oxford Review of Economic Policy*, vol. 6, no. 3, Autumn, pp. 82–92.

Coutts, K. and Godley, W. (1992) 'Does Britain's balance of payments matter any more?, in J. Michie (ed.), *The Economic Legacy 1979–1992*, London: Academic Press, pp. 60–7.

Feinstein, C. and Matthews, R. (1990) 'The growth of output and productivity in the UK: the 1980s as a phase of the post-war period', *National Institute Economic Review*, no. 133, August, pp. 78–90.

Forsyth, P. J. and Kay, J. A. (1980) 'The Economic implications of North Sea oil revenues', *Journal of the Institute of Fiscal Studies*, vol. 1, no. 3, pp. 1–28.

Greenhalgh, C. (1989) *Employment and Structural Change in Britain: Trends and Policy Options*, London: Employment Institute.

Her Majesty's Treasury (1992) 'Supply side performance in the 1980s', *Treasury Bulletin*, vol. 3, issue 2, Summer, pp. 23–36.

Kaldor, N. (1971) 'Conflicts in national economic objectives', *Economic Journal*, vol. LXXXI, March, pp. 1–16.

Kaldor, N. (1977) 'Capitalism and industrial development: some lessons from Britain's experience', *Cambridge Journal of Economics*, no. 1, pp. 193–204

McCombie, J. S. L. (1992) '"Thirlwall's law" and balance of payments constrained growth: more on the debate', *Applied Economics*, vol. 24, no. 5, May, pp. 493–512.

McCombie, J. S. L. and Thirlwall, A. (1992) 'The re-emergence of the balance of payments constraint', in J. Michie (ed.), *The Economic Legacy 1979–1992*, London: Academic Press, pp. 68–74.

Maddison, A. (1982) *Phases in Capitalist Economic Development*, Oxford: Oxford University Press.

Maddison, A. (1987) 'Growth and slowdown in advanced capitalist economies', *Journal of Economic Literature*, vol. XXV, no. 2, June, pp. 469–98.

Muellbauer, J. and Murphy, A. (1990) 'Is the UK Balance of payments sustainable?', *Economic Policy*, no. 11, October, pp. 348–95.

Solow, R. M. (1957) 'Technical change and the aggregate production function', *Review of Economics and Statistics*, August, pp. 312–20.

Thirlwall, A. P. (1979) 'The balance of payments constraint as an explanation of international growth rate differences', *Banca Nazionale del Lavoro Quarterly Review*, March.

Thirlwall, A. P. (1980) *Balance of Payments Theory and the UK Experience*, London: Macmillan.

United Nations Development Programme (1992) *Human Development Report*, Oxford: Oxford University Press.

4

THE COMPETITIVENESS OF UK MANUFACTURED EXPORTS

Tony Buxton

INTRODUCTION

Since the UK was the first economy, around 200 years ago, to 'industrialize', reflecting essentially the wide use of high-volume production processes, its share of industrial products in the world total at the time, were such figures available, would have been close to 100 per cent. The same was presumably true of the share of manufactured exports. A decline was therefore inevitable as other countries industrialized. Once such statistics began to be computed, this indeed happened and continued to happen steadily, though not monotonically. The balance of trade of manufactures followed a similar downward trend until, in 1983, for the first time, it went into deficit. However, at about the same time, the decline in the UK's share of world exports seemed to have halted or even reversed itself.[1] If trading performance depends on 'competitiveness' as argued later in this chapter, then, notwithstanding the trade deficit for the reversal of the share to have taken place, 'competitiveness' must have improved round about then.

The 'competitiveness' of the goods and services produced in an economy is a multi-dimensional affair but is often conveniently separated into 'price' and 'non-price' factors. The two are inextricably linked of course. In principle though, a lower price for a product of the same 'quality' or 'characteristics' represents better price competitiveness. The converse is more difficult, but notionally a product with the same price but less quality has lower non-price competitiveness. Price is the central variable in standard economics. But non-price competitiveness is often regarded as being at least as important in international trade. Japanese producers have increasingly owed their high reputation to non-price factors such as reliability. Casual empiricism certainly suggests that significant changes in the quality of goods and services consumed have taken place in the UK. But, on the other hand, products in which the UK has been traditionally strong are now imported. This should not matter if it reflects specialization in which the UK has shifted resources in response to international competition. Arguably, though, it *does* matter if the shift has been to goods or services which are of lower value-added than our competitors:

57

viz. if in this sense the restructuring of UK industry has not halted the process of relative decline.

In the context of the home economy, the source of improvement of both kinds of competitiveness is more efficient or effective production, and it is here that the 'supply-side' revolution of the 1980s may have had an effect. In an international context though, price competitiveness can also improve, at least in the short term, through currency devaluation. The aim of this chapter is to shed some light on the contribution of aspects of competitiveness to the apparent improvement in the performance of UK manufactured exports. In particular, it attempts to show the effects of exchange rate changes, other price factors and non-price competitiveness, covering manufacturing as a whole.

PRICE COMPETITIVENESS

Domestic prices are usually analysed in terms of costs, and in the short run the important cost is labour. A starting point in the study of international competitiveness is therefore simple comparison of wage costs across countries, and this is graphed in Figure 1. In 1980, Japan's hourly wage costs were the lowest of the G6 economies. The UK was next at about 25 per cent higher. But UK labour costs were only about two-thirds of those in West Germany and by 1990 the UK had become the lowest of the G6 economies. By no stretch of the imagination, therefore, could the UK be regarded as a 'high wage' economy relative to the G6. However, the real cost of labour is in relation to how much

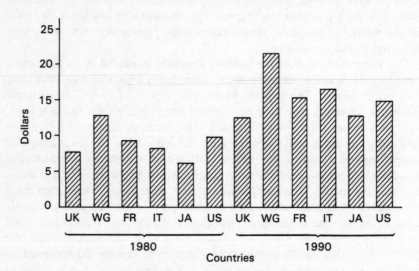

Source: Swedish Employers' Federation and OEF

Figure 4.1 Hourly labour costs (US dollars).

it produces, and a widely used measure of that is unit labour cost (ULC) – the average labour cost of producing a given output. This is based on labour's efficiency which depends on other factors of production, particularly capital and managerial organization. In the shorter term though, these things are fairly constant, so that changes in ULCs are likely to put pressure on prices.

The importance of ULC to pricing in the international marketplace is usually analysed by comparing the UK to its main trading competitors. Relative unit labour costs (RULC), puts the measure in relation to a weighted average of competitor countries,[2] and in terms of a common currency. The paths of RULC and relative export prices (REP)[3] are given in Figure 2. The two follow each other very closely.

An analysis of RULC can therefore help in establishing the source of changes in price competitiveness. One way of doing this[4] is to formulate:

$$RULC = (RWCPP/RLP) \times EER \qquad (1)$$

where:

$\quad$ RWCPP = relative wage costs per person (average wages)
$\quad$ RLP = relative labour productivity
$\quad$ EER = effective exchange rate (weighted average)

The term in brackets in equation (1) is the extent to which wage changes are 'earned' – if relative wages rise at the same rate as relative productivity, the

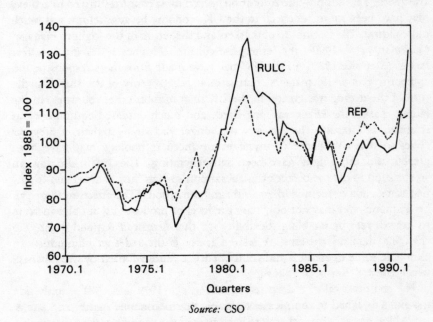

Source: CSO

Figure 4.2 UK RULC and REP.

59

ratio is unity and relative unit labour costs are unaffected, and vice versa. In the UK, much attention has been focused on the extent to which productivity improved in the 1980s as a result of the new regime with its emphases on 'supply-side' policies rather than the 'demand-side' ones which had dominated the period after the Second World War. The issue was regarded as particularly important because the growth of productivity in manufacturing seemed in the mid-to-late 1970s to have fallen to a dangerously low level and also because of the link between productivity and competitiveness in international markets. Whether there had been a sustainable change in productivity became a con-tentious issue. The word 'miracle' was often used to describe the turnaround which seemed to take place in the 1980s and was claimed to have arisen out of the new economic policies.[5]

The debate about the UK's relative improvement received much analytical attention and revolved around the basic question – was it sustainable or not? The issue was whether the UK economic policy changes of the 1980s[6] had had a fundamental effect or was just another cyclical recovery. On the positive side there was the potential for catch-up on the other countries. But other countries were not standing still. They too had to respond to the increased harshness of international competition as impediments to free trade were lowered or removed and the world economy became more competitive. The process of 'catching-up' however, may be easier than setting the pace, so that the UK economic policy changes in the 1980s may have had a stronger effect than elsewhere. The 'supply-side revolution' which most countries strived to achieve may have been more beneficial to the UK economy because reform was much more radical. The freeing-up of markets and the return of the 'right to manage' (Jackman et al. 1990), the 'enterprise culture' (Hughes 1992) and the 'fear factor' (Metcalfe 1989)[7] in the UK may have made firms more responsive and competitive in world markets. Furthermore, the severity of the slump at the turn of the decade was greater in the UK than in most other countries. In the labour market the effect was long-lived, and much outdated equipment was scrapped as a result. The recovery was longer and stronger than in previous cycles so that confidence to invest in advanced technology may have been greater and this might have been self-generating. The 1980s also saw an acceleration in the use of stock control systems such as 'just in time' and 'right-first-time', and of team-working and similar methods. The effects of these can be dramatic, and may not only raise the level of productivity but also increase its growth rate by enabling 'flexibility' so that firms can respond quicker to changing demand patterns. A related factor is the redesign of products to eliminate some operations and components, a route adopted by the Japanese which the UK has been following.

The combination of a deep recession between 1979 and 1981, supply-side measures designed to complement a stable macroeconomic stance, and a rela-tively long recovery, may therefore have created the conditions for a sustainable improvement in manufacturing productivity growth. On the negative side,

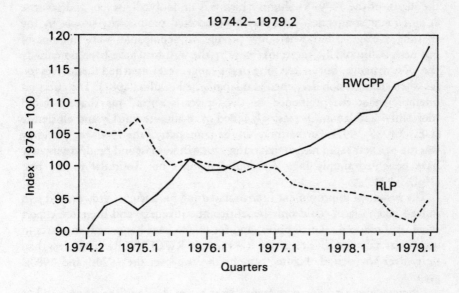

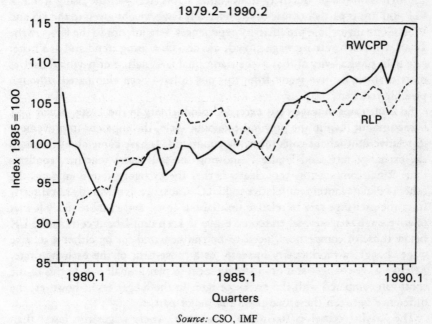

Source: CSO, IMF

Source: CSO, IMF

Figure 4.3 Relative wages and productivity.

however, the length and strength of the recovery might have simply reflected the depth of the 1979–81 slump which was undoubtedly severe and saw the end of many companies. This may have boosted productivity simply by the 'batting average' effect where low productivity companies were put out of business. Additionally, those that went to the wall may have been potentially the most dynamic, but in investing in the longer term stretched themselves too far when the recession deepened and lengthened (Oulton 1987). The effect on unemployment was prolonged, so that 'precariousness'[8] may have reduced 'flexibility' and labour increasingly failed to re-allocate quickly and efficiently (OECD 1986, 1991). Furthermore, in the latter part of the 1980s the economy was run at a very rapid rate so that output growth was fast and productivity may have benefited simply in a 'Verdoorn' manner not dissimilar to the past (NEDC 1988).

The sustained improvement in manufacturing productivity growth, if it had indeed taken place, could only benefit competitiveness, and therefore export share, if it reduced relative prices, and for this to have happened, increases in wage costs must not have exceeded it – the ratio RWCPP/RLP must be less than unity over any period. Figure 3 graphs the two over the 1970s' and 1980s' cycles.

Progress on the productivity front comes across clearly in the rising trend of RLP and this is partly because of the relatively large weight given to the US and West Germany, whose productivity experiences were inferior to the UK's in the 1980s. However, relative wage growth was also on a rising trend and at a faster rate than productivity at that – the traditional UK malaise of paying ourselves more than we deserve seems from this not to have been eliminated although possibly reduced.[9]

So if increases in wage costs exceeded productivity in the 1980s, albeit by a lesser amount than in the previous economic cycle, the apparent improvement in relative unit labour costs must, by equation (1), have come about through the exchange rate, and Figure 4, showing the four series together, confirms that. What comes across very clearly is that the exchange rate dominates the other two in its movement relative to RULC. Causation is obviously not directly from the exchange rate to relative unit labour costs. Rather more likely is that relative wage increases, when too excessive to keep unit labour costs in the UK below those of competitors, need to be compensated for by either a relative wage change, a productivity increase, or a movement of the exchange rate. Relative wage changes and productivity seem to play a small part in this in the short run compared with the exchange rate. In the longer term, however, the difference between these two plays the major part.

The 'paying ourselves too much' syndrome, where wages rise faster than productivity, looked to have improved in the 1980s compared with the 1970s so that the negative effect this had on competitiveness was undoubtedly reduced. But the reduction in RULC which took place, accounting for a significant amount of the improvement in price competitiveness, came about from

1979.2–1990.2

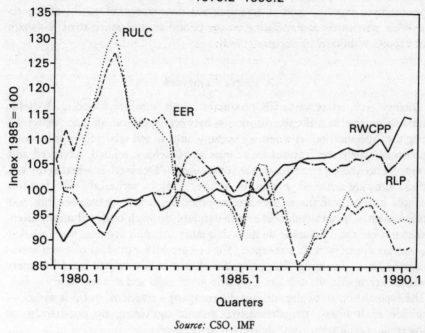

Source: CSO, IMF

Figure 4.4 RULC, RWCPP, RLP and EER.

the decline in the effective exchange rate, amounting to 44 per cent between the trough of 1981.1 and the peak of 1990.2. The reasons for this huge devaluation (which amounts to a comparable cut in costs), were connected to North Sea oil, and are well documented in the literature. But essentially they mean that the improvement in price competitiveness which looks to have taken place in the UK in the 1980s, and which must have contributed significantly to the turnaround in the share of UK exports in the 'world' total, may have been on the back of a series of devaluations which, in the time between joining and leaving the ERM, were described as 'fools gold'.[10]

NON-PRICE COMPETITIVENESS

'Non-price competitiveness' is a useful term but lacks precision, though in practical economics encompasses a myriad of definitions. A catch-all is 'quality' of product. In turn, there is no unique measure of quality and the casual empiricism which suggests that Japan has improved in this respect may be subjective. Because a relative decline in the quality of UK goods has important implications, there is a need to provide objective evidence. The first aim of this section is therefore to discuss the difficulties in defining and estimating relative quality. It then reports on evidence from one indicator of quality itself – value per tonne of exports – and on an important *determinant* of quality of exports – R&D intensity – concentrating on the period around which the UK's share of exports stabilized in the mid-1980s.

A simple framework

'Quality' with reference to UK production has a number of aspects. A useful starting point is to make the distinction between 'specification' and 'delivery'. Highest 'specification' is where a company aims to sell relatively sophisticated products, where the features are at least as numerous, refined, advanced and complex as those of international competitors. 'Delivery' is whether or not these aims are achieved. Failure to 'deliver' may be technical – the features simply do not perform as they are supposed to, involving maintenance and breakdown – or non-technical – sub-standard dispatch or distribution, after-sales service, etc. This static division of quality becomes dynamic when market forces are considered. If a company aims to produce a product of given speci-fication then, assuming that prices for that specification are fixed by inter-national competition, if delivery is inadequate, sales and market share will fall. The eventual outcome depends on the company's reactions, but if it wishes to remain in business, the alternatives include tightening up on delivery or lowering specification until delivery is achievable.

Consider a machine tool as an example of a producer good. If a company claims an accuracy rate of 99 per cent then in terms of specification, quality is high. If, however, only 89 per cent is achieved then in terms of delivery, quality is not. The company may then be expected to reduce its specification so that it can 'deliver' with existing production, or change its technology to achieve its claimed accuracy rate. The same would apply to consumer goods, say the claimed acceleration of a motor car. The process by which specification and delivery interact is complex and variable. In the case of the motor car for instance, motoring journalists would be quick off the mark. For the machine tool, company experience might be necessary. Similarly, specifications can be intricate and complicated so that the extent of under-achievement of delivery may be hard to disentangle.

Taking 'specification' and 'delivery' as simplifying the many aspects of quality of firms' products, how has the UK fared? First, taking the economy as a whole, the UK may be producing increasingly low quality goods. This could have come about: (i) by aiming to produce low specification products and achieving delivery: if UK companies on average have failed to carry out the necessary research, then they may simply realize that attempting to produce relatively sophisticated products is beyond them and settle for a lower quality which *is* achievable; (ii) by attempting to produce high specification products but being unable to deliver so that what actually turns out is low specification delivery.[11]

The difference between these two is that the first is deliberate but may bring some static benefits from trade specification, whereas the second would involve dynamic effects which reduce *ex post* quality as market share is reduced and may have further damaging effects if the process is self-perpetuating.

Considering now an individual industry, the dispersion of quality may change. For any given average, there may be a whole spectrum from high to low, brought about either by (i) or (ii) or both. Another aspect of declining quality in an individual industry is that, even though it might not shrink in size, it could move down-market in its particular product, even though this might not necessarily involve a change in industry structure in terms of size distribution. Similar comments would apply when considering an individual firm's range of products.

Measurement of quality

The theoretical measurement of quality is quite straightforward. For any given product, with perfect markets, quality is reflected in price. In turn, the price is the total value-added in the production of the good, from the basic raw materials to the finished product. In this sense high value-added reflects high quality. Measurement therefore seems easy; compare value-added or unit value across countries, for a product.

However, there are fundamental difficulties in defining a 'good' as discussed later, and there are practical problems of aggregation, exchange rates, etc. But as far as the present discussion is concerned, the measure comes up against the problem of intermediate goods. A country which sells high value-added goods is not necessarily a high value-added producer because it may not contribute much to the productive process; it may import, add some more value then sell. Such a country which assembles high value-added goods from parts made in another country may or may not be called a 'high quality' producer.

Further difficulties arise from consideration of differences between consumer and investment goods and the benefits from international trade. A high income economy may be expected to import high income elasticity consumer goods which would be expected to be of relatively good quality. This in turn begs the question: can high incomes be sustained by exporting relatively low quality goods and importing high quality ones? The intuitive answer is: not in the long run. A more likely case would be where exports and imports were of high quality as specialization generated benefits for exporter and importer. The same is true of capital goods – the use of the highly efficient equipment is most beneficial to an economy, so that importing high quality machinery is a good thing, but exporting low quality investment goods at the same time may not be, again in the longer term.

Given these problems, there are a number of methods which economists have adopted to indicate relative quality. The most technical is the construction of hedonic price indices starting with Court (1939) and developed by Griliches

(1971). The title stems from the 'characteristics' analysis of Lancaster (1966) which analyses demand by the 'attributes' of products. Thus the models and varieties of a particular commodity are made up of a number of characteristics such as size, colour, flexibility, which can change over time. 'New' models are therefore simply a different combination of 'old' attributes. The hedonic approach was developed because of a widespread belief that published price indices do not fully take quality changes into account which causes the published rate of inflation to be biased because it contains the effect of quality as well as straight inflation. The basic method is to split the price of products over time into the effect of raising quality – the weighted sum of characteristics – and the remainder, a 'pure' price effect – how much the same product of constant quality has increased in price. The usual conclusion is that 'quality' accounts for a significant proportion, sometimes all, of published price index movements (Gordon 1990, for instance). This of course gives support to the belief in the importance of 'non-price' factors.

As far as comparing quality over time and across countries is concerned, therefore, in principle the hedonic approach is of great value. It identifies the characteristics of quality as well as their importance. Estimation involves comparison of the size of individual quality improvements but also their contribution to overall quality. Calculation for a single product and/or country is a very big piece of work however; to repeat the exercise for different products and countries is even more so.[12]

Applied economists have therefore often turned to other indicators, including the following:

- comparative trade performance by sector ranked according to R&D intensity (NEDC 1984, 1989; Smith 1986);
- trade performance by sector ranked by rate of demand growth (European Commission 1983);
- geographical pattern of trade, whether countries export to developing or industrialized countries (NEDC 1989);
- UK share of world trade (NEDC 1989);
- share of world trade by sector (NEDC 1989);
- developing the hedonic approach to measure quality through revealed consumer behaviour (Swann and Taghavi 1992);
- econometric studies of specialization (Balassa and Bauwens 1988).

These all provide useful indications of quality differences. Another method which NEDO often used is comparisons of unit values of exports and imports of different products (Williamson 1971; Stout 1977; Connell 1980; Brech and Stout 1981; NEDC 1990). The calculation is simply the total value of exports or imports divided by their weight. The rationale is that, given international competition, price differences between genuinely identical goods will be small; better quality will mean less unnecessary bulk, so that high value per unit weight will reflect, to some extent, high quality. The simplest example is a machine tool which requires a huge lump of cast iron to hold it down will be heavier than one which stops vibrations in another way, but the rationale applies to all goods, viz. if two brands of the same product have the same price then the one with less weight is of higher quality.

The measure has other merits. Weight can be objectively, consistently and accurately measured. The data are extensively available over a wide range of products over long periods. Indeed, an embarrassment of such information exists. On the other hand, there are demerits which mean that the index picks up other effects. Weight and quality are likely to be correlated, but the form of correlation is unknown – does a doubling in value per unit weight double quality or triple it; how do the different facets of quality change in importance; and does the relationship vary between products and over time for any one product? In defence of the measure though, market forces are likely to make the situation the same between countries, and comparisons over time will probably indicate relative *changes* in quality reasonably well.

In relation to the earlier discussion concerning changes in industrial structure, if relative value per unit in a country declines it means either that the mix of products has a lower quality – high quality industries are declining and vice versa – or across-the-board falls are taking place – quality in all industries is falling – or both. The distinction is important, but in an aggregate analysis is impossible to evaluate. Nevertheless, indication of *overall* relative quality change can be obtained from looking at average value per unit weight in the recent past, and this is the starting point following a description of the data.

The source of the data is the OECD Bulletin of Foreign Trade. It consists of the value (in US dollars) and weight (in tonnes) of exports over a ten-year period, 1978–87, for each of four countries – the United Kingdom, France, West Germany and Italy. The US and Japan had 'gaps' in the data and could not be included. These are important omissions but not disastrous given the size and importance of the European economies.

The basic quality measure is value per tonne measured in US dollars, converted from national currencies using exchange rates based on the IMF definition of exports. Thus:

quality of exports = QE = (value of exports)/(weight of exports)

This is taken one step further to make relative comparisons by the construction of RQE, the value of the UK's QE relative to each of the other countries:

relative quality of exports = RQE

= (QE for the UK)/(QE for each competitor)

A value of this ratio above unity indicates the quality of UK exports is high in relation to that of the competitor. A decline in the value indicates a fall in the UK's export quality relative to the country.

The results

As an indication of overall quality of manufactured exports in the economies, Table 1 gives the levels of QE and RQE in 1978 and 1987, and the change in RQE (DRQE) for all products combined. Compositional differences across countries make comparisons difficult when considering manufacturing as a whole. Nevertheless, the table suggests that the UK had the *highest* quality exports on average in manufactured goods in both 1978 and 1987. This is a somewhat unexpected result since the UK is not generally thought of as a high quality exporter relative to other large mature economies. West Germany was second to the UK in both years. The quality of France and Italy's exports were lower, but very similar in 1978. Italy was significantly higher than France in 1987.

The UK therefore comes out well in the comparison of this indicator in both 1978 and 1987 – the quality of the UK's manufactured exports was seemingly higher than that of our large European competitors. Considering the *change* which took place over the period though, the conclusion is very different. The change in RQE suggests that quality has fallen relative to all three of the other countries, albeit by only a very small amount in the case of West Germany. Relative to France, the quality of UK exports fell by about 5 per cent between 1978 and 1987, while relative to Italy the relative decline was almost three times that.

Part of the explanation for this pattern is the conversion to US dollars which is done to the figures, so that different movements in each country's exchange rate relative to the dollar cause the value of exports to change in a way which is not directly related to quality. Removing this influence is not easy of course, because the extent to which changes in the value of exports comes about from either price or non-price factors is unknown. However, an attempt to remove the exchange rate effect can be made by calculating an adjusted RQE, ARQE, by revaluing UK exports in 1987 by the extent to which the pound changed its value between 1978 and 1987 relative to each country:

ARQE = RQE adjusted for the exchange rate

Table 1 Quality of manufactured exports

	1978		1987		Change 1987/78 (%)
	QE	RQE	QE	RQE	DRQE
UK	2.5	–	4.1	–	–
France	1.5	1.7	2.6	1.6	– 5.4
Italy	1.6	1.6	3.1	1.3	– 15.2
West Germany	2.0	1.3	3.3	1.2	– 0.6

Source: OECD

Table 2 Change in the adjusted relative
quality of exports

	DARQE 1987/1978 (%)
UK	–
France	8.0
Italy	10.3
West Germany	– 24.0

Source: OECD, HMSO

DARQE is then the change in the relative quality of the UK's exports when the values in 1987 are measured at the 1978 exchange rate for each country. Table 2 gives the results. DARQE alters the picture somewhat from that given by DRQE in Table 1, and suggests that UK manufactured exports improved in quality relative to those of France and Italy, but worsened significantly relative to West Germany. This is obviously because the pound appreciated against the franc and the lira, but depreciated against the mark. DARQE overcompensates for the exchange rate effect of course because export demand responds to changes in the exchange rate price as well as quality. The 'true' change in quality, to the extent that it is reflected in value per tonne, is somewhere between DRQE and DARE, which implies that quality relative to West Germany almost certainly declined, but may have gone either way in relation to France and Italy.

The implication of this, with the appropriate provisos discussed earlier, is that, while there are absolute differences between the quality of the countries' exports, with the UK apparently the highest, there was a general tendency for relative quality to rise in the large European economies in the 1980s. In West Germany the rise was probably faster than in the UK. In France and Italy the position is not clear-cut. If these results are at all representative, then by this measure the contribution of non-price competitiveness to the improvement in the UK's export share has yet to be proved.

TECHNOLOGY AND EXPORTS

The next stage is to examine further indicative evidence on non-price competitiveness by analysing the technological structure of UK manufactured exports in relation to our competitors, in particular the extent to which there has been a greater shift into 'high-tech'. The argument in Chapter 8 is that relatively high R&D spending can improve non-price competitiveness. An implication of this is that where industries spend relatively more on R&D then their share of the market will rise as competitiveness improves. The mix of products emanating from a given industry structure was discussed earlier. An analysis of the way in which this can be related to technology, and the way in which an economy can achieve an 'effective' export industry structure, is not straight-forward. The presumption though is that the amount of technology embodied in any product would be expected to rise through time and an economy which can generate a relatively large proportion of high-tech industries can take a higher proportion of total exports as the demand for such products rises. In other words, 'non-price' competitiveness and 'high-tech' would broadly be expected to go hand in hand. The approach offered here therefore is to report on the extent to which the exports of the UK economy can be called 'high-tech', and how much changes in the structure of its industries has improved relative to its competitors.

But how can 'high-tech' or otherwise be measured? What has become a widely used measure, gaining its respectability to some extent from the OECD, is the proportion of resources devoted to R&D out of sales (S), otherwise known as research intensity (R&D/S). Thus an industry which has a 'high' R&D/S ratio is categorized as 'high-tech' etc. and is regarded as being more non-price competitive. The benefits of R&D spending can of course come in the form of process improvements – more efficient production methods – as well as in product changes. The assumption made here is that even when R&D is directed towards more efficient production methods, the end result will be reflected in the quality of the good relative to its price, so that the product/process problem does not arise. Another potential difficulty is that industries may change category over the period of the analysis by changing their R&D/S ratio. In fact, the R&D intensity of manufacturing industries varies very little on average. Another problem is re-exports, where a country could look like a high-tech exporter but in fact was not one. Again though, the use of *changes* in structure rather than levels probably eliminates much of the bias from this.

R&D intensity could be used as a continuous variable, but the more conven-tional approach is to split industries into high, medium and low technology ones based on somewhat arbitrary cut-off points using the OECD categories (OECD 1989), based on 1980 R&D/S ratios.[13] The data are measured in current US dollars, but since the main comparative indicators are shares and changes in shares of industry groups out of the total, the prices arguably largely cancel out. Since the improvement in the UK's manufacturing export share appeared to come about in the mid-1980s, and since the effects of R&D would be expected to come about with a lag, any beneficial change in industry technology structure would be presumed to have taken place in the early 1980s. The period 1980–6 was therefore chosen for the empirical analysis.

In 1980, high-tech industries accounted for nearly 21 per cent of the exports of UK manufacturing. By 1986 this had increased to 28.5 per cent – an increase of over 5 per cent per annum in the share. This was significantly faster than in the 1970s, when the high-tech proportion grew by only 1.2 per cent per annum (Buxton and Clokie 1992). The share of medium-tech exports fell in the 1980s, by nearly 2 per cent per annum, and this was significantly faster than in the 1970s. The same was true of the low-tech share. The shift towards high-tech exports was therefore faster in the 1980s than in the 1970s, and suggests that non-price competitiveness improved faster.

The expected, and in all likelihood beneficial, move away from low-tech and towards high-tech is therefore evident and the trend is apparently accelerating. But the pace of technological change is itself commonly thought to be accelerating. Whether the apparent UK improvement in the 1980s is actually an advance depends on the experience of other countries – are the structural shifts of the right size relative to our competitors? The actual shares themselves (for 1986) are interesting though, and are given in Table 3.

The UK had a lower share of high-tech exports than Japan and the US in 1986. However, the UK was significantly higher than in the G6 European economies and reflects to some extent the picture in Table 1 of export value per tonne where the UK was the highest in both 1978 and 1987. However, in terms of improving international competitiveness, the important matter is *changes* in industry shares relative to competitor economies. Figure 5 shows this over the period 1980–6.

Table 3 Technology and exports of manufactures

Shares of high-tech in total manufactured exports in 1986 (%)

UK	WG	FR	IT	JA	US
28.5	18.2	18.9	12.9	33.4	37.3

Source: OECD

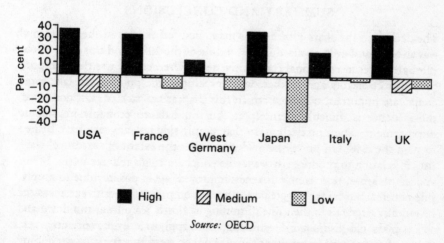

Source: OECD

Figure 4.5 Technology and growth of export shares, 1980–6.

UK industry shifted to high-tech exports in the first half of the 1980s at about the same rate as the US, France and Japan but much faster than Italy and nearly three times quicker than West Germany. Japan reduced its low-tech share the fastest, but the UK rate was about the same as West Germany and France. The UK therefore seems to have participated in the shift towards high-tech exports at least as strongly as the other G6 economies.

The key question is whether 'at least as strongly' would be sufficient to generate an improvement in non-price competitiveness which would contribute towards the rise in the UK's share of manufactured exports. The answer unfortunately has to be 'don't know'. The contribution which high-tech improvement has made could have taken some of the exports of West Germany and/or Italy, which may have helped the overall share, but the data are such that clear conclusions are difficult. On the other hand, the evidence does not point to a worsening of relative non-price competitiveness.

Taking the two pieces of evidence on non-price competitiveness together, what conclusions can be drawn? The lack of information on Japan and the US in the value per tonne data makes strong conclusions difficult. What remains however suggests that the UK's position worsened relative to West Germany in the 1980s, but was probably maintained relative to France and Italy. The technology shares evidence suggests that the UK improved about as fast as France, Japan and the US and significantly faster than West Germany and Italy. The two sets of evidence therefore point to different conclusions, and while the source of the conflict is unknown it has many possibilities. The balance of evidence must be more or less neutral though, with the apparent decline in non-price competitiveness in the first set being offset, in an ordinal sense, by improvement in the second.

SUMMARY AND CONCLUSIONS

The decline in the share of the UK's manufactured exports in the world total was arrested and even reversed in the middle of the 1980s and this came about through better international competitiveness. Whether this was through price or non-price factors and further, whether supply-side policies can take some credit, are important questions which this chapter has tackled. On non-price, the evidence is difficult to interpret, but on balance probably implies no improvement, albeit no decline, so that supply-side policies may have helped to stem the tide. On price, the evidence is that the extent of 'excessive' wage rises in relation to productivity was reduced in the 1980s relative to the 1970s, and in this sense, price competitiveness improved, again possibly due to supply-side policies. But by far the greatest influence on price competitiveness was the historically large fall in the value of sterling as North Sea oil was run down and this is plain old-fashioned devaluation, not supply-side improvements.

It is of course well known that the attempt to stem this trend of depending on devaluation to maintain or raise competitiveness, by joining the ERM, quickly came to an end in September 1992. The subsequent devaluation arguably put UK manufactured exports back on the treadmill of relying on falls in the value of sterling to maintain or improve competitiveness – a treadmill which arguably runs faster as policy-makers stake their credibility on sound currency and then fail to deliver. Meanwhile, possibly as a result, supply-side policies seem to have had limited success so far in improving export performance in manufacturing.

NOTES

1 See the following chapter.
2 The weights used are exports.
3 The weights are again exports.
4 NEDC (1987) for instance.
5 'There can be no doubt that the transformation of Britain's economic performance during the eighties, a transformation acknowledged throughout the world, is above all due to the supply-side reforms we have introduced to allow markets of all kinds to work better.' Chancellor (Nigel Lawson), Institute of Economic Affairs special lecture, 21 July 1988.
6 The main policies are outlined in HMT (1989) and Dicks (1991).
7 Other contributors to the debate include Bosworth (1989), Feinstein and Mathews (1990), Glynn (1992), Kay and Haskell (1990), Muellbauer (1986), Muellbauer and Murphy (1989) and Spencer (1987).
8 The extent of security of employment.
9 NEDC (1987) where RLP is shown to be declining slowly but RWCPP increasing rapidly in the 1970s.
10 Norman Lamont's description of the devaluation option in the days before the UK left the ERM.
11 A third (disaster) scenario which is not considered here for obvious reasons is where the UK aims for lower specification and does not even deliver that.
12 The recently published study of Gordon (1990), which combines the hedonic approach with the conventional specification method for a wide range of US durable consumer and producer goods was first drafted in 1974.
13 The high-tech industries are: drugs, office machinery, electrical machinery, electrical components, aerospace & instruments; the medium-tech are: chemicals, rubber & plastics, non-ferrous metals, non-electrical machinery, other transport, motors, and other manufacturing; the low-tech are: food, drink & tobacco, textiles, wood, cork & furniture, paper & printing, petrol refining, stone, clay & glass, ferrous metals, fabricated metal products, and shipbuilding.

REFERENCES

Balassa, B. and Bauwens, L. (1988) *Changing Trade Patterns in Manufactured Goods: An Econometric Investigation*, Amsterdam: North-Holland.
Bosworth, D. L. (1989) *The British Productivity Miracle*, mimeo., Institute of Economic Research, University of Warwick.
Brech, M. J. and Stout, D. K. (1981) 'The rate of exchange and non-price competitveness: a provisional study within UK manufactured exports', *Oxford Econnomic Papers*, vol. 33, Supplement, pp. 268–81.

Buxton, T. and Clokie, S. (1992) 'Technology and structural change', in C. Driver and P. Dunne (eds), *Structural Change and Economic Growth*, Cambridge: Cambridge University Press, pp. 203–29.

Connell, D. (1980) *The UK's Performance in Export Markets – Some Evidence from International Trade Data*, Discussion Paper 6, London: National Economic Development Office.

Court, A. T. (1939) 'Hedonic price indices with automotive examples' in *The Dynamics of Automobile Demand*, New York: General Motors Corporation, pp. 99–117.

Dicks, G. (1991) 'What remains of Thatcherism?', *Economic Outlook*, vol. 15(5), February, London: LBS. Gower.

European Commission, (1983) 'Competitiveness of European industry, *European Economy*, no. 25, September.

Feinstein, C. and Mathews, R. (1990) 'The growth of output and productivity in the 1980s', *National Institute Economic Review*, no. 133, pp. 78–90.

Glynn, A. (1992) 'The productivity miracle', profits and investment', in J. Michie (ed.), *The Economic Legacy 1979–92*, London: Academic Press.

Gordon, R. J. (1990) *The Measurement of Durable Goods Prices*, NBER, Chicago. University of Chicago Press.

Grilliches, Z. (1971) 'Hedonic price indexes for automobiles: an econometric analysis of quality change', in Z. Grilliches, *Price Indexes and Quality Change*, Harvard: Harvard University Press.

HMT (1989) 'Helping markets work better', *Economic Progress Report*, no. 203, August, London: HMSO, pp. 4–8.

Hughes, A. (1992) 'Big business, small business and the "enterprise culture" ', in J. Michie (ed.), *The Economic Legacy 1979–92*, London: Academic Press.

Jackman, R., Layard, R. and Nickell, S. (1990) *Unemployment*, Oxford: Oxford University Press.

Kay, J. A. and Haskell, J. E. (1990) 'Industrial Performance under Mrs Thatcher', in T. Congdon *et al.* (eds), *The State of the Economy*, London: IEA.

Lancaster, K. (1966) 'A new approach to consumer theory, *Journal of Political Economy*, vol. 74, pp. 132–57.

Metcalfe, D. (1989) 'Water notes dry up, the impact of the Donovan reform proposals and Thatcherism at work on labour productivity in British manufacturing industry', *British Journal of Industrial Relations*, vol. 27, pp. 1–31.

Muellbauer, J. (1986) 'Productivity and competitiveness in British manufacturing', *Oxford Review of Economic Policy*, vol. 2, pp. i–xxv.

Muellbauer, J. and Murphy, A. (1989) *How Fundamental are the UK's Balance of Payments Problems?*, mimeo., Oxford. Nuffield College.

NEDC (1984) *Trade Patterns and Industrial Change*, NEDC(84)21, London: National Economic Development Office.

NEDC (1987) *British Industrial Performance*, London: National Economic Development Office.

NEDC (1988) *Pay and Productivity*, NEDC(88)8, London: National Economic Development Office.

NEDC (1989) *Trade Performance*, NEDC(89)9, London: National Economic Development Office.

NEDC (1990) *United Kindgom Trade Performance*, NEDC(90)80, London: National Economic Development Office.

OECD (1986) *Flexibility in the Labour Market*, Paris: OECD.

OECD (1989) *Main Economic Indicators*, Paris: OECD.

OECD (1991) *Employment Outlook*, Paris: OECD.

Oulton, N. (1987) 'Plant closures and the productivity "Miracle" ', *National Institute Economic Review*, no. 132, August, pp. 71–91.

Smith, M. (1986) 'The output and trade of UK manufacturing industry', *Midland Bank Review*, Autumn, pp. 8–16.

Spencer, P. (1987) *Britain's Productivity Renaissance*, Crédit Suisse, First Boston, June.

Stout, D. (1977) *International Price Competitiveness, Non-price Factors and Export Performance*, mimeo London: National Economic Development Office.

Swann, P. and Taghavi, M. (1992) *Measuring Price and Quality Competitiveness*, Aldershot: Avebury.

Williamson, D. T. N. (1971) *Trade Balance in the 1970s – The Role of Mechanical Engineering*, Discussion Paper 1, London: National Economic Development Office.

5

THE EVOLUTION OF UK TRADING PERFORMANCE
Evidence from manufacturing industry[1]

Paul Temple

INTRODUCTION

In many respects the jury remains out on whether a decade or more of supply-side reform has seen an improvement in the performance of the UK's manufacturing industries. Those who insist that fundamental advances have been made usually point to two main indicators: the rate of growth in labour productivity and the share of world trade.

That there has been some improvement in relation to the growth of labour productivity over the 1970s is widely accepted, although whether this is a useful comparator given the very severe problems of that decade, especially for energy-intensive manufacturing, is very much a moot point. More importantly perhaps, productivity growth appeared to be faster in the UK than in other major advanced economies (with the usual exception of Japan), so that there was some evidence of a 'catch-up' process. What is not so clear is whether this really represents an improvement in the trend rate of productivity advance or whether it is a once and for all 'levels' effect made possible by shedding labour aggressively.[2]

The second piece of evidence relates to the UK share of world manufacturing trade.[3] The remarkable thing about this indicator is that the long-term decline in the UK share appears to have been arrested in the course of the 1980s and may even have gone into reverse. Anderton (1992), for example, uses sophisticated trend analysis to argue that this indeed signifies a definite improvement in 'non-price competitiveness'.

The problem with either piece of evidence is that they are both partial in nature; faster productivity growth is not necessarily synonymous with a healthy industry as those familiar with the 'batting average' analogy in the literature, where a better average is produced by declaring the innings closed and not using the 'tail-enders' – a worse result for the team, since it is the aggregate number of runs that counts. In other words, if faster productivity growth is a result, whether by recession or a lack of competitiveness, of the less efficient firms going under, then there is nothing necessarily desirable about faster

76

productivity growth. Similarly, if as suggested in the opening chapter, weak international trading performance has been at the heart of Britain's economic difficulties, then imports are just as important as exports, and we must look at both to make an accurate assessment of trading performance. In this chapter we examine further evidence regarding supply-side phenomena by looking in a detailed way at the trading performance of UK manufacturing, using data at a rather more detailed industrial level than is customary. We shall be particularly concerned to locate the possible sources of the *relative* variation in performance between manufacturing industries. First of all, however, we assess some of the alternative methods of empirical analysis which are available.

EMPIRICAL ANALYSES OF TRADING STRUCTURE AND PERFORMANCE

The industrial structure of UK trade and the factors underpinning its evolution are of the utmost significance for the economy's prospects. Traditional theories of international trade concentrate on the determinants of comparative advantage, emphasizing the factors determining the relative cost of production of commodities. The Heckscher–Ohlin (or factor proportions) model of international trade reduces this to an individual economy's relative endowments of 'factors of production', while abstracting from differences in consumer tastes and differential access to technology between countries. The fundamental proposition which emerges from this strand of analysis is that economies will tend to export goods which use relatively intensively the economy's abundant factor, since these are relatively cheaper. One important consequence of specialization according to this model, compared to a hypothetical situation of autarky, is to raise the demand for the economy's abundant factor; there will therefore be a tendency for international trade to equalize factor prices around the world, even though factors are assumed to be immobile across international frontiers. In this way international trade sets up an implicit 'flow' of factors between countries. To be generally applicable, the theory assumes perfect competition and imposes restrictions on the possible underlying production relationships.

Attempts to validate the theory empirically began with Wassily Leontief (1953), who used input–output tables to test the proposition for the US, a country widely supposed of course to be 'capital abundant'. By comparing the labour intensity of export industries with those in industries competing with foreign imports Leontief obtained a perverse result – export industries were found to be relatively labour intensive. Over the years, the volume of literature produced by this result has been legendary.

Following the publication of Leontief's 'paradox' many commentators directed a sustained critique at the theory itself, pointing to the relevance of economies of scale, market imperfections, differences in patterns of consumer preferences, and perhaps most significantly to the 'technology factor' in international trade: the proposition that technical change was vital in under-standing trade flows. Especial importance was attached to the 'product cycle' idea that, in some industries at least, an 'availability' advantage (either relatively or absolutely) was more important than any cost advantage at early stages in a product's life. However, in mature phases of the cycle, cost consider-ations prove increasingly significant, and the direction of trade will begin to reverse itself. Product cycle theories added a dimension missing in the traditional account by allowing for the mobility of international capital, and allowing location decisions on the part of multinationals to be based on the cycle itself, with labour costs beginning to dominate the importance of access to sophisticated markets and a highly-skilled labour force. At least one novel theory of international trade drew attention to the importance of the monopoly held by the developed economies (the 'North') in innovative products which helped it to preserve a wage differential against the less developed economies (the 'South'). The North is thereby uncompetitive in mature products and, since new products all eventually mature, it has to keep innovating to preserve the wage differential (Krugman 1979).

The development of alternative theories of international trade proliferated in the 1980s, with many writers concentrating on how producers locate them-selves in terms of product characteristics, competing on the basis of 'quality'. Others, including Leontief himself, were less willing to abandon the conven-tional approach, and instead extended the concept of factors of production to include 'human capital' – investment in skills, training and education. For empirical analysis, the relevant consideration now is how skill-intensive are exports *vis-à-vis* imports? Once this line of attack has begun, of course, it can fairly easily be extended to include technological elements; investment in R&D can be examined through the R&D intensity of exports and imports and so on. However, the extension of the list brings with it the danger (correctly spotted by Posner some thirty years ago[4]) that an *explanation* of trade flows is being replaced with a simple *description*. This is because investment and the resulting stocks (whether of physical, human or R&D capital) are largely *endogenous* with respect to other important variables: that a particular industry has high rates of investment in R&D, up-to-date capital equipment and human skills, is as much a result of a successful trading performance as these factors are a cause of it. This point assumes greater importance when it comes to the formulation of economic policy. To observe that the UK tends to import 'R&D intensive' products does not mean that a simple policy of promoting more R&D will be successful in changing that – indeed it smacks of the 'science push' strategies of the UK in the 1950s and 1960s, which were not notable for their success. Such knowledge gains greater relevance, however, if there is evidence that there are significant barriers (such as market failure) to the accumulation of a particular asset, and here there is much detailed evidence for the UK (see both Chapman (Chapter 9) and Keep and Mayhew

(Chapter 15) for training, and Buxton (Chapter 6) for evidence related to R&D, all in this volume).

Nevertheless the factor proportions approach can generate illuminating pictures of how trade flows develop. Empirical investigation in the UK is surprisingly sparse, however, despite the attention given to it in the US. Looking at the whole world, Balassa (1981) produced results suggesting that developed economies export goods which are intensive in both human and physical capital, tending to import goods which are intensive in unskilled labour. However in a striking study of the UK, covering the years 1910, 1924, 1930 and 1935, Crafts and Thomas (1986) discovered that the development of comparative advantage in the UK had failed to follow this pattern; using a cross-sectional study of manufacturing industries, they found that net exports were positively related to inputs of unskilled labour and negatively related to inputs of human capital throughout the period; this basic result was confirmed in that there was a net inflow, through trade, of human capital services. A study of the more recent past examined the skill, R&D and capital intensities for the period 1968–78 using three benchmark years (Katrak 1982); according to Katrak, the study confirmed 'poor technological performance' in the UK: although the relative skill intensity of exports compared to imports exceeded unity, it declined rapidly over the period 1968–72. The same was found to be true for R&D intensities over the period 1972–8. By contrast, physical capital intensities were found to be rising.

The emphasis in the factor proportions approach is therefore upon supply-side factors in its explanation of trade; the wheel turns full circle with many of the econometric investigations of trade which on the whole tend to emphasize demand relationships. Product differentiation becomes the general rule with oligopolistic producers setting prices and then supplying aggregate quantities perfectly elastically. Provided that there is no rationing, actual observations will fall upon a demand curve. A typical specification of the demand curve for net exports might then be:

$$X/M = A(P_d/P_c)^\alpha (Y_w)^\beta (Y_d)^\gamma (Q_d/Q_c)^\delta \qquad (1)$$

where:

X = exports
M = imports
(P_d/P_c) = price of domestic production relative to competitors' prices
(Y_w) = 'world' real income
(Y_d) = domestic real income
(Q_d/Q_c) = relative 'quality' of domestic goods
constants: $A > 0$, $\alpha < 0$, $\beta > 0$, $\gamma < 0$, $\delta > 0$

Although theory suggests that it is possible for producers to obtain increasing market share through price competition, it also suggests that this is unlikely in the absence of significant differences in the long-term growth rates of productivity; moreover at the economy-wide level differential productivity growth is likely to be offset by long-term trends in nominal exchange rates. More attention is therefore paid to differences in quality (taken to include not only the characteristics of the good itself, but also delivery times and after-sales service) and differences in the income elasticities of demand, β and γ. However, measurement of the relative quality position of producers raises considerable, if not necessarily insuperable, difficulties. Attempts include the tradition at NEDO which explained longer-term shifts in unit values as indicators of quality (e.g. Stout 1977; Brech and Stout 1981) and these are examined by Buxton in this volume. 'Hedonic' or 'characteristics' studies provide a technically superior approach to the investigation of quality but must be conducted at a a very detailed level (e.g. Swann and Taghavi 1992) and are sufficiently labour intensive to make an overall appreciation of shifting quality positions difficult. In practice, therefore, few attempts have been made to include a relative quality term, although a number of attempts have been made to proxy for it, by the use of R&D statistics (Buxton *et al.*, reprinted in this volume) or patent statistics (Greenhalgh 1990) or profitability (Anderton 1992). These are, however, isolated attempts, and in general the relative quality term is dropped from equation (1). Major forecasting models, for example, tend to include only a price competitiveness term (which may reflect costs rather than prices) and substitute the volume of world trade relative to domestic activity for the income terms.

Dropping a quality term from the trade equation may be less serious than it sounds, since much of the literature draws attention to the relationship between product quality and the income elasticity of demand, in which case equation (1) is actually mis-specified since a shift in the relative quality position would alter the coefficient β. Indeed, in a world of homogeneous commodities, in which quality factors had no role, it would be hard to justify differences in β, although one possibility might be if producers in particular economies were for some reason (e.g. barriers to trade) locked in to particular markets which were growing relatively slowly. A little consideration tends to confirm the interaction between a particular quality position and the income elasticity of demand β, since in many instances superior quality indicates characteristics the demand for which is likely to grow rapidly with rising wealth levels: reliability, convenience features and so forth. If this is correct, then the way to test for changes in relative quality positions is via the identification of 'structural breaks' in the econometric model estimating the demand curve. This is essentially the technique used by Landesmann and Snell (1989, 1992) who argue that the 'system shock' engendered by the 1979–81 recession had the effect of altering the quality position of UK producers. This possibility carries more weight if there is a further interaction, not just between quality and the income elasticity of demand, but also between quality and the price elasticity, α, which is likely if at the high end of the quality spectrum, demand is less sensitive to price. In that event, the combination of a recession with a high value of the exchange rate of the sort experienced at that time would have tended to fall disproportionately heavily on producers at the lower end of the spectrum: a 'shake-out' with quality-enhancing effects. In a sense this is a similar effect to that noticed by Brech and Stout (1981), who argued that an effect of recurrent UK devaluations was to cause producers to cluster around the price-competitive end of the product spectrum.

In practice, the supply-side and the demand approach should be viewed as complementary to each other. It is probable that favourable supply-side developments make themselves felt primarily through increases in the income elasticity of demand, which as a catch-all is capable of capturing a wide variety of effects. In what follows we consider both approaches.

INTER-INDUSTRY VARIATION IN TRADING PERFORMANCE: DESCRIPTION

In order to understand the forces shaping trading performance in the UK, it is important to distinguish macro-influences from the myriad of influences on competitiveness at the level of the individual firm or industry. Evidently there has been a quite general deterioration in the balance of payments position of the UK attributable to 'excessive demand' or to an overly 'high' level of the real exchange rate. The key question of whether the UK continues to face a structural problem with the balance of payments relates to whether a sufficient real devaluation can be achieved, or whether rectification of the external accounts can be accommodated only at even higher levels of unemployment than those to which we have recently been accustomed. Within this general deterioration, however, it is important to gauge the extent of variation between industries, and the forces which shape it: to what extent do inter-industry differences reflect widespread views about the problems of the UK economy – perceptions of training deficiencies, management failure, more general techno- logical inadequacy and so forth? Have these been causing a discernible shift in the pattern of trading advantage which is to a degree masked by the severity of the macro phenomenon? The data used to address these questions is a panel of 101 three-digit industries from the 1980 Standard Industrial Classification (SIC) which covers almost the whole of manufacturing industry.[5]

Some idea of the extent of inter-industry variation in performance[6] over the period 1979–90 can be gleaned from Figure 1. On the horizontal axis, industries are ranked according to their export–import ratio in 1979. The vertical axis provides the ordering of the same variable in 1990. Observations which fall on the diagonal line are industries which show no change in the rank order. Observations falling below the line indicate an improvement in relative performance, those above the line show a deterioration. The basic stability of the pattern of trading advantage can be judged by the proximity of many of the observations to the diagonal line. Moreover, many of the outliers are small industries where trade is slight in relation to production and hence the measure

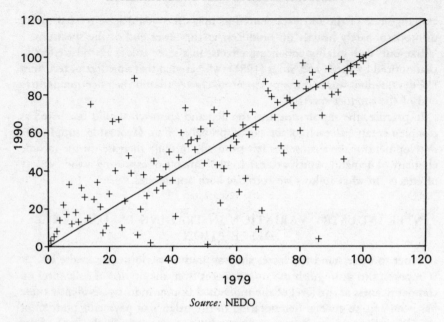

Figure 5.1 Trade performance by three-digit industry: rank orderings by export–import ratio.

of trading performance highly variable. The Spearman rank correlation coefficient for 1990 compared with 1979 was 0.67. An interesting feature is that this correlation coefficient with 1979 as base declines fairly steadily over time without obvious cyclicality; this implies that the recession of 1979–81 either tended to effect trading performance in a similar fashion across industries, or else there is a lack of a 'bounce-back' effect in industries hit hardest by recessionary forces. However, the degree of variation does seem to be markedly higher amongst the engineering group of industries (SIC Division 3), as opposed to chemicals and metals or miscellaneous (SIC Divisions 2 and 4).

Other outliers may be explained by rather special demand conditions: for example, industries displaying particularly rapid declines in rank order are virtually all supplying inputs into the construction sector – industries such as: metal doors, concrete and cement products, structural clay products, and builders' carpentry and joinery. In these industries, a rapid expansion of domestic capacity in line with the explosion of demand in the second half of the 1980s would not have been justified by subsequent events. Moreover, the period showed that cement and other building products were more tradeable than was commonly supposed. Other industries producing durable goods directly associated with a housing and construction boom also did rather badly according to the rank ordering – such as carpets, electric lamps, and wooden and upholstered goods.

Overall, the manufacturing trade ratio, defined as the balance of trade in the output of manufacturing industry expressed as a percentage of the value of total trade (i.e. $100 \times \{X - M\}/\{X + M\}$), deteriorated by about 12 per cent between the periods 1975–9 and 1986–90.[7] This was from a position of broad balance in the earlier period to one of significant deficit (−11.7 per cent) in the later period. At the same time, many individual industries moved into deficit; in 1975–79, fifty-eight of the panel of industries were in surplus, falling to thirty-four in 1986–90. Since the relative importance of different industries to the overall manufacturing balance varies enormously, it is useful to assess the individual contribution of industries to the deteriorating trade ratio. Table 1 shows in each case the fifteen industries making the biggest positive and negative contributions to the change in the trade ratio between the two periods. Only twenty industries in all made a positive contribution to the trade ratio in manufacturing, with food processing providing a significant cluster of improvement. Just a single engineering industry is present – aerospace. On the debit side, by contrast, the chief contributors are almost exclusively from engineering (the exception being plastics processing). The most serious cases from the balance of payments perspective were in motor transport (parts and vehicles), although vehicles began to improve somewhat during 1990 and 1991 under the impact of Japanese inward investment and buoyant markets in Germany and Italy.

Table 1 Largest contributors to change in manufacturing trade ratio: 1975–9 to 1986–90 (in percentage points)

Animal slaughtering, meat processing	0.993	Motor vehicles and engines	−2.224
Aerospace	0.652	Motor vehicle parts	−1.734
Extraction of other minerals	0.626	Other machinery	−1.103
Milk and milk products	0.526	Mining machinery	−0.867
Sugar and sugar by-products	0.480	Agricultural machinery	−0.680
Non-ferrous metals	0.392	Basic electrical equipment	−0.588
Sawmilling planning	0.326	Other electronic equipment	−0.539
Pulp, paper, board	0.296	Hand tools	−0.521
Iron and steel	0.214	Electronic components	−0.455
Wood semi-manufactures	0.181	Plastics processing	−0.452
Organic oils and fats	0.167	Clothing	−0.354
Fruit and vegetable processing	0.148	Miscellaneous industrial machinery	−0.329
Animal feeding stuffs	0.128	Office machinery, data processing equipment	−0.309
Miscellaneous foods	0.125	Shipbuilding	−0.307
Leather	0.041	Rubber products	−0.302
		Total manufacturing	−12.003

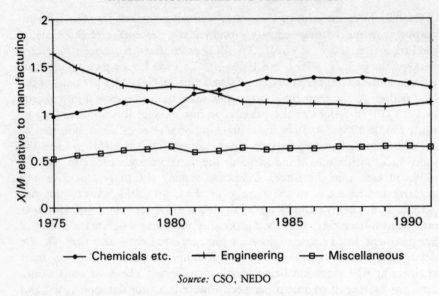

Source: CSO, NEDO

Figure 5.2 Relative trade performance by manufacturing division.

The significance of the weakness of engineering industries is emphasized in Figure 2, which traces the evolution of the export–import ratio *relative to that* of manufacturing as a whole[8] for each of the three SIC Manufacturing Divisions. Note however that much of the decline in the relative strength in the engineering industries occurred between 1975 and 1982. Nevertheless its pre-eminent position in UK manufacturing is a thing of the past.

SUPPLY-SIDE INFLUENCES ON THE PATTERN OF TRADING ADVANTAGE

Much is frequently heard about the respective roles of either a 'technology gap' or a 'skills gap' as pivotal factors in UK economic decline. In this section an attempt is made to isolate the role that these may play in the evolution of trade performance in UK manufacturing. Two further factors will also be considered – the potential roles of foreign investment and industrial structure. In what follows we assume that the influence of these factors can be traced, if they operate at all, at a sectoral level.

The idea of a 'technology gap' combines elements of cost advantage (the relative abundance of specific factors of production closely associated with technical advance) with that of an availability problem (where the gap results from lags in the ability to produce certain goods or services). The consequences of a technology gap are potentially extremely far reaching: a pattern of specialization based on 'research and development' intensive industries is likely to be one where demand is growing comparatively fast and a source of returns to innovation. Indeed for the 'high-tech' sector as defined below, the volume of UK trade (exports plus imports) has been growing by nearly double the rate of total manufacturing trade (close to 10 per cent per annum over the period 1979–90). In some areas of advanced technology, such as computers and other data processing equipment, progress has been even faster than this.[9] A strong trading performance in this sector is therefore a likely source of alleviation from balance of payments problems.

Either of the elements of a technology gap may show up at the sectoral level by an examination of those sectors in which the pace of technological advance is particularly rapid, so that the demand for certain skills and competencies is paramount, and the potential for a lack of availability of certain inputs or outputs is extensive. Such conditions exemplify the so-called 'high-tech' industries. It should not be supposed, however, that there is any fixed mapping between criteria and specific industries, and industries regarded as being in the advanced category fifty years ago would not be so considered today. In practice, the indicator most frequently used for inclusion in the high-tech sector of the economy is R&D intensity (i.e. R&D as a proportion of industry gross output) and this is the approach adopted by the Department of Trade and Industry in the UK. In the US, a slightly more sophisticated approach has been taken by the Department of Commerce, which looks not only at R&D conducted within each industry but also at that of its major suppliers (cf. Butchart 1987). The point is that some industries make extensive use of very advanced processes of production despite the fact that their own in-house R&D may be very low and the actual output not obviously technically advanced. Food processing may be an increasingly important example.

On the basis of R&D intensities and on that of the proportions of administrative, technical and clerical staff on the payroll, Butchart has delineated a number of high-tech industries at the four-digit SIC level whose trading performance can be compared with that of manufacturing as a whole for the period 1975–91. The industries consist of members of the chemical group – synthetic materials, pharmaceuticals; and members in engineering – electronic instruments, components, and capital goods as well as basic electrical equipment, data processing equipment, aerospace, and scientific instruments. Figure 3 traces the export–import ratio for the entire group relative to that for manufacturing as a whole. A further panel is constructed which excludes the aerospace industry, which formed about 25 per cent of UK high-tech value-added in 1989. The major reason for examining the grouping in the absence of aerospace is the latter's heavy dependence upon defence procurement which, quite apart from its general significance in UK advanced technology, has undergone a major policy upheaval in the period under review; after 1985 new forms of competition were introduced, while military defence spending, which had risen steadily in the early Thatcher period, was reined back (Dunne and Smith 1992); in this sense some of the 'protection' offered to a vital part

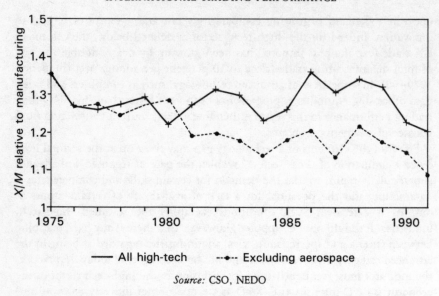

Source: CSO, NEDO

Figure 5.3 Relative trade performance: high-tech industries.

of the UK high-tech sector over the period was removed in the period 1985–91.[10]

Figure 3 presents a thought-provoking story for both groupings. In 1975 they displayed a roughly similar relative advantage over manufacturing as a whole. This deteriorated somewhat up to 1979. The recession years saw the relative advantage shift towards that sector favoured by defence spending with a rather rapid relative deterioration in the position held by high-technology industries, excluding aerospace. While neither panel appears to have lost ground to manufacturing as a whole in the second part of the 1980s, the latest recession has seen a further deterioration in their relative standing – the beneficial effects of contra-cyclical defence spending in the earlier recession being no longer a feature. Moreover, the differential between the two panels is no longer widening. On the evidence, the damaging effects of recession may well be more severe in the high-tech sector. This is perhaps not surprising, particularly if cumulative learning processes are especially susceptible to disruption and curtailment. By 1991, the relative advantage of the high-tech sector over all manufacturing, at least when aerospace is excluded, had all but disappeared, echoing the increasing concerns that are felt, not only in the UK but throughout Europe, about a growing technology gap.

The general picture is consistent with the view that the UK's contact with leading-edge technology has become increasingly based around aerospace and pharmaceutical technologies; it would be helpful if we knew more about sectors responsible for inputs into the aerospace sector, and whether these illustrated a similar robustness in terms of relative advantage as aerospace itself; unfortunately this is beyond the scope of the present chapter. According to Archibugi and Pianta (1993), the particular pattern of specialization reflects the characteristics of Britain's 'national system of innovation' (Freeman 1987; Nelson *et al.* 1992); using patent data from the USA they show that the UK has a 'robust' presence in some of the faster growing areas despite the fact that its overall share of patents was declining.[11]

The advanced technology sector is of course critically dependent upon a skilled and well trained workforce, i.e. upon the supply of human capital. This is doubly so when it is recognized that technology is frequently 'tacit' in nature, depending upon cumulative learning processes on the part of firms, groups, individuals, and increasingly between firms. It may well be that the deterioration in the performance of the high-tech sector is simply a reflection of the oft-cited problem of the accumulation of human capital in the UK economy. Moreover, the problem may have a definite sectoral dimension if there is pronounced sectoral variation in access to the stock of human capital. This may result from the existence of market power – either in the labour market (i.e. a 'mark-up' on competitive wages) or in the product market where monopoly rents may be shared between profits and wages. What evidence as there is suggests that variations in pay across industries (or for that matter between firms) are by no means a simple compensation for differences in individual ability or working conditions. Moreover, differences persist over time and across countries (cf. Layard and Nickell 1991).

None the less, and crude as it is, the standard method of estimating the contribution of human capital to sectoral output is to look at relative wages; given a homogeneous labour market, variations in wages between industries will reflect skill differences. On this basis we can construct industry panels based upon differences in the cost of labour; a division of the three-digit industries into 'high', 'medium' and 'low' groups, based on a comparison made of Census of Production data relating to 1985. The high-wage category includes many of the industries in chemicals and food processing, but very few of the engineering industries – exceptions being in the production of motor vehicles and a number of machinery-producing industries. It is noticeable that not all the high-tech industries are represented in the high-wage panel, exceptions being found in the cases of both precision instruments and surgical and medical appliances. The results shown in Table 2 indicate that it is the medium-wage panel rather than the high-wage panel where performance deteriorates from a position of strength. As might be expected for a developed economy, the low-wage panel performs consistently poorly.

An alternative approach to the investigation of the possible effects of human capital formation is to measure skills in terms of the qualifications of the workforce. In this spirit, Oulton (1993) provides a specific comparison between the UK and Germany. He allocates groups on the basis of comparability between these two countries into: no vocational qualification, lower intermediate, upper

Table 2 Movements in relative trading advantage by industry group (export–import ratio as a proportion of that of total manufacturing)

	1975–9	1986–90
High wage	1.00	1.11
Medium wage	1.40	1.08
Low wage	0.61	0.59
High skill	1.28	1.22
Medium skill	1.22	1.06
Low skill	0.65	0.74

intermediate and higher degree. The use of different qualifications varies in a similar fashion across industry groups between the UK and Germany, but the general German level of qualification in each industry is very much higher. Perhaps the most significant differences are at the intermediate levels. The proportion of the workforce with university degrees is slightly higher in the UK, but the biggest differences are at the lower end: over 60 per cent of Britain's manufacturing workforce had no vocational qualification in 1987, compared to only 29 per cent in Germany. By contrast, the proportions having lower inter-mediate qualifications were 28 and 57 per cent, respectively. Oulton then tests the hypothesis of a skills gap by looking at relative export performance in wealthy third-country markets. He finds that the 'unqualified' skills gap (proportion UK not qualified, less that in Germany) is significant and nega-tively related to export performance in four out of five markets studied. Although Oulton's results are not clear cut, they seem to suggest that deficiencies at the lower intermediate level may be having the greatest impact on export performance.

To examine whether some of these results may have greater generality, the skills data above has been used to construct panels of industries according to their 'skill intensity' based on their use of unqualified, lower intermediate or highly skilled labour (graduate or upper intermediate). Table 2 shows how it is those industries whose requirements are relatively large in their use of lower intermediate skills that have shown the greatest change in their comparative position. There is therefore some support in the data for supposing that the greatest problems for the UK's system of training are to be seen in terms of the sheer number of workers without any vocational qualifications.[12] It is interesting to note that the only industry examined by Oulton in which there is no substantial difference in the gap between the UK and Germany in terms of workers with lower-level vocational qualifications is in aerospace, where trading performance has been satisfactory.

The fact that the engineering sector in particular relies heavily on the supply of well-trained production workers may mean that this variation on the skills gap hypothesis has been a major factor behind engineering's decline. However, the variation in performance between the different engineering industries is considerable, and this raises a further question about the access of different industries to the pool of human capital. Those industries which, because of their structure – low concentration, smaller firm size or both – are rather more dependent upon the external labour market. Larger firms may have significant advantages over small firms in possessing highly developed *internal* labour markets providing more desirable job characteristics quite apart from pay – career structures, greater occupational mobility, training opportunities and so forth. Market power may also strengthen access to human capital. Thus, both market power and firm size may be sources of considerable sectoral variability on the impact of skill and technological deficiencies in the economy. It is precisely in the fragmented, decentralized industries, therefore, where not only the skills gap but also the technology gap may be expected to bite the hardest: Ergas, for example, has pointed out that firms in decentralized industries not only need greater access to an external labour market, they also face difficulties keeping abreast of technological developments and in promoting product quality and compatibility (Ergas 1987). It is therefore worth performing another cut on the data in terms of industrial concentration; official data record the percentage of employment in the five largest enterprises in each industry. Figure 4 illustrates the results and shows that the relative performance of the high concentration sector improves relative to industries with low levels of concentration; the long-term trend deterioration in the performance of this

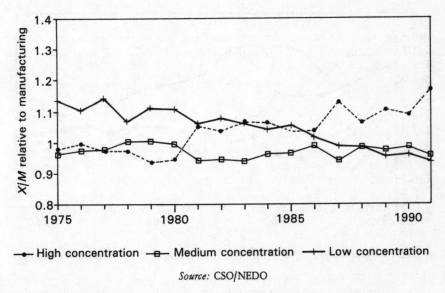

Source: CSO/NEDO

Figure 5.4 Relative trade performance and industrial concentration.

group of industries, although never sharp, is certainly persistent. It is also worth commenting that much of the relative improvement of the high concentration panel occurs in recessionary periods. Figure 5 shows the same information as Figure 4 but restricted to the engineering division. The loss of relative competitiveness of all three panels to manufacturing can be seen in the earlier period, but after the early 1980s, only the low concentration panel continues to decline.

The role of foreign direct investment has received considerable attention, not least because of the economy's great share of gross investment flows within the OECD throughout the 1980s. In 1990 inward investment in the UK had reached a level of $33.8 billion – over one-fifth of the total for the OECD, and two-fifths of that for the European Community. In 1991 and 1992, however, the level of inward investment dropped dramatically, reflecting the recession and the need to be in position prior to the creation of the European single market.

The cumulative effect of this investment has been such that by 1989, over 700,000 people were employed in foreign-owned manufacturing – nearly 15 per cent of the total; this compares with a share of 21 per cent of manufacturing value-added, revealing a considerable productivity advantage for foreign-owned enterprise.[13] The specific impact of industrial investment in certain areas – notably motor cars and some areas of consumer electronics – is quite well known, but a systematic examination of a 'foreign ownership' effect on trade performance does not appear to have yet been made. Unfortunately, it

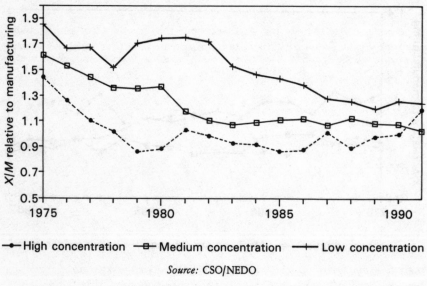

Source: CSO/NEDO

Figure 5.5 Trade performance in engineering by industrial concentration.

is not possible to construct a panel of three-digit industries based on the absolute concentration level of foreign ownership (or on its rate of change) because its extent is not published at this level of industrial detail. Nor is it easy to hypothesize what kind of effects there might be. It is not perhaps surprising that the productivity advantage exists since these are likely to be counterbalanced by other disadvantages – local knowledge about markets being one such possibility. Nevertheless, it is interesting to ask to what extent the aggregate productivity advantage is due to 'structural' factors (the location of inward investment in high productivity sectors) and how much to an 'ownership effect' that remains even within industries.[14] Davies and Lyons (1991) show that much of the increasing advantage of foreign–owned enterprise which has been observed is due to an increasing structural effect, but that a substantial ownership advantage still exists. On their estimate, if domestically-owned firms were able to match foreign-owned firms' performance, industry by industry, then the level of productivity in UK manufacturing would rise by 26 per cent which, as they point out, is of a similar order of magnitude to the observed difference in productivity levels between the UK and Germany or France. The interpretation of this finding depends of course upon the degree to which the sources of the advantage are transferable to other firms. As far as the final impact of foreign investment upon trading performance is concerned, we must of course look beyond the impact within the industry itself and consider the impact on the industries supplying it. It is here that considerable contention has crept in, especially in relation to Japanese inward investment, where the displacement of indigenous production by Japanese imports may more than outweigh the positive effects within the host industry – an effect that EC rules on local content seek to avoid.

Although it is Japanese inward investment that has attracted much of the attention in the literature, it is important to realize that its impact so far has been small, with much of Japanese investment concentrating upon distribution and financial activities rather than manufacturing.

EXPORT DEMAND

Finally, we end this investigation by looking at whether the data confirms the reported sea change in export performance, comparing the 1980s with the 1970s.

Ideally, we would like to consider both export and import performance; unfortunately the modelling of imports presents a number of difficulties in the context of a panel analysis which push it beyond the possible in the present chapter.[15]

Difficulties related to the measurement of quality prevent any simple estimation of an equation based on (1) above; indeed, as we saw, the relationship between 'quality' and 'non-price competitiveness' is not a simple one. High quality is not synonymous with sales as the usual Rolls-Royce analogy makes clear. In practice, however, we can associate non-price competitiveness with market penetration achieved by factors outside the ambit of price – in short, the elasticity of UK manufactured exports to changes in world trade at unchanged relative prices on the one hand, which we call β. This provides simple summary measures of non-price competitiveness – indicating not only the ability of producers to compete within rapidly growing market segments, but also the ability to compete across the range of spatial markets. Both these parameters are, however, influenced by capacity considerations (Landesmann and Snell 1989); in a recession, for example, when UK capacity is disappearing, estimates of β will be biased downwards and γ upwards, as domestic firms disappear from markets. Ideally we would wish to include a capacity variable in our equations. Unfortunately no satisfactory measure appears to be available and not at an individual industry level. Therefore a comparison is made either side of the 1979–81 recession (i.e. between the period 1976–9 and that of 1986–9). It is here that the use of pooled industry level data is especially appealing, since the increased number of observations gives an indication of how the manufacturing system responded 'on average' to changes in demand over quite short periods of time.

The estimated demand equation based on a pooling of the industry data and from a fixed effects model was as follows:

$$x^i = \lambda^i + \beta(wt) + \sum_{j=0,1} \alpha_j(rp^i)_{-j} + u \tag{2}$$

where

x^i = volume of exports of industry i
wt = volume of world visible exports
rp^i = relative export price in industry i
λ^i = industry specific constants
u = normally distributed error term
all variables in logarithms, and data is annual

The existence of lags only in the relative price variable (rp) follows from the fact that measured UK exports can be expected to be coterminous with measures of world exports, so β can be measured directly from the estimated equation. The measure of world trade (WTIMF) derived from IMF data is wider than the more commonly used 'volume of world manufactured exports' which is based only on Divisions 5–8 of the SITC and a list of eleven manufacturing countries; the latter therefore excludes import sections of UK manufacturing industry (especially food processing) and much other trade besides. It was felt that the wider definition was more appropriate. Nevertheless, estimates of β are sensitive to the world trade measure, particularly in the earlier period when world visible trade grew rather faster than world manufactured exports. The lagged effects of relative prices are, however, well established and perfectly plausible; on annual data the addition of a lagged price term (although

Table 3 Estimates of export equation (2)

Coefficient on: (t-ratios in parentheses)	WTIMF	RP1	RP1-1	RP2	RP2-1	adj. R^2	Estimated autocorrelation of residual
1976–9	0.774 (5.7)	-0.414 (-3.0)	-0.161 (-1.1)	-	-	0.990	0.093
1976–9	1.041 (6.9)	-	-	-0.647 (-4.0)	-0.279 (-1.9)	0.990	0.085
1986–9	0.833 (8.0)	-0.593 (-4.8)	-0.116 (-0.9)	-	-	0.988	0.101
1986–9	1.069 (10.3)	-	-	-1.055 (-7.4)	-0.155 (-1.1)	0.989	0.127

frequently insignificant at conventional significance levels) was usually of correct sign, and generated more plausible elasticity estimates. Two alternative relative price terms were used – the relative price of exports relative to imports (RP1) and the relative price of exports in industry i to that of foreign manufactured exports as a whole (RP2) – obtained by using the CSO's published series for relative export prices.

Results for export equation (2) are given in Table 3. There is considerable stability in the coefficients across the two periods depending upon the relative price measure, and this must cast doubt on the hypothesis of a large improvement in export performance. RP2 seems to perform better as a relative price variable, and when this is used the coefficient on world trade is very close to unity in both periods – indicating that, bar relative price effects and recession, the UK was already holding its share of world trade by the late 1970s.

CONCLUSION

This chapter has considered the evolution of UK trading performance in manufacturing industry. Most research has focused on manufacturing in general, but here attention has been paid to the variation between manufacturing sectors for evidence regarding supply-side factors that may be driving trade performance. In fact the data shows reasonable degrees of persistence in the revealed comparative advantage of different industries; the key exception to this is in engineering where not only has performance for the division as a whole deteriorated relative to manufacturing, but the dispersion of outcomes within engineering has been greater.

The implications for the UK of a poorly performing high-tech sector combined with a rapid loss of market share in 'unskilled-labour intensive' industries may be very severe. As a whole, the high-tech industries have maintained some advantage over manufacturing in general. However, the pattern is not uniform and only aerospace and pharmaceuticals can be looked upon as strong performers. This pattern of specialization owes much to the peculiarities of what some have termed the 'national innovation system' which has shown considerable dependence upon defence spending. The disadvantages of this system are comparatively well known and include a lack of civilian 'spin-offs' to R&D activity, an emphasis on product rather than process technology, and the lower risks attached to defence contracts creating a concentration of firms (and activities within firms) in this area (Walker 1993; Sharp and Walker, Chapter 18, this volume; OECD 1992). Excessive secrecy has almost certainly not helped. Of course civilian markets are also important in aerospace and much will depend upon European collaboration in this area. However, the success of projects such as the Airbus has been challenged (Ergas 1993). This particular pattern of specialization is of course similar to that found in US and France.

94

The idea that there may be an important skill gap reflected in UK trade performance finds some support in the data, especially in relation to the poor record of Britain's engineering industries overall. However, the relationship does not appear to be a simple one, and the chief problem may be in the basic training of the workforce, an idea familiar with those who have compared systems in Britain and Germany. In the background is the possibility that these industries have been unable to respond to the challenges of technical change, a problem which may be more acute when industry structure is fragmented.

The idea that there has been a sea-change in export performance in the post-1979 period is not conclusively proven in the data examined, and performance in the late 1980s may have been substantially similar to the later 1970s, when the UK share of world trade had already begun to stabilize. More serious effects on trade almost certainly stem from the impact of recession, which by disrupting the continuity of accumulation processes, may have done considerable damage to trading capability, especially in technology-intensive sectors.

NOTES

1 This chapter has benefited from discussion with colleagues at the Centre for Business Strategy, London Business School.

2 Not all commentators even agree about the improvement in manufacturing productivity advance. Stoneman (1992) has, for example, argued that measurement bias associated with the rapid fall in energy prices around 1986 has led to considerable overestimation of productivity growth in the period after 1985. Moreover, the methods used in other countries (that of 'double deflation' – of both outputs and inputs) may mean that they are not susceptible to the same kind of bias. For further discussion of productivity growth, see Prevezer *et al.* (1993).

3 Somewhat misleadingly in fact, since 'the world' consists, for this series, of eleven major manufacturing countries in Europe and North America plus Japan, and significantly ignores key newly industrialized countries (NICs). For data concerning the UK share of world trade, see below, Chapter 17.

4 Posner (1961), perhaps the first expression of the technology gap theory.

5 The data for this investigation was obtained from the National Economic Development Office with the assistance of Martin Godfrey, and is based on a merger between Census of Production data and the commodity trade statistics made possible by means of DTI 'correlators' between the SIC and trade classifications produced by HM Customs and Excise. Correlations between specific industries and trade classifications are published in the *Business Monitor*. One problem that remains implicit when considering the trade performance of an industry when using this data is that no account can be taken of the ultimate impact of an industry on trade when allowance is made for imports of inputs into the production process; these can change quite radically when, for example, corporate strategy dictates a different sourcing policy.

6 In order to proceed, we need a simple measure of international competitiveness. Since it is wished to consider both export *and* import performance, our preferred measures of trade performance at the industry level are export–import ratios (X/M) or the trade ratio ($\{X - M\}/\{X + M\}$). Although the latter is in some respects a more desirable measure, the export–import ratio has the useful property that it never becomes negative; in practice there is little to choose between the alternatives.

7 Both periods were of economic growth, so possible cyclical influences are reduced. It was felt that taking a run of years would be preferable to considering change between single years because of possible exceptional factors operating within a single year.

8 This ratio provides a measure of 'revealed comparative advantage', i.e. an indicator of movements in relative competitiveness. However, it must be set against the fact that manufacture itself slipped considerably in relation to total UK trade over the period.

9 For electronic data processing equipment, trade has been growing in volume terms by 19.5 per cent per annum over the period 1979–90, although price indices are particularly unreliable in this sector.

10 The new policy aimed to increase the share of competitive defence contracts and reduce the significance of cost-plus contracts; the National Audit Office (1991) has argued that advances have been made in the value for money obtained by the MoD. The combination of falling defence budgets and the change in policy has meant that defence-oriented companies have not shared in the revival of profitability in industry generally (cf. Dunne and Smith 1992).

11 A note of caution should be introduced when using patent statistics to compare performance across sectors. The propensity to patent varies considerably from industry to industry, according to differences in the means by which the gains from innovation are appropriated.

12 Although they may, as Oulton points out, have GCE or GCSL qualifications.

13 These figures are available in the CSO (1991); OECD flows can be obtained from OECD (1992).

14 Although the ownership advantage may be attributable to total factor productivity, it may also be attributable to differences in capital inputs and the quality of the labour force.

15 Specifically, the growth of imports depends upon the interplay of capacity, domestic demand and the growth of international specialization. Satisfactory measures of either capacity at a detailed industrial level, or of international sectoral specialization, do not readily exist.

REFERENCES

Anderton, R. (1992) 'UK exports of manufactures: testing for the effects of non-price competitiveness', *Manchester School*, vol. LX, no. 1, March, pp. 23–40.

Archibugi, D. and Pianta, M. (1993) 'Patterns of technological specialization and growth of innovative activities in advanced countries', in K. Hughes (ed.), *European Competitiveness*, Cambridge: Cambridge University Press, pp. 105–132.

Balassa, B. (1981) *The Newly Industrializing Countries in the World Economy*, New York: Pergamon.

Brech, M. J. and Stout, D. K. (1981) 'The rate of exchange and non-price competitiveness: a provisional study within UK manufactured exports', *Oxford Economic Papers*, vol. 33, Supplement, pp. 268–81.

Butchart, C. (1987) 'A new definition of high-tech industry', *Economic Trends*, vol. 400, pp. 82–8.

Buxton, T., Mayes, D. and Murfin, A. (1991) 'UK trade performance and R&D', *The Economics of Innovation and New Technology*, vol. 1, no. 3, pp. 243–56.

Central Statistical Office (CSO) (1991) *Report on the Census of Production 1989*, London: HMSO.

Crafts, N. F. R. and Thomas, M. (1986) 'Comparative advantage in UK manufacturing trade 1910–1935', *Economic Journal*, vol. 96, no. 383, September, pp. 629–45.

Davies, S. W. and Lyons, B. R. (1991) 'Characterising relative performance: the productivity advantage of foreign owned firms', *Oxford Economic Papers*, vol. 43, pp. 584–95.

Dunne, P. and Smith, R. (1992) 'Thatcherism and the UK defence industry', in J. Michie (ed.), *The Economic Legacy*, London: Academic Press, pp. 91–111.

Ergas, H. (1987) 'Does technology policy matter?, in B. R. Guile and H. Brookes (eds), *Technology and Global Industry*, Washington DC: National Academy Press, pp. 191–245.

Ergas, H. (1993) 'Europe's policy for high technology: has anything been learnt?', mimeo., Paris: OECD.

Freeman, C. (1987) *Technology Policy and Economic Performance*, London: Pinter.

Greenhalgh, C. (1990) 'Innovation and trade performance in the United Kingdom', *Economic Journal*, vol. 100, no. 400, Supplement, pp. 105–18.

Katrak, H. (1982) 'Labour skills, R&D, and capital requirements in the international trade and investment of the United Kingdom', *National Institute Economic Review*, no. 101, August, pp. 38–47.

Krugman, P. (1979) 'A model of innovation, technology transfer, and the world distribution of income', *Journal of Political Economy*, vol. 87, pp. 253–66.

Landesmann, M. and Snell, A. (1989) 'The consequences of Mrs Thatcher for UK manufacturing exports', *Economic Journal*, vol. 99, no. 394, pp. 1–27.

Landesmann, M. and Snell, A. (1992) 'Structural shifts in the manufacturing export performance of OECD economies', *DAE Working Paper No. 911*, University of Cambridge.

Layard, R. and Nickell, S. (1991) *Unemployment: Macroeconomic Performance and the Labour Market*, Oxford: Oxford University Press.

Leontief, W. (1953) 'Domestic production and foreign trade: the American capital position re-examined', *Proceedings of the American Philosophical Society*, vol. 97.

National Audit Office (1991) *Ministry of Defence: Initiatives in Defence Procurement*, London: HMSO.

Nelson, R. (ed) (1992) *National Innovation Systems: A Comparative Study*, New York: Oxford University Press.

OECD (1992) *Technology and the Economy: The Key Relationships*, Paris: OECD.

Oulton, N. (1993) 'Workforce skills and export competitiveness: an Anglo-German comparison', *National Institute of Economic and Social Research*, Discussion Paper no. 47.

Posner, M. (1961) 'International trade and technical change', *Oxford Economic Papers*, vol. 13, pp. 323–41.

Prevezer, M., Small, I. and Temple, P. (1993) 'The competitiveness of UK manufacturing', *Economic Outlook*, vol. 18, no. 1, October, pp. 29–39.

Stoneman, P. (1992) 'The measurement of output and productivity in UK manufacturing, 1979–1989', paper presented to *ESRC Industrial Economic Study Group*, LBS, London, 22 November.

Stout, D. K. (1977) *International Price Competitiveness, Non-price Factors, and Export Performance*, London: NEDO.

Swann, P. and Taghavi, M. (1992) *Measuring Price and Quality Competitiveness*, Aldershot: Avebury.

Walker, W. (1993) 'National innovation systems: Britain', in R. R. Nelson (ed.), *National Systems of Innovation: A Comparative Analysis*, New York: Oxford University Press.

Part II

INVESTMENT AND INNOVATION

6

OVERVIEW: THE FOUNDATIONS OF COMPETITIVENESS
Investment and innovation

Tony Buxton

Just as the introduction of looms is a special case of the introduction of machinery in general, so the introduction of machinery is a special case of all changes in the productive process in the widest sense, the aim of which is to produce a unit of product with less expense and thus to create a discrepancy between their existing price and their new costs. Many innovations in business organization and all innovations in commercial combinations are included in this.

(J. A. Schumpeter, *The Theory of Economic Development*,
English edn, p. 112)

In Chapter 1 it was argued that UK economic performance, along with that of other developed nations, was crucially dependent on international competitiveness – unless the economy can generate sufficient earnings abroad, the balance of payments constraint will restrict development at home. The fundamental source of competitiveness which can enable rapid growth in the long run is investment and innovation. The most widely addressed type of investment is in 'fixed' capital – plant and machinery, buildings and vehicles. But labour is also obviously of considerable importance in the productive process. Improving labour's efficiency requires investment in education and training. It is well known that 'innovation' can enhance product quality and also improve the efficiency with which labour and fixed capital combine. Many factors influence innovation, but investment in 'intangibles' is one of the main sources, and promotional expenditure, education and training, and research and development (R&D) are the three most often discussed. Promotion of UK goods and services abroad is an increasingly important aspect of international competitiveness, but has yet to receive the empirical backup which it undoubtedly warrants. The same is not true of R&D which is seen as vital in the process of innovation by increasing the stock of 'research' capital, or of spending on education and training which can raise the stock of 'human' capital. This chapter explores aspects of investment and innovation over the 1980s.

101

The traditional inputs into the productive process are of course capital and labour. Yet much evidence over a long period of time suggests that these play a far smaller part in economic growth than 'other' inputs, the contributions of these often being aggregated into a single entity labelled the 'residual' or 'technical change'.[1] Innovation has arguably been an integral contributor to this. In view of its historical importance and its likely accelerating role in the future, innovation is given central attention here although fixed capital and labour are not forgotten. Indeed they cannot be since both labour and fixed capital are key vehicles in the introduction of innovation. This chapter therefore begins with a comparative analysis of an important input into technological change – R&D – and of technological output – patents and royalties. It then turns to expenditure on fixed capital and finally to investment in human capital.

INNOVATION

Innovation is often analysed within the context of Schumpeter's (1942) trilogy of the process of technological change; invention, innovation and diffusion. Invention is the creation of new ideas or of technological knowledge; innovation is the process of converting new ideas into marketable products or processes; diffusion is the adoption of the innovation by others. The overall literature on technological change has been surveyed *ad nauseam*, and Baldwin and Scott (1987) and Cohen and Levin (1989) are recent competent compilations. The focus of much research into innovation has been of the technological kind, product and process, and therefore on the main measurable input, R&D expenditure; its effectiveness, often measured by patents; and its effects, through the diffusion of technology, on economic growth and other measures of performance. But a whole host of other innovation questions have been asked.[2] The tempo has risen recently, however, with widespread recognition that the process of innovation is far wider, and that successful implementation requires the satisfaction of a long series of conditions from an original idea to the international marketplace. This appreciation is not new of course as evidenced for instance by Rothwell's (1980) survey,[3] but has now taken a strong hold in the literature. The theoretical difficulties related to property rights have been studied in depth, yet their practical aspects have mushroomed as internationalization has grown. The technological human experience necessary to cope with advancing innovation is increasingly a problem as education institutions grapple with the requirements of industry and training becomes more specialized. Marketing is now seen as an integral part of the process where the most advanced technological developments may fail if not linked to the needs of the user. Similarly, design is now recognized as an ongoing part of the development process, not a once-and-for-all contribution. Stock control methods have meant that innovations may be introduced faster and more effectively. And as part of this, the importance of liaison with suppliers, of both current and capital inputs, is increasingly seen as necessary to ensure success in innovation.

The importance of competition as a stimulant to innovation has long been debated. Schumpeter (1942) and his celebrated 'creative destruction' began the debate by positing whether large firms in relatively monopolistic industries were required in order to 'create' new technology; 'destruction' then came about as new products and processes were copied and competition eventually eroded market power. His work developed into the notion of 'bigness and fewness' where innovation requires big expenditure because technology is expensive and this requires a monopolistic or oligopolistic industry structure. Galbraith's (1952) subsequent famous fiction,[4] and Arrow's (1962) theoretical analysis of the incentive to innovate set in train voluminous studies of the effect of firm size, industry structure and industry characteristics on numerous aspects of technical change (Cohen and Levin op. cit.).

But the benefits of cooperation are increasingly seen as having considerable potential. Collaborative research has obvious attractions, but also many difficulties, particularly relating to appropriability (Katz and Ordover 1990). Similarly 'technology transfer' – how new technology can be used in practice[5] – has long been prominent in evaluating the effectiveness of UK R&D – good ideas are plentiful but exploited by foreign companies rather than home producers (Ray 1989, for instance). Financial aspects of successful innovation have also attracted attention more recently, with the debate on 'short-termism' relevant here. And encompassing many aspects of all of these is the importance of management and business strategy. This includes non-technical aspects of technological innovation – where to put the new machinery – as well as non-technical innovation itself – how to rearrange the existing equipment – reminiscent of the 'embodied' and 'disembodied' technical change classifications.

Governments have for many years played an active role in the process of technical change because of perceived market failure, arising from 'externalities'; increasing returns, public goods or indivisibilities (Stoneman 1987). Government policy affects all aspects of innovation, from the macro-stance to the provision of appropriability laws. Direct innovation policy can either attempt to increase the stock of knowledge or to improve its effectiveness and dissemination. The former is often in the shape of R&D assistance, and the latter can involve helping firms to bring new technology to the marketplace by improving technology transfer and diffusion. The inter-relationship between private and public R&D finance is important partly because the government carries out much of its own R&D but provides much finance for the private sector. The decisions of firms and government are not made independently, however, and interactions – crowding in and crowding out – are inevitable. The call of the 1980s was to reduce the role of the public sector in actively promoting, as well as carrying out, R&D where allocations seem inadequate, and the effects of this can be seen in what follows.

All these are past of the 'new learning' in the economics of innovation.[6] Yet despite the progress of the new, it is important to keep sight of the old. To make improvements in the future we must forgo current consumption, and to generate innovation we must invest in it by allocating current resources. Such spending will by no means always change technology and will certainly not be comprehensively picked up in published R&D statistics[7] but is self-evidently a necessary condition. The effects of R&D as well will not wholly come through in the traditional measures of technological output – patents and the so-called 'technological balance of payments' – the difference between royalties received and paid abroad.

R&D expenditure

The age-old problem in the study of innovation is that the direct spending on technology, mainly R&D, and its impact on patents and royalties, are far easier to measure than the many indirect ones such as the complementary investment in the marketing necessary to carry it through.[8] However, the study of published records of inputs of technology and outputs from it can point to trends and areas of inadequacy in aspects of the process of innovation, especially the extent to which the UK has progressed relative to competitor economies. The empirical analysis therefore begins with R&D expenditure.

For many years, research and development expenditure was virtually equated with technical change and innovation. Now it is regarded by many as only a small part in the process of innovation as a whole. Notwithstanding, this variable arguably requires attention not least by virtue of its maturity. An early criticism of the attention paid to R&D was that it meant different things to people in different firms and industries, to say nothing of countries. To some extent this problem has been reduced by the international use of the so-called 'Frascati Manual' (OECD 1981) so that survey figures are standardized. Published R&D statistics still suffer from many limitations of course, due to their nature and measurement. Nevertheless the data are regularly collected and recognized amongst the OECD countries as a relatively consistent indicator of trends in technological input.

There are three main ways of categorizing the institutions which carry out research: business enterprise, government and 'other' – mainly quasi-public, though non-profit-making bodies such as universities. These three also provide the funds – 'other' here including quasi-charitable bodies such as trusts, and funds from abroad often from foreign-owned companies. In addition, when making comparisons, various levels of aggregation – inter-industry and inter-country – and time-scales are possible. Furthermore, until recently, particularly in the UK, data were available only on a bi- or triennial basis which sometimes necessitated interpolation or comparisons between cyclically different time periods.[9] What follows therefore has its limitations, but the aim is to see the extent to which the UK has compared in the 1980s with earlier years and with our main competitors.[10]

In 1990 £12.1 billion was spent on R&D in the UK. This compared with £106 billion allocated to fixed capital, nearly nine times more. In view of the comments earlier about their relative contributions to economic growth this may seem surprising but is partly explained by the extent to which these investment flows boosted the corresponding stocks, and is discussed later. Also the complementarity of the two is relevant. The more familiar R&D comparison is with GDP, showing the percentage of total resources which are allocated to investment in research – gross expenditure on research and development (GERD). In 1990 the UK's GERD/GDP ratio was 2.21 per cent. This is compared with the same statistic over the last two decades in Figure 1.

The graph suggests a superior performance in the 1980s to that in the 1970s. However, the relatively high percentage in 1981 reflects to some extent a steep fall in GDP since that year was the bottom of the early 1980s recession.[11] Furthermore, after 1986 the proportion of R&D spending fell at a time when the economy was running at a rapid rate and resources were relatively easy to come by. And there are other misgivings about the experiences of the 1980s. The first of these springs from a comparison with the other G6 countries, shown in Figure 2.

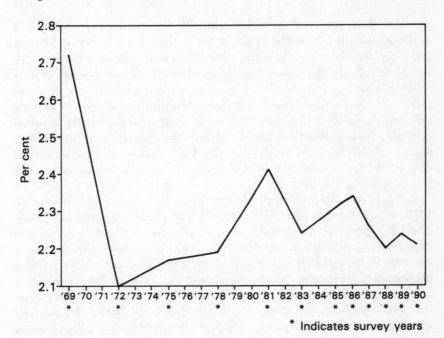

* Indicates survey years

Source: CSO

Figure 6.1 UK GERD/GDP ratio, 1969–90.

105

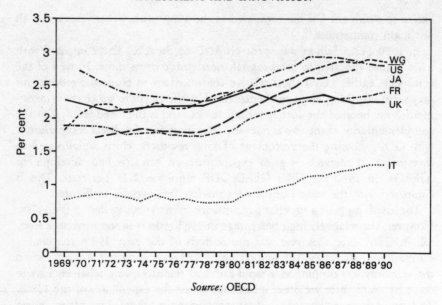

Source: OECD

Figure 6.2 GERD as a percentage of GDP.

In the 1970s, the trend in the UK ratio was upwards and at least as fast as in the other countries. In the 1980s, however, the UK's ratio was at best flat and more likely falling while in the other economies, with the possible exception of the US, the ratio was rising. By this measure, the UK fell well behind in the 1980s.

So far the analysis has been in nominal terms, which is the way the data are collected. In Figure 3 an attempt is made to compare real R&D expenditure. A specific R&D deflator is required for this but in practice, in the absence of an 'official' one, researchers use the GDP deflator. This has obvious difficulties[12] but is used here none the less because, over a long period, the picture is strongly indicative.

In Japan, real expenditure on R&D increased more than four-fold between 1972 and 1990 and in West Germany and Italy about two-and-a-half times. The UK raised real spending by only 20 per cent during this period and expenditure actually fell in the recessions in the early and late 1980s and hardly rose even in the rapid expansion in the middle of the decade – a truly dismal performance.[13] However, when considering the contribution of R&D to economic growth, its rate of increase is arguably the important indicator and the overall poor UK performance in Figure 3 is borne out in the graph of annual growth shown in Figure 4. Although the necessary interpolation of the data in the earlier years masks the annual picture somewhat, after 1978 the UK was behind the others in every year except 1986 when UK growth was momentarily the fastest.

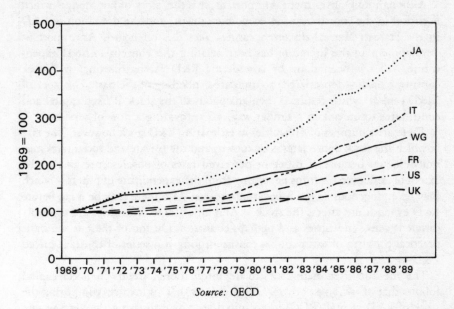

Source: OECD

Figure 6.3 G6 real GERD.

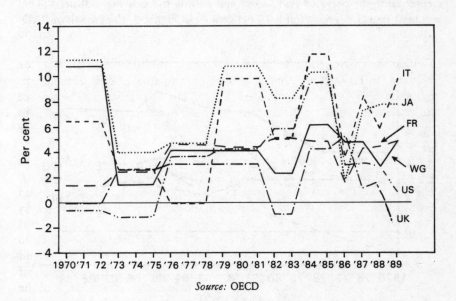

Source: OECD

Figure 6.4 G6 real GERD growth.

Although R&D investment is important, it is the 'stock of knowledge' which is critical in the contribution to economic growth, and the definition of R&D in the Frascati Manual discussed earlier takes this on board. An important development in the literature has been relating this concept to R&D expenditure.[14] It has been done by considering R&D as contributing to a stock consisting of the (depreciated) accumulated spending of the past. The stock of 'R&D capital' which results is then analogous to the stock of fixed capital and contributes to output in a similar way, viz. providing a flow of services.

There are a number of difficulties in estimating R&D stock however. The rate at which the stock depreciates is unknown, and the private and social rates may not be equal because of different perceived rates of obsolescence and of the extent of 'spillovers' – firms benefiting from the expenditure of others – which may be endogenous to the innovation process. Also there may be a lag before R&D expenditure affects the stock.[15] And all of these difficulties are probably different across industries and perhaps countries. On top of these is the basic practical problem of estimating a consistent long-run series of constant-priced R&D figures.

The method used here to estimate international trends in R&D capital follows that of (amongst others) Griliches (1980). This involves computing the stock of R&D capital (RDC) in an initial year by estimating the average rate that R&D expenditure increased up to that point, and then depreciating at a fixed rate.[16] R&D capital for any subsequent year is then calculated by depreciating the previous year's stock and adding the new expenditure.[17] The assumed rate of depreciation is 10 per cent.[18] In Figure 5, the growth of R&D

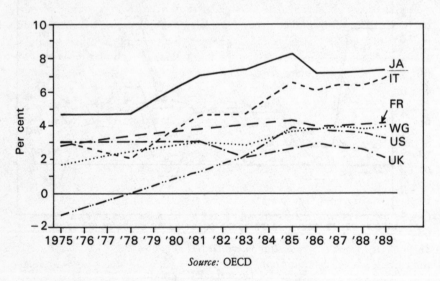

Source: OECD

Figure 6.5 G6 growth of GERD stock, based on R&D growth, 1975/89.

108

capital in each of the G6 is estimated from expenditure figures in constant-priced own currencies.

Japan's stock of R&D capital grew the fastest in the 1970s and 1980s, the rate accelerating from about 5 to 7 per cent. The UK's growth in the early 1970s was actually second fastest and maintained a steady 3 per cent per annum until 1981 when the rate faltered, recovered and fell again to under 2 per cent at the end of the 1980s. The remaining countries' experiences were broadly similar to Japan's in that growth accelerated over the period although less quickly, so that by 1990 the rate of increase of the UK's R&D stock was the slowest in the G6, even including the US where growth slackened after the mid-1980s.

The growth of GDP and the stock of R&D capital is probably a two-way process, where rapid expansion of the economy can release resources for R&D spending on the one hand, or high R&D expenditure can generate fast GDP growth. The combination of the two can generate a virtuous circle which Japan has probably gone some way to achieving. But if, as argued earlier, innovation is the main driving force behind competitiveness, and investment in R&D is a key way to promote innovation which the Japanese experience suggests it is, then the important direction of causation is from R&D to GDP growth, albeit with a lag, so that countries which increase their stock of knowledge the quickest eventually achieve the fastest growth of their economies. This to some extent is borne out in GDP growth figures, but also is portentous for the future – the UK's poor performance in the 1980s means that the stock of knowledge which the UK has to call upon to improve competitiveness in the 1990s may prove wanting.

Explanations for the relative decline in the UK's R&D performance have been many and varied and continue a lingering debate relating to company and industry distribution, basic research versus applied research and development, and many aspects of the 'new learning' discussed earlier. But the most straight-forward explanation relates to the government's contribution to the total. Much has been made in the past of the fact that, despite much government assistance to R&D, such spending may be 'inappropriate' in various ways – too much on defence, purloining top scientists, picking winners, etc., and combinations of these arguments, despite solid ones to the contrary.[19] In the 1980s while these issues were still debated, the undoubted influence of government on the total was that it had reduced its contribution.

This had one or two aspects. Between 1978 and 1989,[20] government R&D financing, intramural and extramural, fell by over 3 per cent in real terms.[21] Over the same period the funding of R&D by business enterprise increased by 60 per cent. Research actually carried out by that sector only rose by just under 38 per cent, however, reflecting the fall in the government contribution. To the extent that government policy aimed to withdraw financial help to private industry so that the 'market' could decide on the optimal allocation of expenditure, the policy seemed to be to some extent successful. Given Figure 3 earlier, however, the apparent 'crowding in' which took place was insufficient to get real expenditure in total rising at the same rate as our main competitors. But this aggregate picture hides the fact that 'crowding in' did not in fact take place. Figure 6 shows real spending in 1978 and 1989 in six broad sectors of the economy.

In 1978 72 per cent of UK aerospace R&D was financed by government. By 1989, this amounted to 40 per cent and total expenditure had actually risen. The increase was risible however at a mere 8.8 per cent or less than 1 per cent per annum – hardly adequate in a highly competitive, 'high-tech' industry. Much of this fall in assistance to aerospace in fact went to electronics, and here the industry raised its own spending hardly at all. Chemicals where government assistance is minimal saw the biggest rise, and second largest was 'other' where government support actually rose significantly. Needless to say, these re-allocations may have been made by the government in the light of indications that the usual criteria for public assistance, mentioned earlier, required it,

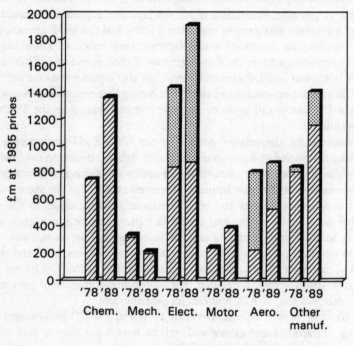

Government financed   Non-government financed

Source: DTI

Figure 6.6 Source of R&D finance, 1978–89.

having regard to our competitors. But another way of looking at this which suggests that they may not have done so is the percentage of the total which was financed by government. This fell from 49 to 36 per cent over the period 1978–89.

Figure 7 takes this further with another international comparison. The percentage of GERD which was financed by governments in the G6 in 1981 had West Germany and Japan a long way below the others. Much of the explanation for this lies in their lack of defence industry. In the 1980s these two countries reduced their relative contributions even more but the UK government reduced its contribution even faster so that by 1990 the UK and West Germany were about the same despite the huge UK commitment to defence.

This happened partly because the UK government reduced its own spending and partly because it reduced its help to the business sector. Figure 8 shows how this changed relative to the other countries. Now the UK looks more like France and Italy in 1990, but this came about by the UK and France reducing their relative contributions and Italy raising its own in the 1980s. The other countries were fairly steady but the US was much higher than the other two, again reflecting maintained defence commitments.

Finally, the changing role of government R&D, as well as the extremely skewed company distribution of spending in the UK with expenditure concentrated into a very small number of firms, can be seen in the analysis of R&D by firm size. Table 1 shows this for the some two years as above.

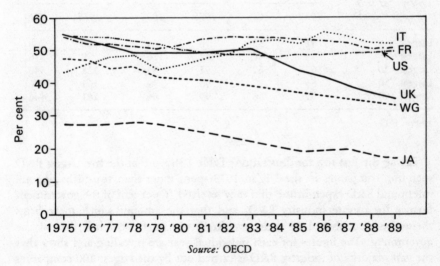

Source: OECD

Figure 6.7 Percentage of GERD financed by government.

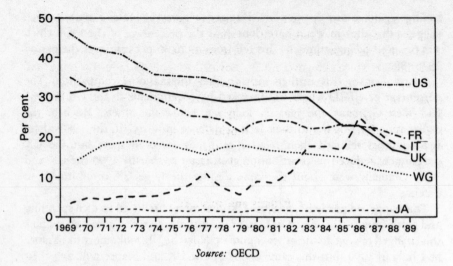

Source: OECD

Figure 6.8 Business enterprise expenditure on R&D percentage financed by government.

Table 1 The 100 UK enterprises with the largest R&D expenditure as a percentage of the total: 1978 and 1989

Enterprises with the largest R&D	Intramural R&D		Government R&D finance		Private/government finance	
	1978	1989	1978	1989	1978	1989
Largest 5	41	32	76	64	68	208
Largest 10	53	46	82	76	98	270
Largest 20	67	62	91	84	123	346
Largest 50	83	77	96	94	161	396
Largest 100	91	86	99	96	181	446

Source: DTI

Taking the first row for illustration, Table 1 shows that the five largest R&D spending companies in the UK in 1978 spent more than two-fifths of total intermural R&D expenditure; that they received 76 per cent of the government finance for private industry R&D; and that the amount which these firms themselves contributed to their own R&D was only two-thirds that of the government. The figures for each individual year are revealing and show that the vast majority of industry R&D is carried out by the largest 100 companies in terms of R&D, but this fell significantly between 1978 and 1989. A case against this change would involve diseconomies of scale, but on the other hand, helping small(er) companies was an important aspect of the industrial policy, such as it was, of the 1980s administration.

The table also demonstrates that these companies received virtually all the R&D finance which the government provided for private industry, but again the proportion has fallen. Finally the figures show how the private contribution relative to government changes as company size (measured by R&D) falls, and how this changed in the 1980s. In 1978, the biggest five companies received the most government support but provided a much smaller amount themselves. By 1989, this had been reversed so that their contribution was twice the government's. This change was true all the way down the line.[22]

Patents and royalties

Patents and royalties are frequently used as indicators of technological output,[23] but both have shortcomings. There are a number of factors that affect patenting propensities so that there are important differences across countries in patent applied for/granted ratios. Some of these are because of differences in the degrees of protection offered. Patenting fees also differ, as the time taken for a decision to be made by patenting offices varies between countries. Furthermore there are variations in technical aspects due to differences in scientific understanding. Due to these problems (and others[24]) it is customary not to compare own-country patents but to contrast external ones, usually those granted in the US. Table 2 therefore looks at per capita patents in the US by country of origin where the earlier 1980s are compared with the period 1963–80 because of the longer-term nature of the phenomenon. The table clearly illustrates the UK falling behind relative to the other G6 except the US with the other countries increasing their patents far faster.

Royalties are paid on a patent if another person or company wishes to use it. It is arguably therefore a good indicator of the worth of a patent although problems abound relating to the propensity to patent across countries and industries.[25] By this measure, though, the UK record compares well with the

Table 2 Per capita patenting in the US
(patents per million population)

	1963–80	1980–5
UK	44	40
West Germany	55	97
France	27	39
Italy	8	14
Japan	10	79
US	236	158

Source: Pavitt and Patel (1988)

113

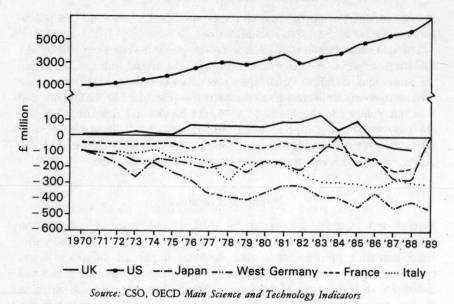

Source: CSO, OECD *Main Science and Technology Indicators*

Figure 6.9 Technological balance of payments.

other G6. Figures for the 'technological balance of payments' – the net receipts for the use of patents, licences, trademarks, designs, inventions, know-how and closely associated technical services – are shown in Figure 9.

Until the early 1980s the UK was a net exporter of technology by this measure. This compared starkly with Japan and West Germany, which over the entire period 1970–89 experienced deficits. This may indicate of course that these countries are better able to exploit available technology and/or that UK companies are reluctant to seek technological potential elsewhere. And Figure 9 as a whole backs up the frequently cited belief that the UK is good at ideas and inventions but poor at exploiting them. However, having said that, starting in 1983 the balance took on a downward trend and by 1986 was negative, although less so than the others except the US. This may mean that the UK has begun to emulate Japan and West Germany, but the decline may not be entirely unconnected with the relative demise of UK R&D discussed earlier.

FIXED INVESTMENT

Fixed capital is central to much economic analysis, not least that relating to economic cycles. For that reason, amongst others, it was much debated in the 1980s. The recovery from the recession of the early part of the decade was often related to changes in investment in stocks, while the extent of scrapping in that period and the consequent loss of capacity as well as the enhanced value of new capital, endowed with the latest technology, was much analysed, particularly in relation to the sustainability of the rapid expansion in the late 1980s (NEDO 1988).

Investment in fixed capital has many aspects and a multitude of comparisons are possible in providing a balanced overview of the 1980s' experience. None the less, Figure 10 begins the story by charting the rate at which real fixed investment grew in the UK in the 1980s. Average growth at an annual rate of about 3.5 per cent per annum, was faster than GDP but, as the graph shows, there was considerable variation. In the early 1980s, fixed investment expenditure declined quite rapidly, bottoming out in the first quarter of 1981 at an annual rate of almost −15 per cent. The mid-1980s' growth was steady except for a short period around 1986 following the removal of tax allowances on fixed investment. Growth then accelerated as the economy expanded in the late 1980s, peaking at an annual rate of nearly 20 per cent in the second quarter of 1988, before falling to zero at the end of the cycle.

Investing in the future requires forgoing current consumption and the extent to which society chooses to do this is often approximated by the amount of resources which are allocated to investment out of the total – the proportion spent out of GDP. This is graphed in Figure 11 for the 1980s. As expected, the path is broadly similar to the growth in Figure 9, with the percentage falling in the first four years and then rising until 1989. Taking the 1980s as a whole, fixed investment was a bit less than in the 1960s and 1970s but higher

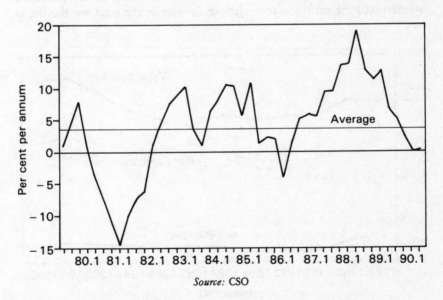

Source: CSO

Figure 6.10 UK fixed investment (growth rate, 1979.2–1990.2).

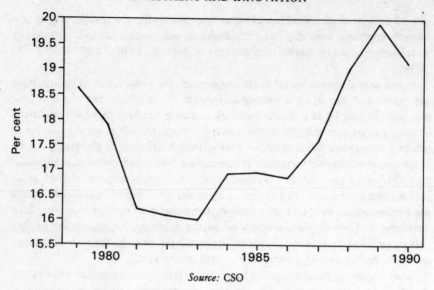

Source: CSO

Figure 6.11 UK fixed investment (percentage of GDP).

than in the 1950s, and more variable than in all three. Figure 12 now dis-aggregates this into the three usual categories – plant and machinery, vehicles and buildings – over the 1980s.

The series representing plant and machinery and vehicles are practically stationary and the main source of the big increase in the total was the rise in

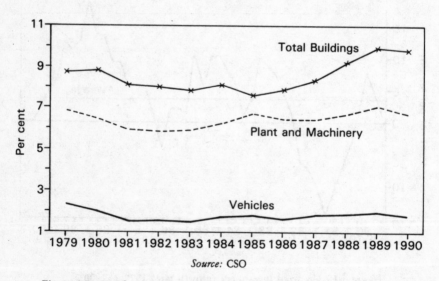

Source: CSO

Figure 6.12 UK fixed investment; by type of asset (percentage of GDP).

116

investment in buildings. The contribution which this pattern – rather than one where investment in vehicles and plant and machinery increase as well – makes to economic growth, is debatable.

Investment in 'building' takes place in dwellings and commercial property. The domestic property boom of the 1980s is well known and was accompanied *pari passu* by a big hike in commercial property prices, partly because of the expansion of the 'city' and other services as discussed in Chapter 16. The effect of this can be seen in Figure 13 where the amount of expenditure on each in relation to GDP is graphed. The very rapid increase in building in total in Figure 12 was due to growth in both parts until 1988, but after that was predominant in the non-dwelling sector, which continued to rise rapidly after the dwellings part had turned down. Its legacy is the huge surplus of floor-space, particularly in London, in the early 1990s.

Comparing investment to GDP is also useful when making comparisons across countries because it makes allowance for absolute differences in size, as was done with R&D. Figure 14 charts the G6 economies in 1979 and 1990 – the two peaks of the UK's 1980s' cycle (though not of the other countries).

Japan stands out in having a far higher ratio than the others, allocating over 30 per cent of its GDP to this type of investment. When put next to growth of GDP where Japan also excels, the implication, like R&D, is fairly obvious. The UK share was lower than all the others except the US in 1990. However, the UK managed to increase its ratio over the 1980s. Japan did the same, but in all the others fixed investment fell in relation to GDP by surprisingly significant amounts. Figure 15 takes the international comparison further by

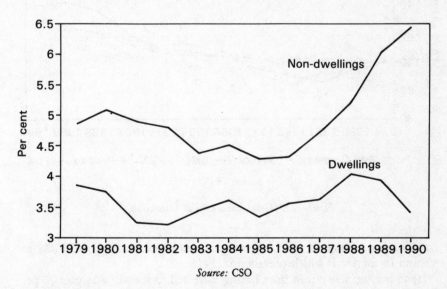

Source: CSO

Figure 6.13 UK investment in buildings; by type of building (percentage of GDP).

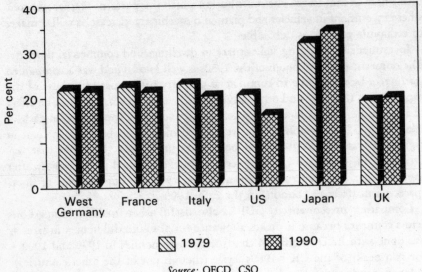

Source: OECD, CSO

Figure 6.14 Gross fixed capital formation as a share of GDP, 1979 and 1990.

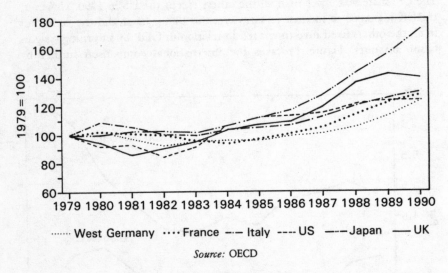

Source: OECD

Figure 6.15 Gross fixed capital formation.

graphing the volume of fixed investment in each country over the 1980s in relation to the levels which prevailed in 1979.

Japan is again way out in front having increased its spending by over 70 per cent. This came about after relative stagnation in the early 1980s but very rapid growth after 1983. The UK's experience was not dissimilar but was even more variable. Between the years 1979 and 1981, UK fixed investment fell nearly 15 per cent. It then grew strongly until 1989 by almost 70 per cent, a rate of about 6.75 per cent per annum before falling back in 1990 so that overall, fixed investment rose by just over 40 per cent – a relatively creditable performance. Though a lot less than Japan, this was higher than the remaining four countries of the G6 by a significant amount, although in general they showed less variation, reflecting the greater proneness to cyclical variation in the UK compared with the others. Also variation in the stages of economic cycles may account for some of the differences. West Germany increased its fixed investment the least by less than 20 per cent, and this again may not be unrelated to the 1980s' G6 GDP growth picture.

In the analysis of economic growth, many attempts have been made to assess the relative contributions of labour, capital and 'technology'.[26] Their importance depends on the services from the three, not just the net flow into them over any time period. And the influence of each on GDP growth is the increase in each weighted by its importance. The growth of the stock of fixed capital is therefore in the end the key measure of the performance of fixed investment in its contribution to economic growth. Figure 16 shows fixed capital growth over the 1980s in the G6 economies. Once again Japan stands out, having a growth rate approximately double the others. The UK's stock grew the slowest except at the end of the decade.

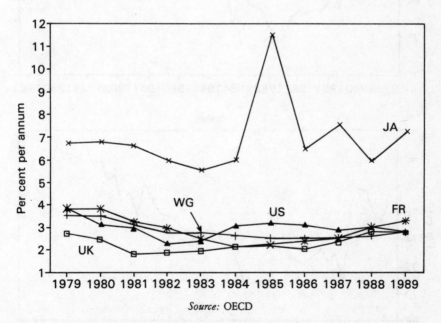

Source: OECD

Figure 6.16 G6 gross fixed capital stock (annual growth rate).

119

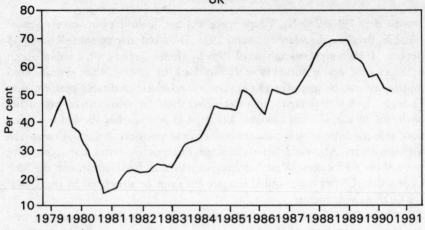

UK

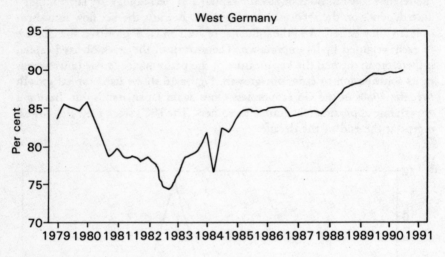

West Germany

Italy

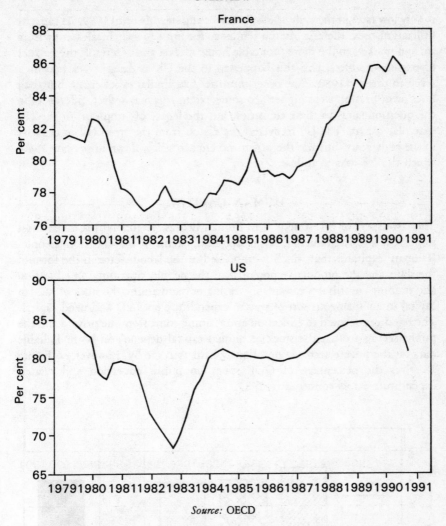

Figure 6.17 Capacity utilization of G6 countries (except Japan).

While the size and growth of the stock of fixed capital is important, its effectiveness, or the services from it, depend to some extent on the rate at which it is used. This is often approximated by the capacity utilization index produced by the CBI.[27] The index only applies to manufacturing companies, but probably tracks the course of capital utilization in the economy as a whole reasonably well. Except for Japan, the other G6 countries carry out similar surveys, and Figure 17 graphs them over the 1980s.

In the UK, capacity was not very high at the cyclical 'peak' in the second quarter of 1979, standing at about 50 per cent. It then fell deeply and sharply to very low rates in the early 1980s, before rising steadily until 1989. As capacity utilization rises, there is often a tendency for firms to switch sales away from foreign markets to the more profitable home market and as a result the balance of payments suffers, and this happened in the UK as capacity reached high levels in the late 1980s. The other countries had similar experiences, but their rates of utilization were higher. To some extent this may reflect differences in the questionnaires in these countries, but the legacy of 'stop–go' in the UK may play a part. The US recovered the fastest from the steep fall in capacity in the early years, but was the first to experience a slow-down in the late 1980s which the UK was to follow.

HUMAN CAPITAL

The last aspect of investment is in human beings. Arguably this is the most important and fundamental since everything stems in the end from people. 'Human' capital is that which is embodied in the labour force in the form of the skills and the productive potential of the people. Spending on education and training contributes towards increasing or maintaining the stock of human capital in an analogous sort of way to expenditure on R&D and fixed capital. The resources devoted to education and training come from the private and the public sectors so that the stock of human capital depends on both. Reliable data on the private sector is notoriously hard to come by, however, so Figure 18 gives the percentage of GDP spent on public education and related expenditure across countries in 1987.

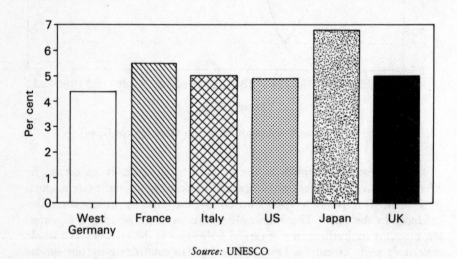

Source: UNESCO

Figure 6.18 Public expenditure on education as a share of GDP, 1987.
Note: Italy is 1986

To the extent that 1989 is representative, Japan again has a very high spend in relation to its GDP compared with the rest. The UK is about on a par with Italy and the US. West Germany is the lowest but this may be partly accounted for by the reputed higher rate of training by the private sector in that country. Demographic differences must also be taken into account in interpreting the figures and, more important, that the effectiveness of this expenditure is as central as its size. Figure 19 graphs the UK's own experience over the 1980s. The percentage of GDP which was allocated to public expenditure fell quite sharply in the early 1980s, but slightly recovered at the end reflecting demographic factors to some extent.

Figure 20 takes the public education story further by examining the equivalent of the 'participation rate' in employment – the percentage of people who are engaged in higher education in relation to the potential. This 'enrolment ratio' is the proportion of 17–22-year-olds who are in university or other higher education out of the total in that age group. The US has by far the highest ratio, almost double the next of France. The UK had the lowest ratio at only 22 per cent in 1987. So in this aspect of investment in human capital, the UK was worse than the other G6, and inferior to its own record on fixed investment.

The actual stock of human capital is not systematically estimated. An indication of it is the number of people with educational qualifications. Comparative estimates of this are not published by 'official' data agencies, but a recent one-off study comparing Great Britain with West Germany and France in the late 1980s revealed the picture shown in Table 3. According to these figures, in the 'degree etc.' category, the UK is on a par with West Germany

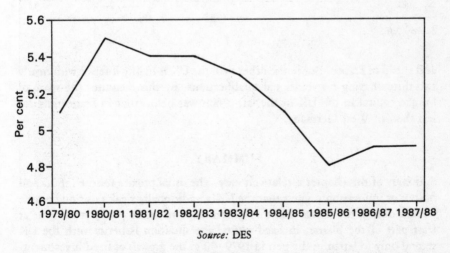

Source: DES

Figure 6.19 Public educational expenditure as a percentage of GDP: the UK experience.

123

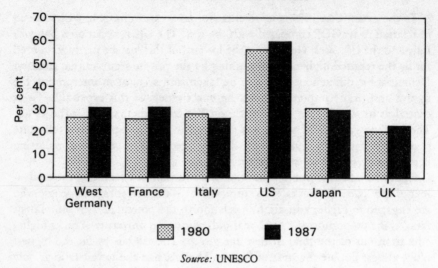

Source: UNESCO

Figure 6.20 Enrolment ratios of university and higher education students.
Note: US is 1986

Table 3 Vocational qualifications of the labour force, 1985–9

	Great Britain (%)	West Germany (%)	France (%)
Degree or higher vocational diploma	17	18	14
Intermediate vocational	20	56	33
No vocational	63	26	53

Source: NIESR

and ahead of France. But in the other two, the UK is highly inferior with nearly two-thirds having no vocational qualifications. By this measure, the stock of human capital in the UK in the late 1980s was below that in France and far less than in West Germany.

SUMMARY

Summary of this chapter is relatively easy. The usual proxies for the inputs and output of innovation suggest that the UK's traditionally weak position became weaker during the 1980s and that government scientific policy must bear at least part of the blame. In fixed capital the situation is better with the UK second only to Japan in the period 1979–90 in the growth of fixed investment. In human capital, the relative position of the UK showed similar poor trends to R&D in the 1980s. Given the ideological emphasis on innovation and on education and training in the 1980s, not least by the National Economic Development Office, the relative regression in these two seems regrettable.

NOTES

1 Abramovitz (1956), Fabricant (1954), Solow (1957) originally, and Maddison (1987) for instance, more recently, where the 'residual' accounts for up to 90 per cent of GDP growth.
2 Kamien and Schwartz (1982: 12–13) provide a useful enduring checklist.
3 Pavitt's (1980: 11) comments on Rothwell at the time included: 'Rothwell also identifies some other specifically British weaknesses in innovative activities: the inadequacy of market intelligence in many of the world's most important markets; and the poor links that often exist between product design and production engineering, with the result that new British product designs are sometimes unnecessarily difficult and costly to make. Rothwell stresses that the management of innovation is demanding and difficult, requiring a high level of professional and technical competence. It is here that the most important changes in British management will have to take place'. One wonders whether they have.
4 'There is no more pleasant fiction than that technical change is the product of the matchless ingenuity of the small man forced by competition to employ his wits to better his neighbour. Unhappily, it is a fiction. Technical development has long since become the preserve of the scientist and the engineer. Most of the cheap and simple inventions have, to put it bluntly, been made' (p. 91).
5 To be distinguished from diffusion which refers to the wider use of existing technology that has already been transformed into an innovation (Stewart and Nihei 1987).
6 Freeman and Soete (1990) contains a number of relevant readings.
7 Hollander (1965), for instance, some time ago established that firms devote a considerable amount of their resources to technological innovation which is outside their formal R&D operations.
8 Kuznets (1962), for instance, provides an early discussion.
9 In the UK, benchmark surveys are now carried out every four years together with annual sample surveys in the intervening years covering the 100 enterprise groups spending most on R&D but ensuring all product groups are covered fully.
10 When there are gaps in the data, the series, in this and subsequent graphs, are interpolated. To make the comparisons consistent, the data for other countries are interpolated for the same years as the UK.
11 Stoneman (1992) has a discussion.
12 The biggest is that, since a substantial proportion of R&D spending is on personnel, wage and salary changes are more important than the prices of other inputs which, because they are subject to the effects of technological change, tend to rise less quickly.
13 The position may actually be worse if the correct deflator was used.
14 Minasian (1961) is an early example, and Griliches (1979) notably more recent.
15 The difficulties are not fundamentally dissimilar to those relating to fixed capital.
16 The actual calculation is:

$$RDC(t) = RD(t)/(r - d)$$

where

$RDC(t)$ = R&D capital at time t
$RD(t)$ = R&D expenditure at time t

$$r = \text{the past growth of R\&D expenditure}$$
$$d = \text{the rate of depreciation of R\&D}$$

17 $RDC(t + 1) = (1 - d)RDC(t) + RD(t)$

18 As an 'intangible', R&D capital is unlike fixed capital where the rate can often be estimated from the length of life of the asset. It is broadly agreed, however, that the depreciation rate of R&D is low – knowledge remains useful for long periods. Griliches (1979) actually assumes a zero rate, but the compromise here is 10 per cent. Clearly the lower the rate the greater the influence of the past is on present stock values and therefore the greater is the error should the assumption be wrong. Individual observations may therefore have large inaccuracies but the trends are unlikely to be systematically biased.

19 Stoneman (1992) and Dasgupta and Stoneman (1987) discuss the issues.

20 The appropriate 'peak to peak' contrast would be 1979 to 1990, but in the absence of 1979 figures, the 'years prior to peak' are compared.

21 Some of the fall was because the UK Atomic Energy Authority was denationalized in 1986. Stoneman (1992) has some estimates of the effect.

22 Clearly the actual companies in the size groups are likely to have changed. In view of Figure 7, chemical companies are likely to have progressed up the ladder.

23 But there are others, particularly diffusion indices, Pavitt and Patel (1988) for instance.

24 Pavitt and Patel (1988).

25 Some companies patent everything 'just in case', others rarely do, etc.

26 See footnote 1.

27 The Confederation of British Industry's quarterly survey.

REFERENCES

Abramovitz, M. (1956) 'Resource and output trends in the United States since 1870', *American Economic Review*, vol. 46, pp. 5–23.

Arrow, K. (1962) 'Economic welfare and the allocation of resorces for inventions', in R. R. Nelson (ed.), *The Rate and Direction of Inventive Activity*, Princeton: Princeton University Press.

Baldwin, W. L. and Scott, J. T. (1987) *Market Structure and Technological Change*, London and New York: Harwood Academic.

Cohen, W. M. and Levin, R. C. (1959) 'Empirical studies of innovation and market structure', in R. Schmalensae and R. Willig (eds), *Handbook of Industrial Organization*, vol. II, Amsterdam: North-Holland.

Dasgupta, P. and Stoneman, P. (eds) (1987) *Economic Policy and Technological Performance*, Cambridge: Cambridge University Press.

Fabricant, S. (1954) *Economic Progress and Economic Change*, Princeton: Princeton University Press.

Freeman, C. and Soete, L. (eds) (1990) *New Explorations in the Economics of Technical Change*, London: Pinter.

Galbraith, J. K. (1952) *American Capitalism*, Boston: Houghton Higgins.

Griliches, Z. (1979) 'Issues in assessing the contribution of research and development to productivity growths', *Bell Journal of Economics*, vol. 10, pp. 72–116.

Griliches, Z. (1980) 'R&D and the productivity slowdown', *American Economic Review*, vol. 70, no. 2, pp. 343–8.

Hollander, S. (1965) *The Sources of Increased Efficiency: A Study of Dupont Rayon Plants*, Cambridge, MA: MIT Press.

Kamien, M. and Schwartz, N. (1982) *Market Structure and Innovation*, Cambridge: Cambridge University Press.

Katz, M. L. and Ordover, J. A. (1990) 'R&D cooperation and competition', *Brookings Papers on Economic Activity*, Microeconomics, Washington DC: Brookings Institute.

Kuznets, S. (1962) 'Invention and activity: problems of definition and measurement', in R. R. Nelson (ed.), *The Rate and Direction of Economic Activity*, National Bureau for Economic Research, Princeton: Princeton University Press.

Maddison, A. (1987) Growth and slowdown in advanced capitalist economies', *Journal of Economic Literature*, vol. 25, no. 2, June, pp. 649–98.

Minasian, D. (1961) 'Technical change and production functions', mimeo., presented at the Annual Meeting of the Econometric Society.

National Economic Development Office (1988) 'Pay and productivity in the UK', memorandum by the Director-General, London, NEDC(88)21, June.

OECD (1981) *The Measurement of Scientific and Technical Activities* (The Frascati Manual), Paris: OECD.

Pavitt, K. (ed.) (1980) *Technical Innovation and British Economic Performance*, London: Macmillan.

Pavitt, K. and Patel, P. (1988) 'The international distribution and determinants of technological activities', *Oxford Review of Economic Policy*, vol. 4, no. 4 Winter.

Ray, R. F. (1989) 'Full circle: the diffusion of technology', *Research Policy*, vol. 18, pp, 1–18.

Rothwell, R. (1980) 'Policies in industry', in K. Pavitt (ed.), *Technical Innovation and British Economic Performance*, London: Macmillan.

Schumpeter, J. A. (1942) *Capitalism, Socialism and Democracy*, New York: Harper & Row.

Solow, R. M. (1957) 'Technical change and the aggregate production function', *Review of Economics and Statistics*, vol. 39, pp. 312–20.

Stewart, C. and Nihei, Y. (1987) *Technology Transfers and Human Factors*, Levington, MA: D. C. Heath & Co.

Stoneman, P. (1987) *The Economic Analysis of Technology Policy*, Oxford: Clarendon Press.

Stoneman, P. (1992) 'Why innovate?', in A. Bowen and M. Ricketts (eds), *Stimulating Innovation in Industry*, London: Kogan Page.

7

THE CASE OF FIXED INVESTMENT

Ciaran Driver

INTRODUCTION

There is a growing consensus on the performance of the UK economy in the 1980s. Sentiments that used to be confined to the inside pages of the *Observer* have now found wide acceptance among more mainstream economic journalists and commentators.

> The profit driven corporate sector has consistently withdrawn resources from underperforming sectors [leading to] ... a structural trade gap.... Britain long ago lost its motor-cycle sector. It has since lost its domestically owned car industry too. As things are going the steel, aircraft and basic chemicals industries will not be far behind.
>
> (Barry Reilly 'The long view', *Financial Times*, 27 February 1993)

> In short, the benefits of higher UK productivity growth in the 1980s were consumed, not invested, and the economy has become unbalanced as a result.
>
> (Andrew Sentance, CBI director of economic affairs, *Sunday Times*, 14 March 1993)

It is important however to see the larger picture. The fruits of higher productivity were consumed because that was part of the grand accord between industry/government and those in work. In exchange for greatly increased work intensity and less job security wages per head of those in work rose.[1] It is doubtful whether productivity could have risen so fast without this accord. But since the 'unbalanced' economy is in no shape to mop up the surplus army of displaced workers, the enduring legacy of the 1980s' economic policies is mass unemployment. If the problem with the Lawson boom was that demand increased too rapidly, we may expect that it will be beyond the end of the century before employment drops to its 'equilibrium' level. Put differently actual employment will have been a million higher than its equilibrium level for about twenty years. When it is realized that this is an *optimistic* scenario based on the belief that it is labour market reforms – rather than technology,

128

Table 1 Gross fixed capital formation (current prices) as a percentage of GDP (market prices)

	UK	EC(12)	FR	WG	IT	JA	USA
1961–70	18.3	19.1	23.8	24.9	24.6	32.2	18.3
1971–80	19.1	22.6	23.9	22.3	24.0	31.6	19.3
1981–90	17.5	19.9	20.4	20.1	20.9	29.2	18.6
1993	15.5	19.6	19.6	21.4	19.3	31.2	15.3

Source: European Commission

training or investment – that galvanizes an economy, the scale of the policy challenge becomes evident. Indeed, *internal* government projections, and those of the Confederation of British Industry, are more sanguine, predicting unemployment still at 2.25 million by the end of the century.

What is an appropriate policy response? The economy needs *long-run supply-side* policies: poor performance cannot be cured by macroeconomic shocks which seem to be most powerful in inducing *real recessions* and *nominal booms* (Allsopp *et al.* 1992). So much is nearly commonplace. But there are sunk costs in the old regime, which is still defended by influential sniper fire and entrenched in political support. Change will be slow and grudging and arguments will have to be won point by point.

This chapter takes up the issue of fixed capital formation – capital investment in buildings; plant and machinery and vehicles. Comparative data on this are recorded in Table 1. Gross fixed capital formation in the UK is lower as a ratio of output than most major competitors.[2]

THE IMPORTANCE OF CAPITAL INVESTMENT

Capital investment is important not only because productivity gains are largely dependent on it, but because it is a discretionary component of demand. If the recovery path of capital investment followed current expenditure as an alert cat follows a mouse there might be little to lose sleep over. But problems arise when the cat itself behaves sleepily. The complacency of some commentators on investment stems from a failure to take this point seriously. The *Financial Times* journalist Samuel Brittan, for example, argues that it is wrong to focus on investment simply because it is a volatile component of demand...

> when there is a deficiency of total spending ... consumer spending is just as good at plugging the hole.
> (*Financial Times*, 'Economic viewpoint', 25 March 1993)

In a purely accounting sense Brittan is right. Consumer expenditure not only accounts for a much larger fraction of GDP than business investment but strong cyclical recoveries are often characterized by an early surge in consumer expenditure before investment responds. When we look deeper, however, at the structure of economic causation and the sustainability of the recovery it is clear that the investment response is crucial. The validity of Brittan's view rests heavily on his second belief that:

> if output can be increased without inflationary effects, the capacity will be created by business.
>
> (*Financial Times*, 'Economic viewpoint', 8 April 1993)

Here we are dancing on thin ice. To avoid digression let us bypass the question of whether a significant output increase can simply be facilitated by a conquest of wage inflation.[3] We focus rather on investment confidence and the time-scale of non-inflationary growth needed to inspire it. Initial investment stimulus is sometimes better than a consumer-led one because the former generates sustainable income-related consumption in its wake – the multiplier, enhanced by productivity gains, is more reliable than the accelerator. That of course should be familiar to all students of the Lawson boom of the 1980s and the Barber boom of the 1970s when the initial investment response in productive sectors was insufficient to prevent capital shortage stoking up inflation. The experience of the inter-war period is also salutary in this respect. Investment failed to respond to output due to a lack of confidence (Matthews *et al.* 1982: 384).

Econometric modelling suggests that UK investment fell in relation to output in most of heavy industry after 1981 (Hunter and Pescetto 1992). Capital investment in the 1980s' upturn in the UK was low not only in relation to output but also in relation to profitability (Driver 1987). Uncertainty, after allowing for interest rate effects, has had a significant dampening effect on investment in the last couple of decades (Driver and Moreton 1992; Artus and Muet 1990). And finally there is evidence that payback periods for capital investment shortened during the 1980s (Driver and Moreton 1992). In the following section we look at two possible reasons for the hesitant performance of capital investment in recent years: the role of risk and uncertainty; and the ability of firms to appropriate private profit from the technological advance embodied in new capital.

FIXED INVESTMENT: EXTERNALITIES, SPILLOVERS, APPROPRIATION AND RISK

The question of whether the social rate of return to fixed investment exceeds the private rate of return is one of the most interesting questions in economics today. If so, countries which happen to have a rapid growth in the capital stock may have higher output growth as well. Of course the issue is one of context. The UK had a high rate of capital growth in the 1960s which did not lead to sustained rapid growth, possibly because of the sectoral composition of investment, or the lack of complementary skills.

Despite this caveat, recent evidence suggests that capital growth confers benefits beyond those captured by the private return to capital represented in the firm's production function. There are several plausible reasons for this. First there may be spillovers of technology from one firm to another – either horizontal or vertical – and the acquisition of skills which benefit the whole economy. Other examples of spillovers are where follower firms benefit from the standard-setting and market testing that the leader performs.

Alternatively, or in addition, to these arguments, the existence of risk suggests that the economy may be well served by higher investment than the private optimum. Marginal investments, while not acceptable in terms of private risk, may nevertheless be justifiable on welfare grounds since society as a whole can avoid borrower and lender risk of default (Meltzer 1989). For both of these classes of reasons then, capital investment should be pushed beyond the point of zero private risk-adjusted return.

Perhaps surprisingly it has been US economists who have made the running in pointing to the importance of fixed investment and technology for high growth. The original contribution of US economist Dale Jorgenson in the 1960s gave us the modern neoclassical theory of investment. As is well known the basic version of this theory states that the rates of savings and investment are irrelevant to growth. But now Jorgenson and his co-worker Ralph Landau have reassessed this view, re-opening the question of whether technology can be regarded as exogenous – a disembodied input separate from the supply of new capital goods (Jorgenson and Landau 1989).

While Jorgenson's own position is equivocal – he argues that the productivity element in the growth-accounting equation has become of increased importance and is silent on the capital-productivity nexus, Landau stresses the endogeneities which make any accounting for growth hazardous – 'Technical change itself is largely determined by capital investment (human and physical) as well as by R&D' (p. 503).[4] Landau (1992) further argues (against the Samuel Brittan view above) that investment is quite likely to be less than optimal because heightened risk and uncertainty mean shortened payback periods. Indeed this has occurred just as technology has lengthened gestation periods for capital supply. Thus 'supply is no longer assured even if demand is stimulated' (p. 56).

In the opinion of these authors, technology has accentuated the opportunities of capital investment to increase productivity simultaneously with heightening the risk that individual companies may not themselves be able to appropriate the gains from investment. This view is supported by economists working on technological trends (Mowery and Rosenberg 1989: 236).

A variant of this view comes from another contribution (De Long and Summers 1992), where it is convincingly shown that cross-country productivity growth is positively related to capital equipment expenditure, with a response (elasticity) of about a third or a quarter (see Figure 1). The paper demonstrates that the correlation is not explained by the omission of other variables such as

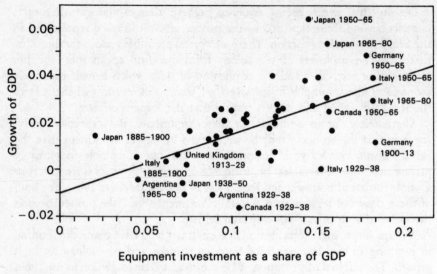

Source: De Long and Summers (1992: 167)

Figure 7.1 Equipment investment and growth for very long panel data.

education. Furthermore, the association is likely to indicate a *causal* role for equipment expenditure, one reason being that the association does not hold so strongly with structures expenditure, where some investment has more the character of consumer expenditure. The authors argue that the most likely explanation for this effect is the spillover to other firms of gains that cannot be privately appropriated. Others argue that the effect being captured here is that of 'catch-up' and that it applies only to countries well below the productivity frontier, e.g. the UK (Clark 1993).

To sum up the externality argument, risk and spillover imply that the market on its own does not optimize the investment decisions for a modern economy. Demand and growth may be depressed on this account. Furthermore, the pursuit of non-inflationary growth as a *prerequisite* for faster capital growth may be a chimera.

UK CAPITAL INVESTMENT IN THE 1980s

In the previous section we showed how investment of the right sort and in the right context could stimulate faster growth. This section examines whether recent capital investment in the UK has been of this character. Was the sectoral composition of investment good for the economy? And was the balance between different categories of investment appropriate?

Sectoral composition

The change in the sectoral composition of capital investment over the 1980s was truly remarkable. This change not only reflected but amplified the changing composition of output away from manufacturing and towards services. There were major changes in investment share over the 1980s. The share in fixed investment of chemicals, metals, engineering, food and vehicles fell from about 20 per cent to 10 per cent. During the same period financial services nearly tripled its share to 30 per cent.

The sectoral composition can be looked at in another way as well. It was non-manufacturing investment, along with private consumption, that underpinned the Lawson boom and kept it afloat for so long. In the three years 1987 to 1989 in which demand was expanding between 3 and 6 per cent, manufacturing investment contributed a cumulative total of less than half a percentage to that growth as compared with nearly five times that for non-manufacturing investment (Milne 1991).

A dramatic deterioration in manufacturing investment relative to Europe from 1979 is evident in Table 2, though this is marked by use of 1981 as the base year. At least with hindsight it appears that the pattern of capital investment was badly judged by the market. Much of the investment in business and financial services suffered low capacity utilization in the recession. Services output in 1991 contracted for only the second year since records began in 1950, with output of the distribution; catering; transport and communications sectors falling faster than the whole economy.

The misallocation of resources reflects more than market instability: government has a role in guiding long-run decisions with macroeconomic implications. The allocation of capital to non-manufacturing sectors implied an orientation of capacity to domestic rather than external demand. Indeed Muellbauer (1990) showed that there was a significant negative correlation across twenty-five sectors between the export-to-sales ratio and the rate of fixed capital formation for the period 1979 to 1987.

The government gambled on the possibility that financial and business services could export a far higher percentage of their output under the proposed liberalized regime in services. That now appears another mistake: these services are price sensitive and competition here is likely to be just as intense as in manufacturing. Contrary to earlier belief, the location advantages of the city of London are not inimitable. Indeed the UK world share of world invisible receipts dropped during the 1980s and invisible receipts as a percentage of GNP stood at 20.5 per cent in 1990, only about 3 per cent above the 1980 figure. The verdict, then, is clear on the sectoral allocation of investment: there was too little put into the tradeable manufacturing sector, resulting in potential capital shortage.

None of this suggests that future rapid growth in non-manufacturing exports should be discounted. Indeed Barker may be right when he argued some years

Table 2 Volume index of investment in manufacturing industry (1981 = 100)

	1977	1978	1979	1980	1981	1982	1983	1984	1985	1986	1987	1988	1989	1990	1991	1992	1993
B	75	68	76	99	100	111	104	109	112	127	135	158	169	189	183	180	146
DK	–	–	–	–	100	98	108	150	197	203	221	234	252	275	292	312	294
D*	89	93	99	107	100	98	96	95	112	124	128	131	143	153	158	147	134
GR	–	–	–	–	100	92	47	22	22	16	14	18	17	16	13	15	16
F	103	105	105	107	100	97	94	106	113	118	122	138	149	170	158	142	135
IRL	125	161	169	153	100	116	108	123	195	213	211	306	379	424	416	458	430
I	132	126	121	110	100	97	88	87	99	106	119	131	143	149	150	138	131
L	108	127	115	121	100	123	136	151	175	243	250	258	204	216	240	247	262
NL	117	114	107	115	100	95	99	126	155	160	160	149	145	204	190	179	187
UK	136	145	141	124	100	95	95	109	113	119	125	141	142	141	120	127	123
EUR*	106	108	108	110	100	96	93	99	111	117	122	132	143	152	147	139	131

*Excluding the five new German Länder
Source: European Economy, February 1993, based on EC investment survey

ago that there was a structural weakness in the manufacturing sector reflected in the trade elasticities which, '...is partly compensated by structural strength in the services sector. It may be just as easy or important to strengthen services as to improve performance of manufacturing' (Barker 1988). However, any such shift must be gradual and organic, especially since the strength of employment linkage from manufacturing to services is stronger than the converse link from services to manufacturing (Driver 1988).

Investment categories

We now turn to the other question at issue – the relative balance between the various functional types of investment expenditure. We will focus here on the two main categories used in European business surveys – expansionary investment, including new products, and efficiency investment which generally involves technology to reduce labour or material inputs.[5]

Capital investment responds to demand and cost pressures. In theory, market signals will provide information on the best response, with companies allocating their capital budgets in a way which makes the marginal return from a unit of efficiency investment just equal to that on a unit of enlarged capacity. This optimistic reasoning abstracts, however, from both risk and spillover.

Efficiency investment is less risky for firms. It probably has quicker payback. It relies more on engineering cost estimation than on gauging demand, i.e. more on local knowledge. Potentially offsetting this are spillover effects which have ambiguous influences depending on whether technological or market influences dominate. Technological spillover of benefits will cause firms to be more cautious in development work. On the market side if there are significant costs in pioneering and testing new markets the expansionary type of investment may be constrained. The business literature is rich in its description of influences that affect the appropriability of private profit and which therefore suggest that private business decisions on the type of investment may be biased (Porter 1987). On my reading of this literature and the associated literature on appropriability of various types of R&D expenditure, investment seems likely to be biased towards the cost-cutting type.

These considerations suggest that in an environment of market risk, firms may be tempted to invest a higher proportion of resources in efficiency investment as compared with expansionary investment than would be the case in a less risky environment. From the firm's point of view this may be a rational response, but it drives a wedge between the interests of the individual firm and the economy or society as a whole.[6] A more formal argument suggesting a capital-intensive bias is given in the Appendix.

Some readers will find the distinction between the two types of investment irrelevant: cost-cutting investment ought in theory to spur expansion via vigorous price-cutting. Furthermore, it may be felt that the charge of excessive efficiency investment sits uneasily with the alleged benefits from efficiency

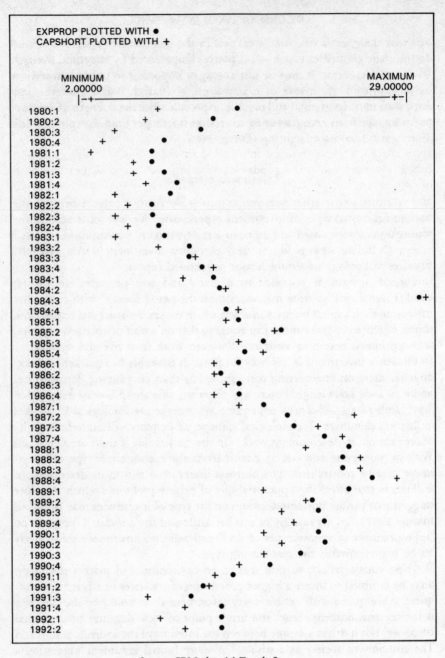

Figure 7.2 Time plot of: expansionary investment intention proportion (EXPROP) and proportion experiencing capacity shortage (CAPSHORT).

investment cited earlier. Nevertheless, a casual look at the data is enough to dispel the notion of a simple link between efficiency investment and growth. UK manufacturing productivity boomed in the 1980s but manufacturing output stagnated. In part this was due to the level of rent extracted by the remaining workforce. But the same phenomenon affected the USA in this period, masked only by growth in the computer industry (Clarida and Hickok 1993). And the worker rent story simply does not apply in the US context. It appears that higher efficiency investment in the US leads to an increased proportion of price-sensitive goods in exports but a reduction in the proportion of quality-sensitive capital goods which are characterized by learning by doing and economies of scale. The story here may be more complex than usually thought. Cutting the critical mass of an industry and retreating into price-sensitive or niche markets may be recipes for low growth efficiency. [7]

The issue of which type of investment is appropriate is partly one of timing. Expansionary investment tends to rise in a boom in relation to other types of investment (efficiency or replacement). But the change in gear is often not effected until companies are sufficiently sure of impending recovery to risk investments that have to be validated by market growth. Indeed, Figure 2 shows that the proportion of expansionary capital *authorizations* is strongly associated with *contemporaneous* capital shortage. This caution may be rational from an individual firm's point of view but it destabilizes the economy and ends in deflation. Some evidence on firm behaviour in this regard is presented in the next section.

EXPANSIONARY INVESTMENT OVER THE CYCLE

We now investigate the suspicion harboured above that UK companies fail to invest in expansionary investment even when it is reasonably clear that demand is about to strengthen. Put differently we look at the charge that excessive caution in respect of expansionary investment creates the conditions that undermine incipient recovery.

The evidence here draws heavily on Driver and Meade (1993) who report a study based on the Confederation of British Industry *Industrial Trends Survey*. We show there that companies' perceptions of shortage of plant capacity (as a constraint on output) is predictable for most industry groups more than ten quarters ahead. This in itself is a remarkable finding. It is possible to explain it by a sluggish response of expansionary investment to capital shortage. This could be due either to a desire to smooth adjustment or because of uncertainty. The cost of adjustment explanation is, however, implausible because typical delivery and installation lags are too short for this explanation to be valid. The alternative explanation – that the observed underinvestment reflects a cautious response to uncertainty – is strengthened by a significant correlation between the ranking of industries according to predictability of capital shortage and the ranking according to instability in industry prospects. This correlation is significant at the 5 per cent level when instability is measured as the variance of industry fluctuations in optimism (the balance of 'ups' over 'downs' in the CBI survey). Thus capital shortages in industries with greatest instability are *most* predictable, suggesting that instability induces a conservative bias in investment plans.

Further evidence that this is the case is provided by statistically relating the expansionary component of investment to future capacity shortages. The evidence again suggests a cautious response: capacity shortages more than five quarters ahead are not generally responded to, though they are predictable.

Yet further evidence that uncertainty matters is presented in Table 3, where the proportion of expansionary investment is related to capital shortage and capital shortage interacted with demand uncertainty. A significant negative interaction effect is present suggesting that firms will not react decisively to expansionary signals in the presence of uncertainty.

From these figures, a doubling of the uncertainty index when the capacity shortage is at its mean level would virtually eliminate the expansionary effect. The implications of all this are serious for employment prospects. The spectre of capital shortage employment is haunting Europe and especially the UK. By this is meant that unemployment, whatever its original cause (obsolescence, wages, demand shocks), cannot be resolved in reasonable time simply by altering relative factor prices. A significant increase in expansionary investment is a necessary condition for resolving unemployment: nevertheless stimulus

Table 3 Explanation of expansionary investment.
Sample period maximum consistent with data availability: 1980. 1–1987.4

t-statistics in parentheses		
Dependent variable EXP		
CONSTANT	0.292	(4.55)
EXP(−1)	0.505	(7.88)
CAPSHORT	0.424	(8.64)
CAPHORT*UNCER	−0.181	(−2.49)
R^2 = 0.96		
D.W. = 2.34		
LM(1) = 0.9 (1.27)		
LM(4) = 1.8 (4.24)		
J-B = 0.83 (2)		

Key: EXP: proportion of responses giving reason for authorization as expansionary investment (CBI data); CAPSHORT: percentage replies with output constrained by plant capacity (CBI data); UNCERT: dispersion across twelve forecasting teams of one-year ahead GDP forecasts (Investor Chronicle data, as transformed in Driver and Moreton 1992) *Diagnostics:* D.W.: Durbin–Watson statistic; LM(1), (4): LM test for first- and fourth-order autocorrelation, F-form; J-B: Jarque-Bera statistic for normality of residuals distributed as $\chi^2(2)$

provided to the private sector to engage in that expansion does not appear to date to have been markedly successful.

POLICY MEASURES

Investment is a proper subject for intervention whether by regulation, tax or direction. This is because business risk biases investment below what it would be in the absence of risk (Aiginger 1987; Driver and Moreton 1992). Despite textbook claims, there is no clear way of diversifying risk since full information is not available to investors and in any case managers, who make the decisions, are vulnerable to bankruptcy. This makes companies shirk commitments that society as a whole would be happy to bear. Furthermore, the benefits of large capital projects frequently have spin-off benefits which do not enter into private calculations of the profit that is appropriable by the investors.

More investment is needed; but only more investment of the right sort. In this paper we have reached some conclusions on this. Equipment investment raises the growth rate more than might be thought because of spin-offs. On the other hand, equipment investment of the cost-cutting kind may take undue precedence over expansionary investment at times of uncertain demand. Academic consensus is that tax and subsidy measures generally only affect the timing of investment rather than its quantity. This suggests a focus on the timing of different types of investment to satisfy the objective of stable and sustainable growth.

I have suggested that the timing of the relative proportions of expansionary investment and efficiency investment is sub-optimal. In particular, too little expansionary investment takes place in anticipation of the upturn. These are important points for the design of policy on investment. It appears, for example,that it would be wrong simply to attempt to stabilize investment, though stabilization may be necessary for the small-firm sector that acts in an uncoordinated risk-accepting way. For the important large-firm sector the aim should be to accelerate expansionary investment in advance of output recovery. In the UK, a countercyclical investment programme – the Accelerated Project Scheme – was introduced in 1975 with some success, though it did not focus on expansionary investment.

A more systematic approach is that practised in Sweden for many decades – the Investment Fund System (IFS). Although primarily intended in Sweden as a stabilization system it can also be used to favour certain categories of investment and to alter their timing (Pontusson 1992). The essence of the approach, illustrated in Figure 3, is that companies voluntarily place profits in a tax-free fund, to be released selectively at later periods. The scheme has been successful in stabilizing investment: MIT economist Stanley Fischer says of it, 'Somewhere, sometime, a government policy worked in a way it was intended to' (Taylor 1982: 'Comment').

Given the aim of accelerating expansionary investment, the release of funds

139

Main elements of the Swedish scheme

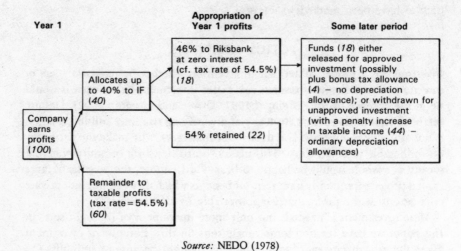

Year 1

Appropriation of
Year 1 profits

Some later period

Company
earns
profits
(*100*)

Allocates up
to 40% to IF
(*40*)

46% to Riksbank
at zero interest
(cf. tax rate of 54.5%)
(*18*)

54% retained (*22*)

Remainder to
taxable profits
(tax rate = 54.5%)
(*60*)

Funds (*18*) either
released for approved
investment (possibly
plus bonus tax allowance
(*4*) – no depreciation
allowance); or withdrawn for
unapproved investment
(with a penalty increase
in taxable income (*44*) –
ordinary depreciation
allowances)

Source: NEDO (1978)

Figure 7.3 The Swedish investment reserve fund system.

could be conditional on a high proportion of this type of investment in advance of the upturn. The scheme does not have to be self-financing and can incorporate permanent subsidies to particular types of investments that are thought to generate large spinoffs.

The introduction of an IFS in Britain was last considered in the mid-1970s when the Machine Tools Economic Development Committee of NEDO supported the proposal. Ironically the resulting NEDO report (NEDO 1978), while recognizing the intrinsic merit of the scheme, rejected it because of the then operation of free depreciation. Introducing the report, Lord Roll suggested that the scheme might be relevant in Britain 'if the tax regime were to change'. Given that these changes – initiated by Nigel Lawson in the mid-1980s – have now been implemented, it presents us with an opportunity to implement an effective capital investment policy. There will be pressure to introduce automatic accelerated depreciation provision to encourage investment generally.[8] However, this should be avoided. Investment is a proper subject for planning and coordination. The recent history of British economic performance suggests misallocation of private investment reflecting extremes of herd behaviour on the one hand and risk-aversion on the other.

CONCLUSIONS

Capital investment affects the chances of sustainable growth. Put differently the conditions for growth depend, not only on labour market considerations, but on the confidence that is both signalled and generated by capital investment.

The investment decision is one in which there is more than usual scope for private and social interests to diverge: consequently it is the arena where state involvement is likely to bear greatest fruit. The resistance to giving priority to investment probably hinges on a distrust of corporatism and the replacement of individual by collective decision-making. However, the pendulum has swung so far in that direction in the UK that the clock is no longer ticking.

The policy lesson is that risky long-run investment markets may not capture the social rate of return any more than is the case with new technology. If these externalities or spillovers are strong there is a compelling case for public support and direction to be given to fixed investment. The downside is that this public support will also be misguided and wasteful. A balanced approach to these concerns is surely possible.

APPENDIX

The intuition of the mathematics below is that if firms underinvest in capacity in response to risk they will aim to increase capital intensity, as labour, but not capital, can be varied *ex-post*.

With a putty-clay production function, capital intensity corresponding to maximum profit is derived in Lambert and Mulkay (1990) for a CES production function:

$$\ln(K^*/L^*) = \text{constant} + \sigma \ln(w/c) + \beta \ln(E[Y]/Y^*)$$

where

K^* = optimal capital stock
L^* = labour corresponding to full use of capacity
σ = elasticity of substitution between inputs
β = demand risk parameter
w/c = relative factor price
$E[Y]$ = expected production = certainty production
Y^* = optimal capacity

Risk neutrality and multiplicative demand-risk apply. Technical change is abstracted from.

Under certainty the final term disappears. For demand elasticities greater than 2, it is positive under risk if price is chosen *ex-ante* (Driver *et al.* 1993). Furthermore, in a fixed-price context, the final term is likely to be positive if profitability does not exceed historical values (Lambert and Mulkay 1990). Thus, risk induces greater capital intensity.

NOTES

1 Hourly labour costs in manufacturing are still a quarter lower in the UK than the EC average, partly reflecting low non-wage costs.
2 For cross-country comparisons, the net figure is preferable. As the UK has tended to have a higher ratio of shorter-lived assets that will inflate the gross figure compared with other countries. The net figures are even less favourable to the UK (*European Economy* 1989).
3 Brittan abstracts from the starting point of mass unemployment with greatly increased capital intensity of production. What scale of output increase is automatically

facilitated by a conquest of (wage) inflation? Is it likely to be sufficient to make a dent in unemployment? We have been around this track before (Bean 1989). When unemployment is due to capital shortage, it cannot be resolved by labour market flexibility because labour can only be substituted for capital on new projects. Expansion of the capital stock is needed at a very rapid rate if unemployment is to be contained, but that expansion is constrained by demand uncertainty.

4 This point has, of course, been repeatedly made over many decades by writers from heterodox schools such as Cambridge UK, and by other political economists.

5 These categories should not be confused with the asset class of capital investment – equipment or structures – introduced earlier. Cost-saving investment may well require moving to a greenfield site and expansionary investment may imply an even higher capital intensity.

6 This last point has greatest force at a time of mass unemployment when there is no indication that the pressure of unemployment is performing any transformative role. The appropriate calculation is then not the savings made by the firm or the public sector on efficiency investment, but the difference between these savings and the extra tax burden of incremental unemployment. Does it make social sense to have automatic ticket barriers at tube stations or self-service at petrol stations? Studies done by NEDO economists during the 1980s suggest that this difference is frequently negative, supporting the case for marginal employment subsidies. Although often unremarked, such subsidies also have the effect of enhancing the return from expansionary as opposed to efficiency investment, since there is only limited substitutability between labour and capital. Furthermore in a world where much unemployment results from a mismatch of qualities inherent in the unemployed and those demanded by employers, those ejected from low productivity jobs have a high probability of exit from the labour market, with no transformative gain to the economy.

7 To avoid misunderstanding I am not arguing against cost-cutting investment in general – the UK has considerable catch-up potential in manufacturing in terms of capital per head (NIESR 1993). Nevertheless, the balance between efficiency and expansionary (directly labour using) investment must be of concern if the social and private returns on these classes of investment diverge markedly, say because of risk, or external economies. Policy-makers should be adult enough to be able to make discriminating judgements here, whatever the prevailing ideology.

8 The Investment Fund System in Sweden was abolished by the Social Democrats as part of tax reform in 1989–90 as the emphasis shifted towards a general encouragement of investment through a reduction in profit taxation.

REFERENCES

Aiginger, K. (1987) *Production and Decision Theory under Uncertainty*, Oxford: Blackwell.

Allsopp, C., Jenkinson, T. and Morris, D. (1992) 'The assessment: macroeconomic policy in the 1980s', *Oxford Review of Economic Policy*, vol. 7, no. 3.

Artus, P. and Muet, P. A. (1990) *Investment and Factor Demand*, Amsterdam: North-Holland.

Barker, T. S. (1988) 'International trade and the British economy' in T. S. Barker and P. Dunne (eds), *The British Economy after Oil*, London: Croom Helm.

Bean, C. (1989) 'Capital shortage', *Economic Policy*, April, pp. 11–54.

Clarida, R. H. and Hickok, F. (1993) 'US manufacturing and the reindustrialization debate', *World Economy*, March, pp. 173–92.

Clark, P. (1993) 'Tax incentives and equipment investment', *Brookings Papers on Economic Activity*, vol. I, pp. 317–48.

De Long, J. B. and Summers, L. H. (1992) Equipment investment and economic growth: how strong is the nexus?' *Brookings Papers on Economic Activity*, vol. 2, pp. 157–211.

Driver, C. (1987) *Towards Full Employment: A Policy Appraisal*, London: Routledge & Kegan Paul.

Driver, C. (1988) 'The employment effects of expanding service industries', in T. S. Barker and P. Dunne (eds), *The British Economy after Oil*, London: Croom Helm, pp. 83–99.

Driver, C. and Moreton, D. (1992) *Investment, Expectations and Uncertainty*, Oxford: Blackwell.

Driver, C. and Meade, N. (1993) 'What explains lagged investment response: gestation lags; adjustment cost; or demand uncertainty?', *Working Paper*, Imperial College Management School, May.

Driver, C., Lambert., P. and Vial, S. (1993) 'Risky production with *ex-ante* prices under monopoly: analytical and simulation results', *Bulletin of Economic Research*, vol. 45, no. 1, pp. 59–68.

Hunter, J. and Pescetto, G. (1992) 'Structural change and manufacturing investment in the UK', in C. Driver and P. Dunne (eds), *Structural Change in the UK Economy*, Cambridge: Cambridge University Press.

Jorgenson, D. and Landau, R. (eds) (1989) *Technology and Capital Formation* Cambridge, MA. MIT Press.

Lambert, J.-P. and Mulkay, B. (1990) 'Investment in a disequilibrium model or does profitability really matter?', in J. J. Gabszewicz, J. F. Richard and L. A. Wolsey (eds), *Economic Decision Making – Games, Econometrics and Optimization*, Amsterdam: North-Holland, pp. 131–55.

Landau, R. (1992) 'Capital investment: key to competitiveness and growth', *Brookings Economic Review*, Summer, pp. 52–6.

Matthews, R., Feinstein, C. H. and Odling-Smee, J. C. (1982) *British Economic Growth 1856–1973*, Oxford: Clarendon.

Meltzer, A. (1989) *Keynes' Monetary Theory*, Cambridge: Cambridge University Press.

Milne, A. (1991) 'Non-manufacturing investment and UK aggregate demand', *Economic Outlook*, June, London Business School.

Mowery, D. C. and Rosenberg, N. (1989) *Technology and the Pursuit of Economic Growth*, Cambridge: Cambridge University Press.

Muellbauer, J. (1990) 'A pattern biased against trade', *Financial Times*, 19 January.

National Economic Development Office (NEDO) (1978) *Investment Reserve Schemes* London: NEDO Books.

National Institute of Economic and Social Research (1993) *Economic Review*.

Pontusson, J. (1992) *The Limits of Social Democracy: Investment Policies in Sweden*, Ithaca: Cornell University Press.

Porter, M. E. (1988) 'The technological dimension of competitive strategy', in R. A. Burgelman and M. A. Maidique (eds), *Strategic Management of Technological Innovation*, Homewood, IL: Irwin.

Taylor, J. B. (1982) 'The Swedish investment funds system as a stabilization policy rule', *Brookings Papers on Economic Activity*, vol. 1, 57–105.

8

RESEARCH AND DEVELOPMENT AND TRADING PERFORMANCE[1]

Tony Buxton, David Mayes and Andy Murfin

INTRODUCTION

The importance of innovation as a major determinant of economic performance is discussed in the investment and innovation overview, Chapter 6. The view that part of the effect of innovation comes through in improved trading performance is an obvious possibility, and a significant body of literature now exists which provides theoretical foundations and empirical backing for this belief. The present chapter seeks to extend this literature by an econometric study in which R&D is included in a model of UK trade, to test the proposition that 'innovation' can significantly affect both export and import effectiveness.

The aim is to extend the literature by:

1 sampling fifteen industry groups in the G5 economies over thirteen years (Table 1 in the Appendix has details);
2 allowing R&D to have a lagged effect on exports and import substitution;
3 estimating the effects of *relative* R&D expenditure rather absolute spending.

THE LINKS BETWEEN INNOVATION AND TRADING PERFORMANCE

International competitiveness is often analysed using demand-based models which incorporate supply factors through additional variables. The traditional variables are of course prices, incomes and 'tastes'. The last is a catch-all which shifts the basic demand relation for any of a number of reasons, some of which can be controlled by the firm, the most obvious being advertising, and some of which are autonomous. In an international trade setting, the residual effects are the 'non-price' factors discussed in Chapter 4. There is now a substantial body of evidence which suggests that a lack of 'non-price competitiveness' has been a major influence on the relatively poor post-war UK trade performance.[2] Non-price competitiveness has many dimensions, including quality, reliability, technical specification, design, service and after-sales support, value for money, perceived and actual characteristics, advertising, marketing support and dealership networks and others. Some of these factors can be analysed in

144

detail for the individual company or establishment (e.g. Leech and Cubbin 1987; Swann 1986). However, an analysis at this level of detail, when applied to the whole economy, is a formidable undertaking.

An alternative which is used here is to analyse 'industries' at some level of aggregation. Aggregate data for whole industries and groups of industries have conventionally used cost and price competitiveness and the exchange rate to explain trading performance. The industry approach to analysing competitiveness can be made compatible with the company approach, however, by incorporating non-price factors in demand-and-supply relationships either by expressing them in terms of price-per-unit and prices adjusted for quality or by adding them as variables to the more usual volume, price and income relationships. This then enables an evaluation of the effects of non-price competitiveness over a wide range of UK industry.

The particular aspect of non-price effects which is examined in this paper is innovation, as reflected in R&D expenditure. Some support for this use of R&D as a proxy exists (Pakes and Griliches 1984; Hughes 1986a). However, the approach is subject to many reservations. First, innovation is a wide concept and much of the most important effort and expenditure in actually bringing innovations into production and onto the market occurs later in the process than the items that are usually classified as R&D.[3] Second, R&D has only a limited link with innovativeness as such; R&D can take place without any innovation occurring; expenditure on R&D is a measure of inputs rather than a measure of the output actually produced. Furthermore, in using R&D as a proxy for innovativeness it is debatable whether it is current expenditure or an accumulated stock of R&D, analogous to physical investment and capital, that is the measure most appropriate to current impact into the innovation process and this is one of the issues analysed empirically below. Nevertheless while recognizing the drawbacks of R&D data, its use has been reasonably well established (Hughes 1986a), not least because, ostensibly at least, it is easier to measure than innovation.

The principal objective therefore is to examine, using industry data, the empirical link between innovation, as reflected in R&D, and UK trade performance. There are two well-established theoretical reasons for expecting this link. The first is that innovation can lead to the opening up of a 'technological gap' between countries such that their products become competitive in both price and non-price respects. New products can be higher quality, better designed to meet customers' needs and more reliable, while new processes may enable significant cost reductions. Much of the early literature (as shown in Gruber *et al.* 1967, for example) sought to explain why it was that the pattern of the revealed US comparative advantage did not follow the relative intensity of US capital compared with labour as expected. One of their most important contributions is to show how the development of R&D and high labour skills is a natural *competitive* reaction to the pressures place on advanced industrial countries by international trade. Thus it is not just that the high skill base is itself a source of competitiveness but that it introduces much greater opportunity for product differentiation as increased entry into the market by low labour-cost producers erodes the competitive position of the existing makers of the less sophisticated products.

The second, or 'product life cycle', theory arises from the first. Here products earn a variable rate of return over their limited lives. In the early stages growth is rapid and firms can earn substantial profits. As the product matures there are gains from economies of scale and from further development, but in the last stages the ideas become readily imitative and eventually overtaken by the next new product. There are thus major gains to the firm which gets in front initially because novelty precludes effective competition and later because scale lowers its unit costs relative to subsequent entrants as they try to catch up. This is set out clearly in de Jong (1987). The crucial feature of both theories is that they embody the ideas of 'cumulative causation'. Once a firm gets in front and has a temporary monopoly it will tend to confirm that position. The competitive edge leads to increased profits which can be reinvested both in cost-reducing capacity and in further research. The technological lead means that the firm is further ahead in the process of *learning* the new ideas and can be benefiting from this knowledge in other areas while the followers are still catching up in the existing areas. Computer chip manufacture is a classic example where in the case of the 8K RAM chips, the US firms were always able to stay in front of their Japanese competitors. Although the Japanese had lower costs at each point on the learning curve, the US firms had even lower costs still because they were further along the curve. The Japanese changed the position by investing in the large-scale technology which became the basis for the next generation of products, thereby leapfrogging the Americans (Baldwin and Krugman 1987).

A more recent development has been to apply to trade the well-established theories of the influence of industry structure on economic performance. Essentially this means that economic power, emanating from entry barriers/ concentration/product differentiation can influence the incentive/ability to innovate which will in time influence the ability to export or keep out imports. This can be seen to some extent as a generalization of the product life-cycle idea whereby the length of the cycle is dependent upon industry structure.[4]

Previous researchers have struggled over how to incorporate R&D activity in the determination of trade performance. Two input measures can be distinguished: the amount spent and the number of people involved. However, both these factors are subject to constraints from the structure of individual industries. In an early study, Keesing (1967) tests whether the export performance of US industries is influenced by R&D activity in 1962. The methodology is simple correlations between variables, but he argues that there is a strong relationship between the two with causation running mainly from the former. He finds economies of scale to be important as well as high requirements for skills in production. Export shares are not influenced by capital

146

requirements, however. Gruber *et al*. (1967) came to similar conclusions using the same methodology. These conclusions can be extended to the UK (Katrak 1973) where the analysis relates to 1962 and 1966. In this model, relative exports in the two countries in different industries are determined by R&D expenditure and employment of scientists and engineers as proxies for the technological gap; skill differentials and a measure of scale. Skill differences are important, and economies of scale have some effect but there is only weak support for the technological gap hypothesis. More recently (Katrak 1982) has shown that *both* skill and R&D intensity of UK exports were higher than those of imports in 1968 and 1978, a result confirmed by Hughes (1986a). Hughes (1986b) in her survey concludes that, overall, the literature supports the view that innovation is an important determinant of trade performance and that the other main aspect of the technology gap notion is factor endowment of human capital and again this is found to be important when proxied by measures of the skills of the labour force. Structural characteristics, particularly economies of scale, also find some support.

Taking these ideas together Schott (1981) attempts to link the relatively poor economic performance of the UK to a decline in innovative activity. During the 1970s the UK demonstrated a decline in resources devoted to R&D and there was a fall in its share of patent applications. Schott argues that the lack of innovation has helped shift the UK into a 'vicious circle' where slow growth is linked with lower productivity and lower product quality (the cumulative causation argument, in a negative direction). This weakens the trade performance which in turn reduces investment, growth and innovation, and so on. More recently, Patel and Pavitt (1987), looking at the period 1967–83, find that output growth and R&D growth were both relatively sluggish in the UK and that UK firms have not committed 'an increasing share of output or profits to R&D at the same rate as foreign competitors'. Katrak (1982) found that both R&D and skill intensities of UK imports rose relative to exports over a similar period (1968–78), suggesting that the UK was, in relative terms, moving towards a less skilled, less technically intensive product-mix.

Over 1975–85, while production has grown fastest in high research-intensive industries, according to Smith (1986) the UK's international position in these sectors has been eroded with rising import penetration and falling export share. Competitiveness has also been eroded in the medium-intensity (mainly engineering) industries, while the low-intensity sectors have witnessed extensive price competition. The relative decline in business R&D spending in the early 1980s, and the real decline in total R&D spending in the UK are important factors governing the UK's loss of competitiveness in manufacturing industry. This is extended internationally by Walker (1979) to the major OECD countries in the 1960s and 1970s. For the US, UK and West Germany, comparative advantage is quite strong in R&D-intensive industries.

There are, however, two important drawbacks to this approach. The first is that R&D expenditure is itself in part related to the performance of the firm as the ability to spend on R&D depends largely upon profitability as it normally has to be met from its own resources (see Hughes (1986a) for a helpful two-equation model and Buxton (1987) for evidence on the financing of R&D). The second is that other 'non-price' factors also influence trade performance. Their omission will bias the coefficients on the included variables.

R&D CAPITAL

Thus far the discussion of measures of R&D has been in terms of R&D expenditure as a measure of the input to the process or patents and innovations as indicators of output (OECD (1986) also used the 'technology balance' of trade). However, much of the ability to undertake successful R&D is embodied in the skills, knowledge and experience of the personnel who undertake it. The proposition that R&D is an important determinant of innovative output not just in current expenditure terms but also in the form of an accumulated stock originated some time ago (Minasian (1961) is an early empirical example) and is now well established. R&D investment today may produce innovative output today or tomorrow, and so may be treated analogously to investment in physical capital, human skills or in advertising, as a stock variable. The treatment of R&D as a capital stock rather than a current input implies accumulation of these inputs, in the form of physical factors or a stock of knowledge. The stock of R&D capital is the depreciated sum of R&D spending past and present.

The R&D stock measure has been computed by the method used by Griliches (1980) and Suzuki (1985). This involves computing the stock in the initial year by assuming that up to that point R&D expenditure has increased by the average rate of growth it showed previously (over 1969–72) and then depreciating it at a fixed rate. R&D capital for any further year, RDC_t, can then be calculated in the normal way by depreciating existing stock and adding the new expenditure, RDE.

$$RDC_t = (1 - d)RDC_{t-1} + RDE_t \qquad (1)$$

where d is the rate of depreciation.

The crucial element here is the choice of d, the depreciation rate. There are no clear estimates for the appropriate rate available from existing sources and it is clear that the appropriate outcome varies substantially both by industry and according to the type of innovation. Since the 'capital' involved is to a large extent human knowledge and experience, whose value can diminish rapidly if someone else patents the idea, it is difficult to decide on the appropriate rate of depreciation. Estimates of 10 per cent and 50 per cent were chosen for the appropriate depreciation rate to illustrate the consequences of different choices of d rather than using a specific measure, as was common previously (for instance Griliches and Mairesse (1984)). Although it is not common in this literature, a possibility for future research is the calculation of a maximum likelihood estimate for the depreciation rate.

The actual R&D data have been compiled consistently in DTI (1986) as constant price expenditures for fifteen industries and five countries for the years 1969, 1972, 1975, 1978, 1981 and 1983. From these, annual data were calculated by linear interpolation. This is undesirable but necessary given the data shortages. The effect is to overstate the degrees of freedom in the regression analysis. The overstatement is likely to be less, however, the lower is the assumed rate of depreciation, since the addition to the R&D stock from any year's R&D investment is smaller.

THE ESTIMATED MODEL

This study draws particularly on the work of Schott (1981), Schott and Pick (1984) and Hughes (1986a) in its specification of trade flow volumes in terms of R&D. Schott and Pick effectively examine a cross-section of British industries in market share equations, where export or import share depends on UK R&D, the relative levels of education, relative export/import prices and appropriate income variables. These are essentially adaptations of the standard trade flow equations where relative prices and income are the primary explanatory variables (e.g. Thirlwall 1986). Hughes (1986a) examines a cross-section of British industries in 1978, where export and import sales intensities, net trade, or volume flows are related to relative R&D intensities, skilled labour intensity in the UK, industrial concentration, the capital labour ratio, a measure of minimum efficient scale and the investment/capital ratio. The Hughes model also allows for the simultaneous determination of R&D intensities.

Our basic model is the demand for UK exports and the UK's demand for imports. in which R&D acts as a shift variable:

$$TP_i = TP_i(RDC_{ui}, RDC_{wi}, P_{ui}, P_{wi}, Y_{ui}, Y_{wi}, KL_{ui}, KL_{wi}) \qquad (2)$$

where:

TP_i = Trade performance in industry i
RDC_{ui} = R&D capital in the UK in industry i
RDC_{wi} = R&D capital in the 'rest of the world' in industry i
P_{ui} = price of UK exports in industry i
P_{wi} = price of exports of the 'rest of the world' in industry i
Y_{ui} = production in the UK in industry i
Y_{wi} = production in the 'rest of the world' in industry i
KL_{ui} = ratio of capital to labour in the UK in industry i
KL_{wi} = ratio of capital to labour in the 'rest of the world' in industry i

These variables are described in the Appendix as is TP_i which took three forms

(a) UK export volumes in industry i, X_i;

149

(b) UK import volumes in industry i, M_i;

(c) the ratio of the UK trade balance $(X_i - M_i)$ to total UK trade $(X_i + M_i)$ in industry i.

The choice of the dependent variable is not easy and we do not claim that these are the correct ones. As the short discussion of previous work shows, a number of alternatives have been used. For (a) and (b), it was felt that in the first instance X_i and M_i reflect the earlier discussion of straightforward demand relationships. In addition though, scaling might show something different and some literature exists on size normalization in trade (Soete (1987) recently, for instance). In both equations there were choices between demand- and supply-related scalers. In the case of exports, a supply-related one would be industry value-added so that the LHS variable reflected the change in the proportion of production sold overseas. Since the model is of demand, however, a demand variable seems appropriate so that exports are normalized by world production as a proxy to world demand, with supply assumed to be infinitely elastic.

The choice of denominator in the import equation is also not unambiguous. The two most often used are production and home demand (production less exports plus imports). The essential problem with the latter is that movements in exports and imports may offset each other which could be misleading in an import equation. So while import penetration has often been used, the procedure adopted here follows Hughes and Thirlwall (1977) and uses production to normalize imports.

The OECD (1986) has recently completed a major study of R&D, invention and competitiveness and the conclusions from this form a helpful building block for the present analysis. While they look at all member countries they remark that 'the preponderant role of the United States, Germany, Japan, France and the United Kingdom in the R&D potential of the West is commonly acknowledged'. The 'world' is therefore defined here to consist of these five countries and the data were calculated accordingly.

It is as well to be aware of the limitations of the data, which in part concern relevant 'omitted variables'. Among these are indices of capacity utilization, minimum efficient scale, industrial concentration and a measure of human capital or skill input. These have been omitted owing to lack of data availability and our intention to focus on the UK's performance *relative* to its competitors. Variables available for the UK alone are not included. This has affected other studies; for example, Hughes has no information on relative human capital and Schott and Pick none on relative R&D. Against these omissions, this study includes relative price variables and a specification of dummy or fixed effects appropriate to pooled cross-section time-series data (Maddala 1977).

The inclusion of fixed effects has recently arisen in some related literature (Geroski 1987a,b; Cohen *et al.* 1987; Levin *et al.* 1985). Their inclusion in the general form is intended to record industry-specific effects which may have been omitted and to allow the constant term to vary by sector. For Geroski's

(1987a) innovation equations, for example, they are presumed to proxy the variation in 'technological opportunities' by industry. Statistically their exclusion from a general model can then be tested. Similarly, time dummy variables are included to register effects peculiar to each time period. This too helps with the removal of 'trend' factors and reduces the likelihood of 'spurious correlation'. A negative aspect of their inclusion is the difficulty of interpreting the precise meaning of significant coefficients on these dummies.

In addition, the inclusion of fixed effects in the regression is often found to weaken coefficients on key variables of interest. For example, in Geroski (1987b), a significant positive effect of innovations on export performance for UK industry is rendered statistically insignificant once industry-fixed effects are included. This suggests that the propensity to innovate and the strength of export performance are correlated with a third factor, perhaps productivity or managerial efficiency, which is best proxied by industry-specific effects. In the present context, for example, one might expect the inclusion of fixed effects to weaken Hughes's (1986a) finding that relative R&D intensity influences export performance.

The model was estimated on annual data over the period 1970–83 using a breakdown of fifteen industries covering manufacturing (listed in the Appendix). The reported results are for OLS but when instrumental variables are used to allow for any feedback from competitiveness on R&D spending, the results are very similar. Estimation was carried out in logarithmic and linear form for imports and exports and linearly for the trade balance. Simple partial adjustment and error control mechanisms were used to model the dynamic adjustment of trade performance to R&D capital. The results are shown in Tables 1–3. Sargan specification tests were used to compare the linear and logarithmic forms.

Taking exports first, Table 1 columns 1 to 6 show the full unconstrained model, estimated using the three measures of R&D, depreciated at 100, 50 and 10 per cent, respectively. In column (1), both UK and World R&D have significant coefficients with expected signs, similarly for UK export prices. The other variables, however, have insignificant coefficients or the 'wrong' signs. Column (2) therefore reports a more parsimonious estimation, retaining both R&D variables. World R&D is now insignificant, and, notably, the coefficient of 1.06 on World production volume suggests that the UK is able to increase its exports at the same rate as world demand.

Similar exercises were carried out for the two other R&D variables, now calculated as R&D capital stock. The R&D t-statistics are highest when depreciation is assumed at a rate of 10 per cent. This accords with other research and goes some way to supporting very low or even zero obsolescence of research as assumed by Griliches (1980), for instance, and going back to Minasian (1961). The coefficient on UK export prices is stable (and plausible) but those on world production volume and world capital/labour are about halved compared with column (2).

151

Table 1 UK export equations: cross-section/time-series, 1971–83 (fifteen industries, log linear)

Dependent variable	UK export volumes						UK export volumes/world production					
	(1)	(2)	(3)	(4)	(5)	(6)	(7)	(8)	(9)	(10)	(11)	(12)
1. UK R&D	0.20 (6.75)	0.10 (2.84)										
2. World R&D	-0.11 (-2.52)	-0.04 (-0.83)										
3. UK/world R&D							0.16 (3.73)	0.18 (4.53)				
4. UK R&D stock 50% depn.			0.25 (7.09)	0.26 (7.11)								
5. World R&D stock 50% depn.			-0.22 (-4.92)	-0.20 (-4.50)	0.22 (5.98)	0.43 (10.60)						
6. UK/world R&D stock 50% depn.					-0.22 (-6.31)	-0.33 (-8.09)			0.22 (4.48)	0.22 (4.77)		
7. UK R&D stock 10% depn.												
8. World R&D stock 10% depn.												
9. UK/world stock 10% depn.											0.38 (5.64)	0.31 (5.55)
10. UK export prices	-0.31 (-4.00)	-0.44 (-6.42)	-0.28 (-3.43)	-0.34 (-4.88)	-0.34 (-4.42)	-0.38 (-6.09)						
11. World export prices	-0.20 (-1.75)		-0.19 (-1.58)		-0.16 (-1.48)							
12. UK/world export prices							-0.32 (-3.72)	-0.31 (-3.68)	-0.32 (-3.72)	-0.32 (-3.76)	-0.29 (-3.51)	-0.30 (-3.63)
13. World production volume	0.30 (1.93)	1.06 (6.72)	0.51 (3.21)	0.55 (3.38)	0.66 (4.49)	0.52 (3.46)						
14. UK capital/labour	-0.74 (-6.76)		-0.31 (-4.28)		-0.54 (-5.33)							
15. World capital/labour	-0.14 (-1.12)	-0.80 (-14.64)	-0.70 (-10.06)	-0.89 (-15.40)	-0.31 (-2.68)							
16. UK/world capital/labour							0.18 (1.15)		0.04 (0.32)		0.27 (1.83)	
17. $\bar{R}^2$	0.97	0.96	0.96	0.96	0.96	0.96	0.96	0.96	0.96	0.96	0.96	0.96

Table 2 UK import equations: cross-section/time-series, 1971–83 (fifteen industries, linear)

Dependent variable	UK import volumes						UK import volumes/UK production		
	(1)	(2)	(3)	(4)	(5)	(6)	(7)	(8)	(9)
1. UK R&D	-0.41 (-3.23)	-0.38 (-3.06)							
2. World R&D × 10⁻²	-0.36 (-0.43)	-0.39 (-0.47)							
3. UK R&D/world R&D							-11.58 (-1.55)		
4. UK R&D stock 50% depn.			-0.24 (-3.32)	-0.25 (-3.59)					
5. World R&D stock 50% depn. × 10⁻²			-0.42 (-0.09)	-0.70 (-0.16)					
6. UK/world R&D stock 50% depn.								-12.41 (-1.55)	
7. UK R&D stock 10% depn.					-0.05 (-3.93)	-0.09 (-5.34)			
8. World R&D stock 10% depn. × 10⁻²					-0.13 (-1.75)	-0.16 (-1.27)			
9. UK/world stock 10% depn.									-7.18 (-1.50)
10. UK import prices	1.45 (2.34)		1.24 (2.05)		1.37 (2.38)				
11. UK home prices	0.51 (0.92)	0.86 (1.71)	0.40 (0.73)		0.52 (0.92)				
12. UK import /home prices							-2.21 (-3.03)	-3.60 (-6.28)	-3.43 (-5.90)
13. UK production volume	3.30 (2.14)	2.65 (1.75)	3.13 (2.04)	2.64 (1.77)	0.52 (0.35)				
14. UK capital/labour	-19.18 (-2.90)	-11.60 (-5.90)	-18.82 (-2.99)	-11.93 (-6.14)	-17.47 (-3.12)	-10.37 (-5.84)			
15. World capital/labour	2.50 (0.57)		2.61 (0.61)		1.83 (0.48)				
16. UK/world capital/labour							-6.03 (-9.65)	-6.97 (-9.79)	-6.09 (-9.22)
17. $\bar{R}^2$	0.92	0.92	0.92	0.92	0.93	0.93	0.86	0.86	0.86

Table 3 Relative trade balance equations: cross-section/time-series, 1971–83 (fifteen industries, linear)

Dependent variable	(1)	(2)	$\dfrac{UK\ Exports - UK\ Imports}{UK\ Exports + UK\ Imports}$			
			(3)	(4)	(5)	(6)
1. UK R&D $\times 10^{-4}$	2.32 (4.42)	2.30 (4.45)				
2. World R&D $\times 10^{-6}$	-9.97 (-2.33)	-2.18 (-2.18)				
3. UK R&D stock 50% depn. $\times 10^{-4}$			1.37 (4.74)	1.62 (6.48)		
4. World R&D stock 50% depn. $\times 10^{-6}$			-6.47 (-2.79)	-8.26 (-3.96)		
5. UK R&D stock 10% depn. $\times 10^{-5}$					4.28 (6.66)	4.12 (6.84)
6. World R&D stock 10% depn. $\times 10^{-6}$					-2.03 (-4.11)	-1.93 (-4.08)
7. UK export prices $\times 10^{-3}$	-3.34 (-7.08)	-3.32 (-6.92)	-3.40 (-7.22)	-3.50 (-7.34)	-3.47 (-7.17)	-3.48 (-7.19)
8. UK import prices $\times 10^{-3}$	1.88 (3.42)	1.97 (3.54)	1.99 (3.63)	2.38 (4.43)	2.48 (4.55)	2.54 (4.72)
9. UK capital/labour $\times 10^{-3}$	1.17 (0.92)	5.77 (9.09)	1.35 (1.07)	4.45 (15.54)	3.53 (3.77)	4.12 (14.96)
10. World capital/labour $\times 10^{-3}$	4.06 (2.56)		3.83 (2.42)		0.89 (0.74)	
11. $\bar{R}^2$	0.82	0.81	0.82	0.81	0.82	0.82

In columns (7)–(12), the variables are relative values as discussed above. The relative export price coefficient is stable and the relative capital/labour coefficient is insignificant. Again though, in terms of t-statistics, the low-depreciation R&D has the greatest explanatory power. The values of the coefficients of the industry and time dummies are not shown, but most of them are statistically significant. So while there is not a great deal to choose between the equations in statistical terms, equation (12) appears to perform best showing that a 1 per cent change in the ratio of UK R&D capital compared to world R&D capital (depreciated at 10 per cent a year) results in an improvement in relative export performance of 0.31 per cent.

The results for imports are given in Table 2. In this case the appropriate form was linear. Columns (1)–(6) give the unconstrained results in which R&D stock has a significant effect in reducing imports, but the equations do not pick any of the expected opposite influence of World R&D. On the other hand, except for the UK capital/labour ratio, the other variables are either insignificant or the wrong sign. The constrained equations in columns (7)–(9), on the other hand, give strong support for relative prices and capital/labour, but not for R&D, presumably because of the apparent unimportance of world R&D for UK imports.

The effect when exports and imports are taken together is shown in Table 3, where the dependent variable is the trade ratio, trade balance/total trade. While the capital/labour ratio variables when included together show some uncertainty, in equations when the world is omitted, in columns (2), (4) and (6), the coefficients are all highly significant. Again while there is not much in it, the 10 per cent depreciated capital seems more appropriate than the 50 per cent, but both are preferable to the undepreciated R&D. Because the dependent variable consists of both imports and exports, however, care must be taken in interpreting these results because any value for the balance could reflect different volumes of exports. Intermediate values of $(X - M)/(X + M)$ are often interpreted as indicating intra-industry patterns of trade – countries both importing and exporting increasing quantities of an industry's goods. The extent of this is hard to evaluate (Greenaway and Milner 1983), but its existence may be important in evaluating the effects of R&D particularly in relation to the product-cycle literature. In particular, it might be expected that high R&D countries would export heavily in the early stages of the product cycle, but import a mass-market variant at the end. R&D in this case would be an important determinant of trade flows, but may not show up in the ratio used, unless the complex lags are modelled accurately. Thus, while very high or low values of $(X - M)/(X + M)$ may be rigorously linked to R&D, intermediate values may not.

Finally we attempt to put these results into context. The size of the R&D effect is quite substantial. In 1983 values, the end period of the analysis, a £0.3 billion increase in UK R&D spending, about five per cent more than the actual, results in a rise in exports and a fall in imports, improving the balance of payments and hence GDP by £0.4 billion. Clearly this relation only holds for small increases in R&D as large increases might change the balance of payments so much that the exchange rate changes and hence the effect is reduced by the relative price terms in the equation.

CONCLUSION

The results suggest that there is a strong relationship between R&D and international competitiveness. There is clear evidence from previous research that increased expenditure on R&D leads to an improved competitive performance. Our research confirms two propositions:

1 It is not simply spending on R&D which counts but investment in R&D relative to that undertaken by our competitors in each industry. Thus a country which puts a more than proportionate share of its resources into industries which are intensive users of R&D internationally, like pharmaceuticals or aerospace, may appear to have a high aggregate level of spending on R&D but in fact be well below the average in comparable overseas industries and hence not very competitive.

2 R&D spending should be viewed as an investment. It is a firm's R&D capital stock largely embodied in a team of skilled people and the product of the continuing sequence of spending over the years, which acts as the basis for successful innovation and development and this stock depreciates relatively slowly. Thus firms like Glaxo or ICI produce their successful new products from the cumulative efforts of dedicated, skilled research teams over a long period. Large cycles in R&D spending induced by short-term financial pressures are heavily counter-productive.

APPENDIX

Definition of variables

X_i The volume of UK exports to the OECD for industry i in 1975 prices. The current price data in $ from COMTAP on an ISIC basis was converted to £ using actual annual exchange rates and was deflated by the nearest equivalent export unit-value index from MRETS (£m).

M_i The volume of UK imports from the OECD for industry i in 1975 prices. The current price data in $ from COMTAP on an ISIC basis was converted to £ using actual annual exchange rates and was deflated by the nearest equivalent import unit-value index from MRETS (£m).

P_{ui} Index of unit values of exports for industry i.
Source: MRETS

P_{wi} Index of unit values of imports for industry i.
Source: MRETS

Y_{ui} Index of the volume of industrial production in the UK for industry i.
Source: Blue Book

Y_{wi} Index of the volume of industrial production of the 'rest of the world' for
            industry i.
            Source: UNYIS
KL_{ui}, KL_{wi} The ratio of capital stock (constant prices) to labour employment by
            industry and country.
            Source: BDS
$RDE_{u,w}$ The volume of expenditure in constant price \$ on R&D for 1969, 1972,
            1975, 1978 1981, 1983 for the UK, (RD_u) and the sum of, USA, Japan,
            France, West Germany (RD_w). The raw data were obtained from the DTI
            and converted to £ using exchange rates. For estimation purposes, RDE is
            simple interpolated series of expenditure in each year, and RDC are
            imputed R&D stock figures as discussed in the text.

Key to sources

UNYIS: United Nations Yearbook of Industrial Statistics
Blue Book: CSO National Income and Expenditure
MRETS: Monthly Review of External Trade Statistics
COMTAP: OECD database of Foreign Trade Statistics
BDS: Database of Statistical Office of the European Communities

Industries used

	(*ISIC Code*)
Electrical group	(383)
Chemicals and drugs	(351, 352)
Petroleum refining	(353, 354)
Motor vehicles	(3843)
Ships	(3841)
Ferrous metals	(371)
Non-ferrous metals	(372)
Fabricated metal products	(381)
Office, computing machinery, machinery NES	(3825)
Instruments	(385)
Food, drink and tobacco	(31)
Textiles, footwear and leather	(32)
Rubber and plastics	(355, 356)
Stone, clay, glass	(36)
Paper and printing	(34)

NOTES

1 A version of this paper was published in Buxton *et al.* (1991). The authors are
  grateful to the editors of *Economics of Innovation and New Technology* for
  permission to reprint.
2 Thirlwall (1986) contains a clear survey of the issues.
3 NEDC (1987) has a discussion as well as chapter 6.
4 Needless to say, the dynamics of this process are such that structure itself is an
  endogenous variable.

REFERENCES

Baldwin, R. and Krugman, P. (1987) 'The persistence of the US trade deficit', *Brookings Papers on Economic Activity*, MIT, Columbia University, no. 1, pp. 1–43.

Buxton, T. (1987) 'Financing research and development in Great Britain', in *Financer le progrès*, Paris, Instiut d'etudes Bancaires et Financier, Berger Levrault.

Buxton, T., Mayes, D. and Murfin, A. (1991) 'UK trade performance and R&D', *Economics of Innovation and New Technology*, vol. 1, no. 3, pp. 243–55.

Caves, R. E. and Barnett, D. (1990) *Technical Inefficiency in US Manufacturing*, Harvard: Harvard University Press.

Cohen, W., Levin, R. and Mowery, D. (1987) 'Firm size and R&D intensity: a re-examination', *Journal of Industrial Economics*, vol. 35, no. 3, pp. 543–65.

De Jong, H. W. (1987) 'Market structures in the European Economic Community', in M. McMillan, D. G. Mayes and P. van Veen (eds), *European Integration and Industry*, Tilburg: Tilburg University Press.

DTI (1986) 'Review of UK technological performance', London: Sunningdale Conference, paper no. 1.

Geroski, P. (1987a) 'Innovation, technological opportunity and market structure', mimeo., University of Southampton.

Geroski, P. (1987b) 'Exports and innovation', mimeo., London: National Economic Development Office.

Greenaway, D., and Milner, C. (1983) 'On the measurement of intra-industry trade', *Economic Journal*, vol. 93, December, pp. 900–8.

Griliches, Z. (1980) 'R&D and the productivity slowdown', *American Economic Review*, vol. 70, no. 2, pp. 343–8.

Griliches, Z. and Mairesse, J. (1984) 'Productivity and R&D at the firm level', in Z. Griliches (ed.), *R&D, Patents and Productivity*, Chicago NBER.

Gruber, W., Mehta, D. and Vernon, R. (1967) 'The R&D factor in international trade and international investment of United States industries', *Journal of Political Economy*, vol. 75, no. 1.

Hughes, J. J. and Thirlwall, A. P. (1977) 'Trends and cycles in import penetration in the UK', *Oxford Bulletin of Economics and Statistics*, vol. 39, no. 4.

Hughes, K. (1986a) *Exports and Technology*, Cambridge: Cambridge University Press.

Hughes, K. (1986b) 'Literature survey on the influence of technology on economic performance', mimeo., PREST, University of Manchester.

Katrak, H. (1973) 'Human skills, R&D and scale economies in the exports of the UK and US', *Oxford Economic Papers*, vol. 25, no. 3.

Katrak, H. (1982) 'Labour skills, R&D and capital requirements in the international trade and investment of the UK: 1968–78', NIESR Discussion Paper No. 51.

Keesing, D. B. (1967) 'The impact of research and development on United States trade', *Journal of Political Economy*, vol. 51, no. 1.

Leech, D. and Cubbin, J. (1987) 'Import penetration in the UK passenger car market: a cross-section study', *Applied Economics*, vol. 10, no. 4, pp. 289–303.

Levin, R., Cohen, W. and Mowery, D. (1985) 'R&D appropriability, opportunity and market structure: new evidence on some Schumpeterian hypotheses', *American Economic Review*, vol. 75, no. 2, pp. 20–4.

Maddala, G. S. (1977) *Econometrics*, Tokyo: McGraw-Hill.

Minasian, J. R. (1961) 'Technical change and production functions', presented at the Autumn Meeting of the Econometric Society.

Minasian, J. R. (1969) 'Research and development, production function and rate of return', *American Economic Review*, vol. 70.

NEDC (1987) 'Innovation in industry', *Memorandum by the Director General*, NEDC 87(15).

OECD (1986) 'R&D, intervention and competitiveness', *OECD Science and Technology Indicators*, no. 2.

Pakes, A. and Griliches, Z. (1984) 'Patents and R&D at the firm level: a first look', in Z. Griliches (ed.), *R&D, Patents and Productivity*, Chichago: NBER.

Patel, P. and Pavitt, K. (1984) 'The effects of price and quality composition in international trade', University College Discussion Paper 84-01, London.

Patel, P. and Pavitt, K. (1987) 'The elements of British technological competitiveness', Paper presented in NIESR Conference, *Manufacturing in Britain*.

Schott, K. (1981) *Industrial Innovation in the UK, Canada and the USA*, London: British North American Comittee.

Schott, K. and Pick, K. (1984) 'The effect of price and non-price factors on UK export performance and import penetration', Discussion Paper, 84-01, University College, London.

Smith, M. (1986) 'The output and trade of UK manufacturing industry', *Midland Bank Review*, Autumn, pp. 8–16.

Soete, L. (1987) 'The impact of technological innovation on international trade patterns: the evidence reconsidered', *Research Policy*, vol. 16, nos 2–4.

Suzuki, K. (1985) 'Knowledge capital and the private rate of return on R&D in Japanese manufacturing industries', *International Journal of Industrial Organization*, vol. 3, no. 3, pp. 293–305.

Swann, P. (1986) *Quality Innovation: An Economic Analysis of Rapid Improvements in Microelectronic Components*, London: Frances Pinter.

Thirlwall, A. (1986) *Balance of Payments Theory and the UK Experience*, London: Macmillan.

Walker, W. (1979) *Industrial Innovation and International Trading Performance*, Greenwich, CT: JAI Press.

9

INVESTING IN SKILLS: TRAINING POLICY IN THE UK

Paul Chapman

THE BRITISH TRAINING PROBLEM[1]

Economists refer to the process of investing in education and vocational skills as human capital formation. This description is more than economic jargon. It is based on the view that investing in human skills is basically comparable with investing in fixed capital. Policies which are concerned with promoting human capital acquisition are referred to as vocational education and training (VET) policies.

It has become widely accepted that one of the major factors in the poor economic performance of the UK economy has been the inadequacy of VET policies. These inadequacies can be traced to the education system but most comment has been made on the poor VET provision after compulsory education.

This chapter examines the basis for this view from several perspectives. The importance of a trained workforce has been emphasized in much of the research on productivity. If the findings from this research are accepted then a radical overhaul of training and education is a necessary condition for improving the competitiveness of the British economy. The evidence from the National Institute for Economic and Social Research has been widely quoted in support of this conclusion. Going beyond this general policy proposition, it is necessary to understand the motivations of firms and workers if this prescription is to be put into practice. What type of training should be encouraged? What incentives are best suited to the British labour market? In this respect it must be admitted that there is an insufficient understanding of the training process. Even so it is necessary to focus on what we do know and one of the essential elements in a successful economy is a mechanism to encourage firms to undertake training. The most obvious way to achieve this would be through publicly supported institutional arrangements to reward firms who train and to discourage the 'free riders'.

The widely perceived deficiencies in VET provision in the UK have been barely addressed by policy developments over recent years. VET policy has suffered from three failings. First, much of policy has been reactive to events,

160

especially rising unemployment. Second, policy has been divorced from any long-term strategic objectives. Third, policy-makers have been caught between a desire to encourage a market-oriented policy (deregulation) but in practice have found that intervention has been the only way to secure any hope of training provision, especially for new entrants to the labour market or the increasing numbers in long-term unemployment.

It is vital now that the lessons from the recent past are absorbed into future policy action. Before progress can be made it is necessary to dispel the myths about the supply-side policies of the 1980s. There has been no fundamental improvement in training provision and, compared with other competitor countries, the UK can more clearly be identified as a low-wage–low-skill economy.

TRAINING AND PRODUCTIVTY

The economic basis for training or education is that it either improves productivity or acts as a signalling or screening device which allows firms to distinguish ability differences for superficially homogeneous workers.[2] Unfortunately there has been very little empirical evidence to compare these alternatives, although the evidence against signalling is perhaps most conclusive. A number of studies have tried to identify the specific effects of training on wages and employment, largely following the method in Mincer (1962, 1974).[3] But perhaps the most important empirical investigation has been concerned with the link between training and productivity.

There are a number of problems in assessing the contribution of human capital formation to productivity. One set of difficulties lies in the measurement of productivity itself. An important aspect of measurement which specifically concerns human capital is the measurement of labour quality by relative wages. Effective labour (l_e) can be defined as in equation (1):

$$l_e = [l_s(W_s/W_u) + l_u] / [l_u + l_s] \tag{1}$$

where l_s is skilled labour and l_u unskilled labour and (W_s/W_u) is the skilled–unskilled wage ratio; $l_e = 1$ if labour is homogeneous.

The contributions of capital and labour quality to total labour productivity can in principle be estimated and any residual attributed to measurement error or unknown factors. O'Mahoney (1992) uses this method for productivity per worker-hour for UK and German manufacturing in 1987. Effective labour is 1.11 in the UK and 1.23 in Germany. The productivity gap between the UK and Germany was estimated as approximately 22 per cent, of which 9 per cent is due to capital differences, nearly 10 per cent due to labour quality and less than 4 per cent to residual factors. From a simple human capital perspective this suggests that both human and physical capital explain the bulk of labour productivity differences and that human capital is as important as physical capital. This exercise measures relative differences in productivity. Labour

161

productivity in an absolute sense may be influenced in a quite different fashion and physical capital is likely to be much more important. The estimates denote the extent to which relative productivity between two countries can be explained by human and physical capital.[4]

In addition to comparing labour productivity for the economy as a whole, or for a key sector of the economy as in manufacturing, it is possible to consider the much more disaggregate industrial sector evidence. Arguably, this has two advantages. First, it may help to provide more accurate estimates of the contribution of human capital and other factors of production. Second, it identifies the contributing factors to growth in the different sectors of the economy. The National Institute has carried out a series of productivity comparisons of matched plants in the UK with plants in selected European countries, including Germany, France and the Netherlands. Daly *et al.* (1985) set out the methodology and findings for the UK and German metal-working industries. Other industry studies have been undertaken mainly in the manufacturing sector, including metal working, furniture, clothing and biscuit production but also hotels in the service sector. Detailed findings are not presented here.[5]

These studies are of major interest as a source of information about the quantity and quality of training provided in different countries and the particular sectoral descriptions. However, their main stated purpose has been to examine the extent to which observed productivity differentials measured on a comparable basis (using matched plants) can be attributed to differences in human capital and the related vocational training. All these studies attempt to 'explain' productivity differentials allowing for as many observable factors as possible. The residual is attributed to human capital differences. It is the link between the residual productivity differences and unobservable differences in human capital which remain unclear in this research.[6]

Where more exact estimates of the contribution of human capital are produced, reliance is made on estimating the contribution of other factors or choosing plants where such differences are negligible. The estimation of the effects of any differences is extremely uncertain, especially with small samples (designed to exclude such differences). In several of the studies the comparability of capital equipment suggests that this may also be a major factor. For example, in the case of metal manufacture Daly *et al.* (1985) used plants with very different types of machine. Fifteen out of sixteen German firms used numerically controlled machines as against only seven of the sixteen UK firms.

Another problem with the matched plants research is that while the empirical findings concern the production of specific products in a small number of plants, the policy conclusions relate to economy-wide training provisions. One of the findings in the study of the metal-working industry was the superior maintenance of German machines. However, it is problematic whether this can be attributed to better supervision or whether the effectiveness of such maintenance may be related to the technical competence of operatives. Prais and Wagner (1988) recognize that 'it is not always easy to detect to what extent greater skills at one level rather than another are important' (Prais and Wagner 1988: 38). What is observed is a production process with many different contributions (team production) and to allocate marginal contributions of different groups of the workforce is to some extent arbitrary.

There will be other unobservable differences in industrial organization which remain unaccounted for, including different attitudes to work and variations in the state of industrial relations. The fact that findings from this research programme have received such widespread attention despite these methodological weaknesses draws our attention to the wholly inadequate research effort to estimate the real contribution of human capital to productivity. There remains a considerable challenge to provide direct estimates of the contribution of vocational training towards the productivity of the workforce and to establish what kind of training, if any, is the most needed. Another issue is whether provision should be targeted at specific groups of workers or particular skills.

THE EVIDENCE

The evidence presented in this section illustrates three propositions which summarize the 'stylized facts' over the 1980s. The data presented are only illustrative and it is generally recognized that there are many difficulties in the interpretation of VET statistics, especially in international comparisons.

The increase in basic VET provision is problematic

The VET system in the UK has undergone major change. In some respects there has been a significant increase in training activity. In the early 1980s there was a transition from work experience and employment-creation programmes towards supply-side policies providing training. For example, Figure 1 measures the increase in work-related training over the period 1984–90, using the Labour Force Survey measure. This evidence implies that the UK record on training has improved. It would also be more favourable if we compared the UK's absolute position using this measure of training across countries.[7] The UK appears to have a better training record than many countries if we rely solely on Labour Force Survey evidence. Also it appears that the UK devotes a comparable amount of resources towards the finance of education. For example, in 1988 the UK spending on education and training was about 4.6 per cent which was just greater than West Germany and Japan although just less than Italy, the US and France.

However, these simple indicators of VET provision are no more than a starting point to assessing the real level of investment in all forms of human capital. The consensus of informed opinion is that the UK has failed in the provision for human capital acquisition. In 1992 a council of seven well-known economists was set up to advise the government on economic policy, and one of the few areas of agreement was that the UK should somehow increase

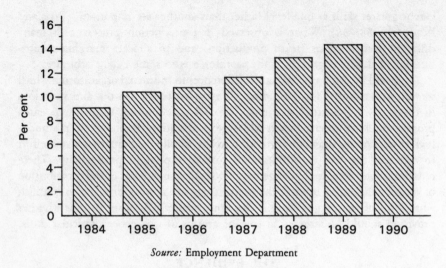

Source: Employment Department

Figure 9.1 The percentage of employees of working age receiving job-related training in the four weeks prior to the ILO survey.

investment in training and education. The changes that have taken place during the 1980s have clearly left many economists, who otherwise hold widely different economic views, unconvinced that the UK is investing sufficient resources in the labour force. Either we need to run even faster to satisfy the need for more trained workers or the quality of training provision is less than it needs to be.

The UK lags behind major competitor countries in terms of both the quantity and quality of VET provision

There remains a skills gap between the UK and other countries. For example, Figure 2 shows that the UK lags behind many other major countries in terms of total VET participation for young persons. Furthermore, the skills gap is greater than such participation statistics suggest because the UK has a high proportion of part-time participants in education and training.

The quality of training provision is clearly of importance. The implication and conclusion of many research studies is that the UK has paid insufficient attention to VET quality. There is considerable evidence that the UK lags behind the productivity levels of competitor countries, and the main reason for this appears to be that training in the UK has been of low quality and is narrowly based. The issue of training quality might be divided into questions about minimum training standards and the quality of a given training duration. Evidence in favour of low minimum standards can be found in many of the studies carried out at the National Institute.[8] For example, the emphasis

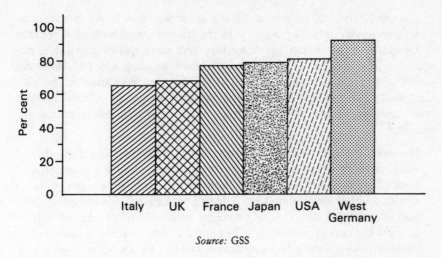

Source: GSS

Figure 9.2 Percentage of young people in education and training (G6, 1987).

in the UK on low-level qualifications associated with National Vocational Qualifications (NVQs) levels 1 and 2 supports this view. Questions about training quality in terms of the productivity effects of equivalent training are much harder to measure.

The UK has a bias towards education rather than vocational training

There has been a significant increase in enrolment in further and higher education. Enrolments in further education over the 1980s have risen by about 30 per cent.[9] In terms of international training qualifications the UK has a strong bias towards academic qualifications. For example, Prais (1989) reports that the UK has a comparable record on training qualifications for bachelor degrees, master degrees and doctorates compared with the US, Japan, Germany and France, but is most clearly behind for vocational qualifications including technicians and craftsmen.[10]

The international evidence on training qualifications shows that at the craftsmen level the UK lags behind other countries.[11] Of course there are many difficulties in international comparisons of this kind, but the main observation which emerges is that the UK compares unfavourably with other countries in terms of lower and intermediate skills. Even with higher-level skills (higher degrees and above) the UK is behind other countries although the gap does not appear to be as great. There is considerable evidence of the UK lagging behind other countries (including Germany), especially in terms of intermediate qualifications. In 1987 the proportion of the workforce with no qualifications was 62.6 per cent in the UK, whereas it was only 29.4 per cent in Germany, and the proportion of the workforce with lower intermediate qualifications was only 26.3 per cent in the UK compared with 56.4 per cent in Germany.[12] The proportion of workers with these qualifications does not appear to be related to the wage differential corresponding with such skills. An earlier international study by NEDO of training and education in the UK, Germany, Japan and the US, concluded that the provision of craft and 'middle level' training in the UK was inferior compared with major competitor countries.

> However, the gap created by the decline in apprenticeship and other initial training will leave industry and commerce without a substantial stock of trained men and women from whom many supervisors, technicians and less well-defined job holders are recruited. It will inevitably lead to severe skill shortages in competent 'middle level' people, not only in crafts but also in marketing, selling, production, financial services and administration, especially once micro-electronics gain a wider foothold.
>
> (NEDO 1984: 86)

The German VET system has been the focus of much attention. It has been frequently cited as a benchmark for other countries, including the UK. The German framework for training, known as the dual system, was seen as very successful for a long time. In comparison with the UK it is the 'middle' group of labour market entrants who stand out as better prepared in Germany. In both countries more than 25 per cent of this group have obtained some form of academic qualification such as a good set of GCSE results. In Germany, in addition to this academic achievement, more than a third of labour market entrants have passed a set of examinations indicating a technical level well ahead of any equivalent UK standard.

There are three significant points about the comparison with Germany which merit special note. First, VET qualifications in Germany are clearly complementary, whereas in the UK they are generally seen as alternatives. Second, the German system provides for a much larger proportion of the population than the UK system. This is reflected in the percentages with no recognizable qualifications. Third, the German system produces a much larger percentage of workers with some form of vocational qualification.[13]

THE ECONOMIC ISSUES

There is no doubt that the importance of training and the investment in human skills in economic performance has become a more fashionable idea in the 1980s and 1990s. It is notable that in 1992 the Nobel Prize in Economics was awarded to Gary Becker, recognizing his work on what has become known as human capital theory.[14] However, our understanding of the economic motivations of firms and workers to undertake training are not well understood. This section examines the economic issues involved in explaining the process of human capital acquisition.

The key economic argument which underpins the shortfall in training provision can be traced to some form of market failure. There are three main forms of market failure which have been identified. First, individuals may be deterred from training because the capital market is unable to adequately finance human capital acquisition.[15] There are various possibilities but in particular human capital cannot be sold by the lender in the case of a loan default.[16] Second, there is the question of 'poaching', where firms fail to train because they fear that non-training firms will recruit trained workers.[17] The latter argument has been the most commonly rehearsed reason given for the lack of training. The basis for the poaching idea is that firms are locked into a prisoner's dilemma game in which training by all firms is Pareto optimal but the Nash equilibrium outcome is no training.[18] Third, employment contracts may restrict employers and workers from achieving the efficient outcome. Unless continual recontracting is allowed to reflect unanticipated changes in the value of human capital, some inefficiency is inevitable.[19] In the case of implicit contracts, recontracting will also be inefficient in a different sense because of risk aversion by workers.[20]

An extension of the prisoner's dilemma model of training is the dynamic equilibrium account of training proposed by Finegold and Soskice (1988). In this model there is either a high-skill–high-wage or low-skill–low-wage equilibrium outcome. Government, firms and workers will find that the equilibrium outcomes are locally stable and many factors will reinforce either equilibrium. The economy can become locked into a vicious circle of low wages and low skills which is self-perpetuating unless some form of intervention is undertaken to shift the economy from one dynamic path to another.[21]

High-skill and low-skill equilibrium

The features of the low-skill and high-skill economies are given below.

The low-skill economy

(a) Individuals perceive the costs of VET to outweigh the benefits, because they have high discount rates.
(b) Firms perceive the costs or risks of upskilling as too high and fear any decrease in managerial control, poaching of skilled workers or disruption of existing work organization.
(c) Government believes that the costs of VET are too high and any change would infringe budgetary constraints or conflict with a market ideology.

INVESTMENT AND INNOVATION

(a) Individuals, who receive high wages and other positive job rewards, perceive the benefits of VET to exceed the costs.
(b) Managers seek improvements in competitive advantage, through short-term flexibility and long-term innovation.
(c) Government aims to avoid both welfare-reducing reductions in real wages and wage-push inflation brought about by workers attempting to counter real-wage reductions with money-wage increases.

This hypothesis is appealing in many ways. It adds a dynamic aspect to the market-failure hypothesis. Market failure leads to a low-skill outcome because profit-maximizing firms are pushed in certain directions by policies which may have many aims, including short-term employment creation. Such policies may have unexpected consequences. For example, policies aimed at strengthening firms in the wage bargaining process may lead to a reduction in the supply of trainees and the development of a low-skill production process to match the low-wage structure. It confirms some of the theoretical literature based on information to agents and suggests that many equilibrium outcomes are possible in the labour market.

There are many strengths of the market failure hypothesis. First, it provides a respectable basis to advocate some form of market intervention to counter the expected shortfall in training. Second, the sub-optimal equilibrium associated with poaching will be more robust than many other similar strategic situations. For example, there will be a lower incentive to achieve a Pareto optimal outcome where there are many firms or where the firms face the repetition of the game.[22] Third, it appears that the optimal outcome can be achieved by appropriate intervention (changing the payoffs for poaching). Finally, the model illustrates the benefits of cooperation as a potential remedy for poaching.

Is the market failure hypothesis an adequate theoretical basis in itself for understanding the training process? Do firms require more information about the costs and benefits of training than it is reasonable to assume? Is this model appropriate to situations where the type of training differs between firms? Perhaps the most severe criticism is that the hypothesis is a 'shell' theory, leaving out more than it explains. It has been widely used to justify market intervention although it is clear that the underlying market failure may be due to many different factors.

Labour markets vary considerably within as well as between economies. An important categorization of labour markets is between internal labour markets (ILMs) and occupational labour markets (OLMs).[23] An ILM functions in much the same way as a labour market with only firm-specific skills, following Becker's distinction between general and specific skills.[24] ILMs are associated with limited ports of entry into the firm, particular workplaces, internal promotions, skills acquisition rather than certification and greater job security. In these markets the firm will be more likely to pay for, and benefit from, training. Given the importance of labour mobility, it is clear that the structure of the labour market cannot be set aside in any discussion of training policy.[25]

It is helpful to categorize training within labour markets under three main types: ILMs in which training takes place within the firm; OLMs in which firms recruit from other firms; and OLMs in which firms recruit new but trained labour market entrants. The impact of different training policies on these three types of labour market are likely to be quite different. For example, a levy on non-training would be effective for within-firm training. Economy-wide training schemes would be mainly effective in promoting training for new labour market entrants. Finally, policies promoting more certification and 'mobility of labour' would be mainly effective outside the firm. Promoting certification can be counter-productive in ILMs. This supports the view that training policies are likely to be ineffective when they are divorced from industrial reality. Economy-wide policies must by definition be wasteful without some flexibility across industries.

The discussion so far is not a comprehensive account of all the economic issues which arise in an examination of training issues. There has been no mention of unions, labour market segmentation and the importance of youth–adult wage differentials.[26] It is also necessary to point out that the economic theory of human capital accumulation is incomplete and much may be required in terms of empirical validation of some of the central hypotheses. Many ideas, including the distinction between general and specific training and signalling, are of more theoretical rather than practical interest. It is problematic to select any common policy themes from such wide-ranging ideas, but it is clear that policy should accommodate the *diversity of labour markets* and market failure issues suggest that significant *state intervention* will be necessary to achieve the optimum quantity and quality of training provision.

VET POLICY

There have been a number of very important training measures in the 1980s. Despite the shift in emphasis in labour market policy towards the supply-side, the British training problem has not been effectively addressed in recent years. VET policy remains one of the limits on the competitiveness of the economy. Some of the major training measures since 1964 are summarized in Table 1.

While there may have been a degree of consensus on one of the major causes of Britain's training problem, the solutions have been many and varied. Policy measures which might be seen as remedies to the market failure problem include:

● subsidies to firms and individuals;
● institutional reforms to promote training;
● economy-wide training schemes financed by government;
● measures promoting certification.

Table 1 The major training policy developments, 1964–93

1964	*The Industrial Training Act* Introduction of ITBs The grant-levy system
1973	*The Employment and Training Act, 1973* Levy exemption Manpower Services Commission (MSC) set up
1978	Introduction of Youth Opportunities Programme (YOP)
1981	*The Employment and Training Act, 1981* Consultation process to abolish ITBs
1982	*The New Training Initiative* Introduction of the Community Programme (CP)
1983	YTS fully operational Enterprise Allowance Scheme (EAS) introduced
1986	New Workers' Scheme (NWS) introduced Restart introduced Two-year YTS introduced
1988	Abolition of MSC Department for Employment takes over training responsibilities *Employment for the 1990s* Setting up of TECs *Training for Employment* Announcement of ET Career Development Loans (CDLs) introduced
1990	Technical and Vocational Education Initiative (TVEI) operational Compacts launched
1991	Training Credits (TCs) introduced (later called Youth Credits) *Education and Training for the 21st Century* National Council for Vocational Qualifications (NCVQ) and National Vocational Qualifications (NVQs) introduced

In recent years, four of the most significant policy initiatives fit in with this categorization; the introduction of the Industrial Training Boards (ITBs) in the mid-1960s, the role of the Manpower Services Commission (MSC) in the mid-1970s and early 1980s, the YTS in the 1980s, and finally the development of NVQs in the 1990s along with more funding for individual training.

In the UK there has been considerable comment on the move away from legislative backing and the current framework is distinct from many other comparable countries.[27] The legal framework in other countries includes: training or leave entitlements, compulsory membership of training bodies and training taxes or levies. Economy-wide schemes may be less effective where ILMs are prevalent and where firms do not retain their subsidized trainees. An important problem with more certification is that firms who operate some form

170

of ILM may reduce training in the face of increased labour mobility. In other words where ILMs are important, better certification may reduce training.

VET provision in the UK favours educational rather than vocational studies, although there has been a plethora of small-scale initiatives which appear to promote vocational skills. These include the Technical and Vocational Initiative (TVEI), Compacts between pupils and employers through the local education authority and city technology colleges (CTCs). None of these initiatives are sufficiently important to detract from the basic outcomes in terms of qualifications and skill training which we can observe for the large majority of the working population.

VET policy cannot be properly considered in isolation from other economic policies. The more interventionist policies on training which were pursued in the 1980s must be set against the backdrop of rising unemployment. This rose from 4 per cent in 1979 to 11.1 per cent in 1986 and then fell to 5.8 per cent in the next trough in the cycle in 1990. In this context it has to be recognized that the economy-wide training programmes operated as employment creation or temporary work programmes as well as measures aimed at training the workforce. One problem in assessing policy has been to disentangle policy measures which were directed at unemployment from measures concerned with training provision. It is also clear that training policy has been too closely tied-in with employment creation. One effect of this has been to encourage low-quality training for the unemployed at the expense of training for workers in firms.

The absence of any clear industrial training policy in the UK is symptomatic of a more general stance towards industrial policy. If policy is designed to remove subsidies and support for industry, including capital investment, it is difficult to formulate effective policies to assist with human capital which are entirely consistent with this hands-off approach. For example, subsidies for human capital investment might distort the optimum production choices. There is a need for a clear view on industrial training policy in the context of an overall strategy for industrial policy.[28]

The whole emphasis in the 1980s on employer-led training has detracted from a serious debate about how training should be funded and organized. Employers have difficulty in responding to training incentives because of the poaching problem. The development of an improved skills base is a *long-term* objective which the private sector is ill-equipped to satisfy alone. The development of the Training and Enterprise bodies (TECs) to draw employers into the training delivery mechanism has not addressed the fundamental dilemma for individual firms and training finance. The ITB system was abandoned in the 1980s without any plans to replace it with an alternative mechanism for dealing with market failure. Training became detached from industrial need and less 'market-necessary'. There was a fundamental inability to grasp the importance of a long-term institutional framework to provide the necessary public support to industry.

171

Accepting the need for planning, it is important to examine what policy objectives are *feasible* and *desirable*. The tendency to pick out 'good examples' of training policy in other countries including Germany, France, the US and Japan without regard for whether any specific policies are transferable is open to many objections. It specifically ignores the social framework which exists in different countries. It is inappropriate to select low relative youth wages in Germany as crucial while ignoring the emphasis on social cooperation with the unions. Without an open debate and the development of a consensus on training it is not surprising that UK policy has tended to be excessively bureaucratic and drifted between competing policy strategies.

There has been a credibility gap between the rhetoric of policy, with the assertion that training should be employer-led and market-based, while in reality greater policy intervention has been necessary. The VET policies of the 1980s may have opened up some minimum training opportunities to the whole workforce and encouraged increased participation in all levels of education, but these same policies have *failed* to:

- develop a long-term programme;
- provide for an institutional structure to support training within firms
- focus on 'market-necessary' VET provision;
- encourage and legislate for higher-level skills.

The UK economy has undergone dramatic structural industrial change in the 1980s and more than ever competitiveness will be based on the skills and adaptability of the labour force working in new industries and producing new products. The case for developing a long-term strategic policy for training and education has never been stronger. With unemployment at historically high levels it is important to ensure that VET policy in the future is not dominated by the demands of the business cycle.

NOTES

1 Parts of this chapter are based on Chapman (1993) which provides a much more detailed coverage of the economic issues relating to training.
2 See Spence (1973).
3 See Main and Shelly (1990) for example.
4 The time-series patterns of manufacturing and economy productivity comparisons including the UK and Germany have been examined in a number of papers. These include most recently, Daly *et al.* (1985), Crafts (1991), Dowrick and Nguyen (1989), Feinstein (1988), Muellbauer (1991) and Oulton (1990).
5 See Prais (1990) for a compendium of these studies.
6 See Daly *et al.* (1985: 60–1).
7 See OECD (1991) for example.
8 See Prais (1990) for example. For a critique of some aspects of this research see Cutler (1992).
9 Enrolments in further education have risen from 1.5 million to 2.0 million and in higher education from 0.78 million to 1.07 million.

10 See NEDO (1984) and Rose (1991).
11 See Prais (1989).
12 See O'Mahoney (1992).
13 See Rose (1991).
14 See Becker (1962, 1975).
15 See Thurow (1970) for example.
16 This is sometimes referred to in terms of property rights. Many economic issues cannot be understood without understanding or knowledge about the legal or customary rights over certain assets. The case of human capital is one such issue.
17 See Oatey (1970) for an early view of this problem.
18 For a review of game-theory concepts see Kreps (1990).
19 See Hashimoto (1981) and Hashimoto and Yu (1980).
20 See Manning (1990) for a simple exposition of implicit contract theory.
21 See also Finegold (1991).
22 See Kreps (1990) on multiple outcomes and repeated games.
23 There is a considerable literature on ILMs and OLMs. The concept of an ILM is sufficiently well known not to require detailed definition here. See Marsden (1986).
24 Training in the Becker human capital model was defined in terms of training which was portable across firms (general training) and training which was only useful to the training firm (specific training). According to the Becker model, firms might be more willing to pay for specific training while workers would be more willing to pay for general training (ignoring government subsidies). See also Jovanovic (1979) and Katz and Zidermam (1990).
25 Marsden and Ryan (1991) argue that the UK is more closely described by an OLM structure.
26 Labour market segmentation and union activity are both potentially important in an understanding of training. However, both these issues have been given little weight in the economic analysis of the subject. The former has, of course, been partly taken into account through gender and age. Recent empirical studies, including Greenhalgh and Stewart (1987) and Green (1990), have identified significant gender differences in training decisions and the effects of training. One aspect of labour market segmentation which has been emphasized is the large difference between the youth and adult labour markets. See Ryan et al. (1991) on the youth labour market. The impact of unions on training remains poorly understood yet it is inconceivable that unions will remain passive on an issue which so clearly affects union members. Furthermore, if interventionist policies are to be followed then the reactions of unions to subsidies, levies and other 'market distortions' need to be considered. While unions may overtly support training, it does not follow that they will have an interest in increasing the employment of trained workers at the expense of agreed wage levels or differentials. The UK has adopted a policy stance which sidesteps the need for union cooperation. In many other countries, including Germany, cooperation would be considered an essential goal.
27 See Chapman and Tooze (1987), Chapman (1991) and Keep (1991).
28 See Senker (1992).

REFERENCES

Becker, G. S. (1962) 'Investment in human capital: a theoretical analysis', *Journal of Political Economy*, vol. 70, Supplement, pp. 9–49.
Becker, G. S. (1975) *Human Capital*, second edition, Columbia University Press.
Chapman, P. G. (1991) 'The crisis in adult training policy', *Studies in the Education of Adults*, vol. 23, no. 1, pp. 53–60.

Chapman, P. G. (1993) *The Economics of Training*, London: Harvester Wheatsheaf.

Chapman, P. G. and Tooze, M. J. (1987) *The Youth Training Scheme in the United Kingdom*, Aldershot: Avebury Press.

Crafts, N. (1991) 'Reversing relative economic decline', *Oxford Review of Economic Policy*, vol. 7, no. 3, pp. 81–98.

Cutler, T. (1992) 'Vocational training and British economic performance; a further instalment of the British labour problem?', *Work, Employment and Society*, vol. 6, no. 2, pp. 161–83.

Daly, A. Hitchens, D. M. W. N. and Wagner, K. (1985) 'Productivity, machinery and skills in a sample of British and German manufacturing plants: results of a pilot study', *National Institute Economic Review*, no. 111, February, pp. 48–61.

Dowrick, S. and Nguyen, D. (1989) 'OECD comparative economic growth 1950–85: catch-up and convergence', *American Economic Review*, vol. 79, no. 5, pp. 1011–30.

Feinstein, C., (1988) 'Economic growth since 1870: Britain's performance in an international perspective', *Oxford Review of Economic Policy*, vol. 4, no. 1, pp. 1–13.

Finegold, D. (1991) 'Institutional incentives and skill creation: preconditions for a high-skill equilibrium', in P. Ryan (ed.), *International Comparisons of Vocational Education and Training for Intermediate Skills*, London: Falmer Press, pp. 93–116.

Finegold, D. and Soskice, D. (1988) 'The failure of training in Britain; analysis and prescription', *Oxford Review of Economic Policy*, vol. 4, no. 3, Autumn, pp. 21–53.

Green, F. (1990) 'Sex discrimination in job-related training', *British Journal of Industrial Relations*, vol. 29, no. 2, pp. 295–304.

Greenhalgh, C. A. and Stewart, M. B. (1987) 'The effects and determinants of training', *Oxford Bulletin of Economics and Statistics*, vol. 49, no. 2, pp. 171–89.

Hashimoto, M. (1981) 'Firm-specific capital as a shared investment', *American Economic Review*, vol. 71, pp. 475–82.

Hashimoto, M. and Yu, B. (1980) 'Specific capital, employment contracts, and wage rigidity', *Bell Journal of Economics*, vol. 11, no. 2, Autumn, pp. 536–49.

Jovanovic, B, (1979) 'Job matching and the theory of labour turnover', *Journal of Political Economy*, vol. 87, pp. 972–90.

Katz, E. and Ziderman, A. (1990) 'Investment in general training: the role of information and labour mobility, *Economic Journal*, vol. 100, pp. 1147–58.

Keep, E. (1991) 'The grass looked greener – some thoughts on the influence of comparative vocational training research on the UK policy debate', in P. Ryan (ed.), *International Comparisons of Vocational Education and Training for Intermediate Skills*, London: Falmer Press, pp. 23–46.

Kreps, D. M. (1990) *A Course in Microeconomic Theory*, London: Harvester Wheatsheaf.

Main, B. G. M. and Shelly, M. A. (1990) 'The effectiveness of YTS as a manpower policy', *Economica*, vol 57, pp. 495–514.

Manning, A. (1990) 'Implicit-contract theory', in D. Sapsford and Z. Tzannatos (eds), *Current Issues in Labour Economics*, London: Macmillan pp. 63–85.

Marsden D. W. (1986) *The End of Economic Man? Custom and Competition in the Labour Market*, Brighton: Wheatsheaf.

Marsden, D. W. and Ryan, P. (1991) 'Institutional aspects of youth employment and training policy', *British Journal of Industrial Relations*, vol. 29, no. 2, pp. 497–505.

Mincer, J. (1962) 'On-the- job training: costs, returns and some implications', *Journal of Political Economy*, vol. 70, no. 5, pp. 50–79.

Mincer, J. (1974) *Schooling, Experience and Earnings*, New York: NBER, Columbia University Press.

Muellbauer, J. (1991) 'Productivity and competitiveness', *Oxford Review of Economic Policy*, vol. 7, no. 3, pp. 99–117.

NEDO (1984) *Competence and Competition: Training and Education in the Federal Republic of Germany, the United States and Japan*, London: National Economic Development Office and The Manpower Services Commission, NEDO.

Oatey, M. (1970) 'The economics of training with respect to the firm', *British Journal of Industrial Relations*, vol. 8, no. 1, pp. 1–21.

OECD (1991) *Employment Outlook*, July, pp. 135–76.

O'Mahoney, M. (1992) 'Productivity levels in British and German manufacturing industry', *National Institute Economic Review*, no. 139, Feb, pp. 46–63.

Oulton, N. (1990) 'Labour productivity in UK manufacturing in the 1970s and 1980s', *National Institute Economic Review*, no. 132, May, pp. 71–91.

Prais, S. J. (1989) 'Qualified manpower in engineering: Britain and other industrially advanced countries', *National Institute Economic Review*, no. 127, February, pp. 76–83.

Prais, S. J. (ed.) (1990) *Productivity, Education and Training*, London: NIESR.

Prais, S. J. and Wagner, K. (1988) 'Productivity and management: the training of foremen in Britain and Germany', *National Institute Economic Review*, no. 123, pp. 34–47.

Rose, R. (1991) 'Perspective evaluation through comparative analysis: youth training in time-space perspective', in P. Ryan (ed.), *International Comparisons of Vocational Education and Training for Intermediate Skills*, London: Falmer Press, pp. 68–92.

Ryan, P., Garonna, P. and Edwards, R. C. (eds) (1991) *The Problem of Youth: The Regulation of Youth Employment and Training in Advanced Economies*, Basingstoke: Macmillan, pp. 82–114.

Senker, P. (1992) *Industrial Training Policy in a Cold Climate*, Aldershot: Avebury Press.

Spence, (1973) 'Job market signalling', *Quarterly Journal of Economics*, vol. 87, pp. 355–75.

Thurow, L. (1970) *Investment in Human Capital*, Belmont, CA: Wadsworth.

10

PROFITS AND ECONOMIC PERFORMANCE

Martin Ricketts

INTRODUCTION

Should policy-makers take an interest in profits? Do changes in aggregate profits and in rates of return signify anything about the performance of the economy as a whole? In spite of the interest shown by political economists from the Physiocrats of the eighteenth century onwards in the distribution of income between capitalists, labourers and landlords, the role of profits in the process of economic development has not been greatly emphasized in policy debates. In this paper the following propositions are discussed:

(a) Low profits are a symptom of a weak competitive position.
(b) There is some evidence that profit rates and shares are higher in other advanced economies compared with the United Kingdom.
(c) Other evidence suggests that the rate of return (particularly in manufacturing) in the United Kingdom increased during the most recent economic cycle and that this was accompanied by a rise in capital formation.
(d) The role of profits both as a measure of dynamic performance and as a stimulus to technical and institutional change is of great importance.
(e) Returns to 'human capital', to entrepreneurial flair, and to the 'architecture' and teamwork of the firm figure prominently in modern discussions of productivity growth. Investment in standard types of physical capital or the use of unskilled labour, is unlikely to form the basis of a highly profitable business. It will be necessary, therefore, to modify our ideas about who receives 'profits' and how they are measured and distributed.

SOME INTERNATIONAL COMPARISONS

Profits and the national accounts

Figure 1 shows the path of gross operating surplus as a share of gross domestic product since the early 1960s in the UK and four other major countries. It is clear that the profit share is cyclical in the United Kingdom, falling in recession

176

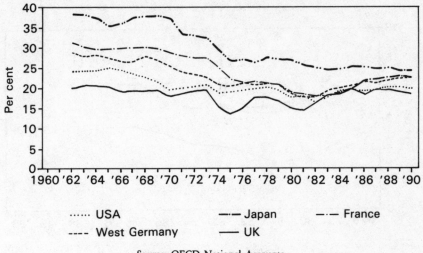

Source: OECD National Accounts

Figure 10.1 Gross operating surplus as a proportion of gross domestic product.

and rising with more buoyant business conditions. The mid-1970s saw the lowest share of gross operating surplus, while in the mid-1980s the profit share rose to the highest levels recorded in the span of twenty years. After 1987, however, a decline began which has persisted to the present.

Rates of return on capital show a similar historical pattern. For the manufacturing sector, the gross operating surplus as a proportion of gross capital stock is recorded in Figure 2. The effect of the recession of 1981 is clearly evident with the subsequent recovery up to 1987. OECD data for manufacturing terminate in 1987 but information on the business sector is available up to 1992. Estimates of the gross rate of return on capital in the business sector for five OECD countries in 1992 are recorded in Figure 3. This confirms that, for the business sector as a whole, the United Kingdom's rate of return on capital is below 10 per cent compared with 14 per cent or above for other major OECD economies.

As can be seen, international comparisons based upon National Accounts data tend to record a rather low average rate of return on capital in the UK compared with other major industrialized countries. This may reflect the difficulty of compiling comparable measures of the stock of capital between countries rather than systematic differences in the rate of return. In particular, estimates of the capital stock in a country require assumptions to be made about the economic lives of different classes of asset and the rates at which these assets depreciate. The United Kingdom assumes that the service life of capital assets is twenty-eight years. Other countries have adopted different conventions for national accounts purposes. In Japan the assumed life of capital assets is

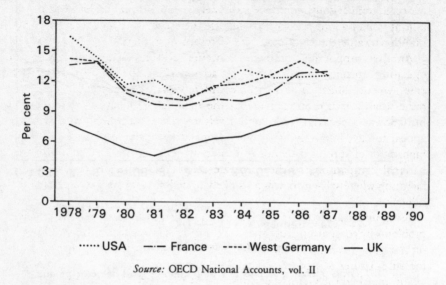

Source: OECD National Accounts, vol. II

Figure 10.2 Manufacturing gross operating surplus as a proportion of gross capital stock.

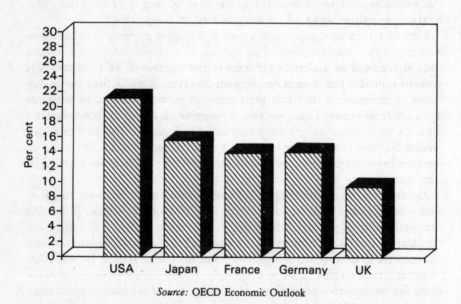

Source: OECD Economic Outlook

Figure 10.3 Rates of return on capital in the business sector in 1992.

eleven years. Adjusting for these variations in conventions when making international comparisons would be extremely complex but it is likely that the assumption of a longer asset life will raise the estimate of the capital stock and bias downwards the computed rate of return on capital.

Another important problem concerns self-employment.[1] Figures of operating surplus in the national accounts include income from self-employment. Much of this income will represent compensation for labour rather than a return on capital, but the national accounts do not attempt a breakdown. Countries with high levels of self-employment will therefore appear to have relatively high levels of operating surplus and correspondingly high ratios of surplus to national income or to capital stock. Confining international comparisons to the corporate sector, or to sectors such as manufacturing where self-employment is likely to be low, may help to overcome this difficulty.

Work undertaken at the Confederation of British Industry[2] allows for these problems by comparing gross operating surpluses in manufacturing to the level of real gross investment cumulated over the preceding fifteen years. By this measure, United Kingdom profitability relative to Germany's rose during the 1980s, matched the German performance in 1987 and 1988, but thereafter fell back rapidly. Even by this measure, therefore, the United Kingdom's ability to maintain levels of profitability comparable with an important European competitor is shown to be lacking, although a rising trend up to the late 1980s is confirmed.

Profits and investment performance

Investment will be undertaken if firms expect the rate of return to exceed the cost of capital. Thus investment depends on expectations of the future returns from additional capital rather than the average returns to the existing stock of capital.[3] Further, at the level of the individual firm, investment decisions will be affected by tax considerations and financial constraints. Nevertheless, assuming that the average return on past investments is some guide to expectations of the future it might be expected that countries with low *ex-post* returns would be those with relatively low propensities to invest. Of course, this would not follow if the cost of capital varied greatly between countries. It might then be possible for the effects of low returns to be offset by a low cost of capital.

With the growing international freedom of capital movements, however, investors will look for the best return wherever it is available. The real cost of capital is unlikely, under such conditions, to remain lower for long periods in one country relative to another. As a rough and ready indication of capital costs, the real long-term rate of interest in five OECD countries is recorded in Figure 4. There it can be seen that during the 1980s real rates of interest were similar in the major countries. The figure charts the yield of long-dated bonds

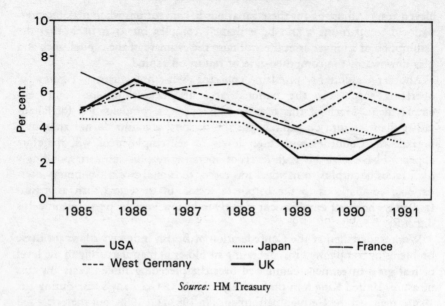

Source: HM Treasury

Figure 10.4 Real long-term interest rates.

less the rate of inflation. Although there is inevitably some variation across countries, the differences revealed by the figure are much less pronounced than differences in the return on capital. Countries such as the United Kingdom with a low recorded return on capital but facing a real cost of finance as high or higher than elsewhere will not be in a favourable position for attracting investment. Given the estimation problems associated with calculations of rates of return mentioned earlier, however, it is the trend rather than the level which is more reliable. The rising trend in rates of return in the United Kingdom until 1988 was accompanied by a recovery in investment which led, by the end of the decade, to a rise in the proportion of national output devoted to capital accumulation.

As a proportion of gross domestic product, gross fixed capital formation in the United Kingdom has tended to remain below the level typical of other countries. Figure 5 records this information for five OECD countries since 1962. However, the general recovery during the 1980s can be seen. The gap between the United Kingdom on the one hand and Germany and France on the other had closed by the years 1988 and 1989. Since then, investment and profits in the United Kingdom have fallen away in the face of a protracted recession. In the case of industrial and commercial companies, however, the level of investment in 1991 as a proportion of GDP still exceeded that achieved throughout the 1970s as well as the early and mid-1980s.[4]

The rising share of capital formation in GDP until 1989 is reflected in Figure 6 which shows an index of real gross fixed capital formation in the

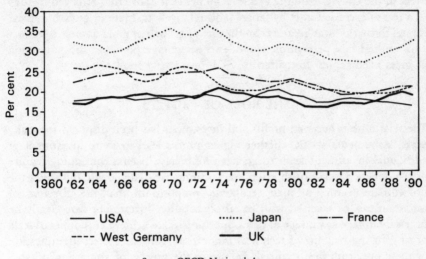

Source: OECD National Accounts

Figure 10.5 Gross fixed capital formation as a proportion of GDP.

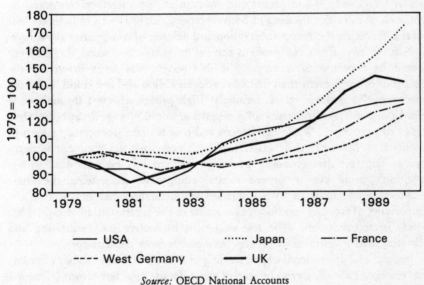

Source: OECD National Accounts

Figure 10.6 Gross fixed capital formation (constant 1985 prices).

United Kingdom and other countries over the years 1979–90. By 1989, investment in the UK was running at a level 40 per cent above that achieved in 1979 – a record exceeded only by Japan. This relatively fast rate of growth in fixed capital formation was greater than the rate of growth of gross domestic product and resulted in a perceptible rise of two percentage points in the proportion of gross fixed capital formation in GDP over that period.

THE ROLE OF PROFITS

The relationship between profits and investment has been disputed for many years. Arguments about whether higher profits lead to more investment or additional investment leads to greater profits have been a continuing feature of the debate about British economic performance. The debate illustrates the unfortunate feature of many economic propositions that the direction of causation can be reversed with equal plausibility. Investment may clearly be necessary to take advantage of new opportunities, to achieve economies of scale or to gain the benefits of technical innovation. But the correct identification of these opportunities is crucial. Failure in the process of appraising suitable areas for investment can simply result in the squandering of scarce resources. Similarly, rising profits may create the confidence and provide the means for greater investment effort. But this is only likely in a competitive environment where profits need continually to be defended and where the option of a quiet life is foreclosed. While profits and investment are therefore connected by channels of influence running in both directions, higher levels of both are best seen as reflecting the successful creation and defence of competitive advantage.

Neither investment nor profit is the key to economic success though both would be expected to accompany it. No society was more driven by the demands of investment than that of the Soviet Union and few could have used investment to so little effect. Similarly, high profits achieved through trade restrictions and the suppression of competition would presage decay rather than renewed dynamism. While investment and profits make poor policy targets in themselves, however, their association with economic development is significant. The fact that economic growth will frequently be associated with a workforce using ever improved capital equipment embodying the latest technical innovations or with upgraded infrastructure, has meant that the importance of creating conditions favourable to the accumulation of capital has rarely been overlooked. The role of profits in motivating, facilitating and directing this investment effort has been much more contentious.

Popular and professional understanding of the role and significance of profits has changed radically in recent years. Only a decade ago, any return on capital above a 'normal' level (a level just sufficient to prevent the providers of capital from withdrawing their support) was widely seen as a sign of monopoly power and social loss.[5] It is almost universally agreed that where government policy protects companies or entrenches public utilities in monopoly positions, such social losses may be sustained. But in conditions where international competition is strong; trade barriers are low; new innovations crowd in one after the other; and rivals, existing or potential, threaten continuously; profits reflect the social gains achieved by successful entrepreneurship. A country whose firms succeeded in generating only 'normal' profits would be a country whose entrepreneurs had discovered nothing new, where there was no freedom of manoeuvre, no resources to facilitate the process of yet further discovery. Institutions would always be precariously balancing at the very cliff-edge of viability, with the minds of managers dedicated to preventing imminent disaster rather than to establishing strategic direction.

This tension between the idea of profit as a return just high enough to persuade people to provide capital for well understood purposes yielding predictable social returns (technocratic profit) and profit as a residual which may be vastly in excess of capital costs and which derives from stealing a march on the opposition (entrepreneurial profit) goes to the heart of the modern reassessment of the role of profits. Whether profits in excess of 'normal' represent social exploitation or social gains from successful entrepreneurship can be debated without end. Monopolies Commission reports have wrestled with this problem for more than thirty years. The general association between high rates of return and economic success both internationally and across industries, however, suggests that entrepreneurial profits are associated with productivity growth and the accompanying technical and organizational innovation. This does not, of course, imply that pure profits derive from entrepreneurship in every instance. But the world as a whole appears sufficiently open and competitive for pure profits generally to represent returns to the establishment of competitive advantage rather than to monopoly restrictions. It is possible to take seriously the idea that the level of profits in an economy under modern conditions is an index of its capacity for change and adaptation.

THE SOURCES OF COMPETITIVE ADVANTAGE

There are many British firms that have established commanding positions in certain fields and whose competitive advantage is reflected in their ability to generate pure profits. Pure profits, in this context, are returns in excess of those which are only just sufficient to compensate the people who provide the various resources used by the firm. A recent study by the London Business School[6] found British firms well represented in a list of the world's large and medium sized firms which generated the greatest pure profits relative to sales. Pure profits were estimated by subtracting from operating profit a charge representing a competitive rate of return on all the capital employed. This suggests that having some of the world's most successful firms does not automatically imply having one of the world's most successful economies. Competitive advantage is not rare in Britain, but neither is it spread widely throughout the economy as a whole.

Of the fifteen firms mentioned in Table 1, four are prominent in the field of pharmaceuticals – Glaxo, Smithkline Beecham, Wellcome and Fisons. Pure profits here derive from the development of patentable drugs. British Gas and British Telecom are regulated monopolies so that profits here may, notwithstanding our earlier comments about the difficulty of distinguishing entrepreneurial from monopoly elements, be derived from access to rents from natural resources or from market dominance rather than technical or other innovation. Other firms such as Guinness and the Rank Organization have built up valuable brand-name capital and exploited it successfully in consumer markets.

Competitive advantage can therefore be derived from various sources. The fact that only three Japanese firms feature in the LBS list of top pure profit earners as a proportion of sales in 1990 suggests that, in Japan, fewer companies receive very large returns than in the United Kingdom, although across the economy as a whole the capacity to generate pure profits may be greater. One possible explanation for this is that companies in Japan typically derive their competitive advantage from different sources from those in the United Kingdom. Competitive advantage requires the development of assets that potential competitors find it costly and time consuming to copy. Such assets can be seen as conferring advantages in access to information or in the ability to cope with imperfect information. They may take the form of technical knowledge of product or process unavailable to a competitor; procedural and organizational knowledge which permits better coordination within the firm;

Table 1 Large British generators of pure profit

Large British companies (*sales exceeding 1 billion ecus*)	*Pure profit/sales in 1990* (%)	*World rank*
Glaxo	28.8	1
Cable & Wireless	23.1	2
Rank Organization	18.9	14
Reuters	18.0	20
British Telecom	17.9	21
Guinness	13.9	44
BPB Industries	13.4	49
Smithkline Beecham	13.2	51
Wellcome	12.3	62
Pearson	11.6	71
BTR	11.6	72
Fisons	11.4	74
British Gas	11.4	75
RTZ	10.8	81
Burton Group	10.8	83

Source: Abstracted from E. Davis, S. Flanders and J. Star (1991) 'Who are the world's most successful companies?', *Business Strategy Review*, Summer.

and 'reputation' which permits the costs of transacting with customers and suppliers in a world of imperfect information to be reduced.

Technical innovation

The development of a new product or process will yield pure profits if it has a sufficient edge over the competition and if others can be prevented from imitating or replicating it. Glaxo, for example, has the highest ratio of pure profits to sales of all large companies in the world, according to the London Business School study. This success was built upon the development of the drug Zantac, a treatment for peptic ulcers. Patent protection clearly plays an important part in keeping competitors at bay in the field of proprietary drugs. A central policy dilemma here concerns whether the benefits associated with the stimulus to innovation outweigh the costs associated with conferring a monopoly (even if of limited duration) on the discoverer. The precarious and imperfect nature of patent protection should be recognized, however. Zantac was not the first effective anti-ulcer drug to be marketed.

Research and development expenditure can be seen as a type of investment, and the profits resulting from technical innovation as a return to a form of intangible capital. Sometimes this capital is represented by tradable property rights in the form of a patent. But it is often the case that technical knowledge is costly to patent and protect, and competitive advantage derives not so much from an ability to *produce* technical breakthroughs as from an ability to *make use* of widely available technical knowledge. This capacity to *use* innovations is more closely related to organizational capability than purely scientific expertise.[7] Japanese firms, for example, seem to rely not simply on patents, but on non-patentable organizational 'know-how' to generate profits. This leads naturally to the second major source of competitive advantage.

Teamwork

Another source of competitive advantage which cannot be patented but which is nevertheless difficult to copy, is the advantage accruing to 'know-how' within a particular team. Over time, workers in a team gain first-hand knowledge and specific skills which are not easily transferable to others and which are more valuable to their existing team than they would be outside the team. Reading a manual on 'lean production' or the operation of Japanese car plants will not permit immediate and effective replication, any more than reading a book on how to ride a bicycle would be expected to produce immediate success. The assets which are required, including the human skills, attitudes and know-ledge, for operating at Japanese levels of efficiency have to be accumulated gradually within the team. Once developed by the members of the team, these firm-specific assets become a powerful source of competitive advantage. John Kay[8] has referred to this source of competitive advantage as the 'architecture' of the firm. Relationships within the team must be such as to make the returns to the team as a whole greater than the returns available elsewhere on all its individual participating resources.

Good teamwork requires a well-trained and flexible labour force. Investment in training does not, however, guarantee good teamwork and 'architecture' any more than investment in R&D can guarantee successful technical innovation. Training in highly specific skills, for example, may be extremely important for the efficient operation of a particular job, but it may do little to improve the ability of people to coordinate their activities with others. Teamwork requires a wide knowledge of the functions and skills of other people to complement in-depth knowledge of particular operations. The proportion of employees receiving job-related training in the UK has risen from 9.1 per cent in 1984 to 15.4 per cent in 1990. There is thus a much increased acceptance of the importance of training to the achievement of higher productivity and international competitiveness. However, competitive advantage and the pure profit which flows from it derives not merely from a skilled labour force but from a cooperative, alert and adaptable one. Training in specific skills may often be arranged fairly quickly. Building a cooperative team will usually take much longer.

Reputation

Successful teamwork requires a firm to develop a good reputation with its employees. Reputation is also important in its links with customers. The value of a good reputation cannot be replicated quickly by a newcomer. Again this was once seen as a source of monopoly power rather than of competitive advantage. Yet reputation in product markets is a form of intangible capital which can only be established over time by continuous attention to serving the customer. Lack of reputation in the important markets can prevent the garnering of rents from innovations. A new product may be functionally superb, but it will not sell unless people believe the claims that are made and have the confidence to try it.

Publishers of magazines and newspapers, for example, depend upon the total reliability of the printing machinery they use. Breakdowns or indifferent or erratic quality have a serious and immediate impact on sales. The market in printing machinery therefore rewards those suppliers who have built up the confidence of publishers that their machines can produce consistently high quality from month to month. Similarly, in supply-chain relationships, reputation is central to the establishment of trust. Long-term associations between buyers and suppliers enable each to develop knowledge of the requirements of the other and to save the costs associated with bargaining and contracting with a continuously changing group of firms. The efficiency gains accruing to these buyer–supplier links are another source of profit to the firms concerned.

ENTREPRENEURSHIP AND PROFITS

The assets that establish competitive advantage and yield pure profits cannot be bought off the shelf. They are non-tradable. A patent can be purchased but not the ability to create innovations. A textbook on organizational structure can be bought but not the specific skills and information which inhere in an already successful team. Even if particular members of a team can be persuaded to leave and join another, they will not thereby immediately be able to replicate the successful formula. The reputation of a team will enhance its own market value as a going concern, but the reputation of one team cannot be sold to another. Because these assets cannot be traded they cannot be acquired through exchange. The assets which yield pure profits must be created by the entrepreneurial effort of the people who make up each team.

It is this entrepreneurial element to the generation of pure profit that explains the importance of foreign enterprise in the transformation of some sectors of industry. In 1989, foreign owned businesses were responsible for 14.6 per cent of employment in manufacturing industry, paid 17.6 per cent of wages and salaries, produced 23.5 per cent of total sales and undertook 26.7 per cent of net capital expenditure. The firms concerned were among the international leaders in their fields. The skills and techniques which enable them to operate at a high level of efficiency, however, are difficult to transfer quickly to others. Were the recipe easily tradable, indigenous firms could purchase the information and skills in the marketplace and transform themselves in a short space of time. Foreign firms could enjoy their entrepreneurial rewards by licensing the secrets of their high productivity and could avoid investing directly in overseas markets. In practice, the organizational and procedural knowledge which underlies the creation of some types of competitive advantage is both created and exploited within a given firm.

If the United Kingdom is to create and sustain a higher level of competitive advantage and gain the pure profit that accompanies it, entrepreneurial skills will be required. This is not to be confused with the assertion that self-employment should be encouraged, or that the small-firm sector should be artificially stimulated, or that the 'wheeler-dealer' should become a role model in the education of the next generation of business leaders. The term 'entrepreneurship' has become gradually encrusted with layers of meaning that are better stripped away. Entrepreneurial rewards (or pure profits) derive from capitalizing on new ideas and innovations (large or small, organizational as well as technical) whose value can be grasped only by the people who develop or stumble across them.

PURE PROFITS AND THE WORKFORCE

It follows from this view of things that entrepreneurial profits will not in the future be received exclusively or even mainly by the providers of capital. The entrepreneurial talent of the entire team requires to be tapped. One of the ways of interpreting the success of Japanese methods is that it derives from the encouragement of alertness to productivity improvements throughout the organization and a willingness rapidly to act upon them. Rents will not therefore appear exclusively as accounting profit because the 'architecture' of Japanese firms permits some of these returns to accrue to a workforce which is, to a significant degree, responsible for generating them. Finding ways of involving the workforce in the entrepreneurial process may in the long run be as significant as ensuring an adequate supply of famous innovators.

In the first place, rents deriving from the scientific breakthroughs of a small, elite group of forward-thinking individuals may not be appropriable unless other features of competitive advantage such as architecture and reputation are in place. The potential benefits derivable from a great discovery may simply be unexploited or used by others. Second, even where advantage can be taken of such breakthroughs, exclusive reliance on them would be a risky strategy. It would reinforce the British tendency to make use of a mere fraction of the talent available, and leave the mass of the population hoping that a far-sighted person will always design a Spitfire in the nick of time. The modern world seems to favour more democratic strategies. Important though the rents derivable from scientific advances may be, they need to be supplemented by the rents generated from continual small-scale entrepreneurial discoveries within the firm. Indeed, some modern writers see the firm as a cooperating group of entrepreneurs who then share the pure profits generated between them.[9] The very distinction between management and workforce is increasingly hard to draw as managerial and judgemental skills are required of more and more people at all levels.

CONCLUDING COMMENTS

It is one thing to recognize the importance of entrepreneurship and pure profit in the process of economic change but quite another to establish reliable guidelines for government policy in this area. Governments are influential, however, in setting an environment which may favour or hinder the establishment of competitive advantage. Three areas in particular are likely to have an important long-run influence on the ability to generate pure profits.

Macroeconomic stability

A stable macroeconomic environment is essential for building the long-term confidence which supports the investment in both physical and human assets required for establishing competitive advantage. Investment in one firm will often require supporting investments elsewhere, and agreements with financiers, suppliers and customers may all need to be adjusted. This process is not helped by the instability and uncertainty associated with macroeconomic disruption.

The rate of inflation, for example, is not regular and predictable. Because rates of inflation have varied greatly over time in the United Kingdom, uncertainty is increased. Business decision-makers are always trying to guess when the government will introduce the next 'squeeze' or attempt to stimulate the economy in the face of falling output and rising unemployment. Where inflation is low it is therefore likely to be easier to plan ahead and for all parties whose cooperation is required if an investment project is to succeed to agree on a suitable course of action.

Inflation has adversely affected profits and investment in the past for other reasons. High inflation rates are associated with high nominal rates of interest. In these conditions interest payments are a combination of a 'real' interest rate plus an element of debt repayment. A great strain is therefore placed on cash flow, especially in the early years of an investment project. This would not matter if borrowing could be suitably adjusted each year to offset the influence of inflation, and if the tax system were neutral with respect to inflation. In practice, neither of these conditions is fulfilled. Inflation reduces the real value of depreciation allowances and results in exaggerated measures of profitability for tax purposes. Further, an economic downturn will make it difficult for a firm to arrange further borrowing and the cash drain implied by high interest rates will be severe. Low and stable rates of inflation should permit lower nominal (and real) rates of interest thus releasing some financial resources as well as management time for the pursuit of competitive advantage.[10]

Maintaining a competitive market

If higher profits are to represent the social gains derived from improvements in technology, in product specification or in economic organization, it is important that they should be earned in a competitive market in which these profits are under threat from rivals. The more protected are industries by artificial trade restrictions or other barriers to new competition, the more likely are firms to seek their profits through political lobbying and the exercise of monopoly power rather than through thinking of better ways to serve their customers and to establish competitive advantage. The importance of maintaining an international trading system which permits as free a flow of goods and services as possible is crucial from this point of view.

Openness to foreign investment

The organizational structures that have led to high rates of productivity growth and innovation in other countries cannot always be immediately understood and replicated by outsiders. Direct experience is often necessary before the best ideas from overseas can be appreciated and adjusted to different domestic conditions. In the 1950s and 1960s the world learned new management techniques from the American multinational. In the 1970s and 1980s, Japanese business practices were changing our attitudes to the organization of the firm and to the management of relationships in the supply chain. The educational value of foreign direct investment is therefore likely to he substantial. By creating an environment conducive to such inward investment, governments can encourage organizational innovation. Profits from good 'architecture' may then come to supplement and augment those that the United Kingdom already derives from patentable scientific achievements.

NOTES

1 Further discussion of this and other problems can be found in James H. Chan-Lee and Helen Sutch (1985) 'Profits and rates of return', *OECD Economic Studies*, no. 5, Autumn, pp. 127–67.
2 See Duncan McKenzie and Andrew Sentance (1992) *Economic Situation Report*, CBI, January.
3 Expectations of the future cannot be observed directly, but will be incorporated into the prices of bonds and shares. This has led some economists to estimate pure profits and the incentive to invest by comparing the market valuation of firms with the book value of assets. This ratio is called Tobin's 'q'. When it exceeds unity there is a clear incentive to undertake investment because pure profits are anticipated. See, for example, James H. Chan-Lee (1986) 'Pure profits and Tobin's q in nine OECD countries', *OECD Economic Studies*, no. 7, Autumn, pp 205–32.
4 See 'Company profitability and finance', *Bank of England Quarterly Bulletin*, August 1992, p. 301.
5 The paper by Keith Cowling and Dennis Mueller (1978) 'The social cost of monopoly power', *Economic Journal*, vol. 88, no. 4, pp. 727–48 is in this tradition.
6 E. Davis, S. Flanders and J. Star, (1991) 'Who are the world's most successful companies?' *Business Strategy Review*, Summer, pp. 1–33.
7 See Paul Geroski (1991) 'Innovation and the sectoral sources of UK productivity growth', *Economic Journal*, vol. 101, no. 409, pp. 1438–51, in which he emphasizes the importance of the ability to use innovations.
8 See John Kay (1992) 'Innovations in corporate strategy', in *Stimulating Innovation in Industry*, National Economic Development Office Policy Issues Series,' London: Kogan Page.
9 For example, Shih-Yen Wu (1989) *Production and Entrepreneurship*, Oxford: Blackwell.
10 These points are emphasized by Walter Eltis in 'The financial foundations of industrial success', Esmee Fairbairn Lecture, University of Lancaster, November 1992. See also 'How inflation undermines economic performance', in *Economics, Culture, and Education: Essays in Honour of Mark Blaug*, edited by G. K. Shaw, Edward Elgar (1991) pp. 81–94.

Part III
CITY AND INDUSTRY

11

OVERVIEW:
CAPITAL AND CONTROL
City–industry relations

Martha Prevezer

Better and more widely diffused knowledge is a remedy for that excessive confidence which causes a violent expansion of credit and rise of prices; and it is also a remedy for that excessive distrust that follows. One of the chief sources of disturbance is the action of the general public in providing funds for joint-stock companies. Having insufficient technical knowledge, many of them trust just where they should not: they swell the demand for building materials and machinery and other things, just at the time at which far-sighted people with special knowledge detect coming danger...

(Alfred Marshall, *Money, Credit and Commerce* (1923))

INTRODUCTION

In assessing the relationship between the financial sector and industrial sector within a country, looking exclusively at the structure of financing and its cost omits much that is significant. In particular the financial sector plays an important role in the control of companies, as an intermediary for other share-holders, and as a collector and storehouse of information about companies. This intermediary role occurs through the connection between the willingness to lend or take equity stakes in a company and the control that such creditors or owners subsequently have over what happens within the company. In the context of equity-holding, the debate has been over the different connections between ownership and control, their separation to varying extents depending on the strength of the stock market, and on the effect such separation has on different types of investment. In Chapter 12, Derek Morris contrasts 'inside control', where concentrated ownership confers control, with 'outside control' where there is dispersed ownership and no overlap of owners and managers, and control comes through a more open stock market and tradeability of the companies.

193

We develop the idea that the type of contractual relationship that is developed between the shareholder or the bank and the company is significant in shaping observed patterns of shareholding or bank lending to the corporate sector. It is the nature of the contractual relationship which is built into the institution, and how this evolves, which has contributed to the perceived characteristics of dependence or otherwise of companies on either markets or banks. Such an approach provides an overview for the more detailed discussion of different ownership and control structures, and their influence on the stock market, which is developed in the chapter by Derek Morris.

This chapter also provides a brief overview of some of the main trends in the financing of companies that underlie the debates that are examined in more detail elsewhere in the book. We look at various aspects of the capital structure of non-financial companies in the UK and US, Germany and Japan. It has been popular practice to distinguish between the UK and US whose companies' financing structures are thought to be more 'market oriented' than Japan's and Germany's, where it is thought that company financing is more dependent on the banks deriving from closer ties between the banking and company sectors. We examine the validity of this dichotomy and look at changes in company capital structures over the 1980s through a variety of measures. It brings out how far differences between countries in their corporate control structures are reflected in debt and equity structures and levels of dividend pay-out. If providers of finance have better information channels, they may be prepared to advance funds more cheaply and for longer periods, thereby permitting higher debt–equity ratios. If firms have long-term relationships with others in a supply chain, as happens frequently in Japan, this may result in larger outstanding claims on one another in the form of trade credits extended and received and this will again increase some measures of the ratio of debt to equity. The funding of employees' separation payments in Japan and pension entitlements in Germany also influences debt–equity ratios depending on whether such implicit or explicit claims on the firm are regarded as debt or equity. So financial ratios, as well as telling us something about the relative cost of finance, are also influenced by the corporate control structures that are looked at in detail in the next chapter.

Finally, we look at the performance and competitiveness of the UK's financial sector, in terms of its growth and productivity in comparison with UK manufacturing, and where its strengths lie in competing with other financial centres. The question is then addressed of whether the particular strengths and expertise developed by this sector, and for which London is famous as a financial centre, have proved beneficial to those parts of the domestic economy most reliant on local sources of finance. The argument here is that, whereas London has excelled above most financial centres in its innovativeness and introduction of new products and services, these have for the most part been geared towards the international global economy, and similar sorts of expertise and local information networks have not existed for smaller companies without access to the international capital markets. It is in these areas that the financial sector has been failing with regard to its support for domestic and smaller-scale industry.

INFORMATION AND CONTROL IN FINANCING COMPANIES

We can think of contractual relationships along a spectrum from specific 'classical' contracts which are legalistic with clauses intended to cover most fore-seeable contingencies, to longer-term more 'obligational' or 'implicit' contracts which do not stipulate exactly what their terms are, where the relationship is assumed to continue over a longer period of time, and where the contract itself is a sign of commitment with the precise terms of the relationship negotiable. Broadly speaking, the Anglo-Saxon world has developed a system making greater use of classical contracts in many areas of business, whereas Japan has developed more obligational relations in many spheres of transactions. In order to have relational or obligational contracts, information flows have to be effective and management time must be invested in their establishment.

It was Coase (1937) who first thought of the firm as a system of contracts which, by reducing transactions costs, improved on pure market transactions between individual agents. Transactions costs are important in the relationship between the provider of finance and the firm for two main reasons – information asymmetries and agency problems leading to moral hazard. Asymmetry of information arises whenever the firm has better information of the details of investment projects and their likely success than an outsider. For an introductory discussion of asymmetric information and the problems arising from it, see Estrin and Laidler (1994). This is coupled with the agency problem arising from the split between owners and managers. The monitoring by owners and the different paths of expansion that managers will take under different ownership structures have been analysed by Jensen and Meckling (1976). It will be hard for an owner who is an outsider to monitor what uses are made of the finance provided; and because decisions about investment inherently involve uncertainty and long payback periods, so the outsider to the firm will find it hard to ascertain whether or not the outcome of the investment has been due to good management.

How do these general observations fit in with the actual institutions that provide finance in the different countries? Different types of contract underlie the relationships between market and company and between bank and company. We look first at the nature of shareholding and the different obligations and rights that it confers in the different systems.

THE NATURE OF SHAREHOLDING IN THE UK, JAPAN AND GERMANY

To a greater extent than with Japanese and German shareholding, the UK shareholder is the owner with ultimate responsibility and rights. In principle it is to the shareholder that managers are accountable and shareholders are entitled to the residual earnings in return for which they are the ultimate risk-bearers (Dimsdale 1994). The system has evolved to cope with this by individual shareholders holding a wide portfolio of shares and consequently reducing risk. In addition, the shares are freely tradeable on the stock market. The consequence is very low concentrations of holdings of shares in any one company by any particular shareholder, even the large institutional share-holders. Shareholders have the right to appoint managers by voting at the annual general meeting. The chairman of the board and non-executive directors on the board are meant to represent and safeguard shareholders' interests in the running of the company. In practice this is not very tightly controlled. The recent recommendations of the Cadbury Committee on corporate governance were intended to strengthen these positions and thereby increase the effectiveness of shareholder representation and lessen managerial autonomy. Another feature of UK shareholding in particular is the equality of shareholder status; thus the small shareholder has equivalent rights as the large, and access to the same information. It is expressly forbidden that groups of shareholders should have privileged access to 'insider' information. Shareholders are all equally outsiders. One of the drawbacks of this is the comparative insulation of shareholders from the type of information they would need to be able to monitor managerial performance more directly. This accentuates the asymmetry of information referred to above, where in effect managers have access to much more detailed and pertinent strategic infor-mation of which shareholders are by definition deprived. Accompanying the exclusion from information is the moral hazard problem of not being able to judge whether the agent, in this case the manager, is acting in the shareholders' interests. A further feature in the UK system is that three-quarters of holding of equity is done by institutional shareholders – pension funds, insurance companies and the like. These have their own constitutions which demand that they serve their pension-holders' or trustees' interests above all. They can best do this by diversifying their portfolios and spreading the risk from any one particular shareholding. It is not in any individual pension fund's interest that the managers of the fund become too involved in either accumulating information about any one company or intervening with the management of the company on the basis of acquired information. In terms of Hirschmann's choice between exit or voice,[1] it is more sensible to exit by selling the shareholding than to voice misgivings and try to change management or management strategy directly.

The countervailing force in the UK system is the strength of the stock market and the development, through the market's openness and liquidity, of what has come to be called the market for corporate control. This means that not only are particular shares freely tradeable but whole companies may be bought and sold. This makes companies more sensitive to their own share prices than they otherwise would be, and in effect the institutions or shareholders can express approval or disapproval for any particular management strategy by buying or selling shares and its consequent effect on the share price, to which management are attuned. This mechanism provides a means whereby share-holders indirectly monitor the activities of managers. Share prices therefore respond quickly to news or information, and when the market reflects all available information in the prices, it is said to be informationally efficient. In terms of our original distinction in the kind of contract that is established, these contracts are classical with the rights to sell shares at any time and no constraints or obligations posed on that right to sell.

Many of these features of UK shareholding stand in contrast to Japanese shareholding practices. Whereas the structure of equity-holding in terms of its split between institutions and household shareholdings is roughly equivalent in the ratio of 3/4 to 1/4 in both countries, the nature of institutional share-holding has some significant differences in Japan from practices in the UK. Such shareholders are more likely to be insiders with some kind of contact with the company whose shares they own. These contacts include being a bank, a supplier, another company where there are cross-shareholdings by each company of the others' shares, or they may belong to the *keiretsu* group which is influential in financing the company. These contacts may provide information. The counterpart to this is that trading is much more constrained. It has been estimated that during the 1980s something like two-thirds of equity was in the form of stable shareholding – *antei kabunishi* – which is distinct from interlocking shareholding – *kabushiki mochiai*. These stable share-holdings amount to an implicit agreement not to sell the shares to third parties or at least to consult the management when wishing to do so. It does not prevent the trading of shares, but certainly mutes it (Masuyama 1994). Accordingly, the most actively traded shares in Japan have been those of the household sector, the opposite of the UK case. Takeover activity has been much less than in the UK and there have been no hostile takeovers. The cost of such stability in shareholding has been the lower rate of return on equity that Japanese shares have given to investors. Management has been freer to pursue higher growth and market-share strategies at the expense of the rate of profit on investment. However, there will be increasing pressure for the market to become more open, for shares to become more tradeable and hence for the return on equity to rise to levels equivalent to those in the West. Precise comparisons between such measures as the rate of return on equity in Japan and the UK or US are fraught by differences in accounting conventions which affect price–earnings ratios and such measures (Corbett 1994). However, it is

197

the balance between the competing interests of shareholder and manager that are likely to change. Another feature of Japanese balance of interests is the greater obligations that are built into company structure towards their employees. This again attenuates shareholder rights in considering the growth path that a company should adopt. Lifetime employment, substantial in-house training, lower mobility of employees and management between companies (but not within companies) than is found in the UK and US, all are part of the system of obligations within companies towards employees. These sorts of contract that exist between company and employees are of the relational, implicit type referred to above (for discussion see Odagiri 1992).

German shareholding does not have as many explicit constraints on it as does its Japanese counterpart. There is no equivalent to stable shareholding agreements, and ownership rights can be sold in a fairly liquid market. However, there are greater barriers than exist in the UK to the transfer of control over a company (Franks and Mayer 1990). These are partly enshrined in the ability to issue non-voting shares so that capital can be raised without ceding control. The banks often have the proxy voting rights for shares held with them. They have to state how they are going to vote and shareholders are informed of their intentions and they must fulfil those intentions. Such proxy voting rights mean that a greater concentration of voting power can be built up through the banks. They may find themselves in a position of being able to block certain decisions and the thwarting of some takeovers has followed from the build-up of that sort of power. Another feature built into the German system that curtails shareholders' rights in comparison with those in the UK is the co-determination system whereby employees' rights are enshrined in company statutes. This affects the structure of boards which we discuss below; it also widens the formal accountability of managers to include employees as well as shareholders. This may in practice not amount to substantial curtailment of managerial prerogative; however, it marks more than a symbolic difference in terms of attitude towards the sovereignty of the shareholder.

THE ROLE OF THE BANKS AND THE MONITORING FUNCTION

The counterpart to having a weaker market mechanism for transferring control rights over a company, as is the case in Germany and Japan, is a more informal but nevertheless substantive network of information gathering and more direct monitoring and intervention in the managers' sphere of influence. The banks perform a central role in this. The main bank in Japan or the Hausbank in Germany, although not having an exclusive banking relationship with its client company, will have built up knowledge about the working and competencies of a company and there is again more of an implicit longer-term relational agreement emphasizing the continuous nature of the relationship (Schneider-Lenne 1994). Banks hold equity stakes in companies, although these are limited to 5 per cent of equity in any one company in Japan and in Germany came to 12 per cent of equity in 1988. They also have a role as lender. As the following section indicates, this in fact in terms of lending as a source of finance for new investment has been more substantial in Japan than elsewhere. Banks also have seats on company boards, in particular on supervisory boards in Germany and they form part of the *keiretsu* in Japan. In addition to the proxy voting rights mentioned above, these features create a concentration of information about companies within the banking sector allied with substantial influence through various channels. This does not mean that the banks dictate activity in the industrial sector in those countries. It does mean that companies may find themselves subject to greater pressure from that quarter instead of from the stock market and via the share price, as happens in the UK. This divergence in the systems of governance partly reflects the structure of ownership, especially when it comes to the smaller and medium-sized companies. Far fewer of the German *Mittelstand*, that body of medium-sized companies on which the strength of the German economy has depended, are publicly quoted companies than their UK equivalent-sized counterparts. It is not surprising therefore that the influence of the stock market should be replaced by other mechanisms, in particular for these medium-sized companies which fits their ownership structure. Aoki (1989) has written of the delegation to the main bank in Japan of the monitoring function by the shareholders and sees the phenomenon of overborrowing in the interests of the bank as a type of agency fee for the bank for doing so.

CHANGES IN THE UK BANK–INDUSTRY RELATIONS OVER THE 1980s

There have been major changes in the UK financial sector, mainly through deregulation, that have affected the way that the UK banks have done business with various parts of the corporate sector (McWilliams and Sentance 1994). The major changes in the financial system included:

- the abolition of foreign-exchange controls in 1979 widening opportunities for lending;
- the removal of the corset in 1980 which had restricted the interest-bearing eligible liabilities of banks;
- the abolition of hire purchase controls on consumer credit;
- the ability of the building societies from 1983 to raise funds through certificates of deposit and further deregulation in 1986 in the Building Societies Act;
- the entry of the clearing banks into the mortgage market;
- the breakdown of informal rules preventing equity withdrawal.

In addition, 'Big Bang' brought major changes from 1986 in the structure of the provision of financial services and the margins on those services. The changes affecting business most acutely have been the globalization and liberalization of financial markets whereby a wide range of new financial instruments became available (such as swaps, options, convertibles). These instruments plus much easier direct access for large companies to the developing Eurobond markets and commercial paper markets, coupled with the internal development of the Treasury functions inside large companies, have meant that the relationship banking which did exist between large UK companies and their banks became less necessary from the companies' point of view. For the banks, their business shifted in composition as a consequence of the financial deregulatory measures listed above, and their proportion of lending to the personal sector increased (from 14 per cent of total bank lending in 1980 to 28 per cent in 1991) and the share of lending to business fell from 70 per cent of total lending in 1980 to under 50 per cent by 1991.[2] To offset this decline in the share of lending going to business there was an increase in leasing and in lending to security dealers, which reflect the changes in method of companies obtaining finance rather than in the amount of finance available. Bank lending to business as a proportion of GDP continued to rise throughout the 1980s from 23 per cent in 1980 to 49 per cent in 1990. However, this has to be seen in the light of bank lending forming a shrinking proportion of large companies' liabilities in the second half of the 1980s, replaced by their issuing commercial paper and other methods of raising finance. It became the case in the late 1980s that large companies could raise finance more cheaply through direct access to capital markets than the cost of borrowing from banks. Below we analyse companies' balance sheets and chart their main sources of finance.

One of the consequences of these changes in the structure of bank lending was increased pressure on banks' profitability. Partly due to the liberalization measures listed above, greater competition in the 1980s squeezed net interest margins, in particular on domestic lending. Margins (interest income as a proportion of interest-earning assets) and spreads (the difference between the rate paid on interest-bearing assets and on deposits) on domestic lending declined. Margins fell from 7 per cent in 1980 to 4 per cent in 1990. This occurred mainly in two periods: between 1980 and 1983 as interest rates fell, margins declined although spreads increased; between 1987 and 1990 there were lower spreads due to greater competition for loans, in turn owing to lower margins on mortgage lending and on lending to large companies and due to changes in the deposit mix on the liabilities side (*Bank of England Quarterly Bulletin*, November 1991). In addition costs did not decline, as retail branch networks have been maintained and there was a greater reliance on labour-intensive fee-generating activities. The broad strategy of the banks was to focus on personal sector customers as large companies looked directly to the markets to satisfy their financial needs. This was despite the fact that banks' most stable sources of non-interest fee income continued to be fees and commissions from the corporate sector.

Whilst bank business with large companies became less of a priority, the number of small businesses registered for VAT rose dramatically during the

1980s. The banks responded to this by expanding its services to small and growing companies. By 1991, 95 per cent of NatWest's commercial customers were small businesses (having a turnover of less than £1 million per annum). Barclays quoted a figure of 80 per cent for the proportion of business customers in 1992 with a turnover of less than £100,000 (McWilliams and Sentance 1994). Small businesses are higher risk and need more servicing, both factors contributing to increasing costs to the banks. In effect, banks provided loan capital to small businesses at rates which, whilst higher than those charged to larger customers, were below those charged by venture capital companies for similar sorts of risk. The Treasury and Civil Service Select Committee of 1991–2 on Banking Codes[3] criticized the banks for insufficient monitoring of companies' performance, making little use of local information which might have been gathered. The committee pointed to the centralization of decision-making in banks with the erosion of authority at the local branch level. It also pointed to the heavy weighting of short-term loan finance and very little use of longer-term loan or equity finance, which was not desired by either companies or banks. Banks have come in for criticism for inadequate assessment of the risk involved in their lending and for adopting too short-term a view of companies' prospects. More information on business prospects and managerial ability coupled with more imagination concerning the forms of finance used may be needed. However, small businesses have to be willing to disclose information and cede some control in exchange for longer-term and more stable financing.

The net effect has been a greater reliance by the banks on higher-risk lending to smaller businesses, which themselves are more exposed to cyclical pressures. This was coupled with the expansion of bank lending to the personal sector and the erosion of longer-term relationships with their more traditional larger corporate customers due to competitive pressures and liberalization of capital markets.

The question of finance for small business has been a recurring theme in the question of Britain's economic performance since at least the time of the Macmillan Committee in 1931 which had identified a considerable finance gap. Many of the features of the financial structure of small businesses are well known – high levels of trade credit, low proportions of equity in total debt and heavy dependence upon short-term borrowing from the banks. With these arrangements the problems of small business are inevitably compounded in times of recession – in 1993 as in 1931. Hughes (1994) has suggested that the situation has probably improved for small businesses in the 1980s as some of the recommendations of the Wilson Committee in 1979 have been implemented – including the Loan Guarantee Scheme (1981) and the Business Expansion Scheme (1983). In addition, new equity markets have been established and the venture capital industry has expanded rapidly. New business start-ups have proliferated during the 1980s, but the death rate is considerable. Hughes, however, points to problem areas remaining in high technology or otherwise innovative manufacturing where finance gaps may still exist. His own suggestion is for clubs of small firms to form Mutual Guarantee Schemes which are quite widespread in mainland Europe. These can be used to reduce problems of informational asymmetry in arranging loans as well as encouraging industrial coordination.

CAPITAL STRUCTURE: A COMPARISON OF GERMANY, JAPAN AND THE UK

Are these differences described above in the relative importance given to share-holders, banks and other stakeholders (such as employees and suppliers) in the different systems reflected in either companies' capital structure or in the pay-out ratios that we observe? There are a number of differences in dividend pay-out ratios, debt–equity ratios and the structure of liabilities and assets on companies' balance sheets that suggest that these differences in the balance of power between different institutions or in conventions are reflected in the way companies organize their financing. Higher dividend pay-outs, more contested takeover activity and higher rates of return on equity may be evidence of greater accountability to the stock market.

Dividend pay-out ratios have been lower in Japan, Germany and the US than in the UK (see Table 1). There are several possible explanations. One is that fear of takeover induces higher distributions. More specifically, pay-outs may be a signal of commitment to some minimum standard of performance, and

Table 1 Ratio of dividends to gross income of non-financial corporations (percentage)

Year	UK	US	Japan
1974	–	24	17
1975	–	20	18
1976	–	20	17
1977	36	19	16
1978	37	20	15
1979	41	20	13
1980	45	23	14
1981	45	22	14
1982	49	25	15
1983	48	23	13
1984	45	21	12
1985	46	20	10
1986	34	22	12
1987	39	22	10
1988	42	21	10
1989	41	28	–

Source: OECD Financial Statistics

failure to achieve that standard sends a bad signal to the market. Below, Derek Morris discusses the possibility that these signals 'jam' and the consequences of that happening. Higher pay-out ratios may also be a mechanism whereby better monitoring by investors of managers can occur. If managers are made to distribute earnings rather than retain them, it diminishes their autonomy and forces them back to the market for more funds than they otherwise would have needed. It provides an avenue whereby, indirectly, shareholders can obtain more information on investment plans and direction that a company is taking than they would otherwise have if distributions were lower.

This is not to suggest, however, that retained earnings are unimportant as a source of finance for new investment; they are particularly important in the UK, US and Germany (see Figure 1). The arguments made as to why retained earnings have assumed such a predominant position in financing for investment in some ways diminish the force of the monitoring argument about high pay-out ratios. It is precisely because of the asymmetry of information about investment prospects for a particular firm where insiders understand the risks better than outsiders, that insiders (managers) prefer to rely on internal finance for riskier projects such as research and development which are particularly hard for outsiders to understand and assess. External financing is deemed unsuitable through posing too many constraints on the use to which the money is put, and managers prefer if possible to exercise their autonomy in areas where they feel the risk aversion and lack of information of investors will make the terms of

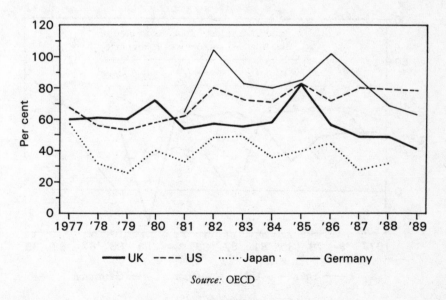

Source: OECD

Figure 11.1 Self-financing ratio.
Note: Germany: Issues of shares included in non-financial sources; break in German series in 1986

external financing more onerous than the opportunity cost of using internal finance.

Lower self-financing and greater use of debt for financing new investment in Japan might also be consistent with this story, if banks are relatively better informed and are effectively insiders to managerial strategy (see Figure 2). Debt financing has been consistently higher in Japan than in the other countries. It has been argued that this use of bank borrowing may be an implicit form of monitoring that reduces the agency costs referred to above. Another distinction between Japanese financing ratios and those in the UK, US and Germany is the greater stability of financing proportions in Japan. There has been a more constant share of debt financing in particular (see Table 2). By contrast, in the other countries external finance has been used as a residual measure as needed, with considerable volatility in debt financing as a consequence. This difference may also be attributable to the banks having more of an insider role in Japan than elsewhere. In this respect at least, German use of bank financing resembles that of the UK more than that of Japan.

These features of corporate control are also reflected in companies' balance sheets. On the liabilities side, in the UK and US there seems to be a higher proportion of equity than in Germany and Japan (Figure 3). In comparisons with Germany this depends on how pension provisions are classified. Table 3 shows debt–equity ratios for Germany defining pension provisions as both debt and equity. They are debt-like having a fixed obligation for repayment at a

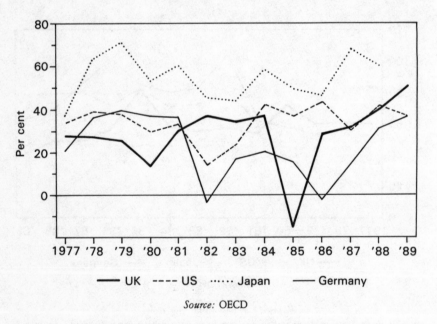

Source: OECD

Figure 11.2 Debt as a proportion of total sources.

Table 2 Sources of finance as a proportion of total sources

	UK		Germany		US		Japan	
	1977–80	1981–9	1977–80	1981–9	1977–80	1981–9	1977–80	1981–9
Debt	23.4	30.4	33.2	18.4	35.1	33.7	56.3	54.2
Of which short-term debt	22.9	21.3	–	–	22.0	10.8	42.2	32.4
Of which long-term debt	0.5	9.2	–	–	13.1	22.9	14.1	21.7
Share issues	9.1	13.2			3.6	−5.3	5.1	6.4
Internal sources	67.5	56.4	66.8	81.6	61.3	71.6	38.6	39.5

Source: OECD Financial Statistics

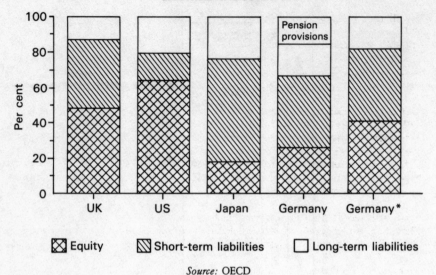

Source: OECD

Figure 11.3 Liabilities of non-financial companies as a proportion of total liabilities, 1977–89.
* Provisions are included as equity
NB: Japanese time period covered is 1977–88

Table 3 Debt–equity ratio of non-financial enterprises*

| | | | | Germany | |
| | | | | Provisions classified as debt | Provisions classified as equity |
Year	Japan	US	UK		
1974	–	0.56	–	–	–
1975	5.60	0.52	–	2.56	1.84
1976	5.72	0.50	–	2.62	1.85
1977	5.49	0.51	1.06	2.60	1.82
1978	5.49	0.50	1.08	2.68	1.84
1979	5.49	0.49	1.06	2.77	1.88
1980	5.16	0.48	1.06	3.02	1.92
1981	5.04	0.47	1.10	3.09	1.96
1982	5.02	0.47	1.13	3.06	1.89
1983	4.84	0.50	1.10	3.05	1.83
1984	4.77	0.56	1.09	3.00	1.76
1985	4.40	0.61	1.04	2.99	1.72
1986	4.22	0.67	1.04	2.90	1.63
1987	4.36	0.71	1.03	4.19	1.51
1988	4.19	0.76	1.03	4.25	1.52
1989	–	0.82	1.14	4.33	1.53

* Gross liabilities less equity as a proportion of equity
Source: OECD Financial Statement

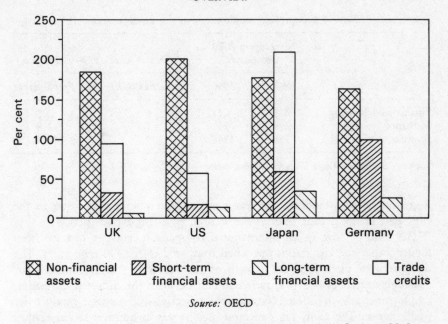

Figure 11.4 Assets of non-financial companies as a proportion of value-added.

certain date. On the other hand they have been represented as social capital and in effect are part of equity over which managers have a relatively free rein. If they are counted as equity, then debt–equity ratios are comparable between Germany and the UK. Treating pension provisions as equity better reflects the type of relational contract that exists between the employee and employer in a German company. Short-term trade credits and short-term borrowing are very important on both the assets and liabilities side of Japanese balance sheets. They are significantly higher than credits extended in other countries. In Figure 3 such borrowing is marked as short-term liabilities; in Figure 4 trade credits are marked separately. Such borrowing and lending between companies reflects the inter-company network of financing and again is an example of the less explicit more relational contracting that occurs between Japanese companies.

THE PERFORMANCE AND COMPETITIVENESS OF THE FINANCIAL SECTOR

The growth of the financial sector of Britain's economy was quite remarkable during the 1980s. On a broad definition of the sector (including business services, such as computing, estate agency and accounting), output growth comfortably outstripped that of the economy as a whole, as shown in Table 4.

Table 4 Output and employment in the financial sector

	Employees (GB) thousands		Growth rates 1979–90 (% p.a.)	
	1979	1990	Output (UK)	Employment
Finance and banking	443	621	6.5	3.3
Insurance	214	261	7.7	1.8
Business services	798	1548	7.7	6.4

Source: CSO Service Trade Statistics (various issues)

Recession notwithstanding, the sector actually grew somewhat faster in the early part of the decade than in the second, post-'Big-Bang', period.

The same is true in an international comparison, and we can see from Figure 5 that the UK stands out when compared to the G6 economies. The disaggregated picture of the growth of the sector in Table 4 shows that, although output growth was rather similar between the different industries, employment growth differed considerably, reflecting differences in productivity performance. The really big generator of jobs was in business services rather than in banking and insurance. As shown elsewhere in this volume, this

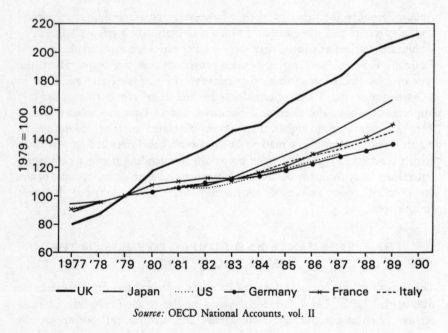

Source: OECD National Accounts, vol. II

Figure 11.5 Growth in the output of financial, insurance, real estate and business services (G6).

reflects a huge structural change in terms of the inputs of business services – which comprises all manner of technical, legal, accounting and advertising services – that are required by other sectors of the economy, including business services themselves (Barker and Forsell 1992). Some have interpreted this as a fundamental shift towards an 'information-intensive economy', a structural shift observed in other advanced economies. In both banking and finance and insurance, similar output gains have been translated into fewer jobs and hence a superior productivity performance. In part this reflects the rapidity of technical change – many of the underlying transactions are on a large scale and relatively homogeneous, so the scope for advance is correspondingly enormous. It should be borne in mind, however, that output measures can be unreliable in this sector, and some have argued that there may be systematic under-recording of output in some of the industries (Smith 1989). An interesting feature of productivity growth in the entire sector, as indicated in Figure 6, is that after the rapid growth in the period 1977–83 it stagnates thereafter, and over the whole period 1979–90 it is little faster than that of the economy as a whole.

The question of the competitiveness of the sector has been heightened by the creation of the European Single Market and the possibility that the dismantling of barriers in financial services might allow rapid penetration of

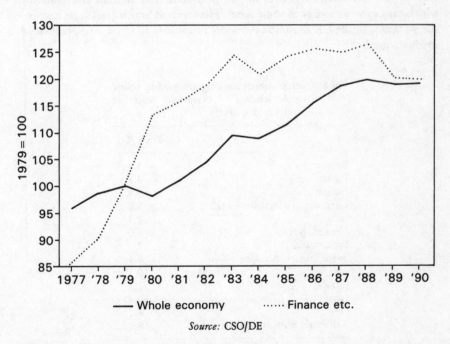

Source: CSO/DE

Figure 11.6 Labour productivity in the UK financial sector against the whole economy.

markets by the most competitive financial institutions in the Community. The Cecchini (1988) report suggested that the UK was a relatively low-cost supplier of a variety of financial services but it is not clear how far higher costs in other markets, especially in Germany, reflect implicit services of the kind discussed above – e.g. the long-term commitments that are attached to bank lending. These 'club effects' amount to significant attributes of non-price competitiveness. It is certainly the case that many commentators are not expecting an easy entry for UK institutions into domestic markets. Smith (1992) cites evidence from the Swiss market, where the relative ease with which it is now possible to obtain banking licences and the abandonment of the banking cartel has made little difference to foreign banks' access to it. In general, entry into the smaller markets in the EC may be easier than into the larger markets of Germany and Italy (Bank of England 1989).

Although it may not be true across the entire range of financial services, the role of non-price competitiveness may be just as great if not greater in this area than in manufacturing. Sources of trading advantage are likely to arise from the specialized expertise and innovativeness of institutions rather than technology (which is relatively accessible to all the major players) and productivity advantages, and so the traditional role of comparative costs may be slight. The sources of competitive advantage for the institutions of a particular country such as the UK stem in part from the peculiarities of its national economy which may give it an edge in some areas. However, as Smith (1992) points out, the weakness of the UK domestic economy is unlikely to stand it in good stead in this regard.

Table 5 International banking analysed by centre (gross lending – percentage share of total world market)

	1990 (Q3)
Belgium	3.3
Luxembourg	4.8
France	6.8
Germany (Federal Republic)	5.0
Italy	2.1
Netherlands	2.9
Switzerland	2.4
Swiss Trustee Account	4.1
UK	19.1
Canada	1.1
Japan	20.4
US	8.1
'Offshore' banking centres	18.7

Source: Bank for International Settlements

The City's strengths have lain in international finance rather than in the provision of finance for the domestic industrial sector. London has been the centre for almost 20 per cent of gross lending in international banking, on a par with Japan (Table 5). London has become the centre of international bond dealing, looking at the number of firms by centre (Table 6). London also has a large number of companies quoted on its stock exchange, both domestic and foreign companies, although many of these are not large companies. Thus London as a financial centre is providing a valuable service to international

Table 6 Association of international bond dealers (number of firms by centre)

	All firms[a]	Reporting dealers[b]
UK	205	73
Switzerland	151	1
Luxembourg	76	5
Germany	68	–
Hong Kong	48	1
Netherlands	58	–
US	29	–
France	49	5
Belgium	39	2
Other	211	10

[a] End September 1990
[b] Those firms which report prices on a daily basis (end September 1990)

Table 7 International stock exchanges (primary market statistics for equities, end-1990)

Exchange	Market value of domestic equity (£bn) end-1990	Number of listed companies, end-1990	
		Domestic	Foreign
Tokyo	1,482.8	1627	125
Osaka	1,221.0	1138	0
New York	1,389.1	1678	96
London	445.0	2006	553
NASDAQ*	736.9	3875	256
Frankfurt	176.5	389	354
Paris	159.3	443	226
Zurich	85.7	182	240
Amsterdam	77.2	260	238
American	35.1	789	70

*National Association of Securities Dealers (USA) Automated Quotations
Source: Bank of England Quarterly Bulletin

companies, and has been more successful than other financial centres by such measures (Table 7).

Therefore in assessing the performance of this sector, we need to consider it in its various parts and for the different functions and services that it needs to perform. There have been many institutional changes centred on the financial sector in the 1980s. These have had mixed effects on the competitiveness both of the sector in itself and in terms of the knock-on effects of what the sector can provide to UK industry.

CONCLUSION

Control mechanisms and relations between the financial and industrial sectors are important for information collection and monitoring by the financial sector of the industrial sector. The relevant financial intermediary may be institutions connected with the stock market or with the banks. In which system do these features work best? We have described here the 'inside' system where financial intermediaries are in the position of accumulating inside information about companies and exercising some measure of control or monitoring as a consequence; the Japanese and German institutions resemble this to some extent. We contrast this with the 'outside' system where information gathering and monitoring occur through institutions that are kept at arm's length from companies and work through markets. Longer-term investment and higher risk investment by companies may be made easier by the types of inside relations that are more prevalent in Japan and Germany than in the UK and US.

The inside–outside dichotomy fits to some extent with some of the features we observe in the capital structures in the different countries, in particular their split between debt and equity. German pension provisions and Japanese trade credits are examples of longer-term obligations and relationships between those stakeholders that constitute the wider nexus of 'inside' financing relationships than occur in the 'outside' UK and US. In the UK and US, on the other hand, the importance of the market is manifest in higher dividend pay-outs and the greater sensitivity that companies display towards their share price.

How well does the UK financial sector perform? In comparison with UK manufacturing, the financial sector broadly defined has grown rapidly over the 1980s and has achieved substantial productivity growth. Its expertise and competitiveness benefits the international community and larger companies with access to global capital markets more than domestic companies confined to local financing mechanisms. The UK financial sector is stronger in areas where outsider control which does not require local and personal knowledge is appropriate and where markets predominate. Thus it has been extremely innovative and competitive in producing new financial instruments, in developing Eurobond markets and in hosting stock markets for international companies. The sector fails in relation to the provision of local domestic finance where detailed knowledge, risk assessment at the local level, and regional commitment and imagination are necessary.

NOTES

1 Hirschmann, A. (1970) *Exit, Voice and Loyalty*, Cambridge, MA: Harvard University Press.
2 *Source: Bank of England Quarterly Bulletin*, various issues, from McWilliams and Sentance (1994).
3 *Source:* House of Commons Treasury and Civil Service Committee Third Report 1991–92 Session, 'Banking codes of practice and related matters'.

REFERENCES

Aoki, M. (1989) *Information, Incentives and Bargaining in the Japanese Economy*, Cambridge: Cambridge University Press.
Bank of England (1989) 'London as an international financial centre', *Bank of England Quarterly Bulletin*, November, pp. 516–29.
Barker, T. S. and Forsell, O. (1992) 'Manufacturing, services and structural change 1979–1984', in C. Driver and P. Dunne (eds), *Structural Change in the UK Economy*, Cambridge: Cambridge University Press.
Cadbury, A. (1992) *Committee on the Financial Aspects of Corporate Governance*, London: HMSO.
Cecchini, P. (1988) *1992: The European Challenge*, London: Gower.
Coase, R. (1937) 'The nature of the firm', *Economica*, vol. 4, pp. 386–405.
Corbett, J. (1994) 'An overview of the Japanese system', in N. Dimsdale and M. Prevezer (eds), *Capital Markets and Corporate Governance*, Oxford: Oxford University Press.
Dimsdale, N. (1994) 'The need to restore corporate accountability', in N. Dimsdale and M. Prevezer (eds), *Capital Markets and Corporate Governance*, Oxford: Oxford University Press.
Estrin, S. and Laidler, D. (1994) *Introduction to Microeconomics*, second edition, Oxford: Philip Allan.
Franks, J. and Mayer, C. (1990) 'Corporate ownership and corporate control: a study of France, Germany and the UK', *Economic Policy*, April, pp. 191–231.
Hirschmann, A. (1970) *Exit, Voice and Loyalty*, Cambridge, MA: Harvard University Press.
House of Commons Treasury and Civil Service Committee on Banking Codes and Related Matters (1992) Third Report 1991–1992 Session.
Hughes, A. (1994) 'The problems of finance for smaller businesses', in N. Dimsdale and M. Prevezer (eds), *Capital Markets and Corporate Governance*, Oxford: Oxford University Press.
Jensen, C. M. and Meckling, W. H. (1976) 'Theory of the firm: managerial behaviour, agency costs and ownership structure', *Journal of Financial Economics*, vol. 3, pp. 305–60.
McWilliams, D. and Sentance, A. (1994) 'The changing relationship between the banks and business in the UK', in N. Dimsdale and M. Prevezer (eds), *Capital Markets and Corporate Governance*, Oxford: Oxford University Press.

Masuyama, S. (1994) 'The role of the Japanese capital markets and the effect of cross-shareholdings on corporate accountability', in N. Dimsdale and M. Prevezer (eds), *Capital Markets and Corporate Governance*, Oxford: Oxford University Press.

Odagiri, H. (1992) *Growth Through Competition and Competition Through Growth*, Oxford: Oxford University Press.

Prevezer, M. and Ricketts, M. (1994) 'Corporate governance: the UK compared with Germany and Japan', in N. Dimsdale and M. Prevezer (eds), *Capital Markets and Corporate Governance*, Oxford: Oxford University Press.

Schneider-Lenne, E. (1994) 'The role of the German capital markets and universal banks, supervisory boards and inter-locking directorships', in N. Dimsdale and M. Prevezer (eds), *Capital Markets and Corporate Governance*, Oxford: Oxford University Press.

Smith, A. D. (1989) 'New measures of service sector output', *National Institute Economic Review*, no. 128, May, pp. 75–88.

Smith, A. D. (1992) *International Financial Markets: The Performance of Britain and its Rivals*, Cambridge: Cambridge University Press.

ACKNOWLEDGEMENT

Figures 11.1, 11.2, 11.3, 11.4 and Tables 1, 2, 3 have been reproduced from Prevezer, M. and Ricketts, M. (1994) 'Corporate Governance: the UK compared with Germany and Japan', in N. Dimsdale and M. Prevezer (eds), *Capital Markets and Corporate Governance*, Oxford: Oxford University Press, with permission of Oxford University Press.

12

THE STOCK MARKET AND PROBLEMS OF CORPORATE CONTROL IN THE UK[1]

Derek Morris

I INTRODUCTION

A major and long-standing source of controversy in the analysis of the UK's economic performance has been the role of the City, and more specifically the London stock exchange, in influencing industrial performance. On the one hand the City represents one of the two major financial centres in the world, provides highly knowledgeable and flexible markets for all manner of financial instruments, includes some of the largest investing institutions in the world and, in conventional terms, has one of the most efficient stock exchanges anywhere providing an easily accessible market for corporate control. This in turn is seen by many as a key discipline on industrial companies' managers and a crucial mechanism for allocating or reallocating resources to their most efficient uses. On this view the City is not only a major contributor to GNP and overseas earnings but a significant and more pervasive contributor to economic welfare.

An alternative view is that the City has had a baleful influence on industrial performance over many decades. On this view the City originally grew as an adjunct to trading rather than production, has been dominated by individuals and institutions with little or no understanding of industry, its workings or its financial needs, is to only a limited extent a source of funds, is often poor at evaluating companies or their opportunities and is obsessed with immediate profit at the expense of successful longer-term development. It is frequently pointed out that a number of countries, most noticeably Germany and Japan, have been notably more successful without any comparably developed institutional arrangements to match the market for corporate control in the UK.

Many in the financial, business, academic and political areas have addressed this controversy, theoretically, empirically and, in many cases, purely speculatively but with little sign of resolution. This no doubt in part reflects the fact that the issue is unavoidably political, being concerned with the disposition

215

and use of power and the consequences for the level and distribution of economic welfare. In part it also reflects quite severe problems of data, methodology and interpretation in analysing the issue, to which we refer later. Whatever the cause, the result is to generate serious policy dilemmas concerning how companies should best be governed, whether or how stock market behaviour should be regulated, what role shareholders can or should play in controlling companies and in particular whether takeovers should be made more or less difficult.

Our purpose here is primarily to review various relevant strands of literature and analyses which only partly intersect, to see what can be distilled concerning this issue, looking at both theoretical considerations and evidence. We will, however, in the course of this, make reference to ongoing analysis concerning the vexed question of 'short-termism', i.e. the allegation that in some way stock markets of the type existing in London inhibit managers from acting in the best long-term interests of their companies.

Our approach is first to summarize briefly some relevant recent literature on forms of corporate governance and control. This starting point, examined in section II, looks at different types and structures of company ownership and the basic considerations which are likely to be important in determining the interaction of the industrial and financial sectors of an economy. Section III then looks in more detail at the motives, consequences and effectiveness of the takeover mechanism in a developed stock market such as exists in the US and the UK. We attempt to draw out from a large number of different studies and indeed different approaches to this issue some reasonably well supported working conclusions concerning the role of takeovers and their consequences. Section IV moves on to the more specific but much less well understood area of short-termism. It looks at two models of rational short-termist pressures which have appeared in the literature and then provides some new perspectives on this issue. The section also reviews the evidence on short-termism, such as it is, and brings out some of the methodological problems in identifying short-term pressures or its consequences in any rigorous or systematic manner.

Section V looks at both the traditional and more recent analysis of the economic behaviour of professional managers, their objectives, activities, the constraints on them and resulting performance. This throws new light on the welfare implications of different types of corporate ownership and control. A key element in the paper is then an attempt to integrate these insights with the earlier analysis of short-termism. Section VI looks at some empirical work that may be interpreted as relevant to the overall picture that emerges of the impact of the stock market on industrial performance, and points the way forward in exploring further these ideas. Conclusions are presented in Section VII.

II CORPORATE GOVERNANCE: SOME BASIC CONSIDERATIONS

Not only elementary economics textbooks but many more advanced analyses of industrial behaviour view firms as individual and indivisible decision-taking units where the decision-taker owns the firm, controls its resources and decisions and receives the profits or accepts the losses made. In practice much of the industrial assets base in the UK is owned and controlled by large, and sometimes enormously large, companies characterized by many thousands of employees, tens or even hundreds of product lines, multi-divisional structures, complex organizational structures, dispersed decision-taking, internal planning mechanisms for allocating resources rather than market coordination and a high degree of separation between the owners who have a legal title to the assets of the company and the managers who direct its activities.[2] This raises a number of questions, not least why in Coase's famous question there are such 'islands of conscious power' in a sea of market transactions, why some resource allocations should occur through market transactions while others (in some cases identical ones) occur through planning and direction internal to a firm, and how efficiency is affected by these considerations.[3] Our present concern is a narrower and subsidiary one, namely the different possible ways in which the various functions of a firm are carried out, how they are integrated, and through what institutional arrangements.

We start by presenting brief working definitions of ownership and control.[4] *Ownership* lies in (i) the legal power to appoint managers and determine their remuneration, and (ii) the bearing of, or reassignment through contracts of residual (uninsurable) risk, the latter conceived of as the surplus (positive or negative) accruing after meeting all contractual obligations. *Management* lies in the direct control and immediate direction of resources, human and otherwise within a company, in the context of spot market transactions and contracts with agents external to the firm and utilizing various types of contract, usually incomplete in the sense that they do not define all possible eventualities, responsibilities, etc., within the firm. Thus even though many people are both owners and managers simultaneously, the conceptual distinction is clear.

In practice the distinction is rendered less clear by the existence of directors on the senior board of a company. These are appointed by the owners and may be thought of as their representatives charged with the responsibility of ensuring that the owners' interests are maximized. Much has been written recently about the need for more non-executive directors who will pursue this responsibility more effectively and more single-mindedly than has often been the case in the past. This is primarily because many if not most directors are executive and hold the most senior managerial responsibilities for directing and controlling resources. In the case of the single owner-manager-director this creates no problem, but where owners and managers are different and their interests diverge, considerable tensions can arise concerning the proper role and duties of the board. The most obvious such tensions arise where directors are inefficient managers or determine their own remuneration. Still further complications can arise where, as is often argued, directors should, either on ethical grounds or efficiency grounds, try to take into account or even represent the interests of other so-called 'stake-holders' in a company besides the owners, e.g., employees, suppliers, customers, etc.

Despite these complications we can use these simple definitions to identify two main characteristics of companies that serve to delineate differing broad classes of corporate 'governance', where this catch-all term is used to span the whole ownership-control nexus. These are, first, the extent of *overlap of ownership and managerial control* and, second, the degree of *concentration of ownership*. While in principle we might define a third, namely the extent to which individual owners have their own direct representation on company boards, in general this is closely related to ownership concentration. Where the latter is high, typically large shareholders will have one or more nominees on a board; where ownership is highly dispersed this is unlikely to occur.

These two fundamental characteristics potentially generate four broad types of corporate governance. (i) Concentrated ownership with high management–ownership overlap. This is the governance structure of the typical unquoted company in the UK and the US. Most if not all of the shares of such companies are held, directly or indirectly, by a small number of shareholders who are also directors holding key management positions.[5] (ii) Concentrated ownership with relatively little overlap between ownership and managerial control. This is the typical form of governance in Japan and most European countries. While there may be a large number of shareholders and an active stock market, for many companies the majority of shares are held by a relatively small number of institutional shareholders, including banks, other financial and industrial companies, suppliers and customers. Many of these will have directors on the boards of the companies in which they hold equity and this general structure is frequently characterized by a series of interlocking shareholdings and directorships. (iii) Unconcentrated ownership with relatively little overlap between ownership and management. This is the typical structure for quoted companies in the UK and US. Individuals and institutions tend to hold relatively small proportions of the shares of any one company, and frequently operate their dispersed investments on a portfolio basis, i.e. spreading investment across a range of shares with different risk–return characteristics.[6] Managers may well hold shares in their company but these holdings will typically represent only a small proportion of the total shares issued. (iv) The final category will be of less interest in our discussion, namely unconcentrated ownership with high management–ownership overlap. This typically applies in partnerships where many or all of those involved in an undertaking each hold a portion of the overall equity. The undertaking is fully owned by the managers but no individual or group has a disproportionately large share.

Before going on to examine some of the differences between these structures, three comments are necessary. First, in some cases a statistically small shareholding may for most of the time be quite sufficient to provide substantial ownership rights. A shareholding of 2 or 3 per cent, particularly if held by managers, may in normal circumstances repeatedly provide majorities at annual shareholders' meetings, partly because many dispersed shareholders regularly decline to get involved and also because many who do frequently assign voting rights to a proxy established by the largest shareholders. This may of course break down in difficult or more controversial circumstances.

Second, although the management–ownership overlap, or lack of it, is important, from the point of view of objectives and incentives it is also important to identify the proportion of a manager's remuneration dependent on his or her ownership of shares or, directly or indirectly, on share perform-ance, for example via share options, profit or share price-related bonuses, etc. There may be much greater convergence of owners' and managers' interests where 80 per cent of the latter's remuneration comes from share-related sources, even though the manager holds only a very small fraction of the shares than cases where the managerial share holding is higher but is not the main source of managerial remuneration.

Third, the four-way classification of corporate governance above, and the typical real-world counterparts mentioned, may appear too dichotomous in that, in principle, there could be a whole spectrum of degrees of ownership concentration and management–ownership overlap, generating a highly heterogeneous pattern of governance. In practice this is largely not the case. While exceptions exist, most undertakings fall rather clearly into one or other of the categories described. This is not an historical accident. There are quite powerful economic forces which make intermediate combinations of ownership concentration and management–ownership overlap relatively non-viable. These are most easily understood in terms of the basic proposition that owners must either have a fairly high degree of control *or* a high degree of market-ability of their ownership rights. This is because, in the absence of both, an owner has no protection or strategy for dealing with poor performance and poor returns. *Ex-hypothesi* the owners cannot step in to change performance as they have no control, nor can they easily sell the ownership right to escape the consequences of any further deterioration. While it cannot be said that there will never be any attraction to such investments, which have characteristics similar to many types of pure gamble, the combination of lock-in and lack of control make this an unlikely basis for corporate governance.

Concentrated ownership structures of the type described above typically confer powerful control functions, either because, as in unquoted companies, the owners are the managers or, as in countries such as Germany and Japan, directors representing major shareholders sit on company boards. Control is also exercised in partnerships. Unconcentrated ownership of the type reflected in the UK and US stock markets does not readily provide influence or control, but such rights are tradable in a highly liquid market. Other theoretical combi-nations do not provide the necessary functions. For example, the issuing of small parcels of shares to a large number of investors in unquoted companies is very rare. Managers may hold some shares for incentive reasons, inheritance sometimes results in a number of individuals uninvolved in the company obtaining an incomes stream, and government incentives for this type of invest-ment exist, but this does not alter the basic premise. Some companies do have a substantial minority shareholder, typically another company, but this does not greatly reduce the concentration of shareholding and is almost always associated with a presence on the board. Even here many unquoted companies see the existence of such a shareholding as a first step, desirable or otherwise, towards quotation, primarily because the shareholder in question may wish to have the opportunity to sell, or may at some point sell to others who wish to have such opportunities. While in theory a majority shareholder group can block this, the presence of minority shareholders on boards, and the scope for competitors, suppliers or customers to become involved may make this difficult.

An alternative hybrid, namely moderate ownership concentration with moderate management–ownership overlap, does exist but is again relatively rare. Typically this involves a company which was unquoted being floated but with the original entrepreneur or family retaining a sizeable grip on the management's structure and composition. In effect most shareholders have marketability, and the small number who might face constraints on this because of the size of their holdings retain a significant measure of management control.

It is worth adding that we have in the above largely ignored another dis-tinction, often made, between individual and institutional shareholdings. This is not unimportant, particularly if it can be demonstrated that institutional investors can get better information, operate more efficient portfolios, exercise superior investment skill or respond to different incentives, though none of these suggestions is uncontroversial. But the main control-type distinction is between concentrated shareholding generating ownership control and unconcentrated holdings permitting managerial control. Highly dispersed shareholdings are both compatible with and just as much associated with institutional shareholdings as with individual ones.

Corporate governance structures involving concentrated ownership repre-sentation and/or control in quoted companies of the type for example generally observed in Germany, we refer to (following recent terminology) as *inside control*. Dispersed ownership of quoted companies in contrast we refer to as *outside control*. It should be stressed that day-to-day control in the latter case is by managers and the more traditional term for such a structure is 'managerial control'. This, however, sidesteps the crucial question of how much discretion managers have when dissatisfied shareholders can sell shares, perhaps precipitating a takeover and a change of management. Hence outside control is quite different in form and effect from inside control but none the less provides some type of ultimate control for owners.

The concentrated shareholding we typically find in unquoted companies we term *entrepreneurial control* and, though we will have little to say on it, the typical partnership format we term *joint control*.

Though we will have cause to refer to entrepreneurial control later, most recent analysis and comment has concerned the differences between, and respective virtues and deficiencies of, insider and outsider control systems. That concentration of ownership is a crucial aspect is seen from the fact that of the 200 largest companies in Germany, nearly 90 per cent have at least one shareholder with a stake of at least 25 per cent of issued equity. In the UK in two-thirds of the largest 200 companies no single shareholder holds more than 10 per cent of the equity.[7] In addition, however, another feature of insider control in Germany and Japan is *reciprocal* shareholdings. It is not uncommon for 20 per cent of the shares of a company to be held by other firms in which the company itself holds shares. In the UK such arrangements are virtually non-existent.[8]

These differences in ownership structure and the differences in board composition to which they give rise generate at least three main differences in behaviour or efficiency characteristics. First, they generate quite different agency relations. When one or more principals (shareholders) recruit one or more agents (managers) to act for them, there is a fundamental agency problem in trying to establish a remuneration schedule which will induce the agents to act as the shareholder would want, in a world where the agent's actions or efforts are not fully observable and company performance is the outcome jointly of the agents' input and the state of the world in which they find themselves. In order to ensure the same profit maximization strategy that the principals would themselves pursue, the agents must, as the principals themselves would, keep all of any additional profit arising from additional effort. The principals can only be rewarded, therefore, via a lump-sum payment from the agents (as for example in a franchise arrangement) if the contract is to generate efficient incentives. This, however, loads all risk on the agents, because the principal gets a guaranteed sum in all states of the world. This is not efficient from the risk-sharing point of view, particularly if, as is likely, managers are risk-averse because all their income is linked to their job, whereas shareholders are risk-neutral because they can diversify across a number of companies.[9]

The two key factors in this are information, i.e. how well can the principals observe, monitor and measure the input of agents; and risk, i.e. how well is it distributed across the parties. In principle, inside control will reduce and perhaps even eliminate the information asymmetry. Under outside control this asymmetry entails a need for some signalling mechanisms by which managers can indicate their views of company prospects and in a manner such that share-holders can systematically attach credibility to those views. In practice much of this function appears to be borne by earnings announcements and dividends. The effectiveness of this, and possible distortions to which it gives rise are considered below. Against the informational advantages of inside control the greater concentration of shareholdings reduces the extent to which risk is diversified away, though it does, at the same time, tend to align the risk exposure of shareholders and managers. Where inherent risk is high, for example for small, single product and/or speculative investment companies, the latter effect may well make outside control preferable.[10] But many such companies will not in any event be quoted on any stock market. Where companies are large enough and diversified enough to reduce the need for portfolio-based diversification of risk, and this appears to be the typical case for quoted companies, then the superior informational characteristics of inside control will tend to make it the preferable form of corporate governance.

The second main difference follows directly from the superior monitoring which inside control permits. Because deteriorating performance and its causes can more easily be detected, corrective action can be instigated earlier, can occur more gradually and with shareholders being better informed in the process. Outside control may result in longer delay before deteriorating performance is observed, indeed strenuous efforts may be made to conceal it; a short-, or even medium-term response by shareholders may be difficult or impossible, apart from selling shares; and corrective action if it occurs may well only be via the threat of takeover.[11] Modest or piecemeal restructuring which would benefit shareholders may not be achievable and significant restructuring may not be feasible without ownership change. This is in sharp contrast to inside control where there typically is little if any correlation between industrial restructuring and/or management control on the one hand, and ownership on the other. In Germany, for example, hostile takeover is extremely rare[12] but it is far from obvious that this has been disadvantageous to the performance or development of German industry. Clearly it does not imply that there is no effective disciplinary mechanism for ensuring managerial effectiveness.

The third main difference lies in the consequences of the board structure associated with each type of control. Inside control typically involves the presence on boards of directors appointed by the owners. This means (i) that effective ownership lies largely in the corporate sector itself, whereas most shares in the UK are owned by financial institutions, in particular pension funds, life assurance companies and investment trusts. (ii) Because such directors are *representatives* of other companies they act for organizations which are quite likely to have an ownership stake for many years and perhaps generations. This may well generate a longer-term perspective than in the typical UK or US case where such representation is relatively rare. (iii) The existence of two-tier boards, with the supervisory board having representatives of employees, trade unions and, in many cases, suppliers and purchasers, means that governance reflects a wider group of 'stakeholders' than just owners, thereby reducing the extent of conflict between shareholders and other parties and the inefficiencies in operation to which such conflicts can lead. A broader spectrum of advice is available and this all reinforces the longer-term stability of inside control.[13] In contrast, in the UK emphasis is placed on the protection of shareholders' rights and maintenance of a fair market in those rights. This can directly curtail the dissemination of information to shareholders, because of the need to ensure that none are discriminated against through receiving it later than others (insider dealing), and to employees and others because of the potential for conflict with the owners who alone are represented on the board.

In many respects these differences appear to favour inside control systems. However, to expand on an earlier conclusion, it seems better to conclude that inside and outside control have different strengths and weaknesses. Outside control may well be best where diversification of risk is important, or where there are divergent views on the risk–return characteristics of company investment projects. The superiority of inside control appears to lie in the fact that it is more appropriate to the conditions that actually face most developed industrial sectors, namely diversified companies relying on complex long-term relationships with customers and suppliers, needing to develop and retain skilled labour and attempting to identify and exploit new products and new models on the strength of those relationships and human skills.

Before proceeding, reference should be made to entrepreneurial control in unquoted companies. In most of the above respects these should function in a manner similar to inside control ones. Agency problems are minimized though potentially at some cost in terms of less risk reduction; and monitoring and adjustment of behaviour in the light of performance is likely to be easier and less discontinuous than in outside control. Control lies within the corporate sector and may be exercised in the light of longer-term perspectives and greater stability, though this may well be family-based rather than enterprise-based. Against this there is little if any institutional representation of shareholders other than the owner-managers, and minority shareholders, who may often have received shares through inheritance, constitute a pressure on management to maintain a dividend stream that would otherwise be unnecessary.

If for most large diversified companies inside control is likely to be superior, it must be asked why outside control as found in the UK and US does not gradually disappear, to be replaced by a more efficient form of governance. As we shall see, however, there may well be quite strong economic forces that prevent outside control mechanisms evolving into inside control (though EC deregulation may well push inside control in the opposite direction).

We conclude therefore that there are agency, monitoring and representation problems in the governance structure of the typical UK quoted company which would in principle militate against corporate efficiency. Support for the system of governance of these companies must therefore be based on the view that an active stock market provides an effective discipline on managers to organize and develop their companies efficiently. The primary way in which this will occur is via the threat of takeover as a result of poor performance, and it is to this that we now turn.

III TAKEOVERS AND STOCK MARKET EFFICIENCY

III.1 Theoretical considerations

The pure theory of takeover or merger is both straightforward and familiar. If managers of companies are fully efficient in their use of resources, act only in the best interests of their shareholders and if the stock market is fully efficient in the use of all information,[14] then mergers will occur if and only if they generate increased market power and/or efficiency gains. The latter may encompass rationalization of production, economies of scale or scope[15] in production distribution or research and development, better economies in obtaining finance, reduction of risk, better information about the marketplace or reduction in transactions costs.[16] While none of these gains necessarily require a merger, as opposed to internal growth, in most cases merger is quicker, less risky, avoids temporary increases in excess capacity and/or competitive pressure and can also offer a low-cost way of overcoming barriers to entry.

While some mergers no doubt occur for such reasons, even at a purely theoretical level, we need to take account of at least two other inter-related elements: the assumptions on which the above picture is based may not hold; and there can be other reasons for mergers to occur. With regard to the first, if managers are not fully efficient then, given that the share price reflects this, there is scope for another company capable of improving performance to take over the firm and realize a higher valuation. These *allocational* takeovers, or the threat of them, are seen by many as the prime means by which an efficient stock market in corporate control enforces efficient behaviour on the part of managers. A firm's efficiency, profitability and valuation can drop below their maximum only to the extent that the takeover mechanism has transaction costs associated with it. In most cases, and certainly for all sizeable takeovers, this leeway is likely to be very small.

In a seminal article, Grossman and Hart suggest that the efficient working of this mechanism may be inhibited by a *free-rider* problem.[17] If a bid is conditional upon 50 per cent acceptance, then each of a large number of dispersed shareholders has an incentive to reject a bid for an underperforming firm. If the bid fails, no shares are bought and those rejecting the bid lose nothing. If it succeeds, those who accepted obtain the bid price but those who rejected the bid gain the necessarily still higher value of the shares once the new management have eliminated the inefficiencies. Desirable allocational takeovers may therefore fail, weakening, perhaps substantially, the disciplinary role of the stock market. Grossman and Hart go on to show that this problem can be avoided if, after the takeover, the raider, as the majority shareholder, can use this position to transfer wealth to another company in which it is the sole shareholder, diluting the share price of the acquired company and eliminating the gains from free-riding.[18] But such practices are normally prohibited because, while they might have advantages in relation to the takeover mechanism, they could also be used much more generally to extract wealth from minority shareholders, and it is not in practice possible to distinguish for regulatory purposes between such cases.

Other means of overcoming the problem exist in theory; for example, legislation permitting compulsory acquisition of minority stakes post-merger can prevent free-rider gains.[19] But in the UK this operates only where the main shareholder holds more than 90 per cent, so that in a takeover which gives the acquirer between 50 and 90 per cent of the target company's shares, the free-rider problem remains.[20] Building up a 'toe-hold' stake at pre-raid prices in principle can generate sufficient profit to cover the cost of paying maximum value in the takeover itself, thereby overcoming the free-rider problem, but building up toe-hold stakes prior to a bid is heavily regulated as are sudden early morning mass-share acquisitions ('dawn raids'), individuals acting together ('concert parties') and other ways of trying to acquire sizeable holdings at pre-raid prices. Unconditional bids, and the actions of arbitrageurs (who buy up shares at prices that reflect the fair gamble on a takeover succeeding but then acquire sufficient shares to be able actually to influence the result), also effect the free-rider problem but in practice do not overcome it.[21] There can be no presumption therefore that a market for corporate control, however liquid, flexible or informed about fundamental values, will necessarily constitute a mechanism for eliminating managerial inefficiency.[22]

A further motive for takeover emerges if we no longer assume that share prices always reflect 'fundamentals', i.e. that they do not systematically deviate from the present value of the future cash flows appropriable by the shareholders. Testing this directly is difficult because the discount rate used by shareholders in such a calculation is unobservable, may vary through time and will be dependent on the perceived risk of individual shares. The familiar capital asset pricing model (CAPM) predicts that this risk will depend on the covariance of a share's return with the market portfolio, but this may or may not hold in practice and, even if it does, this may also vary through time, with the expected value again being unobservable.

Indirect tests, based on the efficient market hypothesis[23] (EMH) tended to show that investors utilize all past and current share-price information and that share prices reflect all publicly available information but not generally *all* information, i.e. including privately held ('inside') information.[24] This rather reassuring picture has, however, been increasingly questioned in recent years. At a theoretical level Grossman and Stiglitz have argued that informationally efficient markets are impossible in competitive equilibria.[25] If they did exist then full information on fundamental value could be freely obtained simply by observing share prices, in which case no one would have any incentive to incur the cost of acquiring the necessary information about and from companies themselves. Equilibrium requires that share prices only partly reflect fundamental values, such that there is a return to investigating fundamentals and obtaining superior information which is not fully reflected in the share price. This suggests that in equilibrium there will be some investors (e.g. fund managers in investing institutions) who will engage in acquisition of information and make a superior return sufficient to cover the cost of so doing. One study in the US by Ippolito suggests this result, though most earlier studies in this field found little if any evidence that institutional investors do make higher returns.[26] In any event, share prices are not fully revealing and there can be an incentive to find and buy undervalued companies. These have been termed *merger bargains* or *acquisitional takeovers*.

It might be thought that such takeovers would lead to the correction of the mispricing which gave rise to them but this is by no means certain. If a better informed trader makes a bid, then this signals that the fundamental value is higher than the bid price. Except where one needs to liquidate an investment it is not rational to sell to a better informed investor. While in practice this does not inhibit acquisitional takeovers occurring, it may well interfere with the efficient functioning of the stock market.

At a more empirical level, numerous studies have suggested that share prices fluctuate far more than can be explained by shifts in fundamental values, that share prices over-react to good or bad news; and that fads or speculative bubbles occur from time to time which cause share prices substantially to depart from fundamental values, followed by generally rather sharp correction.[27] While few such studies can be said definitively to demonstrate that stock markets are not efficient in pricing shares,[28] the general weight of them leaves little grounds of support for the efficiency hypothesis.

Nor are such results necessarily in conflict with earlier support for at least some forms of the efficient markets hypothesis. Summers presents a simple model in which share prices are subject to negative serial correlation.[29] This permits excess volatility, over-reaction and bubbles to occur. He then shows that quite substantial valuation errors in this model are consistent with the efficient markets hypothesis not statistically being rejected. As a result, the fact that neither formal tests of the EMH nor presumably, therefore, investors themselves can identify systematic errors which would permit excess returns to be made, does not mean that market valuations do not vary substantially from fundamental values. Finally we may add that, in the absence of fully effective insider trading, however efficient the stock market might be in its use of available information it will not reflect fundamental values where, as is quite likely in many cases, the latter is fully known, if at all, only to 'insider' managers.

In addition to allocational and acquisitional motives for merger as a result of inefficiency and mispricing respectively, a further motive which it appears may play a highly significant role in takeovers is the managerial pursuit of higher salaries, status, power and security through increased size.[30] Many of the problems and costs of growth can be avoided through growth by acquisition, not least those associated with competing market demand away from competitors where growth is via internal expansion in existing markets. The significance of such *managerial mergers* is three-fold. First, the acquisition of an efficient, well-managed company may be preferable to that of an inefficient one because, although the former does not provide opportunities for post-merger gains, it makes the expansion process much easier and less costly. Second, a company's strategy for growth, in terms of acquisition of resources, personnel, technology etc., market positioning, product development and the like, may in many cases most effectively be pursued via takeover. Third, and somewhat ironically, the factors inhibiting the efficient functioning of allo-cative and acquisitional takeovers may themselves be weakened in a world where managerial takeovers can occur. The latter may systematically entail bid prices above fundamental value, because the bidder acquires greater size to compensate for the capital loss. With regard to allocative takeovers, this can inhibit free-riding because in the event that the takeover was a value-reducing managerial takeover, the free-rider loses by not having sold out. With regard to acquisitional takeovers, a bid from a better informed investor no longer necessarily implies higher fundamental value and hence it may be perfectly rational to sell. Shares can on this approach still end up incorrectly valued in relation to fundamentals but at too *high* a level reflecting the premiums which growth-oriented raiders will pay, as opposed to too low a level, reflecting investors' reluctance to sell to more informed bidders. In practice, of course, elements of both types of deviation from present value may exist.[31]

To summarize this section so far, if stock markets are fully efficient in their use of information, and managers, purely pursuing shareholders' interests, are also fully efficient, then mergers may occur in pursuit of market dominance or real efficiency gains available only from the merged entity. In the absence of those conditions, mergers may occur as the result of, and as a discipline on, managerial inefficiency, as a result of misvaluation of share prices, or as a result of managerial pursuit of growth. In terms of social efficiency, we infer first that pursuit of dominance is undesirable, of real efficiency gains desirable; second that stock market mechanisms to correct managerial inefficiency and inaccurate share prices may be inadequate and perhaps substantially so; and third that while growth maximizing has traditionally been seen as undesirable because of the non-profit-maximizing use of resources it entails, we will have cause to question this conclusion later.

In recent years the list of motives for merger has been extensively added to. Historically conglomerate mergers were seen as a means of reducing risk,[32] but this is an 'uneasy case'[33] given that all such gains to shareholders from merging are equally and more cheaply available by holding an appropriately constructed portfolio of shares in individual companies. It may be that small investors cannot diversify sufficiently to achieve this; or that shareholders have less reliable information on what constitutes the efficient combination of companies in terms of risk and return. In addition, a conglomerate firm will typically experience a lower risk of default which cannot be replicated purely

227

by portfolio diversification, and this may also reduce the cost of debt finance. But the strongest motivation is once again likely to be managerial. If managers are risk-averse, with most of their human wealth tied up in the firm they manage, then they have an interest in the survival and stability of that firm which does not apply to an investor holding shares in the firm as part of a diversified portfolio. It may not be possible to recruit managers at all for some high-risk–high-return companies which investors would like to have as part of their portfolio unless the managers have substantial profit-sharing or profit-related remuneration. In terms of traditional concepts of allocative efficiency, mergers designed to reduce managerial risk may well be undesirable. The same, of course, holds if the objective is increased size to reduce the risk of being taken over.[34]

Another motive for merger which has received increasing attention lies in the potential tax advantages. Acquisition of a firm with losses that can be set against taxable profits of the acquirer may generate gains completely independent of any considerations previously referred to.[35] In the US until recently this applied to past losses whereas in the UK it only applies in effect to losses of the acquired 'division' after the merger, though this could still be a significant motive.

In addition as company taxation will result in lower share prices than otherwise, purchase of another company may be a cheaper way of acquiring assets than purchase of new capital equipment etc., even if the former has some associated adjustment costs. Equally, where capital gains tax is lower than income tax on dividends, acquisition through cash offers is a way of channelling funds from the corporate sector to the personal sector at lower net cost in terms of taxation than payment of dividends.[36] Finally, if a merger lowers risk and, as a result, raises the optimal debt–equity ratio, then this also will lead to a tax saving.

Not unrelated to this is the free cash-flow theory of merger associated with the work of Jensen.[37] Cash flow in excess of that necessary to finance all profitable investment opportunities may not all be paid out to shareholders, either because of tax considerations or because managers prefer to pursue their own objectives with these funds. This may to some extent also reflect the need to reduce cash holdings lest they cause the company to become the target of a raid by another company anxious to obtain liquid resources quickly and/or cheaply.

A final reason for mergers which has become a focus of attention recently is the role of takeovers in allowing the owners of a company in effect to cancel or re-write existing commitments.[38] Managers and other employees may find themselves redundant even though prior to the takeover they had a reasonable expectation of, and in some cases a legal contract determining future employment. Assets may be sold, divisions closed, existing contracts with suppliers or customers terminated, investment, training and research and development activity curtailed or halted even though, in the absence of a takeover, these

228

might not have occurred, or have taken place more gradually and in a manner that allowed the other parties involved to adjust to such changes. The incentive for owners to eliminate or reformulate existing implicit commitments arises because initial arrangements between owners, managers and other parties will be made in the light of the then prevailing circumstances and economic conditions. As the latter change, so an information asymmetry builds up between the managers who have better knowledge about these changes and the shareholders who do not.[39] A principal-agent problem emerges and, unless the shareholder can distinguish between poor managerial performance and externally determined deterioration in performance, there is an incentive for a raider who *can* so distinguish to take over the company and generate a new set of efficient contracts appropriate to the changed circumstances. Even if the raider cannot assess the cause of the sub-optimality it may still rewrite any *ex-post* inefficient contracts after a takeover more easily and more readily than the incumbent owners.[40]

There is therefore no shortage of explanations for takeovers, and little reason to presume that they will necessarily or even normally tend to promote greater productive efficiency, superior resource allocation or higher economic welfare for consumers. The incidence of takeovers and their impact depend on the informational properties and asymmetries in the stock market, the accuracy of stock market valuations, the motives, incentives and control of managers, the tax system and organizational arrangements and contracts, as well as the more obvious factors of the scope for synergistic gains and the impact on product market competition.

III.2 Empirical evidence on takeovers

Evidence on the efficiency of the takeover mechanism is of four types: comparisons of pre- and post-merger performance; comparison of the characteristics of acquiring and acquired companies; examination of share price and company valuation effects; and analysis of the effects of anti-takeover provisions in company articles. We consider evidence from both the US and the UK because these represent the two major markets where outside control and hostile takeovers are prevalent.

In the first category, the most thorough recent investigation is that by Ravenscraft and Scherer.[41] Their analysis of 6,000 acquisitions involving 471 corporations in the US between 1950 and 1976 revealed that post-merger performance was generally poor. In the case of roughly one-third of the takeovers, the acquisition was subsequently sold off, generally having had negative operating income in the last year before resale. The profitability of the other two-thirds also declined on average, especially in conglomerate mergers.[42] The only systematic exception was slightly improved profitability where the merging firms were of roughly equal size. These results are consistent with a large number of earlier examinations of pre- and post-bid performance.

In particular Meeks, in a study of 233 acquisitions in the UK between 1964 and 1972, found that apart from the year in which the merger occurred, profitability showed a mild but definite decline.[43]

These results, however, are not necessarily inconsistent with mergers generating gains, if for example the mergers resulted from an expectation of a deteriorating economic environment, the effects of which were partially *offset* by the merger.

A recent study by Healy *et al*. of fifty large mergers in the US between 1979 and 1984 found that, although the ratio of pre-tax cash flow to market value of assets fell on average in the five years after merger, it fell less than industry averages, so that on this measure of performance, which is largely unaffected by accounting conventions, depreciation provisions, tax considerations, etc., the merged firms did relatively better after merging.[44] They also found that this relative improvement is strongest where the merged firms are mainly in the same line of business; that the relative improvement is associated with higher asset productivity rather than higher profit margins; that longer-term expenditure on investment and research and development does not suffer; and that the relative improvement can explain much of the rise in equity value at the time of merger. This, however, obscures the fact that over the five years after the merger, not only is the performance of merging firms lower than before the merger but both cash flow and assets of these firms increase much less than in the corresponding industries. The ratio improves relatively because the merged firms' assets growth is exceptionally low relative to industry average, whereas cash flow is only half that of the industries concerned. It appears likely therefore that these mergers were predominantly in industries where cash flow in relation to assets was likely to decline, and led to a process of retrenchment, i.e. severe restraint on, or contraction of investment in order to improve average operating performance in the face of industry decline.

Turning to comparisons of acquiring and acquired firms, both with each other and with firms not involved in mergers, there is at best only weak evidence that raiders are more profitable and their victims less profitable. Singh found that the latter did have lower profit and growth rates than other firms in the same industry but that the difference was never statistically significant.[45] Size appeared to be the main discriminant with large firms exhibiting a much lower probability of takeover than small or medium sized firms. Within a given size class profitability was significant over a two-year period but only for the highest and lowest deciles. However, over a six-year period firms with below-average profitability were twice as likely to be taken over as those above the average. A later study by Singh provided general further support for the significance of size and only limited evidence of a profitability effect.[46]

Such results lend relatively little support to the view that the main role of the stock market is to provide a forum in which the control of less efficient companies can be re-allocated to more efficient management. Other studies are still more damaging to this view. Levine and Aaronovitch could find no characteristics other than size and stock market assessment to distinguish raiders and victims;[47] and in an analysis of 287 US companies acquired in the period 1962–72, Mueller found that these victim-firms had slightly *higher* returns on capital than either the average for their industry or a control group matched by size and industry.[48] Harris *et al.* found a similar result for 106 acquired US companies in the period 1974–7, though the difference was not statistically significant.[49] More recently, Ravenscraft and Scherer's evidence, based on a sample which includes a substantial number of unlisted acquisitions, also found that acquired firms tended to have higher profitability than other firms and here the difference was quite large and significant.[50] In addition there was no evidence that units subsequently sold off were less profitable prior to merger than those which were held on to. In a somewhat different type of study, Morck *et al.*, using stock market-based measures of return, found that poor performance by a firm was much more likely to lead to takeover if the whole industry was performing poorly, but more likely to result in internal reform if the firm was underperforming the industry.[51] This is consistent with the above in that companies actually acquired would not necessarily be performing less well than other similar companies, and suggests that internal reform triggered by existing shareholders is the main mechanism by which inefficient management is disciplined, rather than the takeover mechanism.[52] Against this, Martin and McConnell found that the pre-bid performance of firms in which the top manager was replaced after the takeover was significantly worse than its industry average.[53] However, this was not true for takeovers where the top manager was not replaced, suggesting that some takeover may be disciplinary on managerial inefficiency but others not. They also found that takeover targets tended to be in industries which were performing *better* than average, further indicating the significance of motives other than the exploitation of incumbent management inefficiency.

As an interim conclusion, the main thrust of these types of study is that the more traditionally assumed motives for takeover provide at best only a limited explanation for the evidence. In particular, takeovers seem rarely to be in pursuit of either significant monopoly power or conventional synergistic effects, and in many cases appear unrelated to the penalizing of inefficient management. Results also tend to exclude significant financing or tax advantages. Rather, three other conclusions emerge. First, following Ravenscraft and Scherer, pursuit of growth, together with 'hubris', i.e. excessively optimistic estimates of what can be achieved as a result of takeover, is one main explanation. The hubris effect is not necessarily implausible. Suppose there are no real gains from takeover but raiders make random valuation errors. If the latter are negative no bid is made but if they are positive a bid is made and the raider overpays.[54] In this situation only a conviction on the part of the raider that he can do better will explain why bids continue to be made. This can to some extent be tested in the light of the share-price movements which takeovers generate (see below). Second, following Healy *et al.*, takeovers may play an important role in defending firms against severe downturns in performance. Post-merger performance still deteriorates but some mergers may permit rationalization which to some degree mitigates the consequences of cyclical or industry decline.

Third, it is also consistent with the results described that takeovers are, to a substantial degree, a means by which companies can pursue not just expansion but strategic development aims, for example, through building up product ranges, geographical coverage, security of supply, wider distribution, etc. None of these need necessarily increase market power, nor provide any conventional economies of scale observable in subsequently enhanced profit performance. Takeovers may merely represent quick, cost-effective and potentially more stable ways of achieving such company development than internal investment programmes. If so there would be no reason to expect acquirers systematically to be more profitable than acquirers, nor to expect that the latter would systematically tend to be less profitable before a bid or exhibit improvement in profitability after a bid. Indeed in many cases an efficient well-run company may be a more attractive target through which to achieve such aims.[55] Thus, while we would not wish by any means to discount all the other motives for merger, a predominant aim may be the restructuring or strategic development of firms operating in an outsider control world where the assets and goodwill of other companies are easily accessible via the stock market. If so, then it is the *strategy of acquirers* rather than the *inefficiency of acquirees* towards which attention mainly needs to be directed.

We now examine the third type of evidence, namely the movement of share prices during and after takeovers, of which there are now a large number of studies. An early study in the UK by Firth found that, on the day a bid was announced, average gains in the target companies' share prices were 22 per cent (though 80 per cent of the firms had exhibited abnormal gains in the month preceding the bid).[56] But the average movement in the bidding firm's share price was a marginally greater *fall*, suggesting a transfer of wealth from the acquiring firm's shareholders to those of the acquiree rather than any net gain. The great majority of more recent studies however, both in the US and the UK, while confirming that the target firm's shareholders gain significantly, indicate that the raider's share price changes relatively little and if anything on balance tends to rise slightly, suggesting net gains of merger even if nearly all of the gain accrues to the shareholders of the target firm. A survey of studies by Jensen and Ruback found that target company shareholders on average gained 30 per cent in tender offers, 20 per cent in mergers and 8 per cent in proxy battles, while raiders' gained 4 per cent in tender offers and nothing in mergers.[57] A major study by Bradley *et al.*[58] of 236 takeovers between 1963 and 1984 found that 95 per cent of target companies and 47 per cent of raiders exhibited positive share-price effects, and that the cumulative abnormal return for target shareholders was 31.77 per cent, for raiders' 0.97 per cent, and in total 7.43 per cent. Factors such as competitive bidding by raiders and the entry of 'white knights' (i.e. an alternative bidder whom the target firm's management perceive as being a sympathetic vehicle for displacing a hostile bid) both tend to eliminate the small acquirers' shareholder gains. There are also some indications that positive bidder returns may have fallen through the 1960s and 1970s, turning negative though not statistically significantly in the 1980s.[59] A study of 1,800 takeovers in the UK between 1955 and 1985 by Franks and Harris generally echoes these results with the bidder gaining either fractionally or by amounts not significantly different from zero.[60] However, it should be noted that a study by Dennis and McConnell found that convertible preferred stock of acquiring firms showed positive gains which, even though common stock exhibited little if any gains, were enough to generate an increase in the overall share value of acquiring firms.[61]

It seems reasonable to conclude that takeovers typically raise the combined share value of the raider and target companies substantially, and that it is the shareholders of the target company who obtain most if not all of that increase. This raises two important questions. First, what are the sources of the bid premium? Bhagat *et al.* found that on average around 10 per cent to 20 per cent of the rise in the target company's share price could be explained by cost savings arising from lay-offs of employees or managers (though in some individual cases this was a complete explanation) suggesting a combination of improved efficiency and rewriting of implicit contracts.[62] Tax advantages, though quite frequent, tended to explain only about 5 per cent to 15 per cent, but were particularly important in management buyouts (MBOs) (often helped by high leverage) acquisitions by partnerships and, unsurprisingly, by companies carrying tax losses. Across the sample of sixty-two hostile takeovers as a whole, 30 per cent of the bid premium was covered by later sell-offs. While this might in part reflect initial underpricing and in some cases was a way of paying off the debt incurred in the original takeover, it appears that much of this was due to the initial takeover, frequently but not always in the form of an MBO, representing an essentially temporary step in the process of reallocating assets from one public company to another in the same industry. Many such sell-offs were part of a process of concentration or reconcentration on core lines of business. As a result a much higher proportion of takeover activity may ultimately be associated with companies' strategic development and/or acquisition of market power than would be inferred from the initial takeover viewed in isolation. In a number of cases, sell-offs were primarily designed to unscramble unsuccessful conglomerate mergers that had been encouraged by abundant liquidity, availability of debt instruments to finance takeovers and lenient anti-trust provisions. More minor sources of the bid premium were overpayment by the raider's management and cutting back on excessive investment out of cash flow by the target company.

Increases in market power and strategic development can to some extent be distinguished by looking at the effect of a merger on the share price of *rival* companies. Stillman's study of rival firms in eleven horizontal mergers found virtually no evidence of wealth increases such as would be expected if the merger, via increased concentration, were to lead to higher market prices.[63] In two other studies Eckbo found some signs of abnormal returns to rival companies' shareholders, but rejected the view that this was due to increased market power arising from the merger.[64] This was based on correlations with the changes in market structure, and on the share response to challenges to the merger under anti-trust legislation. He concluded that the response reflected identification of cost savings in the merger process that were potentially applicable throughout the industry.

A substantial study by Slutsky and Caves, using a somewhat different approach, found that real synergies explained very little of the bid premium, and that financial synergies arising from the opportunity to infuse more capital to a financially constrained or heavily leveraged firm was more important.[65] The existence of a rival bidder tended to lead to higher premiums despite lower opportunities for real gains. Nearly half of the explained variance in bid premiums is associated with the structure of shareholdings (concentration and/or managerial fraction) in the target or raider company, indicating that the market for corporate control does exercise some effect on managers whose activities depart too far from their shareholders' objectives, but also that managers in raider companies tend to overpay in pursuit of growth, especially where rival bidders are present. Cash bids also tended to increase the premium in comparison with share tender offers.

The significance of overbidding in the presence of rival bidders is supported by Franks *et al.* as is a hubris-type belief by bidding managers in previous undervaluation of the target company's shares.[66] Also, Franks and Harris find that not only contested bids but revised bids and the existence of pre-merger equity stakes held by the raider all increase the premium.[67]

The difference between cash and tender offers is significant not only for the bid premium. Travlos found that raiders' stock returns were average for cash bids but negative for stock offers, perhaps because the use of stock rather than cash is a signal that the bidding firm is overvalued.[68] This is consistent with Brown and Ryngaert's finding that more efficient raiders tend to use cash to avoid any undervaluation of shares following a tender offer.[69] This in turn fits with Franks *et al.*'s evidence that post-bid performance tends to deteriorate after tender offers but not after cash ones.[70]

Therefore, overall bid premiums in takeovers appear to have a number of causes, corresponding to a range of previously identified motives, but with the emphasis on the gains from reorganization of an industry's assets, financial synergies, the consequences of managerial growth objectives coupled with overoptimism concerning the benefits of the takeover, and the reduction in agency problems associated with management control.

The second question concerns whether the evidence for increased shareholder wealth in takeovers can be reconciled with the earlier evidence that post-merger performance often tends to deteriorate, and with the evidence on the relative profiles of raiders and target companies. The evidence on post-merger rates of return tend to direct attention away from synergistic, market power or managerial inefficiency explanations, and also those based on tax advantages or contract revision; even though any of these could be consistent with the share-price evidence. A more consistent explanation would seem to be inefficiency in stock market valuations, leading to acquisitional mergers based not on improvements in performance but on buying assets when they are undervalued. The bid would reveal the true value and hence raise share valuation, the effect would be almost totally on the share price of the acquired firm and there would be no post-merger real gains to be realized.

Franks and Harris argue that at least in relation to *failed* bids, acquisitional takeovers can be distinguished from allocational ones because the former, having revealed underpricing of a company's shares, will result in no subsequent reduction in share price after the bid has failed, whereas the latter, being based on synergistic, efficiency or market-power gains that occur only if the bid goes through will, if unsuccessful, be followed by a reversion of the share price to its earlier level.[71] In an analysis of sixty failed bids between 1981 and 1984 they found on average no reduction in target company share prices in the ten months subsequent to the bid suggesting a preponderance of acquisitional mergers. However, as Williams has argued, this may be too strong an inference because a failed allocational bid may galvanize the existing management to improve its efficiency, thus justifying the higher share price into the longer term.[72] In addition, evidence from the US indicates that the target company's share price does eventually tend to drift back down unless another bidder appears, suggesting that there might be efficiency, synergy or market-power gains to be had from merger, though not any particular merger.[73] Moreover, Pound found that the consensus forecast by stock market analysts of standalone earnings of companies involved in mergers did not change significantly at the time of a bid, and in the case of failed bids was largely correct, suggesting that the bid premiums might reflect real gains available from the merger rather than previous misvaluation.[74] Thus mispricing by the stock market, though no doubt part of the explanation for bid premia but no post-merger improvement, cannot be accepted uncritically.

Apart from misvaluation, this survey of the evidence also directs attention towards three other explanations. First, it is entirely consistent with mergers being a key element in the pursuit of growth by managers and in the strategic development of companies. Takeovers motivated by either of these would typically not lead to any post-merger improvement in profitability, but would lead to a rise in the share price of a target company even if its pre-bid price was an accurate reflection of the present value of future earnings. There would still be a preference, other things being equal, for acquisition of an underpriced company, and this might still play some role in the pattern of takeovers, but the main driving force would be expansion, if necessary paying above the present value; and/or strategic development of the raider's products and market position. The continuation of a higher share price after a failed bid would reflect that a target company was still 'in play', in particular if arbitrageurs had taken sizeable positions in the company; but in the absence of a new growth-maximizing bidder, the price would lapse back towards its original earnings-related value.

The second additional explanation that fits these results is Roll's hubris hypothesis, namely that raiders' management systematically tend to over-estimate their ability to manage an acquisition effectively. The bid would reflect this optimism, generating share-price increases concentrated almost wholly on the target company. Post-merger performance would none the less not tend to improve, and failed bids would be followed by share-price declines if it became clear that no one else shared the same confidence concerning the scope for post-merger improvements. We have already seen that the hubris explanation is quite plausible and the evidence so far provides significant support.

Finally, the evidence is consistent with takeovers being defensive moves to avoid some or all of the consequences of increased competition or industrial decline in the future. Share values would rise because of the relative improve-ment in a firm's prospects but post-merger performance would still decline because of the deteriorating economic environment. Target companies would tend to be those most able to help the merged company survive and hence there would no great tendency for target companies to be relatively weak performers.

We conclude therefore that the stock market provides only a limited role in the efficient re-allocation of resources, from less to more efficient management teams. Instead, it mainly provides (i) opportunities for acquisitional mergers as a result of share-price misvaluations, (ii) a vehicle by which management teams can pursue growth objectives and development strategies relatively easily, (iii) a means for achieving retrenchment or greater consolidation in the face of expected downturns in business but, also, (iv) scope for overoptimistic evaluations by managers of the potential which they can derive from assets currently under the control of other managers. While no doubt there are occasions when an outside management can come in and do better, the evidence suggests that more often the outside management merely has less adequate information and, as a result, too optimistic a view of what is possible.

We now turn briefly to the fourth source of evidence, namely that on the effects of anti-takeover provisions in company articles. These include require-ments for super majorities (e.g. 67 per cent or even up to 90 per cent) of shareholders to approve changes in management control; fair-price amend-ments limiting and/or defining the bid price that can be accepted by the firm; staggered board appointments so that at any one time relatively few of the board can be removed; and various types of so-called 'poison pills' e.g. the power for managers in the event of a bid, to issue preferred stock to share-holders with rights attached, the purchase of which by the raider would make the takeover very, perhaps prohibitively expensive. Such provisions, not surprisingly, reduce the probability of takeover and hence help to entrench the existing management.[75] At the same time they give managers greater bargaining power, in the event of a bid, to achieve a higher price. The former effect would tend to lower share prices, the latter increase it. Although the overall effect appears in practice to be small, most evidence to date tends to suggest that the former effect dominates.[76] It is surprising therefore that such provisions are adopted, given that they require majority approval by shareholders. The usual explanation is that management are able to persuade shareholders of the potential for obtaining a higher price from a bid, even though the overall effect on share prices subsequently is negative; and/or that highly diversified shareholders typically just go along with management proposals.[77]

Similar effects may be involved in the negotiation of 'golden parachutes', i.e. very favourable pay-offs to managers if they lose their jobs.[78] These may not in practice be in the shareholders' interests but can be presented as a mechanism for ensuring that managers will not fight a takeover which is in the shareholders' interests simply to defend their own security.

While this evidence is far from conclusive it is in general consistent with the conclusion above that managerial motivation and managerial perceptions are of primary significance in the incidence and effects of takeovers.[79] If takeovers were mainly concerned to obtain efficiency, synergistic or market-power gains then shareholders would have little incentive to approve anti-takeover provisions. If, on the other hand, there is a danger that undervaluations will occur then strengthening management's bargaining position is attractive but share prices should then rise. However, if managers know that efficiency on their part is no guarantee against takeovers motivated by growth, strategic development, retrenchment and/or excessive optimism they will have strong incentives to persuade shareholders to adopt anti-takeover provisions. The resulting fall in the likelihood of takeover will none the less generate a negative effect on share prices.

Overall, therefore, while there is no reason to reject any of the motives for merger that have been discussed, the evidence taken as a whole indicates that the most significant factors are managerial growth and development strategies, restructuring and consolidation, and errors of valuation, primarily over-optimistic ones by acquiring companies' managers, but also to a lesser extent by stock market investors generally. The effects of all this on economic welfare and the associated policy implications we turn to later.

IV THE STOCK MARKET AND SHORT-TERMISM

IV.1 The debate over short-termism

The previous section looked at the motives for, and consequences of, takeover activity in a stock market. We now go on to consider what impact, if any, the existence of outsider control in a dispersed equity market has on managerial behaviour. While part of this relates to evidence on the relationship between share prices and investment, considered later, we start by looking at the most prominent issue in this area, namely the short-termism debate. Many industrialists are quite concerned that the existence of largely atomistic shareholders, be these individuals or institutions, ready to sell at the first sign that share prices might fall, forces managers to adopt unnecessarily short-term time horizons in their investment decisions and profit planning, to the long-term detriment of company performance and indeed the national economy. This situation is often contrasted with the insider control mechanisms in Germany and Japan which allow managers to pursue, and shareholders' representatives to acquiesce in longer-term strategies particularly with regard to research, innovation and product development, which eventually generate much superior performance. Reference is often made to the generally very short time horizons, often three months or less, over which financial institutions' fund managers are assessed, a phenomenon not present in the insider control structure.

Many if not most of those in the financial world strongly disagree. They argue that sensible investment involves identifying companies with high present values, which may reflect short- or long-term profit potential and indeed more generally both. The short time horizons for assessing fund managers are seen as irrelevant because if new information becomes available concerning long-term profit potential this will tend to be reflected in today's share price and fund managers will want to identify and invest in such opportunities now, with the capital gain reflected in the current three-monthly review. More generally it seems rather implausible to many of them that investors, whose only rationale is to identify good profit opportunities, should systematically miss or ignore good opportunities. If this were the case could not *some* investors identify the profit opportunities, invest and hold until fruition and outperform the market?

Economists have until quite recently had relatively little to say on this issue, though there is some evidence that tends not to support the myopia thesis. For example, McConnell and Muscarella found that share prices tend to respond positively to the announcement of planned investment increases and negatively to announced reductions.[80] In similar vein, Chan *et al.* found that share prices tended to rise in response to increases in research and development expenditure in high technology industries even though earnings might decline, and that this effect was larger than a negative effect in low-technology industries.[81] Other studies by Hirschey and by Pakes gave similar results.[82] Such evidence is not conclusive however. If investors do exhibit myopic behaviour then this would tend to inhibit longer-term strategies and associated expenditures from occurring. In some cases firms might find ways of overcoming the problem, *ex-hypothesi*, generating higher investment or R&D *and* a positive share-price response. This would not necessarily imply that there were not many other cases, and perhaps a majority where myopic behaviour prevented managers from taking a longer-term perspective. Also if *managers* for any reason are systematically myopic then again there would be a positive share-price response in those cases, perhaps infrequent, where managers eschew such behaviour.

A study by the Office of the Chief Economist of the Securities and Exchange Commission in the US found that, contrary to what might be expected from myopic behaviour, high R&D companies were no more likely to be taken over than low R&D ones.[83] But here again interpretation is important. It is quite possible that companies which are more likely to be taken over have to cut R&D as the myopia thesis would suggest. This might lower the threat of takeover to the norm but result *ex-post* in the probability of takeover being the same for low and high R&D companies.[84] The only really telling evidence is a study by Muellbroek *et al.* which finds that firms which introduced anti-takeover provisions subsequently exhibited significant *reductions* in their R&D intensity (ratio of R&D expenditure to sales) relative to their industry averages.[85] That firms might introduce such provisions and simultaneously cut R&D is not necessarily inconsistent with the myopia thesis because an increased threat of takeover would cause both to happen; but a significant decrease in R&D after incorporating the provisions does suggest that the stock market values R&D and that managers who are more secure from takeover face less pressure to engage in such risky activity.

Even here some caution is necessary. Over one-quarter of the sample were subsequently the target of a takeover bid. This high proportion suggests that the sample of firms introducing such provisions was heavily skewed towards those which, for one reason or another, were likely takeover targets. The provisions and the subsequent R&D cuts may both have been a response to this, with the former capable of being introduced much more quickly. Muellbroek *et al.* seek to eliminate this explanation by stating that similar results apply to the subset of firms for which no bid was subsequently made, but the fear of takeover may quite possibly have existed throughout the sample rather than in just those actually receiving a bid.

Against these, a very recent study uses earnings and share price data to estimate directly the implicit discount rate investors use for differently dated cash flows.[86] This finds strong evidence that longer term earnings are discounted at rates appropriate to much later returns, indicating substantial myopia on the part of investors.

A rather different strand of literature questions whether a company's share price is of any great significance at all in influencing investment expenditure. Surveys indicate that over half of investors had not altered their discount rate in three years despite equity yields varying between 4.95 per cent and 11.55 per cent. The 1987 Stock Market crash appeared to have almost no effect on investment intentions, being generally regarded as merely the end of a speculative bubble. Mullins and Wadhwani[87] found that Stock Market variables matter more in the US and the UK in determining investment than in Germany or Japan (where they have virtually no discernible effect) once the usual determinants of investment such as output, relative prices, etc., have been taken into account. However, the effect in both the US and the UK is primarily via the debt–equity ratio which probably reflects the information content of this variable in outside control structures. In neither country does Tobin's q (the ratios of stock market value to replacement cost of assets) add any additional explanatory power. The yield on equity, as measured by the dividend yield plus the growth of the dividend, is significant in the UK, though the effect is small, and not significant in the US.

These results are consistent with another study by Morck et al.[88] This distinguishes between the stock market as (i) a passive informant, i.e. managers assume that it reflects the same fundamentals as those which determine investment, and (ii) an active informant. In this case managers use share prices as a source of information. If the latter reflected only fundamentals then they would not influence investment independently but if they are swayed by 'sentiment' as opposed to fundamentals then they can constitute an additional determinant of investment, (iii) a source of funds, so that variations in equity prices influence investment via the cost of equity funds, (iv) a short-term pressure, such that share-price movements can influence investment separately from fundamentals and financing costs. Models (ii) and (iv) may be distinguishable in that sentiment will be more influential at the aggregate level while stock market pressure will be more influential at the level of the individual company.

Morck et al. examine the extent to which stock returns, financial variables and a combination of them add anything to fundamentals (such as sales, cash flow, etc.) in explaining investment. They find that sentiment and finance do have identifiable effects and that the former is primarily a market pressure phenomenon rather than an 'active informant' one; but the effects are quite small. However, interpretation is again very important. If sentiment effects investment which in turn influences sales growth, cash flow, etc., then stock returns may add little to fundamentals in explaining investment even though, ex-hypothesi, they are influential. Some exogenous shocks can systematically lower stock market prices but raise investment opportunities, for example lower capital prices, higher oil prices, etc. The problem also remains that some investments may not occur because of the share-price reaction it would lead to. Thus short-term pressures may exist but for that very reason neither the investment nor the stock price response occurs, which might constitute statistical evidence for short-termism. More generally, it is necessary to establish a full simultaneous investment model which includes stock market activity and the links between it and investment in both directions if short-term pressures are empirically to be identified using this methodology.

To summarize, there are two fundamental problems about identifying myopia statistically, even if it does occur. First, the probability of takeover will vary across firms. Unless this can be controlled for, it is difficult to infer anything from correlations between share prices and longer-term expenditure decisions by companies. But it is difficult to control for the probability of takeover given, as we have seen, that takeovers appear explicable largely in terms of the objectives and strategy of the *acquirer* rather than the efficiency or other characteristics of the target company. Second, and more fundamental, if myopia exists then it is unlikely, except in error, that firms would carry out the longer-term strategies which would depress share prices. If such errors are few then myopia would leave little trace of a negative correlation between longer-term investments and current share price. The more severe the pressure to short-termism the lower the chance of ever observing such a correlation. It is not therefore surprising that the controversy over short-termism should continue to characterize both discussion on the impact of the stock market, and policy debate over whether takeovers should be made easier in order to improve the disciplinary effect on managerial efficiency, or more difficult in order to avoid the alleged dangers of short-termism.

To try to make some progress we next ask whether there are any intelligible and plausible explanations for why rational agents might end up behaving myopically, given that it implies systematic missing out on profitable opportunities. We present four possible models of rational myopia, before linking this up to the literature on corporate governance to see if other evidence can be brought to bear on the issue, notwithstanding the problems identified above.

IV.2 Models of myopic behaviour

IV.2(i) The signal jamming model

The most common line of argument in support of short-termism is based on the existence of asymmetric information in an outsider-control structure. It is assumed that managers have reasonably sound knowledge of their firms' profit prospects and investment requirements, and associated trends in dividends, retentions and other key expenditure variables. There are none the less likely to be sizeable stochastic elements in all of these in the light of the economic environment, competitive pressures, innovative developments, etc. Where ownership is highly dispersed across many shareholders, the latter will have much less detailed and much less good information and, typically, much less incentive for any one of them to improve this situation. In such circumstances the growth of dividends and/or earnings can be used and taken as a signal of the sustainable position of the firm; and it is well known both that managers do try to smooth the dividend stream over time, and that investors regularly use dividends and earnings as a key guide to share valuation.[89] This means that share prices will be very responsive to dividends or earnings and this is perfectly rational given the signalling role that announcement of them performs.[90]

With insider control, actual or suspected share misvaluations are not particularly significant because there is little scope if any for a hostile raider to buy-up shares, but this is not the case with outsider control. Overvaluation brings no penalties but undervaluation increases the threat of takeover, creating a one-way incentive to raise current dividends or earnings even if this is at the expense of longer-term profit. For example, the dividend can be raised by cutting investment but, more pervasively, earnings can be increased by cutting above the line product or process R&D or other longer-term development expenditures, e.g. training, marketing, export market development, etc., or capital investment again because of its associated running costs; by setting higher prices in the presence of switching costs (which will boost short-term profits at the expense of longer-term ones) or conversely by excessive discounting of durable products to generate a short-term profit boost, again at the expense of the longer term. Development of links with suppliers and purchasers, recruitment and maintenance and repair expenditure are all other areas where short-term improvements in earnings can readily be made by cutting back, at the cost of longer-term efficiency.

The stumbling-block in this line of argument has always been the question, if the stock market does force managers systematically to act in these short-termist ways, why don't investors perceive this and allow for it in their valuation procedures? Stein's hypothesis is that they *do* recognize the problem, but managers are subject to a prisoners' dilemma.[91] If managers could coordinate their activities so that none behaved in a short-term manner then there would be no distortion, a situation investors would prefer. But *any one manager* failing to act in this way would be perceived as less effective than all others, because investors know that the dividend or earnings signal is normally distorted and would presume that this was still occurring. There is an equilibrium degree of distortion, which investors can systematically allow for, but from which no one management can depart without poorer performance being inferred. An interesting property of this model, therefore, is that investors can and do infer the 'correct' position, by allowing for the equilibrium distortion, but managers none the less systematically find that some longer-term expenditures have to be foregone if a drop in the share price is to be avoided.

Stein argues that in principle the problem could be solved by investors getting detailed information about firms and their managers, so that they do not have to rely on dividend or current earnings signals, and such activity is of course important. But if shareholders are highly dispersed, as typically they are in an outsider-control structure, then it will often not be worth any one investor incurring the costs of this, but coordination of such activity by investors may well be impractical. Even if some shareholders followed this strategy they would still be exposed to the risk of capital losses in the event of managers ceasing to act short term (because of the response by the other shareholders) unless they could buy most or all of the shares. This implies that there will be less pressure on managers to act short term in companies with more concentrated shareholdings, the advantages of which might offset any increase in risk resulting from a more concentrated holding. It would also be entirely consistent with insider control, *ceteris paribus*, being a more efficient ownership structure.

Three other inferences may be drawn from this signal-jamming model. First, the pressure to act short term will tend to be more serious in relation to less tangible expenditures such as product and process research and development, marketing, building up customer and supplier networks, etc. Long-term investment in some types of plant and machinery may be subject to the same problem, but it will usually be much clearer as to why the investment is being made, what the likely pay-off will be and the risks involved, etc., thereby facilitating the transmission of information to investors without having to rely on signalling mechanisms.

Second, the holding of shares by managers, which is generally thought of as a way of improving the profitability of managers may, in this model, make things worse because the managers have an additional disincentive to carry out longer-term plans which reduce the current share price. Only if managers hold a controlling proportion of the shares, as is typically the case in unquoted companies, will this cease to hold.

Third, such a model casts a different light on some of the empirical evidence described above. If managers are forced to act in such a manner then, as Miles found, they will apply test discount rates to projects that are systematically too high, reducing investment below the profit-maximizing optimum. If such is the case then any increase in investment, particularly in R&D where the problem is likely to be most acute, certainly will raise the value of the company, leading to a positive share-price response. But this in no way implies that short-termism is not present and a constraint on managerial behaviour.

Thus, while there are cases where short-termism may not be a problem, primarily under insider control, i.e. concentrated share holding of quoted companies, and in unquoted companies, Stein's model provides a model of how it can rationally occur under dispersed outsider control and shows how this might be consistent with the relevant evidence.

IV.2(ii) The mispricing arbitrage model

An alternative but not incompatible explanation for short-termism is provided by Schleifer and Vishny.[92] Consider a capital market in which the interest rate equals the rate of return on assets, in which some mispricing of assets may occur, and in which arbitrageurs, who can borrow at the prevailing interest rate, attempt to profit from such mispricing. In the simplest case the arbitrageur is indifferent how long it takes for the mispricing to emerge, because the present value of an investment in an underpriced share is independent of the period necessary for price correction to occur.[93] In practice the arbitrageur faces two risks; that he may need to liquidate early at a time when the mispricing is worse; and that if price correction takes a long time, the fundamental value of the company may deteriorate. Both these risks are greater the longer the time before the share price corrects itself.

There are two main consequences of these risks. First, the cost of funds to the arbitrageur will rise above the rate of return and, second, because the capital market does not have full information on the skill of individual arbitrageurs, it will to some extent credit-ration the latter.[94] As a result, first, the present value of mispricing arbitrage falls the longer the period to price correction, and second, with limited funds there is an opportunity cost of any individual arbitrage operation.[95] These raise the costs of longer-term arbitrage. Because in equilibrium the return to short- and long-term arbitrage must be equal there must be a higher gross return on long term arbitrage, which in turn implies more mispricing of assets whose mispricing is revealed later. Managers, however, try to avoid mispricing because the disutility of underpricing, with its concomitant threat of takeover, is much greater than any utility from overpricing. Managers will therefore systematically tend to avoid longer-term investments where fundamental value is only likely to be revealed after a long time.

Three mechanisms can exacerbate this pressure towards short-term investment. First, arbitrageurs can reduce their cost of funds by demonstrating success, but this may increase the incentive to make short-term gains from short-term mispricing. Second, if arbitrageurs tend to avoid longer-term mispricing because of the higher costs involved then the market pressures towards price correction will be weaker in the case of long term-assets, exacerbating the effects described. Third, if managers do invest in longer-term assets, then there may be scope for a takeover, followed by adjustment to shorter-term investments which reduce the arbitrage costs, making the company more valuable and providing a capital gain for the raider. In this model, therefore, long-term behaviour by managers may lead directly to an increased takeover threat.

As with the signal-jamming model this approach explains how managers may experience systematic pressure to act short term even though investors, in this case capital market arbitrageurs, act rationally. As before the pressure may evaporate if managers have majority control or if there is sufficient inside control to make share-price misvaluations irrelevant. But small-scale managerial share-holdings may again make the situation worse because managers will suffer capital losses if share prices fall as a consequence of long-term investment activity.

IV.2(iii) Sunk costs and externality effects

In recent years there has been growing emphasis placed on the role of sunk costs in determining competitive behaviour and outcomes, and in particular on the incentives to firms to increase sunk costs as a form of strategic entry deterrence. This has also revealed the potential for sunk costs incurred for other reasons, 'innocently' to deter entry.[96] The significance of sunk costs for ownership and control issues, however, has not been addressed.

In a different context there has been revived interest in the potential for investment and other types of expenditure to have externality effects, for example by lowering prices of inputs to other firms hence increasing their profitability, investment and growth, thereby generating faster economic growth.[97] Here again, however, the implications for ownership and control remain unexplored. This section summarizes recent attempts by the author to explore the interactions between sunk costs, various types of externality, the stock market and short-termism.[98] For simplicity we imagine that a firm, in investing in and producing for a market, incurs initial fixed costs which are sunk and subsequently incurs variable costs which are linearly dependent on output. Traditional models have focused on the extent to which firms can obtain strategic advantage in later periods by adopting levels of investment or techniques of production which involve higher sunk costs initially and lower variable costs subsequently. This advantage occurs because, in the event that another firm considers entering the market, the first entrant will consider only its non-sunk costs in determining its price–output strategy whereas the later entrant, having as yet incurred no cost, will have to consider all its costs. This results in a more favourable outcome for the first entrant.

In practice there are numerous other ways in which increased investment today may lead not just to higher profits in the future but to a strategic change in the future terms of competition with other firms. First, higher investment will tend to be associated with a lower average age of the capital stock, more recent technological advance, higher productivity levels and greater competitiveness.[99] This together with consequent higher profits and higher market share will typically generate more opportunities for future competitive activity, including product development, greater market knowledge, greater security of demand and lower financing costs, all of which can put the firm in a strategically stronger position in the future. More generally, following Scott's analysis of the growth process, any investment will typically create new opportunities for investment.[100] The set of profitable opportunities will not therefore in general decline as a result of the taking-up of one of those opportunities, but will be maintained as a result of the investment carried out. High investing firms, which traditionally would be thought to have moved down their investment demand schedule to a point characterized by low returns at the margin and few further opportunities, may therefore find themselves facing new cost-and-demand conditions, new product opportunities, etc., which were not available previously. In some cases opportunities may become available to other firms and there is a straight externality effect of the original investment. In other cases only the investing firm will be in a position to exploit the new opportunities.

This naturally leads on to a second link, via learning-by-doing. In many firms the key to corporate success is not just the right investment decisions nor even

245

just recruitment of the appropriately skilled personnel, though both will be necessary. Of much greater importance will be the often highly specific knowledge of the product and the market and how each can develop relationships with customers and suppliers, the technology and production processes involved and how all these can best be integrated. Where such effects are important (and it is arguable that this is the typical case) investment may create future investment opportunities which cannot be foreseen initially but which accrue only to the investing firm by virtue of the experience it gains, in one or more aspects of the firm's activities from implementing the investment. Whether the latter involves new technology, new products or new markets, development of new skills, or just embodies new employment, production or distribution arrangements, the result may be the creation of new opportunities, previously unforeseen, which are highly specific to the firm concerned, and which can give it a strategic advantage in future competition with other firms.

The consequence of these various effects is that, in principle, any investment expenditure may generate four different types of profit. (i) The excess of revenue over cost in the shorter term as a result of undertaking the investment; (ii) subsequent longer-term profits as a result of maintaining the investment; (iii) additional profits in the longer term as a result of lower cost (or higher revenues) attributable to the initial investment via the new opportunities, learning effects, etc., described above; and (iv) further profits deriving from the strategic competitive advantage which follows from the cost (or other) advantages generated.

We now focus on four crucial characteristics of a sunk-cost investment which has the knock-on effects described and hence the profit profile outlined above. First, managers will find it progressively harder to identify, still less quantify the profit consequences as one goes down the list. The shorter-term conventional profits will typically be assessed in terms of discounted cash flow (DCF) or other cruder types of investment analysis technique. Managers are likely to be aware of the second but they will generally be harder to quantify. The third and fourth may well be considerations that influence their thinking and judgement but, by their nature, these are likely to be highly judgemental, very imprecisely assessed, unquantifiable and often, as a result, much more marginal to any decision.

Second, any such problems may be of an order of magnitude larger for the typical shareholder in an outside control structure. Assessment of any but the first source of profits may be extremely poorly informed, highly speculative and very prone to swings in fashion, sentiment and the like. Even investment analysis of the sort undertaken by financial institutions may find it very difficult to assess adequately, if at all, the longer-term consequences.

Third, the structure of the profit profile means that there will typically be a level of investment beyond which the present value of the profits under headings (i) and (ii) will fall, but the present value of the profits under (iii) and (iv) will still rise. Thus an assessment which largely or wholly focuses on the first or first and second sources of profit will generate lower investment than one which incorporated all elements of the profit stream.

Finally, the higher the level of sunk-cost investment, and the longer the period until the later elements of the profit profile appear, the greater the risk that a negative shock to the firm's economic position will render it vulnerable to losses, a falling share price and perhaps takeover. This will be evident to both managers and shareholders at the time that the investment is made.

The combination of sunk-cost investment and what may be termed *inter-temporal externalities* (which may accrue to other firms but which will in part accrue to the investing firm), together with the resulting profit-and-risk profiles and the problems of shareholder assessment, can generate a situation in which the net present value of the total profit stream of new investment is positive but the share-price response is negative and the risk exposure to negative shocks increased, in both cases reducing the security of managers and inhibiting the investment from occurring. Neither effect will be very pronounced in an insider-control world where managerial security is not greatly threatened, if at all, by a falling share price; but could be acute in an outside-control one where the shorter-term costs and risks of new investment are a more dominant influence on share prices than longer-term externalities.

In practical terms the consequence is likely to be either the omission of the externality effects in DCF calculations or the use of higher rate-of-return hurdles than otherwise, which in turn reduce the present value of the later profits more rapidly. Managers may want to override the more quantitative shorter-term calculations to reflect their assessment of the externality effects but will often be reluctant to do so because of the potential damage to their own security. The result is a systematic tendency for managers to focus on shorter-term returns where share-price fluctuations matter. As before we would expect these effects to be less severe where managers have majority control, or ownership control is concentrated in a small number of relatively well-informed investors.

The crucial and to some extent unifying features of these three models of short-termism are the informational asymmetry that exists between managers and shareholders in an outsider control structure and the generally poor incentives for highly dispersed shareholders to correct this. Given these problems we might expect to see growing institutionalization of shareholdings in financial intermediaries which can specialize in the acquisition of information, and growing concentration of shareholdings in an individual company. There may well be, however, powerful forces constraining such institutions to a 'local' optimum, i.e. profit-maximizing behaviour within the context of current institutions and forms of operation even though different forms of operation might be superior. Typically under outsider control, investing institutions are highly skilled at assessing a large number of companies relatively quickly, in part using the financial signals used earlier, and in constructing and managing optimal portfolios of shares in a range of companies. They will not generally be well equipped to focus on a small number of companies and become involved in their direction such that they can pursue an inside-control strategy. In these circumstances any attempt to shift towards the latter approach may well reduce profits, but the alternative of a wholesale change in both strategy and personnel will be impractical. Thus even if the costs of short-termism outweigh the gains from diversification of risk under outside control, the latter may well rationally persist, perhaps indefinitely.

V MANAGERIAL OBJECTIVES, GROWTH AND THE MYOPIA DEBATE

The previous sections focused attention on the information asymmetry characteristics of outside- as opposed to inside-control mechanisms. We now look at the other major distinction, namely the different locations of power and constraints that emerge from these control structures. We start from what is now the main framework for analysing the economic characteristics of different company control mechanisms, namely the Marris model.[101] This views managers as equating the growth of supply of funds with the growth of demand, the latter ultimately achieved through diversification. The growth of funds is a positive function of the profit rate, while the growth of demand, after some point, is a negative function of it. The latter relationship derives from the lower margins necessary to increase growth through lower prices, higher marketing, more research and development, etc.; and from the tendency, again after some point, for faster growth to raise the capital output ratio as a result of progressively less successful diversification in pursuit of ever faster growth. The equilibrium growth rate can be increased by managers who are assumed to pursue growth for the greater salaries, status and power it affords but this eventually entails lower profitability, higher gearing and/or new equity issues, all of which jeopardize the share price and hence raise the threat of takeover. The basic model is then one of growth maximization subject to a takeover constraint. The extent of this discipline depends on how easy or difficult it is for shareholders to enforce their own objectives, and these enforcement costs will in turn reflect such things as the concentration of shareholders, the availability of ready benchmarks of achievable profitability and the like.

From this perspective two inferences have traditionally been drawn. First, managerially-controlled firms will tend to have higher growth rates but lower profit rates than owner-controlled firms because the latter, unlike the former, will have a direct concern for the profits they receive. Second, anything which reduces enforcement costs and, therefore, in the event of substantial non-profit-maximizing behaviour by managers, makes takeover more likely, will improve resource allocation and economic welfare.

Further analysis has, however, indicated that both of these inferences may well be incorrect. With regard to the economic welfare effects the seminal work is due to Odagiri.[102] He first argues that, in the industrial sector of an

248

economy containing both growth maximizers and profit maximizers, the former will come to dominate, primarily because they will systematically be prepared to pay more for assets than the latter, reflecting the additional utility they get over and above the present value from increased levels of assets. Increasingly therefore we can think of the whole industrial sector in terms of a representative Marris-style enterprise, with the growth and profitability of the sector reflecting the strength of the growth motivation of managers and the extent of enforcement costs. If, as Odagiri argues is the case in Japan, growth motivation is powerful because managers rarely achieve greater salary, status or power through changing companies, and if enforcement costs are high because the stock market offers relatively little disciplinary effect via the threat of hostile takeover then growth will be rapid. If, as in the US, there is a very flexible managerial labour market and a very flexible and effective market for corporate control then industrial growth will be much lower. Similar comments apply to Germany and the UK, respectively.

Empirical support for this view does not rely only on the faster rate of internal diversification and growth exhibited by Japan in comparison with the US and UK. Evidence also indicates that Japan has typically had quite a low profit rate, which at first sight is surprising in such a successful economy, but is fully explicable within the Marris–Odagiri framework; new product development has typically been faster and product life-cycles shorter than in the US, even though this may lower profits prematurely on existing products, because it drives growth; export markets have played a major role in providing growth opportunities, rather than a marginal role in providing profit opportunities; investment and R&D have been much higher and dividends lower in Japan and Germany than in the US and UK; and the refined DCF criteria, test discount rates and disaggregate profit centres so often emphasized in the UK and US investment techniques and management literature are relatively rare in Japan, replaced by criteria relating to market share, future growth, product diversification and innovation.[103]

The paradox in all this of course is that it is *weak or ineffective markets* – the managerial labour market and the market for corporate control – which generate faster growth and higher economic welfare in Japan. The dynamic welfare gains from growth as a result of ineffective markets exceeds any static welfare gains traditionally associated with profit maximization and efficient markets.

Turning to the other inference from the Marris model, namely that owner-controlled firms will be more concerned with profits than growth, this also appears flawed. In a detailed study of large unquoted companies, which were very largely owned, directly or indirectly, by the senior managers, Hay and Morris found that most were if anything more growth-oriented than comparable quoted companies owned by dispersed shareholders and controlled by salaried managers, for two reasons.[104] First, in most cases the managers wished to pass the company on to the next generation. The major threat to this was inheritance and capital transfer taxes, liability for which could force a sale of the company to raise the necessary funds.[105] As earnings and/or dividends were the main determinants of the valuation of the company for capital taxation purposes, there was a strong incentive not to go above a profit rate necessary to finance expansion. Second, these companies, unlike quoted ones in the UK, experienced no threat of takeover if they should decide to go for longer-term, larger-scale and/or riskier projects which might enhance growth and long-term profitability, but which would, for reasons examined in the previous section, generate a potentially dangerous fall in share price if there had been a market for them and substantial non-managerial shareholdings.[106] Empirically it was found that in the 1970s unquoted companies both grew faster *and* were more profitable.[107]

The work of both Odagiri and Hay and Morris serve to strengthen the significance of the Marris framework if not all the specific inferences. Nearly *all* companies are likely to have substantial growth motivation; quoted managerial companies are the *most* subject to disciplinary pressure to maximize profits; and economic welfare is likely to be *highest* where this pressure is weakest.

This view of the ownership-control nexus throws new light on the question of short-termism. At one level it could generate a quite different interpretation of the traditional conflict between managers who believe that investors are myopic, and financial institutions and others who would dispute this. If managers behave as depicted in the Marris model then rather than it being investors who fail to see the desirability of long-term investment which the managers sensibly work to pursue, it is the managers who in pursuit of their own goals try to over-invest, with the profit-maximizing owners having, as best they can, to curb this through selling shares as a response.

While elements of this are almost certainly present, this none the less ignores both the analysis of short-termism in the previous section and the implication of the Marris model drawn out by Odagiri. Consideration of these leads on to a second, more comprehensive interpretation. We start by assuming an optimal investment[108] programme, I^*, which is defined as a set of investment decisions over time, including both short- and long-term investment projects which, in the traditional manner, would maximize the present value of the earnings of the company. The investment programme actually pursued can differ from this for two main reasons. The short-term pressures described in sections IV.2(i) and IV.2(ii) will tend to reduce investment below I^*, to I', because they will systematically tend to discriminate against the longer-term components of I^*. This will, however, raise share prices. Managers will nevertheless want to invest more than I'. This may be because of the potential externalities as described in section IV.2(iii) which are not reflected in the present value but the inclusion of which we equate with the welfare optimum as derived in the Marris–Odagiri approach. However, the more powerful reason may well be the pursuit of managerial objectives which are helped by higher investment expenditure and greater growth. These forces may, if unfettered, raise investment partly towards or even beyond I^*. Thus, in an outside-control world where takeover is easy, investment may well fall short of I^*. At the other extreme a highly developed insider-control structure is likely to see investment approach I^*. The crucial element stemming from this analysis is that in the case of outside control, if takeover opportunities are limited, the relatively unfettered pursuit of growth by managers for their own purposes may well be welfare *enhancing* because it tends to offset the reduction in investment below I^* caused by outside control and therefore tends to generate an investment programme nearer to I^*. It need not be the case that managers have any greater insight into the externality effects of, or incentives to obtain, these benefits, though in practice both may be true. Rather it is that weak control of managerial pursuit of growth leads to the type of investment programme which generates these effects, whereas tight restrictions on such activities would prevent them being realized.

Within this framework, managers operating under an outside-control structure will tend to view investors as creating short-termist pressures which depress investment below the level they wish to pursue, and below I^*. Investors, however, will see managers as trying to invest beyond the level which maximizes their share price. Insider control then has three separate advantages. First, it tends to eliminate short-term pressures stemming from signal-jamming and arbitrage, raising actual investment, I, above I'. Second, the weakness or absence of the takeover mechanism permits more scope for managerial objectives to raise I above I' towards I^*. Third, in as far as inside control permits greater recognition of, and ability to appropriate externality effects, it directly encourages I to approach I^*. Thus the pursuit of managerial objectives, though distorting activity from conventional profit-maximizing levels, offsets the distortions due to short-termism and tends to encourage investment with externality effects of the type elaborated upon above.

VI TOWARDS EMPIRICAL TESTING

As against the view that systematic short-termist behaviour is not plausible, and that the evidence is against it, we have seen that there are a number of ways in which it might emerge, and that such evidence as exists is in no way inconsistent with short-term pressures on managers arising from outside control. But it must be emphasized that neither of these steps actually substantiates the existence of myopic behaviour on the part of either investors or managers. Nor at present does extensive evidence exist. This section looks briefly at related studies to see what light they throw on this.

Reference has already been made to the work by Hay and Morris which showed unquoted companies investing more, growing faster and generating more profits than equivalent quoted ones in the UK, and this is important evidence that outside control may not be an optimal mechanism for generating maximum economic performance.[109] There are, however, two caveats to this.

First, more recent work by Hay and Morris, updating their earlier study, found that, while similar results held through the recession of the early 1980s and up to around 1983–4, the difference in performance declined and, in the major upswing of the later 1980s, reversed.[110] This may not necessarily undermine the view that outside control generates short-term pressures which reduce performance because there are indications in the data that unquoted companies exhibit more stable performance, experiencing less of a decline in recessions but less improvement in an expansionary phase. But attempts to identify this explicitly measuring the *persistence* of performance give ambiguous results.[111] There are signs of slightly greater persistence in unquoted companies over three years but the difference is small, and from one year to the next it is quoted companies that exhibit greater persistence.

The second caveat is that we cannot assume that any difference in performance between quoted and unquoted companies stems only from the control problems inherent in outside control, still less that it is short-termist problems. Though both assumptions are plausible, there are other differences, most notably that in most unquoted companies the majority if not all of the shares are owned by the managers or their associates. This alignment of motives of managers and owners may have an advantage quite separate from any resulting from the absence of a ready market in ownership rights. While comparisons of quoted and unquoted companies offer some insights, as of course do comparisons of outside control with inside control as found in Germany and Japan, conclusive evidence for, or indeed against, short-term pressures being generated by outside control remains absent.

A few points can, however, be identified in recent work which while not explicitly concerned with short-termism none the less focus on the two factors which we initially identified as important, i.e. shareholder concentration and managerial shareholdings, but in relation to companies quoted on the US or UK stock markets and therefore subject in principle to outside control. In the UK, Leech and Leahy obtained data on share holdings for a sample of 470 quoted companies, 325 of which were in *The Times 1000* list of the UK's largest companies and covering 32 per cent of companies on the London stock exchange.[112] They then split this sample into 'owner-controlled' companies where shareholder concentration was sufficient to give them effective control, and 'managerially-controlled' companies where shareholder concentration was insufficient. In practice, as they point out, it is very difficult to say what degree of concentration of shareholding is necessary to locate effective control with the shareholders rather than the managers, and they carry out all their analysis with six different measures, three relating to the size of the largest shareholder and three, using earlier work by Cubbin and Leach, relating to the probability that the largest shareholder could, given certain assumptions, obtain majority support in any future contested vote.[113] Allowing the data to determine which measure statistically gives the best results they found that on average 'owner-controlled' companies generated 1.89 per cent higher margins, 4.54 per cent higher return on shareholder's capital, 5.06 per cent per annum faster growth of sales and 10.59 per cent per annum faster growth of net assets. They were also associated with higher company valuation and lower salary of the highest paid director but these were not quite statistically significant. While the higher profitability is not surprising the substantially higher growth performance suggests that the reduced threat of short-term takeover pressures as a result of concentrated share ownership permitted these companies to pursue longer-term strategies which eventually generate higher profits as well.

Here again there are two caveats. First, Leech and Leahy also include specific measures of shareholder concentration and the preferred measure is associated with lower valuation, lower profit margins and lower assets growth. However, because concentration and control are included in the same equations this is an association, *given* the control type. On the preferred control definition, with regard to the negative effect on growth, 86 per cent of the sample are classified as managerially controlled. Thus, *given* that concentration is insufficient to shift control from the managers, and given therefore that the problems of outside control are likely to be at their most acute, a higher concentration of shareholding to some degree inhibits managerial pursuit of growth because it is easier for a few shareholders to sell shares and thereby generate a takeover threat. The lower margins and valuations of managerially-controlled companies, when shareholder concentration is higher, may reflect parallel short-term pressures that inhibit longer-term profitable opportunities, but could also indicate the Japanese situation where greater freedom to pursue longer-term strategies, though welfare enhancing, is at the expense of persistently lower margins.[114]

The second caveat is that, while on their preferred definition of owner control based on a probabilistic voting model, the great majority of quoted companies are managerially controlled, none the less in 91 per cent of Leech and Leahy's sample, the largest shareholder held over 5 per cent of the shares; in 54 per cent, the largest three shareholders *together* had a controlling interest; and in all but one, the largest ten had majority control. If these small groups acted together, a matter on which there is no evidence or data, then much tighter ownership control would be possible. Given the advantages of owner control, this cannot be ruled out. Against this, it is not clear that Leech and Leahy would find the results that they do if this coalition potential were being exploited on an appreciable scale.[115]

Comparable studies in the US do not exist. But a study by Holderness and Sheehan compared the performance of quoted companies with a majority shareholder (a condition that applied to only 5.3 per cent of Leech and Leahy's sample) with that of matched pairs of quoted companies exhibiting dispersed shareholdings.[116] This found much higher levels of capital investment amongst corporations with company majority holdings, much higher advertising expenditures amongst individual majority holders and much higher research and development expenditure in both groups than their dispersed shareholding counterparts. However, these differences were in part due to an outlier with median differences tending to be much smaller (though all still in the same direction) and in some cases not statistically significant. In a different type of study, Wruck found that on average a public sale of shares, which typically increases the dispersion of shareholdings, resulted in a negative average abnormal return, whereas private sales, which typically increase the concentration of shareholdings, resulted in a 4.5 per cent positive average abnormal return.[117] There is a significant range of concentration over which the effect of the latter is negative, but this may reflect management purchases and growing management entrenchment which would permit longer-term and/or more growth-oriented strategies but reduce share valuation.

This leads on to the other area which has been examined, namely the effect of managerial shareholdings. A study by Masson and Madhavan found that the value of a firm rose on average with managerial shareholding.[118] Morck *et al.* found that increases in management shareholdings up to 5 per cent of the total and above 25 per cent raised stock market valuation (as measured by Tobin's q) but lowered it in the 5–25 per cent range.[119] They interpret the positive effect up to 5 per cent as reflecting increasing alignment of shareholder and management interests, and the negative effects from 5–25 per cent as reflecting increasing managerial entrenchment, dominating any incentive alignments. Other evidence in both the US and the UK are not consistent with this non-linear relationship[120] but, even if overall there is a positive relation between managerial shareholdings and valuation, this unfortunately does not help much in examining myopia. Higher valuation despite, or indeed because of, the lower threat of takeover would be entirely consistent with the short-termist thesis, but it would not be rejected even if valuation fell, if the stock market was indicating by this its lack of recognition of the longer-term investment opportunities now able to be exploited. It is the impact of managerial share-holding on investment, both tangible and intangible, and on growth which needs to be focused upon, with stock market valuation being a derivative consideration. Indeed, paradoxically, if liquid stock markets are myopic then higher managerial shareholdings in such markets may *exacerbate* the problem because managers not only face a *constraint* on longer-term strategies but an *incentive* not to pursue them.

Overall, therefore, there is some support for the view that more concentrated share ownership generates better performance in quoted companies if it is sufficient to generate ownership control, such that shorter-term pressures arising from the dispersed sale of shares are weakened. But the specific relation-ships between shareholder concentration and managerial shareholdings on the one hand, and myopia, investment and growth, and stock market valuation on the other, remain unclear. That myopia *can* occur is now well established. Identifying its extent needs further data and analysis.

VI CONCLUSIONS

Ownership of corporations in the form of equity shares owned by investors and traded on open markets, such as exists in the UK, is one (but only one) of a number of forms of ownership. We have looked at reasons for believing that the information flows and incentive effects associated with such institutional arrangements may create significant problems for companies which, at least in the circumstances in which many UK quoted companies find themselves, are potentially detrimental to corporate performance. Detailed review of the evidence on takeovers suggests, first, that a market in corporate control may play an important role in permitting or facilitating corporate restructuring, retrenchment and the pursuit of corporate strategies. But evidence from other countries suggests that this is not the only institutional arrangement able to provide such opportunities. Hostile takeovers in the UK appear to provide what in several other industrial economies is provided by internal restructuring, implemented administratively. Second, the stock market does not provide a particularly strong, effective or efficient mechanism for disciplining poor managerial performance or creating incentives to correct the latter, even though there can be no doubt that it has some such effects. In addition the stock market frequently exhibits valuation errors both by investors and acquiring companies, particularly overoptimistic valuations by the latter. These can create opportunities for, or generate takeover activity which has zero or negative effects on company performance.

With regard to the question of whether trading of equity on a liquid stock market generates short-term pressures on companies which prevent them pursuing longer-term welfare-enhancing strategies, it has previously been argued that this is theoretically implausible and rejected by the evidence. However, we have seen, first, that there are a number of reasons why these pressures might systematically occur in developed stock markets. These revolve around the problems of transmitting signals to investors in outside control systems; arbitrage processes coupled with the asymmetric effects of under- and overvaluation; the role of sunk costs, risk and inter-temporal externalities; and the dynamic gains from managerial growth strategies which may offset some or all of any short-term pressures generated by the stock market. All of this is consistent with the generally superior performance of companies, both in the UK and abroad, which are not subject to the economic effects of public quotation on a stock exchange. Concentrated shareholdings which generate inside control reduce the information asymmetry problem, reduce therefore the need for signalling mechanisms which can create short-termist pressures, minimize the significance of the mispricing of shares, make negative shocks more survivable and reduce the threat of long-term implicit contracts being invalidated. Above all, they provide a context in which longer-term growth-oriented strategies can be pursued without the threat of takeover which would otherwise inhibit them.

Second, the limited evidence available is insufficient to reject short-termism. If myopia does exist then the longer-term investments which would depress share prices and generate a confirmatory negative relation between them are precisely the ones that firms will systematically avoid. Against this, direct estimates of the discount rates used by investors suggest that short-term pressures do exist, though the precise reasons still remain unclear. To arrive at a definite conclusion will require further analysis, in the light of the theories we have examined, of the inter-relation between ownership structure, investor and management behaviour and company performance measured not only by profitability but by investment, innovation and growth.

In the meantime, policy can be based only on our present state of knowledge. This suggests, at a minimum, greater scepticism towards the view that a highly developed stock market and ready scope for hostile takeover are bound to improve industrial efficiency overall. Rather it indicates leaning more towards greater constraints on such activity, either relying more on the pursuit of growth by managers to provide longer-term efficiency gains, and/or encouraging greater ownership concentration, the development of structures which bring about more direct ownership involvement in companies, and greater emphasis on internal monitoring systems, all substantially less constrained by external stock market pressures than is the case at present. In the context of current growing European integration, this suggests governments should be wary of a process of harmonization in relation to equity markets if it involves deregulation designed to encourage more extensive, more open and more liquid equity markets such as exist already in the UK. There is little evidence that this is necessary, still less that it is sufficient to promote corporate efficiency or long-term economic growth.

NOTES

1 This paper is one of several resulting from research into the dynamic efficiency characteristics of companies and their determinants, financed by the Economic and Social Research Council grant no. L102251013.

2 For an elaboration and quantification of these characteristics see D. Hay and D. Morris, *Industrial Economics and Organisation* (Oxford University Press) 1991, pp. 273–81.

3 R. Coase, 'The nature of the firm', *Economica*, n.s. vol. 4 (1937), 386–405.

4 While the location of ownership and of managerial control of companies in the UK may appear obvious, there is considerable uncertainty and some semantic confusion about the concept of corporate control. Also, while legal title to ownership may generally be clear (though even this is problematic in some non-trivial cases such as insolvency) the discretionary powers which ownership provides depend heavily on the legal and institutional arrangements surrounding patterns of ownership. For a detailed analysis of the concepts of ownership and control, see D. Hay, D. Morris, G. Liu and S. Yao, *State-owned enterprises and economic reform in China* (Oxford University Press) 1993, ch. 12. In the context of ownership reform, in China and other economies in transition, the concepts of ownership and control are far from

clear-cut, but the analysis of them is equally applicable to Western capitalist economies.

5 For a detailed analysis of the ownership and management structure of unquoted companies in the UK, see D. Hay and D. Morris, *Unquoted Companies* (Macmillan) 1984.

6 The crude capital asset pricing model (CAPM) suggests that *all* investors rationally should hold the *same* portfolio of shares, albeit in differing ratios to their so-called riskless holding of interest-bearing bonds, depending on their risk preferences. However, different companies might provide the same risk and covariance with the rest of the market as each other so that portfolios which are identical from the point of view of the model might contain different companies' shares. For a description of the CAPM, problems with it and empirical testing of it, see Hay, Morris (1991: 499–505).

7 See J. Franks and C. Mayer, 'Corporate control: a synthesis of the international evidence', 1992 mimeo.

8 See W. Kester, 'Industrial groups as a system of contractual governance', *Oxford Review of Economic Policy*, 8, no. 3 (1992), 24–44.

9 For a formal statement of the principal-agent problem, and possible resolutions of it, see Hay and Morris (1991: 311–17).

10 For example, the strength of small biotechnology companies in the US and UK may be partly attributable to this. More speculatively, outside control may have some advantages in economies more exposed to fluctuations and/or external shocks. For example, the strength of small biotechnology companies in the US and UK may be partly attributable to this.

11 To use the useful but often overlooked approach of Hirschman, inside control permits a 'voice' option if performance is poor, i.e. complaint, investigation and adjustment without severing formal or informal contracts, whereas outside control tends to generate an 'exit' response, sale of shares and severance of the economic relationship involved. As Hardie points out, the set of information flows and decision possibilities in inside control are much richer because they do not have to be standardized, whereas outside control regimes require established accountancy procedures and reporting conventions, within which it may be much more difficult to convey idiosyncratic information. See J. Hardie, 'Comment', on J. Franks and C. Mayer, 'Takeovers', *Economic Policy*, (1990), 191–223.

12 Franks and Mayer report that there have been only four hostile takeovers in Germany since the Second World War. See Franks and Mayer (1992).

13 See T. Jenkinson and C. Mayer, 'Corporate governance and corporate control', *Oxford Review of Economic Policy*, 8, no. 3 (1992), 1–10.

14 The notion of stock market efficiency is considered in more detail below. Here full efficiency implies that all formation available at any time, including evidence of systematic errors in the past, is used to determine share prices. The latter therefore do not systematically err from the present value of future earnings, there are no share 'bargains' to be had and no methods by which any investor, on the basis of 'inside' or 'outside' information, can systematically beat the market index.

15 Economies of scope occur when two products are related such that the marginal cost of producing one is dependent on the level of output of the other.

16 See Hay and Morris, (1991: ch. 14) for a fuller discussion of most of these issues. For discussion of the information advantages of horizontal mergers in a stochastic market see E. Gal-Or, 'The informational advantages or disadvantages of horizontal mergers', *International Economic Review*, 29 (1988), 639–61. While merging firms generally gain from greater precision of information and the reduction in the number of rivals whose behaviour must be predicted, they only

gain from consequent changes in responsiveness to information if competition is of Bertrand form, i.e. in prices. In Cournot (quantity) competition, there is no such incentive to merge.

17 S. Grossman and O. Hart, 'Takeover bids, the free-rider problem and the theory of the corporation', *Bell Journal of Economics*, 11 (1980), 42–64.

18 It can be shown that if $d > C/n$ where d is the dilution per share, C is the costs of takeover and n is the number of shares in total, then provided that shareholders in the largest company expect dilution, there will be no free-rider problem.

19 See G. Yarrow, 'Shareholder protection, compulsory acquisition and the efficiency of the takeover process', *Journal of Industrial Economics*, 34 (1985), 3–16.

20 Many bids are made conditional on 90 per cent acceptance, but reserve the right to reduce this figure. The raider generally cannot, and would not wish to pre-commit to this, given that 50.1 per cent gives control.

21 See Hay and Morris (1991: 516).

22 In this context 'inefficiency' covers both underperformance and pursuit of alternative objectives.

23 For the seminal work in this area see E. Fama, 'Efficient capital markets: a review of theory and empirical work', *Journal of Finance*, 25 (1970), 380–423.

24 For a recent survey of this evidence see E. Fama, 'Efficient capital markets II', *Journal of Finance*, 46 (1991), 1575–617.

25 See S. Grossman and J. Stiglitz, 'The impossibility of informationally efficient markets', *American Economic Review*, 70 (1980), 393–408.

26 See R. Ippolito, 'Efficiency with costly information: a study of mutual fund performance 1965–84', *Quarterly Journal of Economics*, 104 (1991), 1–23; W. Sharpe, 'Mutual fund performance', *Journal of Business*, 39 (1966), 119–38; M. Jensen, 'The performance of mutual funds in the period 1945–1964', *Journal of Finance*, 23 (1968), 389–416.

27 For a survey of work on the excess volatility approach see R. Shiller, 'The volatility of stock market prices', *Science*, 235 (2 January 1987), 33–7. On the over-reaction hypothesis, fads and bubbles, see W. de Bondt and R. Thaler, 'Does the stock market overreact?' *Journal of Finance*, 40 (1985), 793–805; W. de Bondt and R. Thaler, 'Further evidence on investor overreaction and stock market seasonality', *Journal of Finance*, 42 (1987), 557–81; O. Blanchard and M. Watson, 'Bubbles, rational expectations and financial markets', in P. Wachtel (ed.), *Crises in the Economic and Financial Structure* (Lexington), 1982; B. Diba and H. Grossman, 'On the inception of rational bubbles', *Quarterly Journal of Economics*, 102 (1987), 697–700; R. Flood and R. Hodrick, 'Asset price volatility, bubbles and process switching', *Journal of Finance*, 41 (1986), 831–42; K. West, 'Bubbles, fads and stock price volatility tests: a partial evaluation', *Journal of Finance*, 43 (1988), 639–56.

28 Dividends may be smoothed by managers to reflect only sustainable earnings changes, resulting in dividends being more damped than the price of the shares which entitle an investor to these dividends. See T. Marsh and R. Merton, 'Dividend rationality and variance bounds tests for rationality of stockmarket prices', *American Economic Review*, 76 (1986), 483–98. Also, in response, R. Shiller, 'The Marsh–Merton model of manager smoothing of dividends', *American Economic Review*, 76 (1986), 499–503. Bubbles could be the result of rational shifts in expected returns. See E. Fama and K. French, 'Business conditions and expected returns on stocks and bonds', *Journal of Financial Economics*, 25 (1989), 23–49. For more explicit rejection of the efficient markets hypothesis see B. Lehmann, 'Fade, martingales and market efficiency', *Quarterly Journal of Economics*, 105 (1990), 1–28.

29 L. Summers, 'Does the stock market rationally reflect fundamental values?', *Journal of Finance*, 41 (1986), 591–601.

30 For the main analysis of these motives and their effect on the economic behaviour and performance of firms, see R. Marris, *The Economic Theory of Managerial Capitalism* (Macmillan), 1963. For a summary and assessment see Hay and Morris (1991: ch. 10).

31 Note that even if allocational and acquisitional takeovers become fully efficient in this way this by no means guarantees resource allocation efficiency in the economy as a whole. Assets may still be transferred from more efficient to less efficient but growth-maximizing managers. See below, however, for potential offsetting mechanisms.

32 Unless there is perfect positive correlation between the earnings streams of two firms, their merging will always reduce the ratio of the standard deviation of earnings to their mean.

33 See H. Levy and M. Sarnat, 'Diversification, portfolio analysis and the uneasy case for conglomerate mergers', *Journal of Finance*, 25 (1970), 795–802.

34 That larger size does in general reduce the probability of being taken over is one of the few empirical results in this field which finds almost universal support. See the discussion of empirical studies below.

35 See, for example, C. Hayn, 'Tax attributes as determinants of shareholder gains in corporate acquisitions', *Journal of Financial Economics*, 23 (1989), 121–53. This shows that loss carry-forwards and expiring tax credits are significant attributes of target firms in the US. In addition, mergers are more likely to be completed (or in some cases will only be completed) where the tax liability on gains from the sale of equity are deferred, usually as a result of the bid being a share rather than a cash offer. These results are consistent with, and may offer some partial explanation for, the widely observed fact that much if not all of the investor wealth gains in a merger accrue to the shareholders of the acquired firm. (This is discussed later in the chapter.) It is similarly consistent with increased merger activity in boom periods when successful firms typically have higher tax liabilities.

36 See 'Takeover activity in the 1980s', *Bank of England Quarterly Bulletin*, 29 (1989), 78–85. If such considerations were important, they are unlikely to be so now, given recent changes in relative rates of personal taxation of income and capital gains.

37 M. Jensen, 'Agency costs of free cash flow, corporate finance and takeovers', *American Economic Review*, P&P 76 (1986), 323–9.

38 See, for example, J. Franks and C. Mayer, 'Capital markets and corporate control: a study of France, Germany and the UK', *Economic Policy*, 10 (1990), 191–231.

39 See D. Scharfstein, 'The disciplinary role of takeovers', *Review of Economic Studies*, 55 (1988), 185–99.

40 This has important effects on what commitments are possible *ex-ante*. In addition the forms of legal contracts will reflect the threat of takeover and influence the probability of takeover.

41 D. Ravenscraft and F. Scherer, *Mergers, Sell-offs and Economic Efficiency* (Brookings Institution) 1987.

42 A detailed examination of the share price movements of thirteen leading conglomerates indicates that, contrary to general perception, they did not make higher returns for their shareholders than other companies. There is no inconsistency therefore between their performance and returns to shareholders. See Ravenscroft and Scherer (1987: 207–10).

43 G. Meeks, *Disappointing Marriage: A Study of the Gains from Merger* (Cambridge University Press) 1977. For a survey of other supporting results see Hay and Morris (1991: 524–5)

44 P. Healy, K. Palepu and R. Ruback, 'Does corporate performance improve after mergers?', *Journal of Financial Economics*, 31 (1992), 135–75.

45 A. Singh, *Takeovers* (Cambridge University Press) 1971.

46 A. Singh, 'Takeovers, economic natural selection and the theory of the firm', *Economic Journal*, 85 (1975).

47 P. Levine and S. Aaronovitch, 'The financial characteristics of firms and theory of merger activity', *Journal of Industrial Economics*, 30 (1981–2), 149–72.

48 D. Mueller, 'The United States, 1962–72', in D. Mueller (ed.), *The Determinants and Effects of Mergers* (Oedgeschlager, Gunn & Hain) 1980.

49 R. Harris, J. Stewart and W. Carleton, 'Financial characteristics of acquired firms', in M. Keenan and L. White (eds), *Mergers and Acquisitions: Current Problems in Perspective* (Lexington) 1982.

50 D. Ravenscraft and F. Scherer (1987). The inclusion of unlisted companies does, however, introduce additional problems of valuing assets.

51 R. Morck, A. Shleifner and R. Vishny, 'Alternative mechanisms for corporate control', *American Economic Review*, 19 (1989), 842–52.

52 They also found that internal reform was more likely if the firm was managerially controlled, but takeover more likely if the firm was effectively run by the founder or some other individual entrepreneur. The effectiveness of internal reform processes is considered further below.

53 K. Martin and J. McConnell, 'Corporate performance, corporate takeover and management turnovers', *Journal of Finance*, 46 (1991), 671–87.

54 R. Roll, 'The hubris hypothesis of corporate takeover', *Journal of Business*, 59 (1986), 197–216.

55 In an interesting 'comment' on the article by Franks and Mayer (1990), Malinvaud argues that many takeovers appear not to be motivated by considerations of poor target company performance.

56 M. Firth, 'The profitability of takeovers and mergers', *Economic Journal*, 89 (1979), 316–28.

57 M. Jensen and R. Ruback, 'The market for corporate control: the scientific evidence', *Journal of Financial Economics*, 11 (1983), 5–50.

58 M. Bradley, A. Desai and E. Kim, 'Synergistic gains from corporate acquisitions and their division between the stockholders of target and acquiring firms', *Journal of Financial Economics*, 21 (1988), 3–40. See also P. Malatesta, 'The wealth effect of merger activity and the objective functions of merging firms', *Journal of Financial Economics*, 11 (1983), 155–81, for further support.

59 See G. Jarrell, J. Brickley and J. Netter, 'The market for corporate control: the empirical evidence since 1980', *Journal of Economic Perspectives*, 2 (1988), 49–68.

60 J. Franks and R. Harris, 'Shareholder wealth effects of corporate takeovers: the UK experience 1955–85, *Journal of Financial Economics*, 23 (1989), 225–49. In addition, Franks *et al.* have shown that the negative abnormal post-merger performance found in some studies may be due to the use of incorrect benchmarks for assessing risk in the estimation of abnormal returns. See J. Franks, R. Harris and S. Titman, 'The post-merger share price performance of acquiring firms', *Journal of Financial Economics*, 29 (1991), 81–96.

61 D. Dennis and J. McConnell, 'Corporate mergers and security returns', *Journal of Financial Economics* 16 (1986), 143–87.

62 S. Bhagat, A. Schleifer and R. Vishny, 'Hostile takeovers in the 1980s: the return to corporate specialization', *Brookings Paper on Economic Activity* (Microeconomics) 1990, 1–84.

63 R. Stillman, 'Examining antitrust policy towards horizontal mergers', *Journal of Financial Economics*, 11 (1983), 225–40.

64 B. Eckbo, 'Horizontal mergers, collusion, and stockholder wealth', *Journal of Financial Economics* (1983), 241–73; B. Eckbo, 'Mergers and the market concentration doctrine: evidence from the capital market', *Journal of Business*, 58 (1985), 325–49.

65 A. Slutsky and R. Caves, 'Synergy, agency, and the determinants of premia paid in mergers', *Journal of Industrial Economics*, 39 (1990–1), 277–96.

66 J. Franks, R. Harris and C. Mayer, 'Means of payment in takeovers: results for the UK and US', CEPR Discussion Paper 200 (1987).

67 Franks and Harris (1989). Bid premiums also appear to have jumped in 1973–4 as a result of the oil shock, more volatile economic considerations, etc., which increased the heterogeneity of investors' expectations. See K. Nathan and T. O'Keefe, 'The rise in takeover premiums: an exploratory study', *Journal of Financial Economics*, 23 (1989), 101–20.

68 N. Travlos, 'Corporate takeover bids, methods of payment and bidding firms' stock returns', *Journal of Finance*, 42 (1987), 943–64.

69 D. Brown and M. Ryngaert, 'The mode of acquisition in takeovers: taxes and asymmetric information', *Journal of Finance*, 46 (1991), 657–70.

70 Franks *et al.* (1987)

71 J. Franks and R. Harris, 'Shareholder wealth effects of UK takeovers', in J. Fairburn and J. Kay (eds), *Merger and Merger Policy* (Oxford University Press) 1989.

72 M. Williams, 'Do empirical studies help identify the welfare effects of merger', Working Paper (Institute of Economics, Oxford) 1992.

73 Bradley *et al.* (1988).

74 J. Pound, 'The information effects of takeovers', *Journal of Financial Economics*, 22 (1988), 207–28.

75 See, for example, G. Jarrell and A. Poulson, 'Shark repellants and stock prices', *Journal of Financial Economics*, 19 (1987), 127–68.

76 See, for example, V. McWilliams, 'Managerial share ownership and the stock market effects of antitakeover amendment proposals', *Journal of Finance*, 45 (1990), 1627–40; Jarrell and Poulsen (1987); S. Linn and J. McConnell, 'An empirical investigation of the impact of "antitakeover amendments" on common stock prices', *Journal of Financial Economics*, 11 (1983), 361–99. G. Jarrell and A. Poulsen, 'Dual-class recapitalisations as antitakeover mechanisms', *Journal of Financial Economics*, 20 (1988), 129–52; P. Malatesta and R. Walkling, 'Poison pill securities', *Journal of Financial Economics*, 20 (1988), 341–76; M. Ryngaert, 'The effect of poison pill securities on shareholder wealth', *Journal of Financial Economics*, 20 (1988), 377–417.

77 See Jarrell and Poulsen (1987).

78 See R. Harris, 'Antitakeover measures, golden parachutes and target firm shareholder welfare', *Rand Journal of Economics*, 21 (1990), 614–25.

79 Further support for this comes from evidence on defensive corporate restructuring by managers in response to takeover bids, which can be large and costly in terms of shareholder wealth. see L. Dann and H. DeAngelo, 'Corporate financial policy and corporate controls', *Journal of Financial Economics*, 20 (1988), 87–127. Note, however, that neither managerial resistance to a bid, nor some other frequently observed characteristics of takeover such as sequential and mistaken bidding, the emergence of white knights, etc., *necessarily* indicate that managers are not trying

to maximize shareholder value. See R. Giammarino and R. Heinkel, 'A model of dynamic takeover behaviour', *Journal of Finance*, 41 (1986), 465–80.

80 J. McConnell and C. Muscarella, 'Corporate capital expenditure decisions and the market value of the firm', *Journal of Financial Economics*, 14 (1985), 399–422.

81 S. Chan, J. Martin and J. Kensinger, 'Corporate research and development expenditures and share value', *Journal of Financial Economics*, 26 (1990), 255–76. This result raises the possibility that institutional investors are rather specialized with those analysing high-technology industry understanding and geared to respond to R&D announcements, but those looking at low-technology industries focusing more on earnings *per se*. There may also have been 'clientele' effects, i.e. investors with high marginal income tax rates preferring to invest for capital gains in long-term opportunities. This could make R&D investment more attractive for these investors than low marginal tax-rate payers more concerned with immediate income.

82 See M. Hirschey, 'Intangible capital aspects of advertising and R&D expenditures', *Journal of Industrial Economics*, 30 (1982), 375–90; A. Pakes, 'On patents, R&D, and the stock market rate of return', *Journal of Political Economies*, 93 (1985), 390–409. More tentative support comes from U. Ben-Zion, 'The R&D and investment decision and the relationship to the firm's market value: some preliminary results', in Z. Griliches (ed.), *R&D, Patents, and Productivity* (University of Chicago Press) 1984; I. Cockburn and Z. Griliches, 'Industry effects and appropriability measures in the stock market's valuation of R&D and patents', *American Economic Review*, P&P 78 (1988), 419–23.

83 Referred to in J. Stein, 'Takeover threats and managerial myopia', *Journal of Political Economics*, 96 (1988), 61–80.

84 See Stein (1988).

85 L. Muellbroek, M. Mitchell, J. Mulherin, J. Netter and A. Poulsen, 'Shark repellents and managerial myopia: an empirical test', *J. of Pol. Econ.* 98, 1108–17.

86 D. Miles, 'Testing for Short-Termism in the UK Stock Market' *Economic Journal*, 103 (1993), 1379–96.

87 M. Mullins and S. Wadhwani, 'The effect of the stock market on investment', *European Economic Review*, 33 (1989), 129–61.

88 R. Morck, A. Shleifer and R. Vishney, 'The stock market and investment: is the market a sideshow?', *Brookings Papers on Economic Activity* (1990), 157–215.

89 J. Stein, 'Efficient capital markets, inefficient firms: a model of myopic corporate behaviour', *Quarterly Journal of Economics*, 104 (1989), 655–70; J. Stein, 'Takeover threats and managerial myopia', *Journal of Political Economics*, 96 (1988), 61–80.

90 In fact, Nickell and Wadhwani provide empirical evidence that investors systematically place too much weight on current dividends in their valuations. See S. J. Nickell and S. Wadhwani, 'Myopia, the "dividend puzzle" and share prices', Discussion Paper 272, Centre for Labour Economics, London School of Economics, February 1987.

91 J. Stein, 'Efficient capital markets, inefficient firms: a model of myopic corporate behaviour', *Quarterly Journal of Economics*, 104 (1989), 655–70; J. Stein, 'Takeover threats and managerial myopia', *Journal of Political Economics*, 96 (1988), 61–80.

92 A. Schleifer and R. Vishny, 'Equilibrium short horizons of investors and firms', *American Economic Review*, P&P 89 (1990), 148–53.

93 Formally, let the share price be P_0, the fundamental value be F_0, the interest rate i, and the time to correction n. Assuming that the fundamental value grows at rate i, the fundamental value at time n is $F_0(1 + i)^n$. The payment to the supplier of

funds is $P_0(1 + i)^n$. The present value of the gain as represented by the difference between these two is given by

$$PV = \frac{(F_0 - P_0)(1 + i)^n}{(1 + i)^n} = F_0 - P_0$$

which is independent of n.

94 See, for example, J. Stiglitz and A. Weiss, 'Incentive effects of terminations: applications to the credit and labour markets', *American Economic Review*, 73 (1983), 912–27.

95
$$PV = \frac{F_0(1 + i)^n - P_0(1 + i')^n}{(1 + i')^n}$$

where i' is the higher cost of funds to the arbitrageur; dPV/dn is then negative.

96 See Hay and Morris (1991: 95–100) for a survey of these issues.

97 For the seminal works see M. Scott, *A New View of Economic Growth* (Oxford University Press) 1989; P. Romer, 'Increasing returns and long-run economic growth', *Journal of Political Economy*, 94 (1986), 1002–37; P. Romer, 'Capital, labour and productivity', *Brookings Papers on Economic Activity: Microeconomics* (1990), 337–67; P. Romer, 'Endogenous technical change', *Journal of Political Economy*, 98 (1990), S71–S102. For a recent survey of the issues see A. Boltho and J. Holtham, 'New approaches to economic growth', *Oxford Review of Economic Policy*, 8 (1992), 1–14.

98 For the formal model on which this is based, see D. Morris, 'Sunk costs, shocks and myopia', Working Paper, Institute of Economics, Oxford (1993).

99 For an elaboration of the mechanism see D. Morris and D. Stout, 'Industrial policy', in D. Morris (ed.), *The Economic System in the UK* (third edition) (Oxford University Press) 1985, 851–93.

100 See Scott, (1989: ch. 6).

101 See Marris (1963). For a summary and assessment of Marris's work see Hay and Morris (1991: ch. 10).

102 H. Odagiri, *The Theory of Growth in a Corporate Economy* (Cambridge University Press) 1981.

103 See H. Odagiri, *Growth through Competition, Competition through Growth* (Oxford University Press) 1992, especially ch. 8.

104 Hay and Morris (1984).

105 While it might be thought sufficient to sell only a minority of the shares, thus still ensuring management control, this was rarely if ever possible, because a minority stake in an unquoted company would provide neither control nor marketability. A holder of such a stake would therefore have no way of avoiding or offsetting poor managerial performance. In practice therefore the only realistic options, in the event that personal funds were insufficient to pay the tax liability, were flotation, sale or break up of the company.

106 There are some unquoted companies, nearly all first-generation ones, where the main motive of the founder-managers is to maximize the value of the company and then float or sell it to make the maximum capital sum on retirement. These were more prevalent in the 1980s but were not generally amongst the larger unquoted companies in the UK.

107 See Hay and Morris (1984). Subsequent work for the 1980s indicates that this pattern persisted in the first half of the 1980s but not in the second half. This may reflect that unquoted companies were less responsive in the short term to *either* the recession of the early 1980s *or* the rapid expansion of the economy in the later 1980s. See D. Hay, D. Morris, S. Evans and R. Macey-Dare, *The Performance of*

Quoted and Unquoted Companies in the 1980s, Institute of Economics and Statistics, Oxford (1991).

108 'Investment' should here be interpreted in the broadest possible sense to include R&D expenditure, product and market development, training, etc.

109 See Hay and Morris (1984). For a review of other studies in this vein, see Hay and Morris (1991).

110 Hay *et al.* (1991).

111 Morris (1993).

112 D. Leech and J. Leahy, 'Ownership structure, control type classifications and the performance of large British companies', *Economic Journal*, 101 (1991), 1418–37.

113 J. Cubbin and D. Leach, 'The effect of shareholding dispersion on the degree of control in British companies: theory and measurement', *Economic Journal*, 93 (1983), 351–69.

114 Only one other UK study has looked at shareholder concentration, but this is mainly concerned with managerial shareholding and the problems of departure from 'one share-one vote'. See R. Curcio, 'Managerial ownership of shares and corporate performance: an empirical analysis of UK companies 1972–86', Working Paper No. 290, Centre for Economic Performance, London School of Economics (1992). Current research by the author, utilizing shareholder concentration data over a six-year span for all quoted companies in the UK, is aimed at identifying the impact of concentration independent of any control type to which it might give rise.

115 We also note Schleifer and Vishny's work which, having found comparable evidence in the US of shareholder concentration, points out theoretical reasons why the incentive to start compiling larger shareholdings might be small if shareholdings are initially highly dispersed. See A. Schleifer and R. Vishny, 'Large shareholders and corporate control', *Journal of Political Economy*, 94 (1986), 461–88.

116 C. Holderness and D. Sheehan, 'The role of majority shareholders in publicly held corporations', *Journal of Financial Economics*, 20 (1988), 317–46.

117 K. Wruck, 'Equity ownership concentration and firm value: evidence from private equity financing', *Journal of Financial Economics*, 23 (1989), 3–28.

118 R. Masson and A. Madhavan, 'Insider trading and the value of the firm', *Journal of Industrial Economics*, 39 (1991), 333–54.

119 R. Morck, A. Schleifer and R. Vishny, 'Management ownership and market valuation', *Journal of Financial Economics*, 20 (1988), 293–315.

120 See, for example, G. Jarrell and A. Poulsen, 'Dual class recapitalisations as anti-takeover mechanisms: the recent evidence', *Journal of Financial Economics*, 20 (1988), 129–52; R. Curcio (1992); M. Jensen and J. Warner, 'The distribution of power among corporate managers, shareholders, and directors', *Journal of Financial Economics*, 20 (1988), 3–24.

Part IV

THE UK LABOUR MARKET

13

OVERVIEW: THE UK LABOUR MARKET

Paul Chapman

The outstanding faults of the economic society in which we live are its
failure to provide for full employment and its arbitrary and inequitable
distribution of wealth and incomes.

(John Maynard Keynes, *The General Theory*, p. 372)

The labour market is of crucial importance in overall economic policy. The
differences in view about overall macroeconomic policy can be generally traced
back to different assumptions about labour market behaviour. Furthermore,
there is now a considerable amount of research which suggests that labour
market structure matters and that these structures differ enormously across
countries, even within trading groups such as the EC. In this chapter we
examine the major changes in labour market policies and the relevant structural
changes in the economy since 1979. It can be argued that many of the problems
in the labour market have been resistant to policy changes. In particular it can
be argued that the UK economy remains prone to both higher inflation and
more severe cycles than most competitor countries.

This chapter is divided into five parts. Part I examines how the labour market
functions. Part II summarizes the key policy developments since 1979. Part III
examines the key structural changes. Part IV examines labour market outcomes
arising from both policy and structural change. Finally, Part V comments on
the future policy agenda.

I THE TEXTBOOK VISION OF THE LABOUR MARKET

Labour market policy since 1979 has been based on a very simple model of the
labour market. This textbook model has had an enormous influence on the
policy developments in the 1980s. In this chapter it is argued that this model
can be misleading and has been the basis for oversimplification of the
arguments about many controversial labour market policies. In what follows,
this simple model is referred to as the market clearing theory (MCT). In general

there are two versions of MCT, both of which are associated with some form of market failure.

(i) In the classical spot market, goods are traded according to the prevailing levels of demand and supply, leading to market clearing if the price is allowed to fluctuate. In the textbook model of the competitive labour market, the wage rate is assumed to be the mechanism which brings about the adjustment of supply and demand into equilibrium. Unemployment occurs because wages are too high and this gives rise to involuntary unemployment as indicated in Figure 1. Alternatively, if wages are too low skill shortages will arise.

There is an essential truth in this simple view of the labour market and there is also a great deal of empirical evidence on relative wages which suggests that firms will increase employment at lower wage rates. It is also very clear in this model that unemployment arises when unions raise wages above the market-clearing equilibrium. This analysis is especially relevant to an individual labour market concerned with a particular type of labour.

(ii) MCT can also be extended to a macroeconomic view of the labour market. A crucial part of this whole economy analysis is that workers will have a *reservation wage* which represents the wage where workers will withdraw their labour. This point could be illustrated by an increasing elasticity in the supply of labour as the real wage falls. Unemployment is an equilibrium outcome but demand-or-supply policies might be used to move the economy towards full employment. In the 1980s it became fashionable to argue that the only permanent method of increasing employment was through the supply-side and this is shown in Figure 1. In general more workers would be willing to work at a given wage and there would also be a lower reservation wage.[1]

According to this view of the labour market unemployment can be reduced by the adjustment of wages to the equilibrium rate and supply-side policies

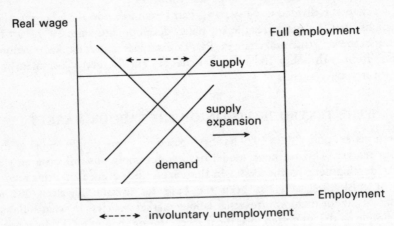

Figure 13.1 Unemployment and the labour market.

which reduce the equilibrium wage rate. A further mechanism through more training might also be effective in increasing skilled employment.[2]

However, there are several problems with this simple view about the causes of unemployment and the implication that a more flexible wage system is the only requirement for full employment. Many of these arguments can be traced to a single idea that labour markets are not like commodity markets – for example, the market for coffee beans. Labour markets are complex and varied. Recent economic theory has focused on why the wage rate may fail to achieve market clearing and furthermore why wage flexibility might in some circumstances be inherently undesirable. Many of these ideas developed because the MCT became increasingly irrelevant to understanding the secular rise in unemployment in the 1980s in many countries, where wage adjustment failed to take place. The unique characteristics of the labour market are explored in the following discussion.

For price adjustment to be effective in a simple spot market other relevant prices must remain the same. MCT often leaves it unclear whether it is real- or money-wage adjustment which is necessary. The theory of the labour market is based on the response of supply and demand to real-wage changes.[3] However, wage bargains between employers and workers are formulated in terms of money wages. Workers and employers might be willing to adjust real wages to a new equilibrium but might find it hard to translate money-wage changes into real-wage changes to secure market clearing.

Keynes argued that changes in money rates might be unable to achieve market clearing because of 'ineffective demand'. As money wages were adjusted downwards, aggregate demand would fall leading to a contraction in the demand for labour. Full employment equilibrium with lower real wages would seem to be forever just out of reach.[4] Pigou, defending the pre-Keynesian macroeconomic theory, had argued that in a downward wage–price spiral a 'real balance effect' would emerge which would, in the long run, boost consumption. This defence for the MCT mechanism is of limited policy relevance if there are alternative options which can bring about a quicker response to rising unemployment.

In addition to an explanation of the level of wages, the rate of change of money-wage rates has been central to labour market policy. Indeed, it is arguable that macroeconomic policy has been overly concerned with inflation in the last decade. For a time the Phillips curve relationship had dominated economic discussion of inflation. Phillips (1958) proposed that there was a stable relationship between the rate of change of money wages and the rate of unemployment and that by implication there was a policy choice to be made across a menu of unemployment–inflation combinations. Following the breakdown of this relationship in the late 1960s and the seminal paper on the Phillips curve by Friedman (1968) it has become widely accepted that the trade-off might disappear in the long-run, and in the case of the extreme rational expectations view of the Phillips curve, where according to Lucas (1972) only surprise demand changes matter, there is no trade-off even in the short-run.[5] The consensus is that the important relationship is the long-run equilibrium unemployment level referred to as the non-accelerating inflation rate of unemployment or NAIRU. When unemployment is below this level, inflation will rise and when unemployment is above it, inflation will fall. NAIRU represents the equilibrium unemployment rate at which expectations are sustained; wage-setters and price-setters achieve the real wage they expected, and inflation should be stable. A more formal definition is given below.

A formal definition of NAIRU

The definition of NAIRU can be based on several model formulations. The version proposed by Layard *et al.* (1991) is as follows. A price equation can be based on a mark-up on expected wages. If the mark-up is fixed we have a 'normal cost' pricing model. Equation (1) is the intended real wage set by price makers.

$$p - w^e = b_0 - b_1 u \quad (b_1 > 0) \tag{1}$$

where p is the log of prices, w^e is the log of expected wages and u is the unemployment rate. The wage rate (in logs) in equation (2) depends on the mark-up on expected prices.

$$w - p^e = a_0 - a_1 u \quad (a_1 > 0) \tag{2}$$

NAIRU will be given by u^* in equation (3) where $p = p^e$ and $w = w^e$

$$u^* = [b_0 + a_0] / [b_1 + a_1] \tag{3}$$

Figure 2 shows the pattern of earnings inflation and the unemployment rate over the period 1979–92. The cost of deflation after 1980 was very high in terms of higher unemployment. From 1980 to 1986 the rate of inflation was reduced from 20 per cent to 7.5 per cent, but unemployment rose from 5.1 per cent to 11.1 per cent over the same period and remained stubbornly high until after 1986. In the period from 1986 to 1990 unemployment fell and inflation began to rise again. By the early 1990s, unemployment was increasing rapidly towards the levels of the mid-1980s while earnings inflation remained at around 7.5 per cent with a significant fall in 1992 to 6 per cent. There is some evidence that inflationary expectations were reduced by the high level of unemployment. This can be observed in the lower inflation–unemployment path in 1987–92 compared with 1979–86, although the fall in inflation which was achieved (around 2 per cent) must be set against the very large rise in unemployment from the start of the decade. This evidence does not seem to correspond with the NAIRU theory of a natural rate of unemployment or at least the short-term deviations from equilibrium may last a considerable time. New theories were sought to explain the increase in unemployment over this period.

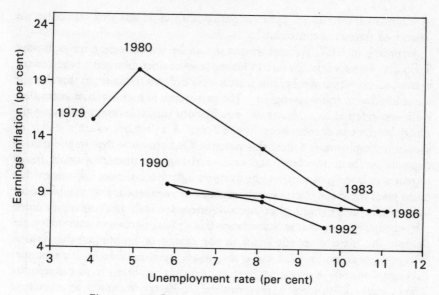

Figure 13.2 Inflation and unemployment, 1979–92.

The relationship between inflation and unemployment shown in Figure 2 highlights another difficulty with MCT. Can wages be treated as an exogenous variable? A more plausible view is that unemployment has been the policy mechanism to control wages. Wage inflation has itself induced measures to control overall demand in the economy.

A further examination of disequilibrium in the labour market is helpful. Out of equilibrium, when inflation is rising or falling, the economy can be thought of as adjusting to demand and supply-side shocks which can be deflationary or inflationary. In the 1960s these shocks were mainly from the demand side, measured by increases in nominal GDP. In 1973–4 and 1979–80 there were large supply-side shocks following the increases in oil prices and other commodities. Positive demand-side shocks increase the price level and reduce unemployment. Positive supply-side shocks also decrease unemployment but the price level falls as well. The period 1979–81 can be characterized by a negative demand shock (unusually tight monetary and fiscal policy). The period 1985–6 included a mildly positive supply-side shock arising from lower oil prices and a reduction in raw material costs. These had a negative inflation effect but the positive demand shock of lower taxes and loose monetary conditions in late 1987 to 1988 overshadowed this effect. From 1989 there was a strong negative demand shock from the squeeze on the economy from tight monetary policy. From this classification of shocks it is clear that the stop–go cycle of the UK economy was largely due to demand-side shocks which were in the main the result of domestic policy. This cycle was well related to the balance-of-payments constraint.[6]

According to MCT, unemployment should be self-correcting through wage flexibility. However, in the late 1970s the level of unemployment began to rise in most economies and it became increasingly difficult to maintain that this rise was solely due to real-wage rigidity. The persistence of high levels of unemployment was referred to as *hysteresis*; equilibrium unemployment following the actual level of unemployment in the form of a 'ratchet effect'.[7] But why should unemployment follow this pattern? One reason is that wage inflation depends on both the level and rate of change of unemployment. Initial increases in unemployment might dampen inflation but once adjustment has taken place the shock effect of such increases was weakened. For example, some workers may judge that higher unemployment levels do not justify continued job search. This is known as 'state dependency'; long periods of unemployment become the main deterrent factor in the chance of finding another job. A further explanation for hysteresis is that wages are too inflexible. For example, in *insider–outsider theory* it has been argued that employers recruit to separate labour markets. Insiders have completely different contracts to outsiders. Markets will not clear as conventionally understood because wages will be determined by bargains between employers and insiders. Outsiders who may be willing to work at lower wages may find themselves involuntarily unemployed.[8] Unless the reasons behind hysteresis can be better understood, it is clear that it may be undesirable and impractical to try to encourage labour markets to mimic the market-clearing mechanism associated with competitive markets.

Even if labour markets could somehow be induced to conform to the MCT model, there might be a further problem that some wage rigidities might serve a useful purpose. In the theory of *implicit contracts* it has been suggested that rigid wages might satisfy the need for workers to avoid risk where employers could be compensated by lower average wage levels.[9] Another idea which has become popular is that worker effort will be linked to wages and that wages should be set to maximize efficiency taking into account the effect of wages on effort. This is known as the *efficiency wage hypothesis*.[10] Employers might prefer to set wages above market-clearing levels in order to encourage worker discipline, or as Lazear (1981) describes it, to discourage shirking.

There are various structural theories of the labour market which explicitly adopt a framework in which competitive wage adjustment is constrained. In the labour market segmentation literature, largely associated with the work of Doeringer and Piore (1971), labour markets can be characterized by *primary and secondary market sectors*. Workers cannot easily move between sectors and unemployment in one sector would not necessarily affect wages in the other. In a related idea the concept of an *internal labour market* has been developed by institutional economists to describe a situation in which workers will only be recruited at certain ports of entry, leaving senior workers less exposed to the vagaries of market surpluses or shortages.[11] One policy view of these structural factors is to argue the case for more competition to break down anti-competitive barriers. An alternative is to reflect on why labour markets might have evolved along different paths compared with markets for commodities and to seek policies which can accommodate the existing labour market structure.

At this point it might be helpful to summarize the objections to the MCT model of the labour market:

(a) What is the standard model of the labour market? How does it imply that unemployment might be reduced? There are two sources of unemployment: disequilibrium and underemployment equilibrium. The ways to improve things (ignoring demand) are:
    (i) improve wage flexibility;
    (ii) reduce the reservation wage;
    (iii) increase training.

(b) Are wages a potential lever for policy? Can unemployment be controlled by wage adjustment? In practice it is easier to control wages by controlling unemployment. Furthermore, this view is consistent with the evidence on inflation and unemployment.

(c) The MCT hypothesis is a simple paradigm. It suggests that the labour market policy should be concerned solely with the wage level and the wage adjustment process. Even in its own terms there is room for debate. Would any other institutional arrangements help? Notably the simple story has no good account, and takes no account, of regional differences and international differences in labour markets.

(d) The MCT approach assumes that the wage question can be dealt with in isolation. This is a fundamental error. It is made clear in this book that Britain's trading performance is important. If policies designed to control wages also reduce productivity then lower wages are irrelevant. This is really an issue about wage efficiency. There is a case for reconsidering supply-side policies not as a means of reducing the reservation wage but as a means of moving from a low-wage–low-skill to high-wage–high-skill economy.

(e) Finally, surely the idea that the labour market should be more flexible is an appealing one? But this too is not beyond criticism. First, labour markets just do not work that way and there is a considerable literature on why they do not adjust. Second, the focus on wage flexibility detracts again from the crucial objective of competitiveness and underlying productivity. One part of this is flexibility in working practices.

II LABOUR MARKET POLICY, 1979–90

The labour market policies in the 1980s attempted to increase the competitive basis for wage setting. Labour markets were deregulated and the power of unions and statutory bodies was diminished. However, against this background of promoting a more competitive labour market, various new forms of market intervention were also introduced, including special employment measures (SEMs) and various policies to promote training. An important element of the new policy approach was that government could best assist by improving the conditions for supply-side factors and measures to improve labour mobility, training and wage flexibility were especially favoured.

Various fiscal measures were introduced to change incentives. In particular it was argued that a key supply-side measure was to reduce the disincentive effects of high marginal tax rates on earned income. The main marginal tax rate was reduced from 33 per cent in 1979 to 25 per cent in 1988 and the highest tax rate was reduced from 83 per cent to 40 per cent. At the same time indirect taxes, especially VAT, were increased to compensate for these changes. VAT rose from 8 per cent in 1981 to 17.5 per cent by 1991.

One problem which was recognized as important was the incentive structure for the low paid and the unemployed. The low paid faced a system of benefits and a tax regime which left many in a 'poverty trap' where the effective marginal tax rate was extremely high, well above 40 per cent the rate for high earners. The unemployed faced a similar problem known as an 'unemployment trap' where the benefit from being in work was small or even negative.[12]

Many other supply-side measures were introduced in the 1980s including significant changes to unemployment benefits. Earnings-related payments were abolished and unemployment benefits and social security were linked to prices rather than earnings. In the long run this will have a major impact on the benefits out of work. In addition to large income tax reductions offered to high-income earners, measures were introduced to encourage savings especially in the form of tax breaks for high-income earners, including special subsidies for the accumulation of shares.

The attempts to deregulate the economy have been conspicuous in the labour market. The main agenda concerned the status and role of unions; the rights and privileges of unions were gradually abolished through a series of legislative measures. Unions could be sued for damages, secondary picketing was to be prohibited, closed shops became illegal, secret ballots became compulsory, and unions could be sued for unofficial strikes. Not surprisingly, union membership fell steadily over this period although some of this reduction was also due to the changing employment structure of the UK economy (discussed below). Total trade union membership fell from 11.7 million in 1980 to 9.2 million in 1989.[13] The increase in unemployment after 1979 and the legislation designed to curb union power had a clear impact on strikes and militancy.[14]

In addition to the legislation to reduce union power, several other policy measures were introduced to deregulate the labour market. In 1986 the minimum wages set by the Wages Councils for under-21s were abolished. Many measures reflected the changing social background. For example, the restrictions on the employment of female labour were removed in 1989 and other measures were designed to create a more competitive labour market. For example, the rights to unfair dismissal were reduced by extending the scope of this legislation to a minimum of two years with an employer. In 1992 it was decided to abolish the Wages Councils for all workers and this in effect eliminated the remaining regulation on minimum-wage levels. This is perfectly consistent with an MCT view of the labour market; minimum wages lead to higher unemployment than would otherwise be the case. However, minimum wages may also perform a useful employment function. If they are not set too high, higher wages may improve productivity to compensate (efficiency wages theory) and low wages may lead to problems of labour turnover which reduce employment in the long term. The balance of these arguments and other social arguments in favour of minimum wages suggests that the simple application of MCT ideas can be misleading.[15] Furthermore, the scale of any employment losses of minimum wages remains unclear. In contrast, MCT assumes that labour productivity is entirely technologically determined and wages can and must adjust according to the simple textbook model.

Many other policy actions had an indirect influence on the labour market. Two areas of great importance were in the housing market and the financial sector. In the housing market the 'right to buy' for council tenants reduced the public sector housing stock. Whatever motives there may have been for this policy, it can be argued that it should in principle have led to a more mobile labour force which was now free from the restrictions of council house tenure. In practice this policy was thwarted by the failure of the private sector to meet the demand for new housing in the expanding regions. It might be argued that the reduction in council housing, along with a small and insignificant rented sector, actually decreased labour mobility. In the financial sector, deregulation (along with the expansion of the demand for financial services through housing policy) led to a large increase in the demand for labour for financial services at the expense of other activities, especially manufacturing.

The policy measures designed to create a more competitive labour market were complemented by direct intervention in the labour market. Policy consisted of a raft of measures designed to assist job seekers to find employment, job experience and training. In the early 1980s this assistance was geared towards the increase in school leavers who flooded the unemployment queue. In the late 1980s this assistance shifted to the adult labour market. For example, Employment Training was introduced in 1988 to assist older workers with training. For a short period there was great concern about growing skill shortages, especially in certain regions in the south of England. This increasing imbalance in regional labour markets was to reverse itself when the recession in the late 1980s was most evident in the south, just as the recession in 1980–1 had been concentrated in the peripheral regions where heavy industry was more important.

III STRUCTURAL CHANGE

It must be emphasized that there are wide variations in labour market structures across countries. This reinforces the view taken here that institutions matter and the simple MCT model cannot be universally applied as the only guide to the operation of the labour market. As far as the G6 countries are concerned there are certain important differences which might be kept in mind. Table 1 summarizes some of the main factors.

The UK wage-bargaining system has some features of a centralized system (high union density, important public sector subject to government incomes policies). It is also evident that it has some significant decentralized features (lack of coordination, firm-level bargaining). At the present time the UK has a mixed system which is, according to Calmfors and Driffill (1988), to have the worst of all possible worlds.[16] This might be because a halfway-house system will lead to confusing signals and the potential benefits of either a decentralized or centralized system are both forgone. This is discussed further in the chapter below.

The labour force is only a proportion of the total population. The participation rate is defined by the numbers in work or available for work compared with the total number of working age. The UK participation rate (high compared with other G6 countries) has been subject to two opposing factors; an increase in female participation and reduced male participation. On balance the participation rate has increased and the labour force (especially females) has been growing in all G6 economies. This is much the same pattern in other countries shown in Table 2.

Table 1 Wage bargaining systems in G6 countries

Country	Coverage	Bargaining system	Coordination	Minimum wage	Incomes policy	Union density
UK	Medium	Mainly firm level	None	None	Minimal through public sector pay	High
Germany	High	Industry level	High	None	Minimal	High
France	High	Industry level	Low	Established by law	None	Low
Italy	High	Industry level	Medium	None	Various measures in 1980s	High
US	Low	Firm level	None	Low level	None in 1980s	Low
Japan	Medium	Firm level	High (employers)	None	None	Medium

Source: Based on Layard *et al.* (1991), Annex 1.4

Table 2 Labour force growth 1980–9, G6 countries, annual growth rates (per cent)

	Germany	France	Italy	US	Japan	UK
All	0.7	0.4	0.8	1.6	1.2	0.7
Females	1.2	1.3	1.9	2.3	1.7	1.7

Source: OECD

The main occupational changes in the UK from 1979–90 are shown in Figure 3. There has been a substantial long-term shift towards non-manual occupations. Technological change has enabled certain sectors to economize on labour. Service-oriented sectors have been less able to increase productivity with new technology or more capital-intensive production methods.[17]. The occupational shift reflects the de-industrialization of the economy.[18]

The broad sectoral changes in employment for agriculture, industry and services in the G6 countries are shown in Figure 4. Industry is defined as manufacturing plus construction and energy. There are several key points to note. First, there was strong employment growth in services in all G6 countries. The growth in services can be expected to reduce the potential for economic growth. Second, employment in agriculture fell significantly in many countries. In Italy and Germany the loss in employment in agriculture was equivalent to

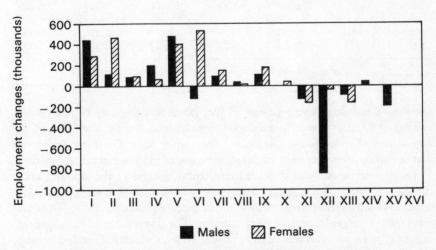

Figure 13.3 Occupational changes in Great Britain, 1979–90.

Notes: **I**, Professional, management and administration; **II**, Professional, education, welfare and health; **III**, Literary, arts, sports; **IV**, Professional in science, engineering and others; **V**, Managerial; **VI**, Clerical; **VII**, Selling; **VIII**, Security and protective; **IX**, Catering, cleaning, personal; **X**, Farming, fishing; **XI**, Processing, repair; **XII**, Processing, repair, metal engineering; **XIII**; Painting, assembly, packaging; **XIV**, Construction, mining; **XV**, Transport operating, moving; **XVI**, Miscellaneous

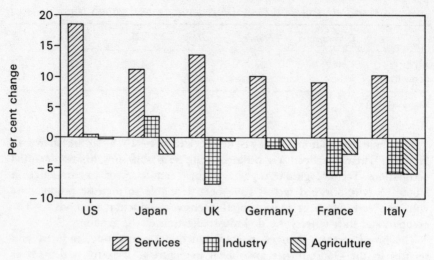

Figure 13.4 Growth in employment, 1979–89 (percentage of employment in 1989).

Table 3 UK employment, 1979–91 (thousands)

Year	Full-time		Part-time		Self-employment	
	Males	*Females*	*Males*	*Females*	*Males*	*Females*
1979	13,480	9,665	728	3,224	1,550	357
1991	11,611	10,637	952	4,623	2,396	747

Source: Department of Employment

the loss in industrial employment. Third, Japan was the only G6 country to exhibit significant growth in industrial employment. Finally, the UK had the largest loss of industrial employment, but unlike Italy, Germany and to an extent France, there has been no substantive loss of employment in agriculture.

There were many other important structural changes in the labour market during the 1980s. The population and labour force were both ageing and part-time, and self-employment became much more significant. Table 3 summarizes these changes in employment patterns. The importance of the supply of labour is often underestimated in economic analysis which has tended to exaggerate the role of demand factors in the labour market.[19]

IV OUTCOMES

Unemployment arises for many reasons. Workers will be moving between jobs (frictional unemployment), new industries emerging while others decline

278

(structural unemployment) or there may be insufficient short-run demand raising unemployment above the equilibrium level (demand-deficient unemployment). The UK record on unemployment for the period 1979–90 suggests that the rate of unemployment in the UK has been above other G6 countries. The rise in unemployment in the UK from 1979 to 1983 was one of the most significant and unsatisfactory outcomes of this period. Also the cycle for the UK has been more severe than the EC average. This is indicated by the standardized unemployment rates in Figure 5.[20]

The economic changes over the 1980s were associated with extreme effects on unemployment and house prices. Whatever market forces were operating across regions their effects were not obviously consistent with the concept of market clearing. Severe regional imbalances developed and this was reflected in the discussion about a north–south divide. By 1991 this new regional imbalance had been reversed and a more equitable distribution of unemployment returned. However, this came about by increasing unemployment in the south rather than by reducing unemployment in the north.

The increase in disparities in regional unemployment followed in part from a labour market which had failed to deliver regional pay flexibility. It was only when demand adjustments came that regional unemployment dispersion began to lessen. Brown and Walsh (1991) have shown that regional pay dispersion has not changed in any significant way during the 1980s except for pay in Greater London where the ratio of pay to the Great Britain average rose from 1.14 to 1.29 between 1979 and 1989.

Given the stated aims of economic policy over the period it is especially important to examine the UK record on inflation. Figure 6 gives the inflation

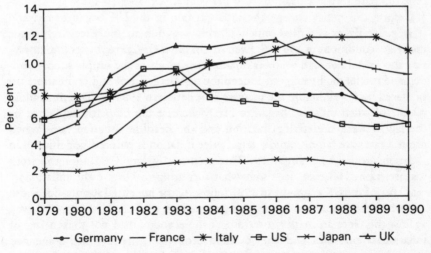

Figure 13.5 Unemployment rates, 1979–90 (standardized G6 economies).

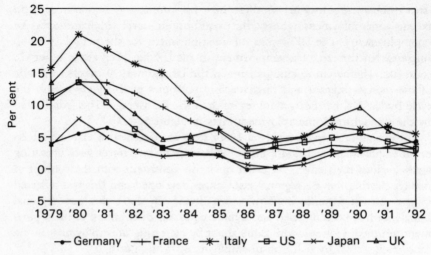

Figure 13.6 G6 inflation, 1979–92 (percentage change of retail prices).

rate over the period 1979–92.[21] A feature of UK performance is that inflation remained stubbornly high in the early 1980s when unemployment rose to record levels. This data also shows the fall in inflation over the period and a degree of convergence in the late 1980s. UK inflation began to rise after 1986 and was higher in 1988–9 than for other G6 countries. The policy reaction to this outcome was to attempt to bring down inflation by a monetary squeeze and UK base interest rates rose from 7.5 per cent in May to 15 per cent in October 1989. By August 1992 the inflation rate had been reduced to 3.6 per cent compared with a peak of 10.9 per cent in October 1990.[22]

Despite this policy change the inflation rate in the UK began to rise and it is generally agreed that much of this was due to the excessively loose monetary conditions in 1987–8. Even so, for other OECD countries the supply-side shocks did not lead to lower inflation as quickly as the simple supply-and-demand model might suggest. Indeed the re-emergence of higher inflation can be traced back well before the increase in inflation in 1988–9. This misleading picture of when inflation began to firmly increase can be partly explained by the lag between underlying inflation and the headline inflation rate. When interest rates are falling rapidly retail price inflation is reduced but this fall in inflation cannot be maintained. This occurred in late 1987 after the stock market crash. However, it is somewhat surprising to observe the inflationary tendency of the UK economy in 1987 following the beneficial supply-side shock and when the pound was appreciating strongly against the US dollar and even against the German mark. In retrospect the economy had not shaken free of inflationary pressures and the so-called economic miracle which some had referred to was just another period of go in the familiar stop–go cycle of the

UK economy.[23] Furthermore, the go period in the late 1980s had probably been allowed to develop further than usual because the economy was benefiting from North Sea oil revenues and the balance-of-payments constraint did not immediately bring a halt to expansion.[24]

Part of the problem in interpreting wage inflation in the UK is the different patterns of pay for public and private sectors. While the UK has not operated a pay policy in the private sector for some time, this has not been the case in the public sector. Pay norms, pay ceilings and selective judgements on various pay commissions have all played a part in public sector pay policy, whatever the formal position of the Treasury. Public sector workers have found their pay lagging in the go phases and catching up in the stop phases.[25] In the late 1980s, as the economy slowed down, the catch-up effects on public sector pay led to levels of wage inflation which appeared to be at odds with an economy slipping into severe recession. Calls for controls on public sector pay can lay the seeds for this dislocation of wage demands with the economic cycle. While the application of MCT to private sector pay was being emphasized, a system for setting public sector pay was required. In this context MCT seems especially unhelpful. Many public sector workers have no immediate alternative employment and in some cases no comparable private sector job. In these circumstances decisions on pay cannot simply be based on a simple textbook supply-and-demand model.

The effects of labour market policies must be assessed in terms of the effects they might have had on competitiveness and the real economy. Of course these real effects may be partly the result of more labour market flexibility and lower inflation: competitiveness can be improved by keeping wage inflation below that of other countries or by improving labour productivity. The overall outcome is measured by unit labour costs which are defined as the labour cost of a unit of output.[26]

Changes in unit labour costs are somewhat difficult to interpret in several respects. First, aggregate data can combine very different sectors which may be misleading. Second, unit labour costs in the short run are determined by the business cycle because firms will not shed labour or hire new workers as quickly as output changes. For example, in the late 1980s the severity of the recession in the UK has considerably pushed up unit labour costs. This creates particular problems for international comparisons where cycles are different. Third, unit labour costs do not allow for different methods of production, based on higher or lower capital–labour ratios. Where UK productivity has been relatively high this appears to have been cancelled out by higher wage inflation. The growth in unit labour costs over the period 1977–87 in the UK business sector was slightly above the EC average and well above for the period 1988–92.

It is also helpful in assessing the performance of the economy to examine whether changes in labour costs are based on changes in productivity or wage and salary costs. Productivity growth in the UK economy fell from a peak of 5 per cent in 1986 to zero growth from 1988 onwards; at the same time average earnings were growing at around 7 per cent and only began to fall as late as 1991. The rise in unit labour costs over this period was clearly an important factor in the UK recession. An MCT view of this data is that it reflects a labour market which is too inflexible: earnings growth should have fallen more rapidly. Alternatively it might be argued that the supply-side of the economy is the root cause of the problem and that the methods to free the labour market have run counter to the necessary investment in human and physical capital which is required to sustain long-run growth consistent with real-wage expectations. The reality is that both these explanations are relevant. There is no evidence that the labour market reforms of the 1980s have provided for sufficient wage flexibility and there is no evidence that the particular supply-side reforms have improved long-run economic growth.

V LABOUR MARKET POLICY ISSUES

The controversy about how the labour market operates is central to policy discussion. The following agenda is intended as a guide to the main issues which will have to be addressed in the 1990s.

(i) *The UK has acquired a reputation as an inflation-prone economy.* The withdrawal of the UK from the European Exchange Rate Mechanism (ERM) in September 1992 and the subsequent devaluation of the pound suggests that inflationary problems may recur despite two major recessions since 1979. Both of these recessions were the outcome of the policy for low inflation. If the UK economy is to ever attain a reputation for low inflation, a system of wage bargaining is required which can deliver. Calmfors and Driffill (1988) have argued the case for a clear choice between a more decentralized or a more centralized wage bargaining system. The UK has a significant union presence, many forms of national bargaining, and a large public sector. It is in many respects well placed to pursue a system based on more centralized and coordinated pay systems. On the other hand, there has been a steady movement, encouraged by governments since 1950s, towards a more decentralised pay system.[27]

(ii) *The UK has also been prone to more severe cycles than other countries.* There is no evidence that the 1980s were different in this respect and the effects of the stop–go cycle on the labour market are clear. There are two policy issues which arise. First, has domestic policy itself been destabilizing? This can only be answered by an examination of overall macroeconomic policy. Second, has the labour market become more flexible and therefore more able to respond to shocks? The evidence on the effects of labour market reforms is hard to assess without observing an actual shock to the system such as a large increase in oil prices.

(ii) *There has been a rise in equilibrium unemployment.* There is scope to debate the importance of various supply-side measures to reduce unemployment, without becoming trapped in old controversies about the possibility of involuntary unemployment. In this context it is desirable to have an unemployment target although this has not been widely discussed in recent debates on UK economic policy. The causes of unemployment are complex and various. Reductions in unemployment can be achieved by various supply-side policies, including active manpower policies, limited duration benefits and appropriately targeted subsidies.[28] Appropriate use of demand management policies are now openly discussed in the debate on economic policy along with the use of supply-side measures.

(iv) *The productivity in the economy depends on supply-side measures.* Whether the supply-side measures undertaken in the 1980s have tackled the fundamental problems of the UK economy must be assessed in terms of outcomes: economic growth, unemployment and inflation. The evidence is very weak and there is a case that the supply-side measures of the 1980s have been ineffective, even counterproductive, in achieving improvements in economic performance. However, there can be no doubt that improvements in the operation of the labour market provide one of the main methods to increase competitiveness, by increasing labour productivity and reducing money-wage inflation relative to other countries.

(v) *Labour market institutions matter.* According to the MCT model there is little scope for labour market intervention except to increase competition. By implication the institutions which govern labour market behaviour perform a marginal role in improving labour market performance. However, it is time to recognize that institutional issues must be debated and it is mistaken to ignore arrangements in other countries which might provide a model.

Much of the new legislation outlined above was designed to deregulate, leading to elimination of certain restrictions on wages, hours of work, the employment of female labour, etc. These measures had implications for many institutions including Wages Councils, the Industrial Training Boards as well as the private sector. The most important labour market legislation during the 1980s was concerned with reducing the power of trade unions. The radical reform of existing institutions broadly conformed to the policy of deregulation. The Industrial Training Board system, the Manpower Services Commission and Wages Councils were all abolished or greatly diminished during the 1980s. New forms of regulation were introduced, most especially the new Training Initiative in 1981 paving the way for the Youth Training Scheme, Training for Employment in 1988 which introduced Employment Training and the Employment Act in 1990 which introduced Training and Enterprise Councils (TECs). More recently the most significant innovation has been the development of a system for skills certification through the National Council for Vocational Qualifications.

What is the rationale and scope for intervention in the labour market? The period since 1979 has been noteworthy for many supply-side measures including union legislation, incentives and the overall policy of deregulation. However, many measures were concerned with policy intervention designed to

283

deal with the increasing level of unemployment. The case for a pure market forces view of the labour market has been found wanting in the discussion in this chapter. Only if this is accepted is it possible to start a serious debate on how to encourage the labour market to really become more flexible through both market and institutional reform. This is necessary if the labour market is to better perform its function of matching workers to jobs and encourage increasing labour productivity.

The UK economy in 1993 has the lowest inflationary pressure for more than twenty-five years but an increasingly urgent unemployment problem. A new agenda for labour market reform needs to be thought out which must include an examination of institutions for the regulation of the labour market.

NOTES

1 The basis for supply-side policies might be seen either as a new lower minimum reservation wage or a larger number of workers prepared to accept the minimum. In terms of Figure 1 the effectiveness of these two policies would depend on the overall state of demand. For example, increasing the numbers of workers who will accept the reservation wage will not help if there are unemployed workers already willing to work at that same wage.

2 This is not illustrated but would require two labour market diagrams with full employment reductions in the unskilled market allowing the expansion of supply in the skilled market. This might lead to an overall reduction in unemployment.

3 Changes in real wages and money wages will only be the same if the price level is constant.

4 The substance of this argument was rather obscure in the original form in Keynes's *General Theory*, and the idea achieved wider acceptance following the work of Leijonhufvud and Clower. See Clower (1965) and Leijonhufvud (1967).

5 This is known as 'the Lucas critique'.

6 See Chapter 2.

7 See Blanchard and Summers (1986, 1987).

8 See Lindbeck and Snower (1986, 1989) for example.

9 See Azariadis and Stiglitz (1983) for a survey of the main ideas.

10 See Yellen (1984) for an account of the main views on wage efficiency.

11 See Jacoby (1990) for a survey of these ideas.

12 A measure of the magnitude of the unemployment trap is provided by the replacement ratio which measures the benefits available out of work against the benefits in work.

13 See OECD (1991) on international comparisons of union membership. The fall in union membership in the UK is high compared with many other countries. For example, in Germany and Japan membership was stable and in Italy membership increased. In France membership lost was higher than in the UK.

14 There is probably an effect of changing industrial composition on strikes as employment has increased in the service sector compared with manufacturing and as the number of part-time, self-employed and female workers have increased. But the fall in strike activity over the decade cannot be seriously disputed. Working days lost in all industries averaged 2.6 billion in 1986–91 compared with 10.2 billion in 1979–85.

15 An additional point is that the labour market is a mixed system of competitive and non-competitive elements. It will not necessarily improve overall efficiency if we make only some parts of it more competitive. This is an implication of the so-called second-best theory.

16 This conclusion was also reached in a National Economic Development Council Paper in 1991.

17 This is a complex issue. Some parts of manufacturing have been contracted out to the service sector and the increase in manufacturing productivity does not allow for this purely accounting factor. The comparisons of labour productivity over time are beset with many difficulties.

18 See Part I of this book.

19 Both Keynesians and monetarists can be criticized for the failure to take sufficient account of the demographic influences on the labour market.

20 There has been a great deal of concern about the reliability of unemployment measures in the UK over this period. By using the OECD standardized unemployment rates, based on the Labour Force Surveys, this problem is minimized.

21 There are two main alternatives to measuring inflation. The two methods are based on the retail price index (RPI) and the GDP deflator. The GDP deflator is based on national income data measured in current and constant prices. The RPI measures the price over time of a basket of commodities. The RPI index is very sensitive to the interest rate in the UK because mortgage payments are included in the index.

22 The inflation rate indicated in the text is based on the retail price index. It is commonly described as retail price inflation.

23 See Chapter 1 on 'the economic miracle'.

24 See Chapter 4.

25 The National Economic Development Council voiced some concern about this problem in a 1990 Council Paper.

26 Unit labour costs are defined by W/Y where W = total labour cost of production and Y = total physical output.

27 See Brown and Walsh (1991) for example.

28 See Layard *et al.* (1991: 508–9).

REFERENCES

Azariadis C. and Stiglitz, J. E. (1983) 'Implicit contracts and fixed price equilibria', *Quarterly Journal of Economics Supplement*, vol. 98, pp. 1–23.

Blanchard, O. and Summers, L. (1986) 'Hysteresis and European unemployment', *NBER Macroeconomics Annual*, Cambridge, MA: MIT Press, pp. 15–77.

Blanchard, O. and Summers, L. (1987) 'Hysteresis and unemployment', *European Economic Review*, vol. 31, pp. 288–95.

Brown, R. and Walsh, J. (1991) 'Pay determination in the 1980's; the anatomy of decentralization', *Oxford Review of Economic Policy*, vol. 7, no. 1, Spring, pp. 44–59.

Calmfors, L. and Driffill, J. (1988) 'Centralisation of wage bargaining and macroeconomic performance, *Economic Policy*, no. 6. pp. 13–61.

Clower, R. W. (1965) 'The Keynesian counter-revolution: a theoretical reappraisal', in F. H. Hahn and F. Brechling (eds), *The Theory of Interest Rates*, IEA Series, London: Macmillan, Ch. 5, pp. 103–25.

Doeringer, P. and Piore, M. (1971) *Internal Labour Markets and Manpower Analysis*, Lexington, MA: D. C. Heath.

Friedman, M. (1968) 'The role of monetary policy', *American Economic Review*, vol. 58, pp. 1–17.

Jacoby, S. (1990) 'The new institutionalism: what can it learn from the old?', *Industrial Relations*, vol. 29, no. 2, pp. 317–59.

Layard, R., Nickell, S. and Jackman, R. (1991) *Unemployment: Macroeconomic Performance and the Labour Market*, Oxford: Oxford University Press.

Lazear, E. P. (1981) 'Agency, earnings profiles, productivity and layoffs', *American Economic Review*, vol. 71, pp. 606–20.

Leijonhufvud, A. (1967) 'Keynes and the Keynesians: a suggested interpretation', *American Economic Review*, vol. 57, no. 2, pp. 401–10.

Lindbeck, A. and Snower, D. (1986) 'Wage setting, unemployment and insider–outsider relations', *American Economic Review, Papers and Proceedings*, vol. 76, pp. 235–9.

Lindbeck, A. and Snower, D. (1989) *The Insider–Outsider Theory of Employment and Unemployment*, Cambridge, MA. MIT Press.

Lucas, R. E. (1972) 'Expectations and the neutrality of money', *Journal of Economic Theory*, vol. 4, no. 2, pp. 103–24.

OECD (1991) *Employment Outlook*, July, Paris.

Phillips, A. W. (1958) 'The relation between unemployment and the rate of change of money wage rates in the United Kingdom, 1861–1957', *Economica*, vol. 25, pp. 283–99.

Yellen, J. (1984) 'Efficiency wage models of unemployment', *American Economic Review*, Papers and Proceedings, vol. 74, pp. 200–5.

14

THE QUESTION OF PAY

Paul Chapman and Paul Temple

INTRODUCTION

In the period since the Second World War, the related issues of pay, employment and productivity have been central to the debate about Britain's
economic decline. Indeed, a major thrust of economic policy since 1979,
whatever the monetarist rhetoric of the early years, has been reform of the
labour market and especially the system of pay determination. Undoubtedly
this emphasis was partly a result of the experiences of the 1970s, when inflationary performance in response to the severe supply-side shocks was markedly
inferior to that of other comparable economies. In this chapter we examine the
role of pay in the generation of inflation and recession; we then turn to the
question of the growing inequality in the distribution of income, before
assessing the consequences of the fundamental changes now taking place in the
way pay is determined.

The key-note cry behind policy has been the need for greater 'flexibility'
(however defined) in labour market behaviour, and the greatest barrier to
achieving that aim was widely believed to be the power of the trade unions.
In fact, however, the concept of flexibility reflects at least three quite distinct
notions. The first is the idea that the transmission of inflation in the economy
owes much to identifiable rigidities in the labour market, related to inherited
systems of collective bargaining. The second notion refers to the responsiveness
of the labour market to the market signals provided by pay and unemployment; advocates of flexibility argue that these should be enhanced by
improving incentives to occupational and geographical mobility as well as
individual performance. This was primarily to be achieved by ensuring that
outcomes be more heavily dependent upon the market – punishing periods of
unemployment more severely and generally widening the dispersion of post-tax
incomes. In the public sector this has meant that pay should tend to 'mimic'
outcomes in the private sector, and more precisely reflect performance. Finally,
flexibility also has connotations with regard to the 'right to manage' and the
ability of employers to control the human resources at their disposal in a
fashion closer to that of other inputs. The very rapid climb in unemployment

in the latest recession may be a pointer to the effectiveness of policy in this regard.

PAY AND INFLATION

Although doubt was cast in an earlier chapter on the causal connections between inflation and the growth process (see Chapter 3 above), the relationship between pay and inflation remains one of considerable importance and interest: first, because of the importance that policy has attached to it over the last decade (so that policy can be assessed in its own terms) and, second, because 'convergence' in inflationary performance is viewed as a vital element in the process of European integration as envisaged in the Maastricht Treaty. Although the role of the UK in monetary union is cloaked in doubt, as indeed is the process itself, it should be noted that the progress of each nation towards union is dependent upon the satisfaction of four criteria related to inflation performance, public sector borrowing, exchange rate stability and nominal interest rates. Whatever the position of the government regarding eventual union, it would be deeply ironic if these criteria, which more or less define macroeconomic performance for those of a monetarist persuasion, were not to be satisfied in the UK. Although inflation has currently reached quite low levels, touching a level in 1993 not seen since the 1960s, the question as to whether this is *sustainable* or not is quite specifically referred to in the protocol defining convergence. Political pressures arising from persistently high levels of unemployment may mean that current levels of inflation are not sustainable in the longer term.

The relationship between pay and inflation can be thought of in terms of an interaction between labour costs and prices – the specific way in which rises in pay feed through into price rises on the one hand, and the reaction of pay to rises in prices on the other. How such a 'wage–price spiral' develops (and hence differences in national performance in terms of inflation) is conditioned in its turn by a number of factors to which we now turn.

The importance of the labour market for the generation and transmission of inflationary pressure stems from the large share taken by labour costs in the total costs of production at the level of the entire economy. This is illustrated by the data in Table 1, which is based on the 1984 input–output tables for the UK, published by the CSO. It shows for example that the labour cost content of the final demand of consumers was about 37.9 per cent; it was significantly higher in the case of exports and investment, however, where indirect taxation is rather less important. Labour costs form an even larger share of government purchases, but this is a rather special case because much government output is not marketed and hence no conventional price is attached to it. The table also makes it clear that labour costs are not the only potential source of inflationary pressure – import costs, indirect taxation and profits all can and do play significant roles. It is important, however, to note that for many firms labour

Table 1 The primary cost content of final demand, 1984 (per cent)

Primary input	Consumers' expenditure	Government purchases	Fixed investment	Exports	Total
(1) Imports	21.9	12.8	33.7	23.7	22.5
(2) Taxes less subsidies	17.9	6.1	6.1	2.5	10.9
(3) Income from employment	38.1	58.7	42.1	44.8	43.6
(4) Gross profits etc.	22.1	22.3	18.1	29.0	23.0

Source: CSO, Input–Output Tables for the United Kingdom 1984

costs are generally a much smaller proportion of total costs than those indicated in the table. This is because at the level of the entire economy, intermediate costs (inter-firm purchases) are netted out. The point is significant, because wage increases granted by one firm are felt as price increases by other firms: microeconomic units may therefore underestimate the inflationary impact of rises in their own labour costs and prices.

It can also be seen from Table 1 that the cost composition of the various items of final demand is quite different and so alternative measures of inflation can behave quite differently, especially in the short run. We may note that:

1 consumer price indices (for example the *retail prices index*[1] (RPI)) will tend to be more heavily influenced by indirect taxation than other familiar indices;
2 the broadest measure of inflation is the *total final expenditure deflator*, the cost composition for which is given by the final column;
3 if import costs are excluded, then we have the composition of costs for *GDP at market prices*.
4 Finally, if we look solely at domestic costs of production (rows 3 and 4) we are looking at the cost composition of GDP at factor cost. The *deflator of GDP at factor cost*, sometimes termed the *index of total home costs*, can be thought of as an economy-wide indicator of output prices *before* indirect taxes and subsidies are included. So for this widely used inflation indicator, labour costs are an even more important component, at something like two-thirds of the total, the remainder constituting profits. Its popularity as an indicator stems from its relevance as a broadly based indicator of purely *domestic* inflation.

The RPI is naturally of great relevance to employees concerned with living standards since it can be used to measure the *real consumption wage*; moreover, as a widely publicized indicator, movements in the RPI form an important backdrop to wage negotiations.

To understand the position of employers in an inflationary context, the index of total home costs (a measure of *output* prices) has greater relevance than the RPI, since the movement of labour costs *per unit of output* (or unit labour costs) relative to this indicator provides evidence of falling or rising profitability. Wages measured in terms of output prices are sometimes termed *real product wages*. It is clear from Table 1 that movements in real product wages can differ from those in the real consumption wages if, for example, import costs or indirect taxes (per unit of output) are changing relative to other costs.

When real product wages are rising in line with labour productivity, then this is generally regarded as consistent with a given level of employment, and will not provide incentives for employers to shed or take on more labour. But it is, however, quite possible for equi-proportionate increases in real consumption wages and productivity to provide incentives for employers to lay-off workers, if for example, import costs were rising faster than domestic inflation. The 'oil shock' of 1973–4, when the price of oil quadrupled, provides the classic case in point: rising prices of imported fuel warranted a reduction in the real consumption wage if the then existing levels of employment were to be maintained. The incomes policy operating at that time involved threshold payments which were triggered whenever the RPI rose more than a given amount; because the rises in this index stemmed largely from imports, the payments actually caused real product wages to rise – in this sense, wages were linked to the wrong index!

An 'equilibrium' rate of inflation is therefore possible when real product wages rise in line with labour productivity. If, in addition, money wages were also rising in line with labour productivity, then unit labour costs would be constant and there would be no tendency for the economy to generate any domestic inflation. Some people have thereby concluded that if, in every firm, pay increases are always based on productivity improvements, then inflation would cease. Such arguments are naive, because if this practice were to be followed rigidly, the remuneration of similar occupations in different industries and firms would rapidly begin to diverge. Recruitment would rapidly become impossible in sectors where productivity was rising slowly. Moreover, relative price change would falter and a vital mechanism of adjustment, tending to redistribute demand away from less progressive sectors towards the more progressive, would not operate. Clearly similar work must receive a similar reward and this recipe for the control of inflation is unworkable. Money-wage increases across the economy need to be based on *average* productivity growth. This implies that a zero rate of inflation, if ever achieved, would be made up of a distribution of price increases, many of which would be negative.

The process of inflation is therefore dependent upon the way in which rises in employment income feed through into rises in unit labour costs – on the balance between compensation per employee and labour productivity. Usually this means that individual wages and salaries before tax are rising faster than productivity, but it could also reflect growing rates of employer contributions to pension schemes, employers' national insurance contributions and so forth. In theory, these additions to the wage bill could also act as a stimulus or check to inflationary pressure.

Whether rising unit labour costs actually feed through into higher output prices then depends upon the ability of producers to set higher prices. This may differ significantly (at least in the short run) between the tradable and non-tradable sector of the economy, depending upon the exchange rate regime in operation. A central feature of the Exchange Rate Mechanism (ERM) of the European Monetary System (EMS), for example, is that it is intended to impose greater discipline on producers to hold the line on price increases, since attempts to raise prices are translated into losses in sales. On the other hand, a floating exchange rate which adjusts in accordance with any price increase simply accommodates any increase in wages and prices.

A fixed exchange rate therefore acts as a disciplinary force on the inflationary process. It is here that the idea of 'credibility' can usefully be introduced, since the disciplinary effect only works if the commitment to holding the exchange rate is a credible one. If it is, the rate of inflation will tend to converge on the member of the regime which has the most anti-inflationary credibility – in the case of the ERM this means Germany, where anti-inflation credentials are believed to have been bolstered by the independence of the Bundesbank from political pressure, and of course have been built up over a long period of time. Of course a single economy can in principle achieve similar results by announcing monetary or other targets implying that inflation of more than a certain amount would not be tolerated – this was the basis behind the Medium-Term Financial Strategy (MTFS) of the Conservative government in the period of Sir Geoffrey Howe's chancellorship. However, it may take considerable periods of time for such credibility to become established, and it may be extremely difficult in a system where the government is effectively the monetary authority and is actively engaged in an ongoing 'political cycle'. If there is some evidence that the early 1980s helped to establish the Conservative credentials, there is probably even more that this was thrown away during the period of the 'Thatcher–Lawson' boom. It was no doubt hoped that entry into the ERM in 1990 would provide a short-cut to credibility and lead to a modification of behaviour in the labour market. However, as we shall see below, the attempt to maintain the sterling exchange rate was simply not a credible one. Subsequent events have re-emphasized the difficulties in using a quasi-fixed exchange rate regime (such as the ERM) to preserve price stability, echoing the death throes of the Bretton Woods system in the late 1960s and early 1970s.

However, it is important to consider what happens when price rises are constrained (via the effects of a fixed exchange rate) from following wage increases. Real-product wages start to rise and if, as is commonly assumed, employers remain on their demand curves, employment will start to fall. A key element in the performance of the labour market is the degree to which unemployment must rise before wage increases moderate sufficiently for an equilibrium to emerge at the sustainable rate of inflation. This will in turn depend upon a number of factors, including the degree of 'mismatch' between the location of lay-offs (in terms of industries, geographical locations or types of worker), and the occurrence of vacancies. Mismatch is widely regarded as a key ingredient in Britain's poor inflationary record. It is not unusual in Britain for vacancies to exist in large numbers in the south-east while unemployment is growing in other parts of the country; and to the extent that wages are a national, rather than a local, phenomenon, wage pressure may continue to mount – a situation described as 'regional mismatch'. Although mismatch tends to move in a cyclical fashion, it has been rather less important in the current recession than it was in the mid-1980s, when unemployment was also at high levels (Bank of England 1993).

There is no doubt that the failure of wages to respond more closely to conditions in local labour markets has been a source of considerable disappointment to a government which has actively encouraged an ongoing trend towards greater decentralization in pay bargaining. Walsh and Brown (1991a) report that although the degree of inter-regional pay dispersion increased during the 1980s, this was almost entirely due to the increase in relative pay in the south-east (especially London). They suggest that greater decentralization has not made wages more responsive to local labour market conditions because pay bargaining is frequently set within a national corporate framework. Decentralization has been occurring along product-market lines rather than geographic ones, reflecting a trend towards multi-divisional forms of organization; in this context, firms increasingly see pay in relation to corporate performance (profits and productivity) rather than to the external labour market. The problem has possibly been exacerbated by the increasing share of corporate headquarters situated in the south-east.[2]

Regional imbalances in the labour market are intensified by the well-documented geographical immobility of manual labour and the peculiarities of the housing market in Britain. Both owner-occupied housing and council housing have substantial transactions costs associated with moving, and the private rental market in the UK remains small. In contrast to the US, for example, manual labour mobility in Britain is reckoned to be lower than that for non-manuals, a situation which sales of council houses was intended to alleviate (Hughes and McCormick 1990). House price differentials between the more prosperous regions and the rest of the economy almost certainly tend to intensify labour market mismatch. According to Bover et al. (1989) and Muellbauer (1990), there is considerable evidence of the effect of fluctuations in relative house prices between the north and south upon the mobility of labour. This stems from a lower elasticity in the supply of housing land in the south, creating a cycle in regional house-price differentials and a consequential 'mobility trap' – as house prices begin to rise relatively in the south, households there become reluctant to move elsewhere, releasing little housing for inward migration, which may in any event become too expensive for northern households. Towards the peak of the price cycle, outward migration plus increased housing capacity in the south reverses the process – house prices in the south begin to fall (at least relatively, but recently in an absolute sense) and again northern households may be reluctant to move because of negative rates of return associated with southern housing. There is therefore 'overshooting' in both directions. Of course in the longer run, as Muellbauer concedes, investment and location decisions may be influenced by the higher levels of house prices as well as lower unemployment in the south. Although the cycle was already in evidence to some extent in the 1970s, financial liberalization in the course of the 1980s (especially the removal of mortgage rationing), in conjunction with the fiscal incentives in favour of owner occupation, has probably intensified its effects. Moreover, the probability is that financial liberalization did help to increase the volatility of consumer spending, and since mortgage lending is a particularly cheap form of finance for consumers, the phenomenon of (housing) equity withdrawal is important as a source of demand and credit expansion in inflationary periods.

The interaction between the housing market and the labour market is therefore important in explaining the high levels to which unemployment has to rise for inflationary pressure to moderate. Regional mismatch is in fact only a part of this story; overall, the key element is the degree to which the unemployed are actively engaged in the search for jobs and providing real competition for vacancies. Discouraged workers (frequently the longer-term unemployed) effectively leave the labour market. The role of the long-term unemployed is explored in Layard *et al.* (1991).

If some classes of unemployed workers no longer compete for work, then the failure of earnings growth to slow further in the mid-1980s, despite the existence of a high 'headline' figure for unemployment, can be explained. In this view of things the labour market can display considerable 'hysteresis', in which the equilibrium rate of unemployment can follow the actual rate upward. It follows that active labour market policies aimed at getting the unemployed back into work and keeping the long-term unemployed active within the labour market, could be a potent means by which the unemployment cost of disinflation as well as the level of unemployment itself could be reduced. Evidence from the current recession certainly does not suggest that the terms of the trade-off between the rise in unemployment and the fall in inflation (sometimes termed the sacrifice ratio) has improved significantly over time (see Figure 2, Chapter 13). If so, this is a sad result from a decade of labour market reform. We return to this point below.

The progress of inflation depends not only on the way in which wages feed through into prices, but also on the way in which price increases react back upon wages. The British labour market is generally characterized as possessing considerable 'real-wage rigidity' so that increases in consumer prices are rapidly translated into wage increases: the labour market behaves 'as if' wages were indexed to the rate of consumer price inflation. In the 1970s, this characteristic was generally held to be a result of trade union power. This argument has considerably less force today.

It is important to realize that although the bargain over the wage is conducted in *nominal* terms, the objective for management and the workforce in the period between negotiations is over the *real* wage and, as we have seen, a different real wage to boot. In consequence, the *expected rate of inflation* over the coming period provides an inescapable *macro* component to wage negotiations which no amount of decentralization or increased flexibility can avoid. Moreover, uncertainty over the anticipated rate of inflation can create pressure for more frequent wage negotiations and even indexation of the sort seen in Italy until quite recently. The macro uncertainty surrounding the wage bargain is compounded by the need to interpret price rises correctly. When the 'shock' to the labour market comes from the output market, i.e. from the prices of goods and services, the correct functioning of the economy requires a different response depending upon whether the shock is nominal or real. If, for example, excess credit expansion triggers a demand-pull inflation on output prices, then there is no obvious reason for real wages (however measured) to change – wage increases should follow the price increase. If, however, the shock emanating from the goods market is a real one, acting for example through lower productivity growth or an adverse movement in the terms of trade, then real consumption wages should alter in consequence, at least if rises in unemployment are to be avoided. Clearly, the macro state of the economy poses quite complex informational problems for negotiators which cannot be resolved by making the labour market more decentralized – indeed this may intensify the problem in making the extraction of relevant macro information more difficult. A number of policies that may help to alleviate the impact of a decentralized structure are discussed below.

The discussion of inflation has so far made no mention of public sector pay, which currently makes up something like 60 per cent of government spending on goods and services (excluding the public corporations). Up until the 1970s, average earnings in the public sector had been a relatively quiescent factor, tending to follow private sector earnings in a reasonably stable manner. Over the last two decades, however, a distinct cycle has emerged with relative public/private sector pay tending to fall over a period of years, before experiencing significant 'bounce back' – the financial years of 1975/6, 1980/1 (the Clegg comparability awards) and 1987/8 stand out in this respect. The time profile reflects the tendency to rein back on public sector pay when possible (aware of the considerable implications for public sector borrowing) before the realities of the labour market – the need to recruit and retain staff – force a reappraisal. The government itself has consistently denied the operation of a *de facto* incomes policy for public sector pay but in the context of expenditure restraint, this is hard to sustain. In any event, the difficulties of operating an incomes policy in only a part of the economy are all too obvious. Although there is not (in most instances) a direct impact of public sector pay on inflation because output is not marketed, the indirect effects are various – through pay relativities, through possible effects on the money supply or through the 'signals' which pay awards may give on the direction of government policy. Rapid adjustments in public/private pay differentials are unlikely to assist the control of inflation, especially in the longer term.

It is now of importance to understand the forces shaping the relationship between the inflation of the late 1980s and the ensuing recession, and to this topic we now turn.

INFLATION PERFORMANCE 1979–92
THE BACKGROUND TO RECESSION

It would be easy, but mistaken, to suppose that the twin problems of inflation and the balance of payments that emerged in the course of the 1980s were simply caused by an 'excessive' growth of nominal demand. However, it is part of the conventional wisdom that it was excess demand and inflation that led to the period of punitive interest rates after 1988 which, in conjunction with record levels of private sector indebtedness, provided the proximate cause of recession. According to this view of things, it was a mixture of policy errors which led to a quite unsustainable consumer and investment boom between 1985 and 1988, financed largely by increased borrowing. Various factors have been blamed – financial deregulation, an unnecessary loosening of monetary policy after the stock exchange 'crash' of October 1987, income tax reductions,

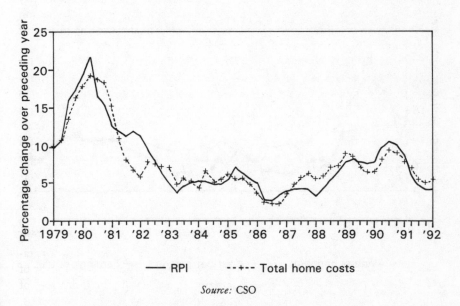

Source: CSO

Figure 14.1 Inflation, RPI and index of total home costs.

295

misleading economic forecasts, even the announcement by the then Chancellor that the 'economic miracle' had arrived. In any event, wildly unrealistic and unjustifiable expectations of future prosperity were sufficient to drive up the volume of consumption by 21 per cent over three years, and investment by 28 per cent, albeit from a low level.

Yet a little further analysis reveals that the supply-side problems were just as important as the demand surge in creating the inflationary conditions. First, it is instructive to consider the two alternative measures of inflation discussed above. In Figure 1, the 'headline' measure provided by the RPI is compared with the index of total home costs. As we have seen, the RPI is intended to provide an idea of the increase in the cost of living. It is therefore affected by such things as indirect taxation, the cost of a mortgage and, critically, the price of imports. It is not therefore a very useful indicator of the purely *domestic* component of inflation, which is better described by the deflator of GDP at factor cost.

Over longer periods of time, the two indicators tend to move together, but considerable divergence is possible in the shorter term. It is significant that the GDP deflator accelerates rapidly from just over 2 per cent to over 6 per cent during the course of 1987 alone, a path not initially followed by the RPI. Although the source of the domestic inflationary pressure came from the side of labour costs, it can be seen from Figure 2 that the problem was not one of an autonomous acceleration of average earnings but rather from the side of productivity. Indeed average earnings growth remained remarkably stable over

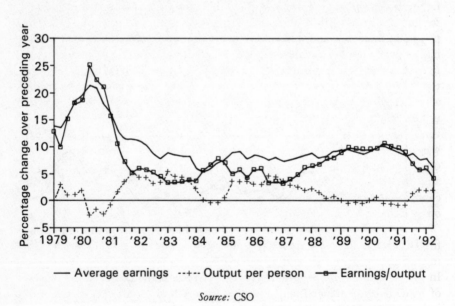

Source: CSO

Figure 14.2 Earnings and productivity growth (whole economy).

the period at around 7–8 per cent. The figure shows that the rate of productivity advance for the whole economy had peaked in 1986, before declining
rapidly towards zero during 1987 and 1988.

That the slowdown was not widely recognized at the time may owe something to the preoccupation with *manufacturing* productivity, of which it had
become fashionable to speak of a productivity 'miracle'. Productivity advance
was rather faster in manufacturing after 1979, largely achieved by reductions
in employment and manning levels. By the late 1980s, employment in
manufacturing was only about 20 per cent of the labour force, compared with
29 per cent in 1979 – rather too small to have any great impact on the overall
rate of productivity advance.

That there was a significant problem of economy-wide productivity does not
imply that the labour market did not have an important role as a generator of
the damaging rise in inflation after 1986. An effective labour market should
deliver low inflation because of its responsiveness to a variety of real shocks. In
essence, the slowdown of productivity growth should have caused average
earnings growth to moderate and inflation to be contained. That nothing of
the sort happened poses key questions about labour market performance
despite a decade of reforms aimed specifically at making the labour market
much more responsive to the 'forces of supply and demand'.

The rise in unemployment needed to moderate earnings inflation since the
onset of the recession does not suggest any dramatic improvement in the
unemployment cost of lower inflation compared to the early 1980s. It was this
failure which spelled the death-knell of the attempt to maintain the parity of
sterling within the ERM after the decision to enter in October 1990. The
process of 'nominal' and 'real' convergence envisaged in the Maastricht Treaty
had evidently not been achieved in the case of Britain. Certainly, inflation rates
in the UK and Germany did converge rapidly, as Figure 3 makes clear. But with
the failure of the economy to recover in 1992, it was a mere charade to describe
a similar rate of inflation in the UK and Germany coping with the strains of
unification as 'convergence'. It can be seen that France's inflation record at this
time shows a much closer profile to Germany, and although unemployment
was substantially higher it was not rising. In Britain, with the current account
of the balance of payments not recovering with any rapidity, and with the
authorities failing to take action to halt the steady slide in sterling during the
course of 1992, the government found that its bluff was called by the markets
on so-called Black Wednesday.

To summarize, the poor UK inflation performance may be attributed in the
first instance to a combination of the ineffectiveness of rises in unemployment
in curbing wage pressure and a lack of flexibility in inflationary expectations.
In the background lie deeper structural problems relating to both the process
of matching unemployed with vacancies and also the credibility of the anti-
inflationary resolve of the government.

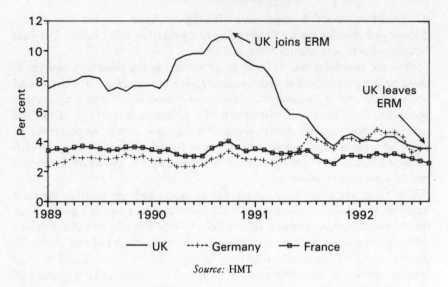

Figure 14.3 Consumer price inflation in the UK, Germany and France (percentage change over previous year).

THE DISTRIBUTION OF INCOME

If pay from employment has a major role to play in the generation of inflation, it also has a key (if declining) role in determining the income of individual households and the distribution of income between households. Although it is gross pay which is important in the transmission of inflation, it is net (take-home) pay which is important to the household, at least if the 'social wage' is ignored. A central aim of government policy since 1979 has been to reduce the tax burden on the community whilst at the same time sharpening the economic incentives to increased effort. The two objectives are of course quite distinct. The former involves reducing the *average* rate of taxation while the latter requires reductions in the effective *marginal* rate of taxation. It is unfortunate that popular debate on both of these components of the tax-and-benefit system has focused so much upon the rate of income taxation, because there are many other influences on the overall impact of the tax-and-benefit system.

Whatever the effect of government policy since 1979 has been on the *perceived* tax burden, the fact is that once the increases in VAT rates are taken into account, it did not reduce the actual average tax burden. Tax revenue as a percentage of GDP rose from 34.3 per cent in 1970–79 to 37.4 per cent in 1980–9 (Johnson 1991). Unless the recovery is faster than anticipated, it seems highly likely that this will increase in the 1990s as announced tax increases take hold.

Of course, rates of income tax have been reduced successively during the 1980s, particularly at the top end of the income scale, where there have been dramatic falls in the top rate of income tax, from 83 per cent in 1979 to 40 per cent in 1993, compared to the reduction in the standard rate from 33 to 25 per cent. At the lower end, a new lower rate of 20 per cent has been introduced. However, National Insurance contributions have tended to raise marginal rates for lower incomes. Moreover, the policy of increasingly targeting social security benefits where most needed, has tended to exacerbate disincentive effects (high *effective* marginal rates) for those out of work and for those on low pay.[3]. Attempts to alleviate these particular disincentive effects were limited to a range of measures introduced in the late 1980s. Following the DHSS Green Paper in 1985, they were intended to address five main problems: complexity, lack of targeting, the poverty and unemployment traps, limited freedom of choice and concerns about the future burden of the system. In retrospect what at first sight appeared to be a more fundamental review became a series of modest reforms which did not radically alter a system of social welfare provision which dates back to the principle of social insurance introduced by Beveridge, and in which 'full employment' formed the essential backcloth. There were some simplifications and revisions to existing support payments; Income Support replaced Supplementary Benefit; Family Credit replaced Family Income Supplement; Housing Benefit was reduced; there were some adjustments to National Insurance contributions to limit the possibility of small income changes triggering large increases in contributions. However, none of these measures really began to deal with the essential disincentive effects of the welfare system. For the unemployed, the abolition of earnings-related benefits reduced the ratio of benefits to the net wage (the *replacement ratio*) and may have acted as a spur to job search for those recently unemployed; a more intractable problem was the disengagement of the long-term unemployed from active job search – the so-called 'state dependency' effect (Layard *et al.* 1991).

It is important to realize that policy-driven changes to the tax-and-benefit system were only a part of a trend towards greater income inequality. In Table 2 we can observe three main trends in income distribution between 1979 and 1989. First the original and post-income tax earnings of the top 20 per cent has increased greatly, at the expense of all other quintiles but especially in terms of the bottom 40 per cent. Second, the original and post-tax shares of the bottom 20 per cent have decreased, while the relative importance of benefits to the same group has also increased, raising its share from 2 to 7 per cent compared with a rise from 4 to 9 per cent in 1979.

Increasing inequality marked a fundamental reversal of the secular trend towards growing equality visible for much of the twentieth century. It can be seen that the increase in inequality mainly arises from original income rather than benefit and tax changes. The latter was only of much import for the top quintile of households.

Table 2 Shares of household income, 1979 and 1988 (1979 figures in parentheses)

	Bottom fifth	Next fifth	Middle fifth	Next fifth	Top fifth	Implied Gini coefficient[a] (%)
Original income	2 (4)	7 (10)	16 (18)	25 (26)	50 (43)	46 (37)
Final income (including benefits)	7 (9)	11 (14)	16 (17)	22 (23)	44 (37)	34 (26)

[a] The Gini coefficient measures the extent of income inequality in society. A value of 100 represents one extreme where all income is concentrated in the hands of a single household or individual. On the other hand, if all households received identical incomes, then the Gini coefficient would be zero. The computed figure in the text is based on the information in this table.
Note: These figures are measured for equalized income which corrects for differences in household size. Final income includes all tax-and-benefit effects.
Source: CSO and own estimates

The increased dispersion of household *income* is the outcome of a number of factors, only one of which is the increased dispersion of pay from employment: unemployment and a declining share of employment income in household income have also been important (Atkinson 1991). Moreover, the picture of household income dominated by the earnings of a male in full-time employment today needs reassessing: between the trough of the recession in 1981 and 1989, there were 636,000 fewer full-time jobs for males, roughly balanced by 670,000 extra full-time jobs for females.[4] The increasing numbers of self-employed and the nature of the work being done may have had an important impact – real income from self-employment on a per capita basis has not risen significantly over the period. Nevertheless, earnings from employment also show considerably more dispersion today than they did in 1979. Moreover, this is no simple composition effect (due, for example, to the increased proportion of women in the labour force) – the effect persists when more detailed subgroups are considered, e.g. non-manual men, non-manual women, manual men, manual women (Hughes 1992). In addition, the distribution has become particularly stretched at the top end, and although these results are typical for the private sector, a similar process has been occurring in the public sector (Walsh and Brown 1991b). At the bottom end the decline in importance (and eventual abolition in 1993) of Wages Councils may be having similar effects.

As far as the ultimate causes of growing inequality in pay are concerned, it is important to stress that trends in Britain are an example of a very similar trend within the advanced economies of the OECD. Davis (1992) found that rising inequality was a common (if not a universal) feature. Note that economies do, however, differ markedly in the degree of inequality observed. There was a general tendency towards higher experience and education differentials as well as greater inequality among 'observationally equivalent' workers. This pattern reverses earlier trends in the same economies towards

Table 3 Average annual growth rates, 1979–89 (per cent per annum)

	Output per person employed	Net average real earnings
UK	1.7	2.4
Germany	1.4	0.3
France	2.1	-0.4
Italy*	1.6	0.8

* 1980–88 only

Note: Net average real earnings = (wages and salaries less direct taxes less security contributions deflated by consumer prices)/ employees in employment

Source: OECD National Accounts, vol. II, 1977–89

growing equality found in the 1970s. Although the rise in inequality in Britain has been quite sharp, this was also the case in the US (which has a markedly higher *level* of inequality), Canada, Australia and West Germany. France provides a counter-example where little change has been observed. The cross-country nature of the phenomenon naturally suggests common origins. The increasing openness of economies to international trade is one interesting possibility in which greater imports of unskilled-labour-intensive products may have similar effects to an expansion in the supply of less-skilled workers.

The increased inequality of pay and income must, however, be set against the central tendency of the distribution; here the interesting phenomenon is that *average*[5] real take-home pay almost certainly increased faster in the UK than the overall rate of productivity growth. Table 3 is derived from the OECD National Accounts and shows that the UK was quite exceptional in this compared to other major European economies, where there appears to have been quite exceptionally slow growth in real take-home pay. In the US, this phenomenon has been widely commented upon. In the final analysis, the precise characterization of gainers and losers over the period remains to be written – there can be little doubt that a sizeable minority of those who managed to remain in employment did quite well. Ultimately this may go down as the dividend from North Sea oil. In the future, tax revenues can be expected to be rather less buoyant than in the 1980s, and the problems of financing welfare and other government expenditures can be expected to intensify.

THE DECENTRALIZATION OF PAY BARGAINING

We have already alluded to the major changes occurring to systems of pay bargaining in the UK. According to the *1990 Workplace Industrial Relations Survey* (WIRS, see Millward *et al.* (1992)), the system of regulating relations between employers and employees up to 1980 could usefully be described as one of voluntary collective bargaining, the central feature of which was the direct bargaining between employers and unions over wages and workplace conditions. By 1990, however, fewer workplaces recognized trade unions (53 per cent in 1990 compared with 66 per cent in 1980), fewer employees were covered by collective agreements, and fewer sites had union representatives; above all else there has been a steep decline in union membership, especially in the private sector.

At the same time, employer associations have declined in importance as far as wage bargaining has been concerned. The number of establishments using multi-employer negotiations to establish at least minimum terms and conditions declined significantly between 1984 and 1990. This is also consistent with the increasing organization of industry along 'profit-centre' lines. Amongst the most important casualties was the famous agreement covering the engineering industry, although we might add agreements in cotton textiles, buses, commercial television, banking, food retailing, docks, cement and newspapers (Walsh and Brown 1991b). Research has tended to confirm the growing importance of 'insider' factors (both firm profits and productivity) in the determination of pay; for econometric evidence see Nickell and Wadhwani (1990) and for evidence from the CBI Pay Databank see Ingram (1991).[6]

It was therefore thought that there would have been an increase in the extent of plant-level bargaining. In fact WIRS found no such increase in the unionized sector, but rather an increase in negotiating structures at company level in unionized companies. However, in the non-union sector, the increasing autonomy of local managements on pay matters was evident so, overall, there was a slight increase in local pay determination.

Fundamental changes have also been occurring in the public sector, with delegation of pay bargaining to agencies, greater autonomy for NHS trusts, and the contracting-out of services in local government all extending the number of bargaining points. Performance-related pay schemes have also proliferated.

Although such a system must in some sense possess greater flexibility it may well be that it has disadvantages in terms of inflation. It is frequently contended that national (or centralized) bargaining systems offer inherent advantages over those which are decentralized. On the employee side, bargainers will be wary of reaching inflationary settlements, because the higher prices will be felt directly by the employees themselves. Evidently as the system becomes more decentralized, this effect is reduced, and an inflationary wage increase on the part of a small group of workers will not, other things being equal, show up as a general increase in prices. Similar effects exist on the employers' side: where bargaining is highly decentralized, individual employers may feel that they have much to gain by offering better wages in an effort to retain and motivate the existing workforce. If employers were bargaining nationally, these benefits would cease to exist. The Nordic countries are commonly thought of as having more centralized bargaining structures and here the unemployment and inflation outcomes have been more favourable than in many other Western European economies. Precise analysis of cause and effect is difficult because of significant variations in aspects of labour market policy towards the unemployed. Sweden in particular has very active policies designed to create jobs, to match the unemployed with vacancies and provide them with training. Moreover, centralization is far from absolute in any of the Nordic economies, and given the existence of 'wage drift', it is far from clear that central bargains dominate the formation of average earnings. Finally, despite a similar degree of centralization, Denmark has had an unemployment record which is very similar to that of Western Europe generally.

In one variant on the centralization thesis, Calmfors and Driffill (1988) have argued that there is a 'hump-shaped' relationship between centralization and inflation outcomes. The UK, it was contended, was on the hump, and there-fore possessed an inferior record. However, such has been the pace of decentralization it is no longer clear that the UK should be classified as an intermediate case.

There are, of course, likely to be gains and losses in any system of bargaining. The process absorbs economic resources, and so centralized systems, quite apart from any advantages in the control of inflation, are clearly efficient in the sense that there are economies of scale attached to the coverage of a single bargain. On the other hand, flexibility and the special knowledge that may come from localized bargaining, will be missing. Moreover, if 'drift' from the central bargain is commonplace, and involves further bargaining, the economies of centralization may be lost; there is some evidence that this may be happening in the Nordic economies. In any event, policy in the UK must be restricted to feasible changes, and it may well be that more can be learned from other decentralized structures, some of which clearly have better macroeconomic outcomes, including Switzerland, Japan, the US and Germany (although here industry-level bargaining is the norm). The US has a decentralized structure but no substantial collective bargaining. Japan offers an interesting comparator to the UK in that the chief difference is in the much greater degree of employer coordination, and the fact that pay bargains are 'synchronized' in the *Shunto* or 'Spring offensive'. Soskice (1990) has in fact argued that favourable inflation outcomes may owe more to employer coordination than to centralization as such. Germany is rather more centralized than the UK, but a key feature of the system, which may be transferable to the UK, is the *Sachsverstandigenrat* or Council of Economic Advisers which has a role in providing credible macro-economic data and projections. This macroeconomic data is clearly important in providing a foundation for the position of the 'social partners' in the linchpin agreement provided by the metal-working industry.

Elements of both the German and Japanese systems are detectable as the ingredients of a pay-policy strategy for the UK which advocates refer to as 'coordinated pay bargaining' (cf. Layard 1990). The essential ingredients include:

1 A national economic assessment (NEA);
2 Synchronized pay bargaining;
3 The formulation of government economic policy.

The logical starting point for a movement towards greater coordination in pay bargaining is the NEA which could be viewed as initially providing better, more credible information for bargainers. It is important that no element of compulsion is involved in the arrangement but that it is based on improved information flows to the bargainers as well as real incentives towards greater coordination. A number of outputs are possible, but the determination of a 'competitive' rate of price inflation for the coming year is one possibility. Such a figure could provide an alternative macroeconomic 'anchor' to the current system which is currently lacking. Importantly, it would also be forward-looking, and related to the rate of *producer* price inflation. Credibility would almost certainly require independence of the members of the council. Having achieved this, average wage settlements would need to be based on the average rate of productivity growth in the economy as a whole. It is of course important that successful firms should be able to bid labour away from unsuccessful ones, but the indicator of success in competitive markets is not its peculiar rate of productivity growth but its profitability. Profit (but not productivity) related pay is a way in which better firms could procure better quality labour without potentially inflationary pay settlements.

The announcement of a competitive rate of price increase would not of course prejudice pay negotiations one way or another, but may order them in a forward-looking manner. The next stage would be the 'synchronization' of pay bargaining in the manner of the Japanese, so that deals are struck at approximately the same time, after discussion of the NEA. Public sector deals might then follow those in the private sector. Knowledge of the progress of the pay round might then assist in the formulation of government policy if pay settlements were bunched in the period prior to the budget. Pay synchronization will not necessarily resolve problems of 'leapfrogging' in a decentralized system, but the fact that bargaining is taking place in a number of different locations, at the same time, and where similar issues are forthcoming, may provide real incentives on employers to coordinate their activities, and improved employer coordination would appear to be a prerequisite for a more successful bargaining system. Synchronization is not likely to prove a complete panacea, and may bring distinct problems, not least in terms of the emphasis it will give to pay relativities – where staggered awards can be expected to allow some 'fudging' of the issue.

CONCLUSIONS

Whether the supply-side measures undertaken in the 1980s have tackled the fundamental labour market problems of the UK economy must be assessed in terms of their wider outcomes: economic growth, unemployment and inflation. The tackling of inflation has been a key focus for labour market reform, yet it is by no means clear that the UK has better performance on this front than it possessed in 1979. Despite the serious decline of the power of trade unions in collective bargaining, 'insider' power seems to be as important as ever and this may partly reflect new systems of pay determination.

At the same time, the dispersion of outcomes for both individuals and households has widened considerably for reasons that are still being explored, but the impact of higher levels of unemployment and a decline in employment for full-time males has been vast. Although other advanced economies have experienced rising inequality in income distribution, the speed of the effect does seem to have been very rapid in Britain, with tax–benefit policy imparting a further twist in the same direction. Experience in other countries suggests that more active labour market policies towards the unemployed could do much to reduce long-term unemployment.

While it is hard to contest the idea that more flexibility in the labour market is desirable it does not follow that this will be achieved by even more decentralization. Considerable changes have been taking place in the way pay is determined in Britain; decentralization is the driving force, but this does not appear to have meant very much in terms of local labour market flexibility.

What remains in question is the role of the labour market in improving competitiveness, and what kinds of labour market reforms are now appropriate. A new direction for supply-side policies might be to reconsider the incentive effects of taxes and benefits. At the present time: (i) any reductions in benefits and taxes are seen as necessarily beneficial to the economy whatever the implications for incentives; (ii) there are weaker incentives for all low-paid workers and the unemployed; (iii) a decentralized system of pay bargaining has been encouraged but the potential consequences for inflation of this change in the pay bargaining system have been largely disregarded. The current system sadly lacks the macroeconomic anchor that might prevent further inflationary booms and this is exacerbated by the housing market.

NOTES

1 Note that the RPI is not based on national accounts data but upon the cost of purchasing a typical basket of consumption goods and services; these include items which are not part of the basic national income data (e.g. mortgage interest payments). The consumer price index, which is entirely based on the national accounts, is the consumer expenditure deflator.

2 For evidence, see Begg and Guy (1992) – a trend which accelerated with the merger and acquisition boom of the late 1980s.

3 For a general survey of problems of incentives for the low paid, see Bowen and Mayhew (1990).
4 Data are from the Censuses of Employment for 1981 and 1989, summaries of which are published in the *Employment Gazette*.
5 Median earnings would perhaps be more appropriate, given the considerable positive skewness in the distribution.
6 For a detailed appraisal of new systems of incentive pay, see Cannell and Wood (1992).

REFERENCES

Atkinson, A. B. (1991) 'What is happening to the distribution of income in the UK?', *Keynes Lecture*, British Academy, London, 15 October.
Bank of England (1993) *Inflation Report*, London, August.
Begg, I. and Guy, N. (1992) 'The changing regional structure', in C. Driver and P. Dunne (eds), *Structural Changes in the UK Economy*, Cambridge: Cambridge University Press, pp. 45–78.
Bover, O., Muellbauer, J. and Murphy, A. (1989) 'Housing, wages, and UK labour markets', *Oxford Bulletin of Economics and Statistics*, vol. 51, pp. 97–162.
Bowen, A. and Mayhew, K. (eds) (1990) *Improving Incentives for the Low Paid*, London and Basingstoke: Macmillan.
Calmfors, L. and Driffill, J. (1988) 'Centralisation of wage bargaining and macro-economic performance', *Economic Policy*, no. 6, pp. 13–61.
Cannell, M. and Wood, S. (1992) *Incentive Pay: Impact and Evolution*, London: Institute of Personnel Management.
Davis, S. J. (1992) 'Cross-country patterns of change in relative wages', National Bureau of Economic Research, *Macroeconomics Annual 1992*, Cambridge, MA: MIT Press.
Hughes, J. (1992) 'Earnings and pay bills in the 1990s', *Labour Market Issues No. 10*, Trade Union Research Unit, Oxford.
Hughes, G. A. and McCormick, B. (1990) 'Housing and labour market mobility', in J. Ermisch (ed.), *Housing and the National Economy*, Aldershot; Avebury.
Ingram, P. (1991) 'Ten years of manufacturing wage settlements: 1979–89', *Oxford Review of Economic Policy*, vol. 7, no. 1, pp. 93–106.
Johnson, C. (1991) *The Economy under Mrs Thatcher, 1979–1990*, Harmondsworth: Penguin.
Layard, R. (1990) 'How to end pay leap-frogging', *Economic Report*, vol. 5, no. 5, Employment Institute, London.
Layard, R., Nickell, S. and Jackman, R. (1991) *Unemployment: Macroeconomic Performance and the Labour Market*, Oxford: Oxford University Press.
Millward, N., Stevens, M., Smart, D. and Hawes, W. R. (1992) *Workplace Industrial Relations in Transition* (1990 Workplace Industrial Relations Survey), Dartmouth Publishing.
Muellbauer, J. (1990) 'The housing market and the UK economy: problems and opportunities', in J. Ermish (ed.), *Housing and the National Economy*, Aldershot: Avebury.
Nickell, S. and Wadhwani, S. (1990) 'Insider forces and wage determination', *Economic Journal*, vol. 100, no. 401, p. 496–509.
Soskice, D. (1990) 'Wage determination: the changing role of institutions in advanced industrialized economies', *Oxford Review of Economic Policy*, vol. 6, no. 4, pp. 36–61.

Walsh, J. and Brown, W. (1991a) 'Regional earnings and pay flexibility, in A. Bowen and K. Mayhew (eds), *Reducing Regional Inequalities*, London: Kogan Page.

Walsh, J. and Brown, W. (1991b) 'Pay determination in Britain in the 1980s: the anatomy of decentralisation', *Oxford Review of Economic Policy*, vol. 7, no. 1, Spring.

15

THE CHANGING STRUCTURE OF TRAINING PROVISION

Ewart Keep and Ken Mayhew

INTRODUCTION

The demise of NEDO is symbolic of the end of a corporatist era in British policy-making. Most other institutional arrangements had changed earlier, including in the area of training policy which was an important item on NEDO's agenda throughout its existence, not least under its penultimate director-general, Sir John Cassels. This paper describes the changes that have been occurring in the institutional landscape of the training system since the start of the 1980s, and considers their likely contribution to improving this vital component of the economy's supply-side.

In order to make sense of these changes, two issues need to be considered at the outset. The first is the ideological context in which debate about training in Britain has traditionally been framed. The second concerns the nature of the system that the reforms of the 1980s aimed to transform.

THE STATE AND TRAINING

Since the mid-nineteenth century the central focus of argument has concerned the role of the state in the provision of vocational education and training (VET). In the nineteenth and early twentieth centuries Britain was unusual among the industrialized and industrializing nations in leaving VET provision to the individual or his employer. Even the development of elementary education was for a long period left largely in the hands of religious charities, with much agonizing about the role of the state in providing financial and legislative assistance for their efforts. In marked contrast to Britain's voluntarist, *laissez-faire* approach, in Germany, France and Japan the state took the lead in stimulating industrial development, and as part of these efforts invested in the creation of VET structures (see Gospel and Okayama 1991; McCormick 1991; Uchida 1991).

Given this divergence in approach it is not surprising that comparisons between British and overseas VET systems have formed one of the major stimuli to debate about training over the last 150 years (Perry 1976; Reeder 1981). In particular, since the late 1970s a growing awareness of the UK's deficiencies *vis-à-vis* other developed countries has led to widespread agreement across the political spectrum that improvement of the UK's skills base is a vital pre-requisite for economic success. The means by which such an improvement might best be secured have, unfortunately, not been the subject of the same degree of consensus; and the role of the state, and the degree to which training provision can be left to market forces, have been the focus of controversy.

THE VOLUNTARIST TRADITION

Until the early 1960s, training 'was, at least in peace time, almost solely the responsibility of industry and commerce' (MSC 1980: 3). The state had only a limited role to play, particularly through the provision of vocational educa-tion in further education (FE) colleges. At the same time, the Ministry of Labour 'provided some skill training, mainly for adults but including some first year apprentice training, in Government Training Centres ... it was also a significant supplier of instructor and supervisor training through its "Training Within Industry" (TWI) services' (1980: 3). The individual firm had primacy, but its activities and thinking were subject to influence by a range of outside bodies, such as trade unions, professional institutes and associations, employers' organizations, Joint Apprenticeship Councils in some industries, the Industrial Training Service, the Institute of Personnel Management, and the British Association of Commercial and Industrial Education (BACIE).

Craft apprenticeship for a select group of young entrants was the dominant form of training provided within manufacturing industry, with little in the way of structured training for adult workers. In the non-manufacturing sectors of the economy, apprenticeships were rare (the major exception being in hairdressing), but there were various forms of clerical training and cadetships for some young entrants. However, as in manufacturing, there was little provision for adult employees.

The early 1960s witnessed a period of change, as a number of forces tended to impel policy-makers towards a new consensus on the role of the state in training. The first of these was the failure of the UK economy to match growth rates on the Continent. A second force was a growing belief that the uncoordinated decision-making of individual employers militated against both the quantity and quality of training provision that the well-being of the national economy required (MSC 1980: 3; Kenny and Reid 1985). Third, since the Second World War there had been criticism of some of the rigidities of the traditional craft apprenticeship system – particularly the fixed length of the traineeship and the restrictions upon who might undertake it (Perry 1976; MSC 1980). It was felt that reform of apprenticeships was overdue, and that such reform would be more easily accomplished within the context of a training system where there was greater coordination of employers' efforts. The pressure for reform of apprenticeships was heightened by demographic change, which meant that the numbers of young people likely to be entering the labour market were set to rise sharply (Perry 1976). Finally, there was parallel change and reassessment taking place within the education sector. This activity included reports and inquiries into 15–18 education, management education and business studies, that is those parts of the sector 'bearing most directly on the relationship between formal education and industrial training' (MSC 1980: 3).

THE INDUSTRIAL TRAINING BOARDS

A combination of these pressures and an apparent failure on the part of employers to undertake change sufficiently rapidly on a voluntary basis led to the Conservative government's 1962 White Paper on industrial training, which in turn led to the succeeding Labour government's 1964 Industrial Training Act (for a detailed account of the genesis of the Act, see Perry 1976).

The Act, which marked a watershed in peacetime state intervention in British training, had three aims: to relate decisions on the amount of training undertaken more closely to economic needs and changes in technology; to upgrade the overall quality of training and to set minimum standards; and to provide mechanisms whereby the cost of training could be more fairly spread among employers. The most important provision of the Act was the power it gave to ministers to establish Industrial Training Boards (ITBs). The Act also set up a Central Training Council (CTC) to advise the government on training matters.

The ITBs covered specific industries or sectors. Each board consisted of employer and trade union representatives, usually with some additional educational members. The boards were empowered by the Act to establish a levy on firms within their industry. The levy was used by each board to fund its operating costs and to promote greater training activity. Companies could obtain training grants funded by the levy if their training plans and provision met minimum standards set by the board.

The ITBs were concentrated in manufacturing industry, though large boards were established in some other sectors, such as distribution and retailing, and hotels and catering. The boards concentrated their efforts on identifying skill shortages and fostering relevant training by employers through grants financed from the levy (for detailed accounts of the structure and operations of the ITBs, see Perry 1976; and MSC 1980). By 1969 there were twenty-seven of them in operation (later reduced to twenty-five), plus the Foundry Industry Training Committee (which operated in ways similar to an ITB). These boards covered 15 million employees out of a total national labour force of 25 million (Lindley 1983). The CTC tried to coordinate the work of the ITBs, stimulate policy debate and encourage attempts to deal with cross-sectoral skills. As Perry (1976: 311) underlines, the new system did not require direct financial support from the state, and control of training remained in the hands of employers and unions. The state's role was essentially catalytic.

At the start of the 1970s, after most ITBs had been at work for no more than five years, it was decided to review their operations and those of the CTC. The main reason for this was a growing chorus of complaint about the operation of the levy/grant system (Ainley and Corney 1990: 16–17). Complaints came from those on the political left who wanted training to be taxation-funded, and, more vocally, from those on the right such as Enoch Powell, who characterized the ITBs as bureaucratic and inherently wasteful. In addition some economists, such as Lees and Chiplin (1970), attacked them for distorting th: operation of training and labour markets.

The resulting report, published by the Employment Department as *Training for the Future, A Plan for Discussion* (ED 1972), concluded that the changes ushered in by the 1964 Act appeared to have made a considerable contribution. Survey data supported the contention that there had been an increase, somewhat tailing off in the late 1960s, in the volume of training. Liaison with education had improved, and apprenticeships had, in a limited number of cases, been shortened. However, not everything in the garden was judged to be rosy. The boards were seen as ineffective in dealing with training issues that straddled several industries and were also accused of excessive bureaucracy. Rates of levy were often quite high (1 per cent or more of company payroll costs), and companies which saw themselves as good trainers were having to spend much time and effort reclaiming money from the ITBs. The problem of small firms, who lacked training departments, and saw themselves paying out levy with little hope of its recovery, was judged to be particularly important. Very little had been done to ease the long-standing problem of apprenticeship age entry restrictions or to improve adult training provision. The report suggested, among other things, the abolition of the levy and the transfer of all ITB staff to a National Training Agency.

THE EMPLOYMENT AND TRAINING ACT AND THE MSC

After heated discussion followed the publication of *Training for the Future*, the Employment and Training Act 1973 made a number of significant reforms. These included the replacement of the ITBs' mandatory duties (for example to impose a levy) by enabling powers to exercise such duties if they so wished; and a requirement for each ITB to define small firms (the definition to be confirmed by government), and then to exempt them from the levy. ITBs were also to exempt all those establishments, 'whose training arrangements met their own needs adequately – as measured against criteria specified by the ITB and approved by the MSC and Secretary of State' (MSC 1980: 4). The aim of this measure was to concentrate the efforts of ITBs on those companies that had made little progress, and upon improving the forecasting of future skill needs. Henceforth an ITB could only set blanket, non-exceptable levies if there was 'consensus' among employers in the industry. Consensus was defined as the support of organizations representing at least 50 per cent of the employers liable to the levy (providing the firms so represented were also liable to pay over half of the sum raised by the levy). A ceiling of one per cent of the payroll was also set on levies. The only way an ITB could establish a levy higher than this was with Parliamentary approval. The costs of ITBs' operating expenses (chiefly staff wages), capital spending and training advisory services were transferred to the public purse.

The final change was the winding-up of the CTC which was replaced by a national, tripartite body, the Manpower Services Commission, to oversee national manpower planning, the operation of government training schemes and employment services, and the activities of the ITBs. The government's original intention had been to create a national training agency, but pressure from the TUC, and to a lesser extent the CBI, led to a broadening of the organization's remit to include national manpower planning and employment services (Jackson 1992). The MSC reported to the Secretary of State for Employment, and was governed by a tripartite commission normally comprised of three representatives nominated by the CBI, three by the TUC, two local government representatives, and one educational, one Scottish and one Welsh representative. It was initially organized into two executive agencies – an Employment Services Agency and a Training Services Agency. A separate but essentially similar Scottish MSC operated in parallel with its larger English and Welsh counterparts. For detailed accounts of the MSC and its activities, see Ainley and Corney 1990; Evans 1992; and, for a radical critique, Benn and Fairley 1986).

Following the 1973 legislation, training policy at national level was dominated by concern about endemic skill shortages and by the problems posed by rising levels of unemployment in the UK economy (Ainley and Corney 1990). To deal with the first of these challenges the MSC launched numerous measures aimed at reducing persistent cyclical skills shortages, particularly in the engineering industry. Debate about the need for more fundamental reform of the apprenticeship system and for improvements in the quality and quantity of training for adult workers intensified, though with little immediate practical effect. At the same time the development of various special temporary employment measures and training and work experience schemes for the unemployed proceeded apace. There was one specific attempt to deal with skill problems across industrial boundaries. In 1976 the MSC produced a report, *Training for Vital Skills* (MSC 1976), which proposed an additional levy to collectively fund training in a small number of key transferable skills. The levy was to have covered the whole employed population (not just companies in scope in industries with ITBs), but the report failed to win the backing of employers.

In the years following the Employment and Training Act a number of problems emerged with the new levy/exemption arrangement and with the relationship between the boards and the MSC. The move from levy/grant to levy/exemption meant a sharp fall in ITB levy income as more and more companies reached the criteria necessary to gain exemption. The result was an increasing reliance on support from the MSC. MSC figures indicate that in real terms total levy income for all ITBs fell by 81 per cent between 1971/2 and 1978/9. By contrast, exchequer support rose by nearly 500 per cent (MSC 1980: 6). The boards' growing dependence upon government money exacerbated tensions in their relationship with the MSC, the fundamental cause of which was a conflict between the MSC's national policy goals – particularly those dealing with unemployment – and the specific needs and interests of each board's industry or sector.

CHANGING POLICIES SINCE 1979

The election in 1979 of a Conservative government marked a dramatic change in training policies. The government's approach was to be shaped by a number of ideological principles, and the clearest and most coherent exposition of these is to be found in the White Paper *Employment for the 1990s* (ED 1988).

The first of these principles is that market forces, rather than statutory rights and duties, are the best means of determining the type and levels of training undertaken. It is up to employers and, to a lesser extent, individuals to choose for themselves how much, or how little, to invest in training. As a corollary, the government has felt that the role of the state should be confined to the provision of education, with interventions in the training market limited to supporting disadvantaged groups and the provision of pump-priming money for developmental purposes, and exhortation. It should be noted that this approach is in marked contrast to that in other European countries, most of which provide some form of legislative backing for training (see Keep 1991). This either takes the form of individual rights to training and educational leave and the imposition of a remissible training tax or levy on all employers (as for example in France), or it is expressed through compulsory employer member-ship of training bodies (as in Germany).

Second, the government has believed that vocational education and training provision should be employer-led and employer-controlled, and that the influence of educationalists and trade unions on training should be diminished. To quote from *Employment for the 1990s* (ED 1988): 'Employers as both providers and consumers of training have the primary responsibility for ensuring that our labour force has the skills to support an expanding economy'. Again, this view takes Britain in the opposite direction from most of the rest of Europe, where notions of 'social partnership' mean that tripartite control of training policy and delivery is important (Keep 1991).

The government's market-based, employer-led approach towards training needs to be seen as part of a wider continuum of policies aimed at reform of the British labour market. As *Employment for the 1990s* (ED 1988) makes

313

clear, the government has perceived training as being inextricably linked to issues such as pay and industrial relations. Thus during the 1980s reform of the training system took place within the context of wider attempts to increase the static efficiency of the British labour market by means of deregulation and measures to stimulate labour market competition. These labour market reforms included legislation aimed at weakening the power of trade unions, the weakening of the wages councils, and the repeal of the Fair Wages resolution and Schedule 11 of the 1975 Employment Protection Act. More recently legislation securing the outright abolition of the Wages Councils has been introduced. Training policy can be viewed as that element of the government's labour market strategy that has attempted to improve dynamic efficiency within the labour market by stimulating greater volumes of more effective training.

The change of government coincided with further rapid rises in the levels of unemployment, particularly among young people, and with heightened perceptions of the strength of international competition. These factors produced among MSC officials, academics and other commentators on the training scene, a new awareness of both the scale and urgency of the UK's education and training problems. As a result of the conjunction of ideological, economic and social forces, the 1980s were to witness radical reform of the structure of training provision.

THE DEMISE OF THE ITBs

The first demonstration of a new approach came in 1981 with moves to abolish the majority of the ITBs. The process by which this momentous decision was reached is as follows.

In 1980 the MSC launched a review of the operation of the 1973 Employment and Training Act, the product of which was a lengthy report – *Outlook on Training* (MSC 1980). It concluded that, while there were numerous problems with the operation of the ITB system, there was a significant body of evidence that suggested that ITBs had improved both the quality and quantity of training. The majority of CBI members accepted the need for a training board system of some kind – provided that industry had sufficient control of its ITB (MSC 1980: 14). The report recommended that there was a continuing need for government involvement in training provision, largely because of problems of externalities, the poaching of skilled labour, and instances of market failure (MSC 1980: 25–6); rejected any moves to abolish the boards; and suggested a number of ways in which their operation might be improved.

In the wake of *Outlook on Training*, the MSC decided upon the need for further consultations, including a sector-by-sector review of the ITBs. In November 1980, the new Secretary of State for Employment, Norman Tebbit, announced that the sectoral review of training arrangements must consider in detail the possibility of substituting voluntary for statutory arrangements and made clear the government's intention to retain statutory ITBs only in a few key sectors where they were likely to be essential to securing wider national training objectives. Furthermore, the government increased the pressure on industry to move to voluntary training arrangements by warning that it would in future no longer be willing to support the boards' operating costs from public funds, and that these costs would be passed on to industry in sectors where employers decided to retain their boards. In response, employers in many sectors scrambled to divest themselves of their ITB, and submitted plans for voluntary training arrangements to the MSC.

The result of the sectoral reviews was published by the MSC in July 1981 as *A Framework for the Future* (MSC 1981). The MSC recommended the retention of ITBs in seven sectors – including clothing and allied products, engineering and construction. In the cases of the other seventeen boards, the Commission judged proposals for voluntary training arrangements to be insufficiently advanced to allow a firm decision to be reached. The government accepted the retention of the seven boards as a temporary measure, and, after encouraging the MSC to enter into further consultations with industry, sanctioned the winding-up of the other seventeen boards. In 1981 the government had indicated its intention to move as swiftly as possible towards the abolition of the remaining seven boards, and, in 1988, it announced a further review of their activities with a view to securing voluntary training arrangements in their sectors. This resulted in all but the Construction Industry Training Board being wound up.

Thus the experiment with a legislative framework for training in Britain came to an end in a majority of sectors after less than fifteen years. The original levy/grant system of ITB financing had survived for less than eight years.

How justified was the government's hostility to statutory training arrangements and its assertion that the boards had largely failed to improve training (and particularly the training of those already in employment) in Britain? There is a surprising absence of detailed research on their work, the major exception being Senker's (1992) book on the Engineering Industry Training Board. Most of the evidence on ITB performance comes from the official reviews conducted in 1972, 1980 and 1981. The 1980 review in particular represents a comprehensive and relatively neglected source of information. In the course of the review submissions of evidence were received from the CBI and ninety-nine employer organizations and chambers of commerce, the TUC and seven unions, thirty-six educational organizations, 122 employers and group training organizations, and bodies such as the Institute of Personnel Management (IPM), the British Institute of Management (BIM), the Industrial Society and NEDO. The review body also commissioned research on issues such as the operation of the levy exemption system, and companies' relationships with their boards. As outlined above, the general conclusion of the reviews, and of the consultation and research process that surrounded them, was that the ITBs had made a significant contribution to improving the quality and quantity of training, but that there were significant areas, such as adult training, cross-sectoral skills and apprenticeship reform, where progress had been either slow or negligible.

Many of the deficiencies that were laid at the door of the ITBs stemmed, at least in part, from the actions and attitudes of both government and employers. As Senker (1992) indicates, some of the problems faced by the boards can be traced back to a failure by employers to embrace the need for radical reform of training, and an unwillingness to pay for change and improvement. Employers, if not in the driving seat within ITBs, at the very least had an effective power of veto over major developments, and often exerted a conservative influence over planning. As Lindley points out (1983: 356) when employers criticized the ITBs for their lack of achievement, they were often criticizing in part the brake which they themselves had imposed on progress. The MSC's 1981 sector-by-sector review made the point, in relation to several boards, that in their search for employer consensus, change had been slowed.

Moreover, Senker argues that 'ITBs' failure was as much attributable to governments' actions and inaction as to deficiencies in the ITBs' performance' (Senker 1992: 5). Some of the difficulties that attended relations between the MSC, as the guardian of national training policy, and the ITBs have been touched upon above, in particular conflicting political messages and priorities concerning the emphasis to be placed on training the unemployed, and the MSC's insistence on ITBs' efforts being geared to meet its targets, rather than the needs of the industry it was supposed to be representing.

Two other aspects of government policy, it has been suggested, clouded the ITBs' fortunes. The first was the change from a system of levy/grant to one of levy exemption following the 1972 review (Perry 1976; MSC 1980; Senker 1992) which rendered many boards increasingly reliant upon government funding. The 1980 review (MSC 1980: 50) indicated that in twelve out of twenty-five boards more than half of the employers eligible to pay levy had gained exemption (these figures excluded all those firms who were additionally exempt from paying levy because of their small-firm status). The second factor was the uncertainty over the future of the boards engendered by political hostility to them after 1979 (Senker 1992). In particular, the activities of the seven boards that survived after 1981 were materially affected by the government's publicly-stated desire to see them replaced by voluntary arrangements as soon as was practicable.

The government's views regarding the ITBs' performance notwithstanding, it is noticeable that ministers have had very little to say about the situation that existed prior to the 1964 Act. This is not surprising given the history of failure that attended UK training policies based on a *laissez-faire* approach prior to the establishment of the ITBs. Indeed, it should be recalled that it was the persistent apparent inability of employers to improve training of their own volition that had forced a Conservative government to accept the need for legislative intervention (Kenny and Reid 1985: 273; Perry 1976; Sheldrake and Vickerstaff 1987).

THE NEW VOLUNTARY SECTORAL TRAINING SYSTEM

The voluntary sectoral bodies with which the government were intent upon replacing the ITBs were to be designed, run and financed by employers in each industry. They were originally called Non-Statutory Training Organizations (NSTOs). Involvement of trade unionists and educationalists was no longer guaranteed, but was only at the invitation of employers. At the same time, individual employers were free to choose whether to join or support their NSTO. The NSTO had no powers to raise a levy from members or to compel companies to train or cooperate with its plans.

The NSTOs were not expected to replicate the full range of activities undertaken by the ITBs. It was envisaged that their main roles would be to disseminate information, help define future skill needs, organize group training schemes, and act as 'ginger groups'. With the move to develop a system of National Vocational Qualifications (which is discussed at greater length below), many of the NSTOs assumed responsibility for helping to formulate standards of occupational competence for their sectors.

About ninety NSTOs were established in the wake of the 1981 round of ITB abolitions (Berry-Lound *et al*. 1991). Early indications of their likely effectiveness were not auspicious. Many of the original proposals for NSTOs that were submitted to the MSC as a precondition for the abolition of the industry's ITB were little more than shells (MSC 1981), whose minimal functions were seen by companies in the industry as the price required from them for the removal of the likely financial burden of an ITB (Coopers & Lybrand 1985: 13), and CBI staff were privately alarmed at the prospects for the effectiveness of some of these bodies (Stringer and Richardson 1982: 37). Moreover, government-commissioned research in the mid-1980s indicated that the majority of NSTOs were 'ineffective' when judged against the MSC's targets for their activities (Rainbird and Grant 1985; Varlaam 1987; Anderson 1987).

Latterly the NSTOs have renamed themselves Industry Training Organizations (ITOs), and more recent studies of their operations suggest that their general effectiveness has slowly improved (Berry-Lound and Anderson 1991). Between 1987 and 1991 the number of ITOs rose by about a fifth (Berry-Lound *et al*. 1991: 537), partly as a result of the post-1988 wave of ITBs converting themselves into voluntary bodies. There are currently 123 ITOs operating in Britain. These cover 'five out of six of employees in the national workforce' (Berry-Lound *et al*. 1991: 535). In 1988 the ITOs set up a National Council for Industry Training Organizations (NCITOs) which produced a code of conduct which outlines a set of 'ideal outcomes' from ITO activity.

Government-sponsored evaluations suggest that nevertheless there remained significant doubts about the lack of stature and influence of some ITOs, about their tendency to be forced by their members to concentrate on short-term issues, and about the confusion surrounding their role *vis-à-vis* the growing local focus for policy-making and provision (Berry-Lound and Anderson 1991). Of particular concern were their frequently low levels of resourcing. Out of eighty-one ITOs in 1991, 27 per cent employed fewer than two full-time equivalent staff, and a further 49 per cent employed between two and six full-time equivalents (Berry-Lound and Anderson 1991). In 1990/1, out of seventy-eight ITOs, 54 per cent had annual incomes of less than £200,000 (Berry-Lound *et al*. 1991: 539).

Moreover, when the activities of the ITOs were measured against the NCITO's twelve-point list of 'ideal outcomes', it was apparent that while many of them were still working towards these, relatively few had actually achieved them. For instance, the HOST Consultancy estimated that only 35 per cent of ITOs had been able to establish means whereby their sector's current and future skill requirements and training needs were defined, monitored and periodically reviewed; and only 26 per cent could demonstrate continual development in their sector's overall training performance (Berry-Lound *et al*. 1991: 541). Indeed by 1991 only two of the NCITO's twelve 'ideal outcomes' had been achieved by more than 50 per cent of the ITOs covered by the HOST Consultancy survey.

A NATIONAL SYSTEM OF VOCATIONAL QUALIFICATIONS

The creation of a unified system of national vocational qualifications (NVQs) was a vital element in the new training system. In the mid-1980s, the MSC launched a Review of Vocational Qualifications (RVQ), which was charged with examining the vast array of existing vocational qualifications. The RVQ concluded (MSC/DES 1986) that there was massive overlap and duplication which was confusing to employer and trainee alike, poor coverage of some occupations and sectors, limited access to training for adults, inadequate provision for progression and credit for prior learning and achievement, and too much stress on the testing of knowledge rather than skills or competencies. 'In aggregate this resulted in a low take-up of vocational qualifications and an inadequately qualified workforce' (Raggatt 1991: 62). The review recommended that the qualifications jungle should be rationalized and brought within a single, coherent system of National Vocational Qualifications that would be readily comprehensible to employers and trainees alike.

A new, employer-led National Council for Vocational Qualifications (NCVQ) was established to oversee the creation of NVQs in England, Wales and Northern Ireland. In Scotland an existing body – the Scottish Vocational Education Council (SCOTVEC) – was charged with creating parallel Scottish Vocational Qualifications (SVQs). The role of these bodies was set out in the White Paper *Working Together – Education and Training* (ED/DES 1986). The intention has been that the NCVQ should ultimately become self-financing through fees generated by 'kitemarking' qualifications. More recently the NCVQ has been charged with developing a set of General NVQs (GNVQs) which are meant to provide broad-based, vocationally-oriented qualifications for use in schools and further education, to run alongside A levels.

The NCVQ set about constructing an NVQ framework within which it recognizes and approves existing and new qualifications submitted to it by awarding bodies. There were initially four NVQ and SVQ levels. A fifth level covering professional qualifications is now being developed. NVQs are meant to have a broad equivalence with educational qualifications. Thus NVQ level II is taken to be roughly equivalent to five GCSEs, and NVQ level III to possession of two A levels and five GCSEs (CBI 1989: 16).

NVQs are designed by Lead Industry Bodies (LIBs), whose activities have been directed by employers rather than educationalists. They are based on the standards of competence, as defined by employers, that are required to undertake specific jobs (for details of this process, see Debling 1991). The notion of competence-based qualifications was pioneered in the USA, where it was used to support new forms of training for schoolteachers (Prais 1991). For a detailed discussion of the emergence of competence-based learning in America, see Grant et al. (1979).

NVQs are always modular, and broken down into component 'units of competence'. The trainee acquires an NVQ by achieving the standards for each of these units, and for each unit the trainee receives a credit. Credits can be achieved either through undertaking training, and/or through the accreditation of prior learning (APL) – the formal acknowledgement and record of skills previously acquired by whatever means. Credits, whole NVQs and other qualifications can be accumulated and recorded as a portfolio in the National Record of Vocational Achievement (NROVA). The competencies required to gain an NVQ are to be assessed primarily in the workplace, rather than the classroom or through written examinations, and assessment is normally to be undertaken by the candidates' supervisor or by other managerial staff.

Most NVQs are sectorally specific, but some cross-sectoral bodies have been founded to deal with, for example, trainers and clerical and administrative workers. In many cases the LIB has been the sector's Industry Training Organization (ITO). In 1992 there were about 160 LIBs. The Employment Department has indicated that it would like to see many of these merge to form a smaller number of Occupational Standards Councils (OSCs) (Reid 1992). To date little progress has been made on this front.

Progress in introducing NVQs proved initially to be far slower than originally had been hoped. The NCVQ eventually set itself a target of putting in place NVQs for levels I to IV covering 80 per cent of the workforce by the end of 1992. During 1992 the rate of development of NVQs, and the numbers of NVQs being awarded, increased rapidly. By the end of the year there were 516 NVQs available and the target of 80 per cent coverage had been met. However, many of the NVQs had only provisional accreditation from the NCVQ, and more lower-level qualifications had been accredited than higher-level ones. In 1991/2, 117,089 NVQs were awarded. It is expected that in 1992/3 the total should be about 200,000 (*Times Higher Education Supplement*, 8 January 1993).

In the long term much is expected of NVQs. They are seen as essential to ensuring that vocational qualifications meet the needs of employers, and to raising the status of vocational qualifications *vis-à-vis* traditional academic qualifications. It is also believed that they will encourage more training, by removing barriers to learning and providing a more flexible pattern of learning which places less stress on factors such as the trainee's age or formal writing skills (Debling 1991; Jessup 1991).

More fundamentally, NVQs provide the glue that holds the new devolved training system together. As the focus of policy has shifted to local delivery mechanisms the role of national standards as a means of providing uniformity and coherence has increased. Local delivery to national standards has become the watchword. NVQs form the key element in future evaluation and monitoring mechanisms for training policy, for individual Training and Enterprise Councils (see below for details), and for companies involved in government-funded training programmes. Government funding for training is increasingly being tied to 'outcomes', which are expressed in terms of NVQs achieved, and tax relief to individuals who are financing their own training is only available to those pursuing NVQs.

NVQs are undoubtedly a radical innovation. The new framework for competence-based, workplace-assessed qualifications gives Britain a VET qualifications system which possesses a structure and assessment methods that are in marked contrast to those of vocational qualifications in other European countries.

This radical departure has certainly not been without its critics. Some commentators have accused employers of defining NVQ skill levels in a very narrow and task-specific way, in contrast to their European counterparts who demand a broader mix of training and general education (Prais 1989; Steedman and Wagner 1989: 48–9; Jarvis and Prais 1989: 62–70; Raggatt 1991; CBI 1989; Marshall, 1991; Callender 1992). The danger is that NVQs stipulate the minimum level of skills currently required to perform a particular job, rather than allow broader-based learning that will provide employees with the transferable skills required to cope with change (McCool 1991). Callender (1992) points to there being an inherent conflict between the short-term needs of individual employers and long-term needs of trainees and the wider economy. It has also been felt that employers are often being tempted to define competencies in terms that are backward- rather than forward-looking (Golzen 1991), and which enshrine current structures of work organization and skill. Hence the ability of NVQs to cope with changing technology, skill requirements and methods of work organization have been questioned (Raggatt 1991; Field 1992).

There has been concern that the levels of skill being specified are often very low, particularly when contrasted with those being required by overseas employers. NVQ level I has been described as providing 'a standard of qualifications that is said to be significantly below the lowest level found in most European systems' (*Recruitment and Development Report 26*, February 1992: 16). Jarvis and Prais talk of the possibility of NVQs creating, 'a certified semi-literate under-class – a section of the workforce inhibited in job flexibility and inhibited in the possibilities of progression' (1989: 70).

Furthermore, doubts have been expressed, particularly by Prais, about the reliability of workplace assessment. He argues that overseas VET systems ensure quality through an externally assessed mixture of practical tests and written examinations (Prais 1989, 1991), and that the NCVQ's heavy reliance on workplace assessment of the trainee conducted internally by their employers will weaken the status and credibility of NVQs. Broadly similar doubts have been expressed by the Institute of Directors (1991). The potentially high cost of workplace assessment may also prove to be a problem.

Moreover, the NVQ assessment system is predicated on there being an effective personnel and training system within the workplace (Callender 1992). In many British organizations, particularly amongst small firms, it is open to question how justifiable that expectation really is. For example, the NVQ assessments rely upon the existence of a supervisory workforce able to train and to assess competence. Yet what is known about the supervisory workforce in the average UK company indicates that this is often simply not the case.

At the same time, there is some evidence that the mass of employers remain to be convinced of the value of NVQs (Golzen 1991: 30; Davies *et al.* 1992). ASDA's decision to cease using NVQs, the Department of Social Security's suspension of involvement with NVQs (Field 1992: 7), and the public disputes within the NHS's management about the worth and relevance of NVQs, point to the fact that securing employer commitment may, at best, prove to be a lengthier and more problematic process than was at first hoped. Indeed, knowledge and understanding of NVQs among employers (NTTF 1992) and the working population also appears to be more limited than the NCVQ might have hoped. A survey conducted by Gallup for the NCVQ indicated that 61 per cent of the adults questioned claimed not have heard of National Vocational Qualifications (*IPM Plus*, February 1992: 10). Finally, in the education sector, particularly among the Further Education colleges, reactions to and preparations for the introduction of NVQs has been mixed (Davies *et al.* 1992; (*The Times Educational Supplement*, 22 May 1992; Tysome 1992).

A big question mark that hangs over the NCVQ concerns its ability to fulfil its original objective of simplifying the 'qualifications jungle'. The NCVQ operates within the context of a voluntary training system, where employers, and other actors such as professional and examination bodies, are free not to cooperate. For instance, there is nothing to stop existing vocational qualifications that do not meet NCVQ criteria from continuing to be offered and awarded in parallel with NVQs. The relationship between the NCVQ and the various awarding bodies has not always been smooth (Raggatt 1992; Jackson 1992), and the NCVQ is to some extent dependent upon winning their cooperation. Many awarding bodies exist to make money, and it is unclear whether they will be prepared to rationalize what are profitable product lines. It is perfectly possible that the proliferation of qualifications will continue within the NVQ framework (*Recruitment and Development Report 26*, February 1992: 16). For example, in 1990 there were estimated to be 279 different vocational secretarial qualifications, offered by eleven examination bodies, at five different levels of attainment (Employment Department 1992). It will be interesting to see whether this situation changes significantly in the next few years.

THE RISE AND FALL OF THE MSC

Despite the government's desire to move towards a market-based, employer-led training system in which the role of the state was minimal, events during the early to mid-1980s conspired to render this objective highly elusive. The necessity for the government to be seen to be taking steps to tackle mass unemployment meant that large-scale, government-funded training programmes catering for the unemployed were deemed unavoidable. The result was that the MSC, through both its employment services and training functions, found itself as the primary agency for managing the problem of unemployment via programmes such as the Youth Training Scheme. The cost of such schemes meant that the MSC's budget soared. Training spending rose in real terms by over 300 per cent between 1976/7 and 1988/9.

However, in the 1987 Employment Act, with youth unemployment no longer rising and the Youth Training Scheme in place, the government restructured the MSC by removing its responsibility for employment functions. Control of the Job Centres, the Enterprise Allowance Scheme, and the Careers and Occupational Information Centre was transferred from the Commission to the Department of Employment. It was also decided to rename the MSC the Training Commission in order to underline its new focus of activity. Finally, it increased the number of CBI representatives on the Commission and upon its local Area Manpower Boards which had been set up in the early 1980s to monitor the development of YTS.

In September 1988, following a refusal by TUC representatives on the Commission to endorse the proposed Employment Training scheme for the adult unemployed, the government announced the abolition of the Training Commission. In its place there was to be a new, employer-led structure. At its head was a National Training Task Force (NTTF) made up of a small group of senior business leaders, who invited other individuals, such as a trade union leader and educationalists, to join them. Its role was to offer advice and guidance to the government on the development of national training policies, and to encourage the promotion of greater investment by employers in the skills of their employees.

The NTTF was wound up in late 1992 and was replaced by a similar body styled the National Advisory Council for Education and Training Targets (NACETT). The main functions of this new employer-led forum are to encourage the introduction and use of NVQs, and to monitor progress towards the strategic performance targets in vocational education and training established in the National Education and Training Targets (NETTs) (for details of which see below). NACETT reports to the Secretaries of State for Education, Employment and Wales.

With the demise of the Training Commission, the civil servants who formerly staffed it became part of what was termed the Training Agency and, after this was abolished in 1990, were transferred to the Department of Employment. Their role is now to offer support, advice and developmental services to employer-led bodies, as well as overseeing the running of government-supported programmes of training.

A second change of direction was the move towards the privatization of the Commission's Skills Training Agency (STA). The STA ran sixty government-owned and funded training centres (Skillcentres), which had originally been established after the First World War to train ex-servicemen, and were now being used to retrain unemployed adults in craft skills. The Skillcentres were quickly sold off, many to a management buy-out. The newly privatized company, Astra Training, closed seven of the remaining Skillcentres and in July 1993 went into receivership.

The third and by far the most important element of the government's vision for a new training system was a shift in the focus of training policy decision-making away from national and sectoral levels towards the local labour market. This was embodied in the creation of a nation-wide network of local Training and Enterprise Councils (TECs) in England and Wales, and in Scotland a set of broadly similar bodies called Local Enterprise Companies (LECs).

A NEW LOCAL FOCUS FOR TRAINING POLICY

In the 1960s and 1970s the focus for policy formation and the organization of training delivery above the level of the individual firm was almost exclusively national and sectoral. During the 1980s there was an increasing interest in developing a local dimension to the training infrastructure that would allow policy and programmes to become more responsive to the diverse needs of individual local labour markets.

The review body charged with examining the workings of the Employment and Training Act considered, among other possibilities, the replacement of the ITBs with a locally-based training system (MSC 1980: 27). This option was rejected in favour of the continuance of the statutory boards, but the review body stressed the need to improve arrangements for consultation and for the planning of education and training at the level of the individual local labour market. The next year's sector-by-sector review of the ITBs again threw up suggestions for moves to a locally-based alternative to the ITBs (MSC 1980: 33–4). In particular, in the engineering industry a paper prepared by the Electrical and Electronic Manufacturers' Training and Education Board advocated, 'a structure based primarily on local and regional manpower committees. Within such a structure there would be no place for statutory industry training bodies, though there would be advantage in retaining voluntary industry committees on a national basis' (MSC 1981: 17). In the event, the sectoral review witnessed the demise of the majority of the ITBs and moves to a voluntary system of sectoral bodies, but there was little immediate progress on a local focus for training policy.

The catalyst was the arrival of the Youth Training Scheme in 1983, which prompted the MSC to create a network of fifty-five local Area Manpower Boards (AMBs). These were bodies, made up of local employers, trade union officials, and local authority and educational representatives, whose function was to advise, 'the MSC on the planning and implementation of its programmes locally, including manpower intelligence on the types and quantities of training required' (Ainley and Corney 1990: 64).

By 1987 the increasingly apparent inadequacies of the local labour market information available to those attempting to plan training provision (Keep 1987: 27–9) prompted the creation of the Local Employer Networks (LENs). These bodies, jointly sponsored by the CBI and the British Chambers of Commerce, were introduced by the MSC 'to establish formal mechanisms that will match training to local needs' (MSC, *Focus on Adult Training*, March/ April 1987). The intended nation-wide network of LENs was barely getting under way when the decision to abolish the Training Commission and develop TECs and LECs rendered them superfluous.

Though AMBs and LENs offered a precedent for a local dimension for training activity, the creation of TECs and LECs nevertheless marked a radical break with the past. AMBs and LENs were bodies with relatively limited powers and functions, and had existed within the context of a strong national, tripartite training system, of which they had constituted but a small part. In future, voluntary, employer-dominated local bodies were to be afforded primacy in controlling and delivering government-funded training.

Furthermore, although there had been precursors to an enhanced local focus for training activity, there is little evidence to suggest that much in the way of detailed planning had been undertaken by government to support moves in such a direction before the decision to set up the TECs and LECs was reached. The inspiration for TECs came from the USA, where a network of Private Industry Councils (PICs) were attempting to tackle the training problems of disadvantaged groups. The then Secretary of State for Employment – Norman Fowler – had made a study visit to America to view two of the most successful PICs, and returned convinced that similar bodies could form the major institutional delivery mechanism for training in Britain. There is nothing to indicate that any research had been undertaken to confirm the validity of this conclusion. In fact many US commentators and researchers have judged the PICs to have been relatively ineffective (Finegold *et al*. 1993).

THE STRUCTURE OF TECs AND LECs

TECs are employer-led bodies. They are essentially self-appointed groups of business people, two-thirds of whose board members must be the managing directors or chief executives of local private sector employers. Members of each TEC's board serve in a personal capacity and are not deemed to represent their company or organization.

TECs are limited companies. Their purpose is to administer existing government training schemes for the unemployed, to monitor and tackle skill requirements within the local labour market, to persuade local companies to undertake more training, and to stimulate local enterprise and economic growth. More recently they have been charged with responsibility for various aspects of business/education links (Davies *et al*. (1992). They have a contractual relationship with the Department of Employment, from whom they receive funding for those training schemes aimed at the unemployed, plus a small basic grant towards operating costs and promotional activities. Though some senior TEC staff have been recruited from the private sector, the majority of their employees have been civil servants seconded from the old Training Agency area offices.

It was originally envisaged by ministers that it would take about four years to establish a fully-fledged nation-wide system of TECs and LECs. In the event, this was accomplished within two years. The greatest delays and difficulties in establishing TECs appear to have been encountered within Greater London (*IDS Study*, 485, July 1991: 1). The completed system sees eighty-two TECs covering the whole of England and Wales, along with twenty Local Enterprise Companies (LECs) covering Scotland. A group of ten TEC chairpersons (G10) represented the TECs in dealings with the Department of Employment. The relationship between G10 and the National Training Task Force in influencing the broad direction of national training policy remained unclear throughout the NTTF's life. In July 1993 the TEC directors agreed to replace G10 with a National TEC Council.

The Scottish LECs differ from TECs in that they have taken over not only the training functions of the old Scottish MSC and Training Agency, but also some of the powers of the Scottish Development Agency and the Highlands and Islands Board. As a result LECs have a slightly greater emphasis on their economic development role than do the majority of TECs. LECs came into operation in Scotland on 1 April 1991. The LECs report to a body called Scottish Enterprise rather than to the Employment Department (for further details of the LECs, see Danson *et al*. 1989; Emmerick and Peck 1991, 1992).

THE PROGRESS OF TECs AND LECs

Major studies of TECs include Emmerick and Peck (1991, 1992); Coffield (1992); Evans (1992); IDS Study 485; and Barnes (1991). However, attempts to evaluate whether the achievements to date of TECs and LECs match up, or are likely to match up, to their optimistic prospectus are hampered by the lack of publicly available information. One of the chief characteristics of the new locally-based training system is the problem which its institutional fragmentation has posed for the quality and volume of information obtainable not only by potential customers and academic commentators, but also by those charged with monitoring the system. There are 102 local bodies, each pursuing different goals and objectives, in often quite markedly different ways, and each responsible for deciding what and how much information to provide to outsiders about its activities – the only significant requirement on information disclosure that has been imposed upon the TECs is a duty to publish an annual report. To date, the amount of hard, detailed information that many of the TECs have volunteered about their plans and activities has been less than overwhelming (Coffield 1992).

Even if more information were available, definitive judgements would be impossible at this early stage of their existence. However, a number of observations can be made. These focus on their funding, their relationship with government, their contacts with other parts of the training system, and their representativeness and accountability.

Funding

The decision to establish TECs in 1988 was taken at the height of a boom. Economic growth, coupled with demographic trends that meant declining numbers of young people entering the labour market until the mid-1990s, nourished the view that unemployment would continue to fall, and that tight labour markets would encourage employers to compete to recruit young people and to invest more in training. The initial levels of funding available to the TECs were calculated on the basis of declining levels of youth and adult unemployment. Unfortunately, the onset of the recession and rapidly rising levels of unemployment swiftly rendered these assumptions unrealistic. At the same time, Treasury pressure has meant that overall levels of government expenditure on training have fallen.

These difficulties were important because in most cases 90 per cent of the budget provided by government to each TEC was allocated to supporting the costs of existing Youth Training and Employment Training programmes. In fact, delivery of the government's guarantee to the unemployed of places on YT and ET schemes formed the first, and over-riding, clause in the TECs' contract with government. Reductions in levels of funding for TEC programmes have also been compounded by the uncertainty that surrounds government decisions about public expenditure and the fact that TECs operate only on the basis of a one-year contract with the Employment Department (Emmerick and Peck 1991, 1992). Demands from the TECs for three-year rolling contracts with the Department have to date been rejected.

There was a growing chorus of complaint from the TECs that funding was inadequate. Tight funding, coupled with problems in securing enough employer-provided training places during a recession, meant that in some parts of the country TECs found themselves failing to meet the government's guarantee to offer all unemployed 16- and 17-year-olds a place on a YT scheme (*The Times Educational Supplement*, 15 May 1992). The TECs made clear their desire for the government to free them from a contractual obligation to meet the guarantee, and indicated that they would prefer to allocate their limited funds to a smaller number of higher quality traineeships. The government's response was to reiterate their commitment to the guarantee (*Employer Development Bulletin 32*, August 1992: 15).

Whilst substantial extra government funding for the TECs has not been forthcoming, the government did try to provide some help via the 1990 Budget, which offered tax relief to companies on any money which they gave to TECs. The government has also been keen to see TECs raise money via commercial activities. The amounts that have been raised in these ways have proved to be extremely limited and are believed to be likely to diminish (Davies *et al.* 1992: 6).

Relations with government

While the TECs have generally tried to keep their disagreements with ministers and officials at the Employment Department (ED) out of the public limelight, there have been numerous press reports indicating sharp battles. There is little doubt that cuts in government support have put the TECs under considerable strain and have tended to sour relations between them and the government. In response to a House of Commons Select Committee on Employment survey, Derek Jackson, the chief executive of the Heart of England TEC, stated that cuts in YT and ET funding make

> it virtually impossible to develop the role envisaged for the TEC as an active leader in training, enterprise and economic regeneration. We are in danger of becoming a purely reactive organisation funding short-term solutions to the present economic and social problems.
>
> (quoted in *The Guardian*, 4 November 1991)

Sir Brian Wolfson, chair of the National Training Task Force, suggested that 'we now have a movement fighting to make do with the crumbs left on the table' (*Times Higher Education Supplement*, 18 December 1992).

The mechanisms for, and degree of, departmental supervision of TECs has also proved to be contentious (Wood 1991a), and G10 complained to ministers

that TECs wanted less interference, less detailed monitoring of their performance and more freedom to use public funds as they saw fit. The chair of G10,
Mr Eric Dancer, head of Devon and Cornwall TEC, commented that, 'as TECs
become established and develop a track record and show that they can be
trusted they should be given responsibility for monitoring themselves' (Wood
1991b).

In 1991 the ED, assisted by Coopers & Lybrand Deloitte, undertook an
examination of relationship between the TECs and ED's Training Enterprise
and Education Division (TEED) which was formally responsible for monitoring
the TECs' performance (Wood 1991b). Despite these efforts there continue to
be indications that at times the relationship between the TECs, and the government and the ED remains strained. A survey of TEC board members conducted
by the *Financial Times* in 1992 (Wood 1992) found that 95.4 per cent wanted
greater flexibility in their contractual relationship with the ED. One board
member commented that, 'I do not see how businessmen of any calibre will
continue to tolerate the suffocating and unnecessary bureaucracy' (Wood
1992).

The relationship between TECs and other parts of the training system

When the government decided to develop TECs, it gave little thought to such
relationships. The result has been a measure of conflict and confusion. For
example, the relatively uncoordinated network of locally-based organizations
finds it difficult to interface with other organizations operating on the national
level, such as Industry Training Organizations (ITOs) (Wood 1991a),
professional bodies and large companies (*Financial Times*, 31 July 1991). There
are inherent tensions between the government's decision to devolve responsibility to the local level, and the considerable transaction costs and diseconomies
created by the subsequent need for national organizations to enter into a
multiplicity of individual negotiations with TECs.

Thus, for example, the relationship that is meant to exist between locally-
based TECs and national-level industry or sectoral training bodies has remained
remarkably unclear. Some ITOs are major providers of training, especially with
regard to the organization of industry-wide Youth Training provision. Before
the advent of TECs such schemes had been covered by a single national contract
with the MSC. Many ITOs have been extremely unhappy about having to
negotiate YT contracts and funding with each individual TEC where their
members are operating the industry's nation-wide YT scheme. In June 1991
the British Printing Industries Federation pulled out of participation in YT
because of this (Wood 1991a). Large companies, particularly banks and
retailers that have outlets across the country, have experienced similar
problems. Business criticism of this state of affairs caused the government to
exempt large companies from the need to negotiate with their local TECs about
accreditation under the Investors In People initiative. Instead an Investors In

People Central Support Unit has been established to arrange nation-wide accreditation for large employers (*Financial Times*, 31 July 1991).

At local level, the TECs have generally been careful to forge good working relationships with other organizations, such as Enterprise in the Community, local authorities and the Prince's Trust, but there has been conflict between some TECs and their local chambers of commerce. G10 were recorded as being of the view, in a leaked memorandum of a meeting with the Department of Employment, that 'there was a clear potential for conflict in the enterprise side between chambers and TECs' (*Financial Times*, 7 June 1991). There have also been problems over the provision of business advice. The chambers often offer such a service to their members, who pay a subscription in return. Some newly established TECs set up rival services (Wood 1991a). Meetings were held between G10 and the Association of British Chambers of Commerce (ABCC) in an attempt to achieve closer cooperation.

More importantly, because the TECs were left to define their own boundaries, those that resulted in some cases did not coincide with existing local authority and therefore local education authority (LEA) boundaries. Some TECs cover several complete LEAs, while others cover only parts of different LEAs. This situation does not help the TECs' ability to liaise with the education system or more closely integrate the design and delivery of vocational education and training in their areas. Another source of difficulty has been TECs dealings with local training providers, particularly those in the voluntary sector who have specialized in provision for particularly disadvantaged groups, such as ethnic minorities, young offenders and those with learning difficulties (*Financial Times*, 23 September 1991; Phillips 1991; Emmerick and Peck 1992). Partly in order to free-up funds to cover training not aimed at the unemployed, some TECs have been exerting pressure on those bodies that provide training places for YT and ET, in an attempt to force them to offer lower unit prices.

The representativeness and accountability of TECs

Many TEC boards, as a self-selecting group, are probably not representative of local employers. Initial analysis indicated (Emmerick and Peck 1991) that manufacturing industry was often over-represented in relation to the proportion of employment it provided in the locality. The government's preconditions on board membership have also ensured a structural imbalance in their composition. For example, the Equal Opportunities Commission has pointed out that, as a consequence of the chairmen- and chief executives-only membership rule, TEC boards are likely to look 'very white and male' (*Personnel Today*, 27 June 1989). These fears proved well-founded. In November 1991 only 10.7 per cent of board members were female, and only 3.5 per cent were from ethnic minority backgrounds (Emmerick and Peck 1992: 13–14).

At a broader level, TECs have been designed by the government to be explicitly unrepresentative of other stakeholders in VET – educationalists trade unions, community groups, local authorities and the unemployed. In November 1991 local authority representatives made up 8.5 per cent of all TEC board seats, local education authorities accounted for a further 4.2 per cent, trade unions 5.1 per cent and voluntary organizations 3.7 per cent (Emmerick and Peck 1992: 13–14). While some TECs have made efforts to overcome this difficulty and have evolved elaborate advisory structures in order to allow representation for non-employer stakeholders (NTTF 1992; *IDS Study*, 485, July 1991) other TECs have appeared either hostile or indifferent towards their local authorities (Beckett 1992; Emmerick and Peck 1992). Moreover, the legal status of TECs as limited companies, and the lack of any compulsory formal linkages between them and the communities within which they operate, mean that their accountability to their local communities remains at best uncertain. As Barnes underlines (1991: 38), 'issues of representation and accountability are not abstract debating points but will determine whether TECs are to warrant and sustain the local support they need to achieve lasting success'.

TECs – AN OVERVIEW

On the credit side, perhaps the greatest success of the TEC movement has been its ability to harness the interest and energy of large numbers of senior private sector executives (NTTF 1992; Wood 1992). As a form of 'action learning' the TECs may have offered a significant opportunity to improve knowledge about, and to alter attitudes towards, training in Britain among an influential segment of the business community. On the debit side, the greatest problem which TECs face is the fact that nine-tenths of the funding they receive from government is committed to schemes that are, in the main, aimed at the unemployed, and which only cover entrants or re-entrants to the labour market rather than existing members of the workforce – a difficulty which was sharply compounded by the recession and rising unemployment.

The crucial issue for the future is therefore going to be the degree to which TECs can promote and improve training for those in employment. The questions that remain to be answered are how TECs can change the low-wage, low-skill, low-quality culture that arguably characterizes large parts of our economy; alter companies' attitudes towards the value of training; and address the needs of the adult in employment? The major vehicle for achieving change in employers' outlook and behaviour, besides exhortation, is the Investors In People (IIP) scheme.

INVESTORS IN PEOPLE

Investors In People (IIP), launched in November 1990, is a national standard for effective investment in employees, and was developed by the NTTF, in collaboration with CBI members, the Association of British Chambers of Commerce (ABCC), the TUC, ITOs and other training organizations.

The aim is to encourage more organizations to invest in training, to help them to do so more effectively, and to reward this commitment with a nationally-recognized 'kitemark' of training quality. It is also believed that giving firms that are good trainers a recognizable 'kitemark' will aid the development of the desired 'training market' by making it clearer to prospective employees which companies offer them the best prospects of adequate training and development. There has also been talk of eventually tying the supply of TEC funds to the kitemark (*Financial Times*, 12 March 1991). To date, one TEC – the Central England TEC – has warned all the training and business counselling providers with which the TEC does business that they must commit themselves to gaining IIP status before November 1993 or be struck off its list of contractors (*Personnel Management*, September 1992: 17).

Achievement of IIP status is dependent upon an organization's owner or chief executive making a public commitment to develop all its employees in order to achieve its business objectives; the organization regularly reviewing the training and development needs of all its employees; demonstration of action to train and develop individuals on recruitment and throughout their employment; and evidence that the organization regularly evaluates and reviews its investment in training. Assessment of most organizations in England and Wales applying for IIP status is made by their local TEC, though large companies can deal with a national Employment Department unit. In Scotland IIP assessment is undertaken by a national body – Investors In People (Scotland). The award of IIP status is made for three years, after which it is necessary for the organization to provide evidence of continued achievement and development.

The pace at which organizations have achieved IIP status has been extremely slow. In September 1992 only seventy-six companies had become IIPs, with a further 1,100 organizations committed to achieving the standard (*Employee Development Bulletin*, no. 33, September 1992; 16). This limited rate of progress is perhaps not surprising given the results of a 1990 survey, commissioned by the ED, and undertaken by Deloitte Coopers, which found that out of seventeen leading companies, only two would currently qualify for the kitemark. In particular, problems were noted about the ability of firms to review investment in training against business plans (*Financial Times*, 4 December 1990).

THE NATIONAL EDUCATION AND TRAINING TARGETS

The final element of the new training system is the set of National Education and Training Targets (NETTs), which form a series of performance objectives for British vocational education and training to the year 2000.

In the late 1980s there was much talk about establishing a set of over-arching national training targets, the achievement of which would offer strategic goals for the newly-emerging TEC-based training system. In December 1989 Norman Fowler, the then Secretary of State for Employment, announced that the government was setting a series of ambitious national targets. Just four months later, in April 1990, Mr Fowler's successor, Michael Howard, quietly announced that these targets were no longer part of official policy. Tim Eggar, the junior employment minister, commented, 'the Government cannot impose targets over which it has no control. If you devolve you no longer have direct control over the achievement of targets' (*Financial Times*, 25 April 1990).

In the absence of any clearer leadership by government, the CBI took up the tasks, and following bilateral talks with other employers' groups, trade unions and educational bodies, in the summer of 1991 it launched what it termed a list of 'world class targets' (CBI 1991). Bodies such as the TUC offered their support for these, and the government has subsequently decided to endorse them. Indeed achievement of the National Education and Training Targets (NETTs), as they are now called, form a central element of the 'mission' which the Employment Department sets in its annual guidance to TECs and LECs (see, for example, ED 1991). The main targets set by the CBI are as follows.

(a) Foundation learning

1 By 1997 at least 80 per cent of young people to attain NVQ/SVQ level II or its academic equivalent in their foundation education and training.
2 All young people who can benefit should be given an entitlement to structured training, work experience or education leading to NVQ/SVQ level III or its academic equivalent.
3 By the year 2000, at least half of the age group should attain NVQ/SVQ level III or its academic equivalent as a basis for further progression.
4 All education and training provision should be structured and designed to develop self-reliance, flexibility and broad competence as well as specific skills.

(b) Lifetime learning

1 By 1996, all employees should take part in training or development activities as the norm.
2 By 1996, at least half of the employed workforce should be aiming for qualifications or units towards them within the NVQ/SVQ framework.
3 By the year 2000, half of the employed workforce should be qualified to NVQ/SVQ level III or its academic equivalent as a minimum.
4 By 1996, at least half of the medium-sized and larger organizations should qualify as 'Investors In People', assessed by the relevant TEC or LEC.

332

By any standards the targets are ambitious. They assume the acceptance and use of the NVQ system by all employers, major increases in employer expenditure on training, and a radical increase in the degree of sophistication to be found in the planning and evaluation of in-company training activities. For instance, in order to meet the first attainment target by 1997, the annual rate of growth in 18-year-olds achieving NVQ/SVQ level II or its academic equivalent (four GCSEs at grades A–C) between 1990 and 1997 needs to be double the rate achieved between 1985 and 1990 (*Labour Market Quarterly Report*, February 1992: 17). Moreover, the targets' originators are clear that a key aspect of achieving the targets is the elimination of all employment for 16–18-year-olds that offer no training leading to nationally recognized qualifications (*Labour Market Quarterly Report*, February 1992: 19). Similarly, the objective of half of all large and medium-sized companies reaching IIP status by 1996 needs to be set against the currently very slow rate of IIP accreditation.

Since the NETTs were launched it has become increasingly clear that many of those upon whom responsibility rests for reaching the targets, such as TECs, schools, colleges and small employers, perceive them as something that has been imposed upon them without any reference to their opinions or needs. TEC officials often find it hard to relate the national targets to demand for skills within their local labour markets. Some employers take a similar line. For example, it is often difficult for firms within the retail trade to relate to the national foundation target that by the year 2000 at least 50 per cent of young people should attain NVQ/SVQ level III or its academic equivalent (A levels), given the current skills needs and employment patterns within their industry. The ED is now encouraging TECs to set their own targets, which reflect their individual starting points in terms of differing stocks of skills and qualifications in each local labour force, and which help involve schools, colleges and local employers (*Skills and Enterprise Briefing*, Issue 16/92, June 1992).

The reaction of employers to NETTs has been mixed. For example, the hotel and catering sector has already announced that it regards the national targets of half the workforce aiming towards NVQs by 1996, and half the workforce as qualified to NVQ level III by the year 2000, as unrealistic, and have set themselves targets at half the national level (*Employee Development Bulletin* 40, April 1993: 3). The industry lead body estimates that even this will be hard to achieve, and that without the promotion of NVQs and the action plans which they have devised, only 1.2 per cent of the workforce would be likely to be aiming at NVQs in 1995/6. When sectors as large as this decide that the NETTs are unrealistic, the achievement of the targets must be open to question.

The importance of NETTs to those who run the training system is considerable. They set a series of easily identifiable strategic goals for the new training system which 'offer a framework that binds together a wide range of other initiatives in the education and training field and gives them coherence' (*Skills and Enterprise Briefing*, Issue 16/92, June 1992). Rates of progress towards their achievement also provide a set of measurable performance indicators or benchmarks for TECs and LECs. Finally, the process of achieving the targets is meant to help foster a 'learning culture' among British employers and employees (*Labour Market Quarterly Report*, February 1992: 16).

THE NEW INSTITUTIONAL LANDSCAPE OF TRAINING: AN OVERVIEW

The result of the government's reforms has been to shift the focus of decision-making from a national body (government, trade unions, employers, educationalists) – the MSC – and industry-level bodies (NSTOs and ITBs), towards locally-based, employer-dominated TECs. The model is one of nationally-based standards coupled with local delivery of training. At a broader level, these developments represent not only the dismantlement, but also the emergence of a new model of policy formation, in which the exclusion of bodies such as trade unions and local authorities from any significant role in training policy is regarded as desirable, and in which the state delegates powers over policy formation and the delivery of publicly-funded programmes to self- or state-appointed employer-led bodies (Emmerick and Peck 1992).

Structurally, the new system looks broadly as shown in Figure 1. Attempts to arrive at any judgement about efficiency and appropriateness are hampered by the fact that this system is still evolving and that most of the major bodies within it are very new. Nevertheless there are some reasons for concern.

Fragmentation

The Central Policy Review Staff, in its 1980 report *Education, Training and Industrial Performance*, observed that the 'fragmentation of the training system appears complicated and unwieldy' (1980: 21). Since 1980 the fragmentation has increased very significantly. Instead of twenty-five ITBs and a limited number of non-statutory bodies, we now have 123 ITOs and the Construction

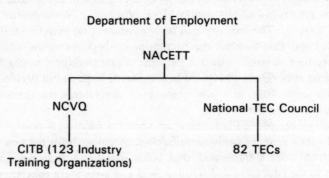

Figure 15.1 The training system in England and Wales.

Industry Training Board. Instead of the MSC, we now have the NACETT, the National TEC Council, and 102 TECs and LECs. Moreover, the linkages and mechanisms for coordination between many of the bodies within this new institutional constellation remain extremely unclear. These problems are mirrored within the education system, where opting out, grant-maintained status, and Local Management of Schools aim to create a system of competing individual schools. Such fragmentation renders liaison between education and industry more difficult (Davies *et al.* 1992). To give just one instance, as more and more schools opt out, and the coordinating role of LEAs correspondingly dwindles, the work of TECs in seeking to liaise with and influence educational provision in their areas will be greatly complicated.

Perhaps the most noticeable lacuna is the current lack of a national forum for training policy with some genuine strategic capacity and powers of direction. The National Training Task Force did not appear to have wished to attempt to supply this strategic vision; and G10, while undoubtedly fulfilling a useful role in coordinating communication between the TECs and ministers, also appeared neither interested in nor capable of providing more than the very vaguest strategic 'leadership'. Indeed there is a fairly open tension between the TECs and any attempts by national bodies to coordinate policy or offer a lead in its formulation. The *Financial Times*'s 1992 survey of TEC board members indicated that nearly 70 per cent of those surveyed rejected any increase in the powers of the NTTF (Wood 1992).

Examination of other European national training systems would suggest that a coherent and effective training system requires three mutually inter-dependent elements: a national focus for strategic planning and policy-making, a set of industry or sector-based training organizations and a local training delivery mechanism. Britain's training system unfortunately has never possessed all three elements simultaneously. We have moved from a world which in the early 1980s had a national policy focus (the MSC) and an industry-based system of provision in the shape of ITBs (at least within most parts of manufacturing), to a situation where we now have no real policy national focus, a patchwork of sectoral bodies of varying degrees of effectiveness, and are relying on locally-based TECs and LECs to address all issues of skill-supply from a local perspective. How sensible such arrangements are is open to question, not least at a time when an increasing proportion of jobs are shifting into the technical, professional and managerial occupations, where national labour markets are often more important than local ones.

The role of employers

The government has sought to characterize the new training system as being employer-led. Though in one sense this is plainly so, it is important to recognize that it is a fairly select group of employers who are involved (Field 1992). They are often self-selected enthusiasts. Moreover, they are explicitly appointed to serve only in a personal capacity. They are hardly representative and hardly meant to be representative of the mass of British employers, particularly small companies, the self-employed and those who do not train. Implicit in this situation is the danger that the enthusiasm of this vanguard of employers will outstrip the willingness of the majority of companies to act to improve training.

This is particularly worrying when it is apparent that within the new system improvements in the quality and quantity of training depend upon the attitudes and actions of individual employers. In future, responsibility for the success or failure will rest almost totally in their hands. The obverse of this is that ministers, whether intentionally or otherwise, have tended to distance themselves from responsibility – the difficulties in establishing the NETTs being just one example of this tendency. Put baldly, the government's message in handing over control of training to employers is, 'It's your problem now'.

In this respect it is interesting to note that there are now a significant number of people within the TEC movement who do not believe that a purely voluntarist approach to training can succeed (Rainbird and Smith 1992). A *Financial Times* survey of TEC directors (Wood 1992) showed that 36.7 per cent of them were prepared to support the re-imposition of some sort of training levy – a figure which had risen to nearly 40 per cent when a second *FT* survey was carried out in 1993 (Wood 1993). Other suggestions have included a corporation tax incentive for those achieving IIP status (Coffield 1992: 21).

It may be that there is an even more profound problem. There is increasing evidence that the country's VET deficiencies are at least as much a problem of lack of employer demand for skills as of lack of supply of them (Keep and Mayhew 1993). To the extent that this is the case then a policy which relies upon employers to achieve a fundamental transformation of the skill base is liable to be of limited effectiveness. Economists have often presumed that employers make privately optimal training decisions, but that because of externality problems the aggregate of these decisions adds up to something which is socially sub-optimal. In fact employers' training decisions may not add up to even a privately optimal strategy in the medium term.

The style of policy-making

The policy-making process has been heavily influenced by short-term economic pressures. In particular the need to be seen to be doing something about mass unemployment may have led to a stress on speed at the expense of coherence. This problem may have been exacerbated by the short tenure of employment ministers – since 1964 less than two years on average.

In terms of strategic thinking the 1980s saw what Clive Ponting described as a 'hole in the heart of government'. There was no effective replacement for the Central Policy Review Staff (abolished early in the decade) as a mechanism for formulating a coherent strategic overview of policy issues that impinged on more than one department. In the field of training this has led to confusion and inconsistencies between policies formulated by the Department of Employment and the Department for Education.

The need for speed and the lack of strategic policy-making machinery have helped to contribute to an often apparently wilful refusal to integrate research into policy-making. Thus, for example, the move to Training Credits was announced before there had been any evaluation of the various pilot schemes. Another example was the decision to move to performance-related funding for government funded schemes like YT and ET. This produced perverse and unintended incentives. It has offered the TECs encouragement to concentrate on training provision for those trainees most likely to succeed rather than helping the less able, and to concentrate on providing training places in low-cost occupations which aim at lower-level NVQs which are more easily attained. A funding system based on value-added would have avoided these pitfalls.

The shift to an employer-based system has gone beyond a denial of corporatism, and has involved the deliberate exclusion of certain interest groups from policy formation. For instance there seems to be an active hostility towards educationalists. Thus John Hillier, the chief executive of the NCVQ, was forced to remind employers that although they might wish to lead and education to follow, educationalists were 'entitled to a seat on the bus, even if it was at the back' (St John-Brook 1992: 6). This attitude may be responsible for an NVQ system that has been compared unfavourably with qualifications on offer elsewhere in Europe and widely criticized for their narrowness and lack of any general educational element.

This is but one example of lack of acknowledgement that there is in fact a community of stakeholders. The consequential danger is that the insights and concerns of other actors are ignored, with the potential costs of poorly designed policies and of absence of enthusiasm for and possibly hostility towards the initiatives that are produced. The failure of many groups to relate to the NETT is a case in point. As Sir John Cassels has argued (1985: 44), there are good reasons why consultation with interested parties and the achievement of consensus might be valuable:

> People in this country on the whole find education and training uninteresting to talk about. It is very important to promote genuine public debate to get people to understand what is involved. I hope that we can do that, because most of the things that need to be done in education and training are so controversial that they cannot be done without a considerable public discussion.

Unfortunately it is hard to escape the conclusion that policy-makers have sought actively to avoid genuine public debate and consultation. The problem is thus how to achieve coordination and cooperation in the context of an economy and culture that has placed increasing emphasis on unrestrained competition and institutional autonomy and fragmentation. The government's

337

outright rejection of anything that smacks of collectivism or corporatism makes it difficult to envisage how progress in this area can be made. The fate of first the MSC and then of NEDO illustrates the difficulties that attend any attempt to concert opinion within the context of a government whose ideology stresses the need for change to spring from the atomized activities of individual agents via the agency of market mechanisms. As a result of this approach Britain finds itself without the kind of forum for debate about VET that is commonplace in most of our international competitors.

A final feature of policy-making style has been a marked lack of stability. This is not simply a matter of the inevitable upheavals associated with any revolution. It is also a function of the overly experimental nature of some of the programmes (e.g. TVEI) associated with a lack of prior research, and of the failure of earlier waves of reform to deliver the expected gains and their replacement by fresh initiatives. Examples are CPVE, ITOs, LENs and YT itself. If at the same time policy formation is exclusionary, then inevitably the average employer is likely to have a limited comprehension of what the system is and of what it is meant to do.

The long-standing nature of our VET problem suggests that its origins are deep-rooted. Recent policy has been formulated on the basis of little diagnosis and has led to a system where the blind might well be leading the blind.

REFERENCES

Ainley, P. and Corney, M. (1990) *Training for the Future: The Rise and Fall of the Manpower Services Commission*, London: Cassell.

Anderson, A. (1987) *NSTOs: Their Activities and Effectiveness*, London: Manpower Research.

Barnes, G. (1991) 'An examination of the formulation of policies by training and enterprise councils', *Small and Medium Enterprise Centre Working Paper*, no. 7, Coventry: Warwick Business School.

Beckett, F. (1992) 'Trading places', *Times Educational Supplement – Update Vocational Education and Training*, January.

Benn, C. and Fairley, J. (eds) (1986) *Challenging the MSC on Jobs, Education and Training*, London: Pluto Press.

Berry-Lound, D. and Anderson, A. (1991) *Review of the Industrial Training Organisation Network*, Sheffield: HOST Consultancy/ED.

Berry-Lound, D., Chaplin, M. and O'Connell, B. (1991) 'Review of industrial training organisations', *Employment Gazette*, October, pp. 535–42.

Callender, C. (1992) 'Will NVQs work? Evidence from the construction industry', *IMS Report*, no. 228, Sussex: Institute of Manpower Studies.

Cassels, J. (1985) 'Educating for tomorrow – learning, work and the future', *Royal Society of Arts Journal*, June, vol. 133, no. 5347, pp. 438–49.

Central Policy Review Staff (1980) *Education, Training and Industrial Performance*, London: HMSO.

Coffield, F. (1992) 'Training and enterprise councils: the last throw of voluntarism?', *Policy Studies*, vol. 13, no. 4, pp. 11–51.

Confederation of British Industry (1989) *Towards a Skills Revolution*, London: CBI.

Confederation of British Industry (1991) *World Class Targets: A Joint Initiative to Achieve Britain's Skills Revolution*, London: CBI.

Coopers & Lybrand Associates (1985) *A Challenge to Complacency: Changing Attitudes to Training*, London: Manpower Services Commission/National Economic Development Office.

Danson, M., Lloyd, G. and Newlands, D. (1989) 'Scottish enterprise: towards a model agency or a flawed initiative?', *Regional Studies*, vol. 23, pp. 557–63.

Davies, P., Collier, A., Foster, E., Gill, A., Millar, G., Nicholls, S., Rowarth, M. and Warwick, D. (1992) 'TECs and education. Report to the National Training Task Force', London: NTTF (mimeo.).

Debling, G. (1991) 'Developing standards', in P. Raggatt and L. Unwin (eds), *Change and Intervention – Vocational Education and Training*, London: Falmer Press, pp. 1–21.

Emmerick, M. and Peck, J. (1991) *First Report of the TEC Monitoring Project*, Manchester: Centre for Local Economic Strategies.

Emmerick, M. and Peck, J. (1992) *Reforming the TECs – Towards a New Training Strategy*, Manchester: Centre for Local Economic Strategies.

Employment Department (1972) *Training for the Future, A Plan for Discussion*, London: HMSO.

Employment Department (1988) *Employment for the 1990s*, Cmnd 540, London: HMSO.

Employment Department (1991) *A Strategy for Skills: Guidance from the Secretary of State for Employment on Training, Vocational Education and Enterprise*, London: Employment Department.

Employment Department (1992) 'Clerical and secretarial skills: a neglected resource?', *Skills and Enterprise Briefing*, Issue 33/92, November.

Employment Department/Department of Education and Science (1986) *Working Together – Education and Training*, Cmnd 9823, London: HMSO.

Evans, B. (1992) *The Politics of the Training Market – From Manpower Services Commission to Training and Enterprise Councils*, London: Routledge.

Field, J. (1992) 'The pedagogy of labour', paper delivered to the University of Warwick VET Forum, February, University of Warwick, Department of Continuing Education (mimeo.).

Finegold, D., MacFarland, L. and Richardson, W. (eds) (1993) *Something Borrowed, Something Blue? An Analysis of Education and Training Policy in the US and Great Britain*, Oxford: Triangle Books.

Golzen, G. (1991) 'Is training out of touch with the 1990s?', *Sunday Times*, 18 August.

Gospel, H. and Okayama, R. (1991) 'Industrial training in Britain and Japan: an overview', in H. Gospel (ed.), *Industrial Training and Technological Innovation – A Comparative and Historical Study*, London: Routledge, pp. 13–37.

Grant, G. and associates (1979) *On Competence*, San Francisco: Jossey-Bass.

Institute of Directors (1991) *Performance and Potential – Education and Training for a Market Economy*, London: IoD.

Jackson, M. (1992) 'Coping with a history of gentlemanly punch-ups', *Times Educational Supplement – Vocational Education and Training*, January.

Jarvis, V. and Prais, S. (1989) 'Two nations of shopkeepers: training for retailing in Britain and France', *National Institute Economic Review*, vol. 128, pp. 58–74.

Jessup, G. (1991) *Outcomes: NVQs and the Emerging Model of Education and Training*, Brighton: Falmer.

Keep, E. (1987) 'Britain's attempts to create a national vocational education and training system: a review of progress', *Warwick Papers in Industrial Relations*, 16, Coventry: Industrial Relations Research Unit.

Keep, E. (1991) 'The grass looked greener – some thoughts on the influence of comparative vocational training research on the UK policy debate', in P. Ryan (ed.), *International Comparisons of Vocational Education and Training for Intermediate Skills*, London: Falmer, pp. 23–46.

Keep, E. and Mayhew, K. (1993) 'UK training policy – assumptions and reality', paper presented to the CEPR conference 'Training and the Skills Gap', Birkbeck College, April.

Kenny, J. and Reid, M. (1985) *Training Interventions*, London: Institute of Personnel Management.

Lees, D. and Chiplin, R. (1970) 'The economics of industrial training', *Lloyds Bank Review*, April.

Lindley, R. (1983) 'Active manpower policy', in G. S. Bain (ed.), *Industrial Relations in Britain*, Oxford: Blackwell, pp. 339–60.

McCool, T. (1991) 'Making standards work together', presentation to the CBI conference 'Leading Standards Forward', London, 3 December.

McCormick, K. (1991) 'The development of engineering education in Britain and Japan', in H. Gospel (ed.), *Industrial Training and Technological Innovation – A Comparative and Historical Study*, London: Routledge, pp. 38–69.

Manpower Services Commission (1976) *Training for Vital Skills*, London: MSC.

Manpower Services Commission (1980) *Outlook on Training, A Review of the 1973 Employment and Training Act*, London: MSC.

Manpower Services Commission (1981) *A Framework for the Future*, London: MSC.

Manpower Services Commission/Department of Education and Science (1986) *Review of Vocational Qualifications in England and Wales*, London: HMSO.

Marshall, K. (1991) 'NVQs: an assessment of the "outcomes" approach to education and training', *Journal of Further and Higher Education*, vol. 15, no. 3, Autumn.

National Training Task Force (1992) 'Draft copy of the Cleaver report', London: NTTF (mimeo.)

Perry, P. J. C. (1976) *The Evolution of British Manpower Policy*, London: British Association of Commercial and Industrial Education.

Phillips, M. (1991) 'Bigger holes mean net loss', *The Guardian*, 19 April.

Prais, S. J. (1989) 'How Europe would see the new British initiative for standardising vocational qualifications', *National Institute Economic Review*, vol. 129, pp. 52–4.

Prais, S. J. (1991) 'Vocational qualifications in Britain and Europe: theory and practice', *National Institute Economic Review*, May, pp. 47–59.

Raggatt, P. (1991) 'Quality assurance and NVQs', in P. Raggatt and L. Unwin (eds), *Change and Intervention – Vocational Education and Training*, London: Falmer Press, pp. 61–80.

Rainbird, H. and Grant, W. (1985) *Employers' Associations and Training Policy*, Coventry: Institute of Employment Research.

Rainbird, H. and Smith, J. (1992) 'The role of the social partners in vocational training in Great Britain', report prepared for the Istituto di Studi sulle Relazioni Industriale e di Lavoro, on behalf of the Italian Ministry of Labour, Coventry, University of Warwick, Industrial Relations Research Unit (mimeo.).

Reeder, D. (1981) 'A recurring debate: education and industry', in R. Dale, G. Esland and M. MacDonald (eds), *Education and the State: Volume 1, School and the National Interest*, Lewes: Falmer.

Reid, W. (1992) 'Setting standards for the future', *Personnel Management*, August, pp. 28–35.

Senker, P. J. (1992) *Industrial Training in a Cold Climate*, Aldershot: Avebury.

Sheldrake, J. and Vickerstaff, S. (1987) *The History of Industrial Training in Britain*, Aldershot: Gower.

Steedman, H. and Wagner, K. (1989) 'Productivity, machinery and skills in Britain and Germany', *National Institute Economic Review*, vol. 128, pp. 40–57.

St John-Brook, C. (1992) 'Industry rattled by new training plan', *The Times Educational Supplement*, 30 October.

Stringer, J. and Richardson, J. (1982) 'Policy stability and policy change, industrial training 1964–1982', *Public Administration Bulletin*, no. 29, pp. 22–39.

Tysome, T. (1992) 'Unloved, unwanted and full of fear', *Times Higher Education Supplement*, 5 June.

Uchida, H. (1991) 'Japanese technical manpower in industry, 1880–1930: a quantitative survey', in H. Gospel (ed.), *Industrial Training and Technological Innovation – A Comparative and Historical Study*, London: Routledge, pp. 112–35.

Varlaam, C. (1987) *The Full Fact-finding Study of the NSTO System*, Brighton: Institute of Manpower Studies.

Wood, L. (1991a) 'Training on trial', *Financial Times*, 10 July.

Wood, L. (1991b) 'Tecs look for marriage guidance', *Financial Times*, 10 June.

Wood, L. (1992) '"Urgent need" found for government to examine Tecs funding', *Financial Times*, 25 March.

Wood, L. (1993) 'TEC chiefs call for wider action', *Financial Times*, 10 May.

Part V

INDUSTRIAL CHANGE
AND INDUSTRIAL POLICY

16

OVERVIEW:
THE AGENTS OF CHANGE
Notes on the developing division of labour

Paul Temple

> Full employment ... is an adventure which must be undertaken if free society is to survive. It is an adventure which can be undertaken with confidence of ultimate success. Success, however, will not come by following any rigid formula but by adapting action to circumstances which may change continually.
>
> (W. Beveridge, *Full Employment in a Free Society*, p. 192)

INTRODUCTION

The pivotal aspect in economic development is an increasing division and specialization in the utilization of labour. There are sufficient common elements to this process amongst the more advanced economies to have led observers to speak in terms of a plethora of unifying themes: the rise of the 'new service economy', 'deindustrialization', 'globalization' and 'Euro-sclerosis' provide some illustrative examples. This chapter addresses some of the relevant issues by commenting on some of the principal features of the advancing division of labour and the changing international political economy, assessing each in terms of the peculiar circumstances of the UK. In such a vast area, any attempt to be comprehensive would almost certainly be a mistake, and so we focus on issues which seem especially germane to the performance debate: first, the growth of service activities; second, the nature of international economic integration and its relationship to technological change; finally, the policy implications of some of these processes are discussed in the context of the UK experience.

DEINDUSTRIALIZATION AND THE GROWTH OF SERVICES

The rise of the service sector in mature economies has provoked considerable debate as to its economic significance and its relationship to the concept of 'deindustrialization'.

In this section we comment upon three aspects of this new division of labour with important ramifications for policy debate – differential productivity

345

growth rates between goods and services, potential market failures in service provision and the international tradability of services.

Structural change is most often described and assessed in terms of shifts in the division of labour in an economy. In fact, economic development in the advanced economies of the world has certain features which all economies have shared in the transition from an agrarian base to an industrial one.

Initially the agrarian sector provides the major share of employment. Industrialization begins when a sustained process of economic growth establishes itself; this involves *inter alia* a rapid shift in the share of employment away from the land towards the so-called 'secondary' sector – manufacturing, construction and energy. The service sector provides an important accompaniment to this process – especially in transport and distribution activities which permit markets to expand, although other service activities, associated with domestic service, urban development and trade are also important.

As Rowthorn and Wells (1987) show, this pattern of development is not sustainable. Widening employment opportunities eventually tend to reverse the process of increasing domestic service and the shrinking employment share on the land means that agriculture can no longer act as a huge labour reserve for the expansion of industry. When employment shares in domestic service and agriculture cease to be significant in terms of those of the secondary and tertiary sectors, then expansion of the service sector necessitates declines in the share of industry. This provides one possible definition of 'deindustrialization' or 'economic maturity'. In the UK at least, this stage was decisively reached by the 1960s when the share of manufacturing employment peaked and the rapid expansion in the employment share in health and education – activities primarily associated with the emerging welfare state – could no longer be accommodated from sources in agriculture, domestic services and the post-war run-down in the armed forces.

In other advanced economies, and with the exception of the US, the stage of maturity was reached rather later than in the UK. In the 1960s, this produced a lively debate as to whether the UK had reached a point of 'premature maturity', and whether there was disguised unemployment in the service sector as in agriculture. By the 1970s the debate concerned the apparent relationship between the growth of public (and non-marketed) services and the decline of manufacturing. Aspects of this question are explored by Mayes in Chapter 17 below.

Productivity, prices and the fiscal problem

It is of course important to understand why the employment share of services tends to rise through time. A number of powerful but sometimes contradictory forces are at work which combine to determine the size of the service sector. The first of these is how the demand for goods *vis-à-vis* services responds to the demands of an increasingly wealthy society. It is sometimes suggested that the demand for services is particularly 'income elastic'. However, empirical studies have not actually confirmed that the demand for marketed services in general is any more responsive to growing income than manufactured products. Other considerations suggest that productivity and prices have as big, if not a bigger, role to play. Moreover, technological change has set up fundamental possibilities for substitution of goods for services which are well documented: television for the services of live entertainers; the automobile for public transport; the washing machine for the laundry and so on. All these cases are well established.[1] The element on which we focus here is that key parts of the service sector are inherently less 'progressive' than other economic activities, limiting possibilities for technical and productivity advance.

In a seminal paper on 'unbalanced growth' written over twenty years ago, William Baumol drew attention to some of the simple, but quite startling, implications for economies characterized by a dichotomy between 'progressive' activities and those which, by their very nature, were not susceptible to the beneficial effects of advances in technology and labour productivity (Baumol 1967). In these activities, it is the labour itself which is essential to consumption – a theatre production or waiter service in a restaurant would be suitable examples. In such cases the quality of the labour performed is, to a large extent, the quality of the output itself. Many but not all such occupations are to be found in the service sector – manufacturing for example makes use of designers, marketers, many of whom may well fall under the heading depicted by Baumol. Moreover, a large number of these kinds of service fall within the public sector – the most important of which can be found in education and healthcare. In any of these cases, opportunities for productivity growth, if not entirely absent, are at least severely circumscribed. As Baumol himself remarks, we tend to judge the quality of education in terms of labour input – declining average class sizes being frequently used as an indicator of 'progress'.[2]

Given some simplifying assumptions, the most important of which is that wages in the long run will tend to equality in both the progressive and the non-progressive sectors, then there will be a persistent tendency for prices in the non-progressive sector to rise in terms of those in the rest of the economy, so that what is happening to relative output cannot be inferred from either expenditure data measured at *current prices* or from employment data. What happens to demand will depend upon both price and income elasticities; many services will simply disappear (except perhaps in luxury niches) either because prices become prohibitive, or else because wages fall behind that obtainable elsewhere – 'the shoe-shine' and the 'butler' are examples. In other sectors the existence of, for example, 'family workers' or the labour of illegal immigrants may prevent wages from growing as fast as in the progressive sector. However, some services are clearly relatively income elastic and here price and income effects may tend to cancel out.

For this reason it is equally interesting to consider what will happen if, either through market or non-market forces, the relative output of the two sectors were to be maintained. In this case, the unprogressive sector will (over time) absorb an ever-increasing fraction of the nation's workforce. Moreover, the overall rate of growth in the economy will tend (asymptotically) towards that recorded in the unprogressive sector.

It is an empirical question as to how far productivity growth in services as a whole actually falls short of that in manufacturing, although one not easily resolved, not least because of the difficulties we have mentioned of measuring 'quality' in services.[3] Nevertheless, evidence is provided in Table 1 on productivity growth in the service sectors of the G6, relative to that in manufacturing and the economy as a whole for the period 1960–90.

It turns out that the officially recorded growth of real value-added per person employed in services is typically between one-third and two-thirds of the growth recorded in manufacturing. With substantial proportions of the populations of these economies now working in services, it is not surprising that recorded growth rates there are much closer to those for the economy as a whole.

It is important to realize that it is in the public sector where activities perhaps most closely resemble those classified by Baumol as unprogressive. Official statistics are more or less useless in this regard since, in the UK, the Central Statistical Office actually measures output of many public sector activities by means of employment, so nothing can be said about productivity growth without circular reasoning. Nevertheless we may be able to infer something about productivity movements on the basis of changes in relative prices. The issues raised by Baumol are particularly relevant when the output is publicly provided, since there is no direct counterpart to rising prices from the consumers' point of view. What people do experience is the ongoing debate about the level of funding of the educational and health services. The often expressed disagreement about whether there have, or have not, been 'real cuts' in education or health services (or for that matter, police, fire, street-cleaning, etc.) often boils down to a question of the standard of measurement. Figure 1

Table 1 Growth of labour productivity in services compared to manufacturing and the whole economy (1960–90)

	Services (% p.a.)	Ratio to manufacturing (%)	Ratio to whole economy (%)
US	0.9	33	75
Japan	3.8	54	75
Germany	2.0	69	71
France	2.2	50	69
UK	1.6	52	76
Italy	2.0	37	54

Source: OECD Historical Statistics 1960–90

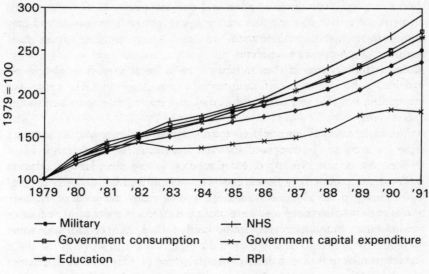

Source: CSO; National Income Blue Book

Figure 16.1 Relative price movements in government purchases, 1979–91.

shows some relevant deflators estimated from the National Income Blue Book for three major components of government spending: health, education and the military. When measured in 'own prices', it turns out that current 'real' government spending rose by rather meagre amounts between 1980 and 1991: 0.4 per cent per annum for military spending, 1.4 per cent for the National Health Service and 0.5 per cent for local authority spending on education.[4]

Of course, measuring spending in terms of an overall standard – the retail prices index (RPI) or the GDP deflator – does have meaning as an indicator of the 'opportunity cost' of utilizing resources in that particular way – what must be foregone in terms of other goods and services not produced. In practice this is what most commentators tend to do, but this can be severely misleading if the point of contention is the *volume* of the service being delivered.

The fact that all these areas are largely financed by general taxation of course adds a certain spice to the fiscal problems of government. The French have a saying – 'avoir le coeur a gauche et le portefeuille a droite'[5] – which may go some way to explaining how people's expressed desire for a better health service is not necessarily matched by any corresponding vote at the polls. As far as current debate in the UK is concerned, it needs to be stressed that the relative cost of education and health provision will tend to rise through time quite irrespective of whether provision is in the public sector, the private sector or a 'pseudo' market. This is not to deny that 'efficiency' cannot be improved in these areas by more effectively marshalling resources, but this is going to be a short-run, *level* of productivity effect and does not affect the argument based on trends. Nor is it to deny that technological change is important and may become increasingly so in these areas, but that this seems unlikely to raise crude measures of productivity (students per teacher, patients per nurse) by very much. It follows that if these activities are to be funded through general taxation, a rising burden of taxation as a percentage of GDP seems the inevitable price that must be paid if standards are to be maintained in the longer term.

Although sectors of low productivity growth tend to cluster within the service sector, it must not be supposed that this is an essential characteristic of all services. As we saw in Chapter 11 in relation to the financial and business service sector, productivity growth can be quite rapid and it is clear that technological change in the ability of machines to process many thousands of relatively homogeneous transactions may have profound effects in some areas of finance and insurance. In transport and communication there is also considerable scope for productivity advance and in these industries recorded growth over the 1980s was very similar to that recorded for manufacturing (as Mayes shows in Chapter 17 below). Distribution has also shown gains, comparable to those seen in the economy as a whole. On the other hand, hotels and catering has been one area of marketed services where productivity growth has been non-existent in the recent past. Between 1979 and 1990, the growth in employees in hotels and catering actually exceeded output growth,[6] suggesting that productivity levels may actually have fallen. Although a different measure to a crude headcount may modify the position somewhat, it does not contradict the general picture (NEDO 1992). Smith (1989), however, believes that, in an area where labour turnover is often critical, the existence of a generally slack labour market in the 1980s allowed hotel, restaurant and public-house proprietors to adjust staffing levels to their desired position.

Differences in long-term productivity growth between goods and services in the course of development generate quite different price structures between the developed and less developed economies. A price of a haircut in terms of, say, washing machines, in Stockholm will typically be much higher than in Kinshasa.[7]

There is also considerable variation in productivity *levels* across the service sectors, as Mayes shows below in Chapter 17, Table 4. Distribution tends to have low productivity relative to the economy as a whole, transport and communication about the same, and banking, finance and insurance rather higher. Wages also differ substantially.[8]

Market failure and tradability in international markets

In addition to secular trends in productivity performance two other aspects may be important in assessing the significance of the service sector – potential market failures in service provision and the issue of international tradability.

Services can be distinguished from goods on a number of counts, including their tangibility, their stockability and the frequent need for close interaction between buyer and seller or between producer and user. Intangibility for example leads to a classification which includes distribution and transport; financial, business and professional services; healthcare, education and other personal services; public administration; etc. But the economic significance of these possible distinctions is somewhat elusive and it is generally more satisfactory to speak of the general tendencies which typify services as a whole rather than every individual service. As we have seen, a tendency for lower long-term productivity growth is one example with clear implications for the structure of economies in the course of development, but not one which can be applied to all services. Other tendencies include one towards market failure and hence for provision to occur within the public sector or for regulation within the private sector; also of vital importance is a tendency towards lower tradability in international markets.

The market failure literature recognizes the public-good argument for government provision – provision by private firms is problematic; because of the free-rider problem, firms are unable to appropriate the returns. The classic example is the service provided by the armed forces. However, there are many examples of rather more imperfect public goods, in which a case can be made for public provision. Research and development (R&D) activity is an especially important example where private returns may fall short of the underlying social benefits. In areas such as this the involvement of the public sector varies enormously across countries. In Japan, for example, state involvement is much lower in R&D than in the UK. This might reflect missed opportunities for increasing welfare in Japan but it may also (and more likely) reflect the relative ability of firms in the UK and Japan to exploit innovation successfully (see Ricketts, Chapter 10, above).

A rather different strand to the market failure argument is based on the quality of provision. Informational asymmetries may create a strong case for regulation of service sector activities. Although Ackerlof (1970) originally applied the idea to the market for secondhand cars, his strictures may be even more generally applicable to the supply of services, not least because 'irreversibility' is an essential aspect of many services (e.g. once your hair has been cut or a court case lost, there is no return to the *status quo ante*). If customers have difficulty in either observing the characteristics of the supplier or the diligence with which the duties are undertaken, then better quality practitioners may have difficulty extracting premiums for quality: a form of Gresham's law applies and the 'bad will drive out the good'. The market itself has devices for improving information flows which include guarantees, reputation effects, consumer and producer organizations, and so on. Sometimes contracts can be drawn up which are contingent upon certain outcomes (e.g. the 'no win no fee' contract is common in US legal practice) but the sharing of risk in these situations is not necessarily optimal.

Systems of intervention which embrace institutions such as licensing aimed at reducing these informational sources of market failure are generally more common in the service sector (and especially in professional services) and they can create potent barriers to entry especially across national boundaries, and these of course have been important in the EC's attempt to create a unified market. The principle behind the European Single Market has been one of 'mutual recognition' rather than 'harmonization' of bodies and standards, which is generally seen as a second-best strategy in which a downward spiral of standards is seen as a possibility.[9]

Interventions in markets based on the need for ensuring quality in provision may for such reasons reduce the international tradability of services, but there are of course many other reasons for lower tradability, largely stemming from two factors: first, that many services exist which are dependent upon the close proximity of the customer (a haircut or a visit to the cinema) and, second, because many services depend upon special national circumstances (e.g. a tax consultant). However, as Kierskowski (1987) points out, services can be traded through other means, for example by:

1 moving the customer to the location of the supplier (international tourism is the most important example of this, but education and health may be increasingly relevant);
2 moving the supplier to the location of the customer (e.g. civil engineering consultancy);
3 relocating of services overseas through foreign direct investment.[10]

It is clear that the generally lower tradability of services is not immutable but is highly contingent. Technological change in the field of information technology may be having the effect of making services rather more tradable, while economic integration can be expected to increase the contestability of markets. Both the Single European Market and the Uruguay Round are clearly important in this respect. Nevertheless, estimates of world trade in services indicate that it is only a fraction of trade in goods. According to the data presented in Hoeckmann (1993), world merchandise exports totalled $3,500 billion in 1990 against $820 billion for service exports. Low tradability in services has meant that foreign investment in service activities has been a key feature in the globalization of the world economy, as we shall see below.

THE GROWTH OF SERVICES IN THE UK SINCE 1979

As we have seen, a shift of labour into the service sector can be regarded as quite normal for mature economies. To what extent is the UK atypical in this regard and to what extent has the growth been in some fundamental sense 'unbalanced', as suggested (for example) by Wells (1989)? The answer to this question depends upon a more precise picture of the nature and causes of service sector growth in the UK since 1979.

As we have seen, the share of total employment in services rises with economic development. A crude indicator of the latter is provided by GDP per capita and this is plotted against service employment share for the OECD economies in Figure 2, together with an estimated regression line. Evidently, for the stage of development reached, the UK displays a very high level of service sector employment. Caution is needed, however, since GDP per capita serves only as a shorthand for a number of factors closely related to the development of services, but which may vary substantially from one country to another – the degree of urbanization and the participation rate amongst women being among the more important. While the UK is not exactly an outlier, the closest observations are for the Netherlands and Norway, countries notable for high levels of welfare and merit good expenditure.

Viewed over time it can be seen from Figure 3a that the shift into services since 1979 was rather more rapid in the UK than in the US, Germany or Japan, but only a little faster (in terms of percentage points) than in France. The UK was already rather heavily specialized in services in 1960 compared to France and Germany, and this position has been maintained. The sectoral pattern of growth is, however, distinctly different. Figure 3b shows how uneven the

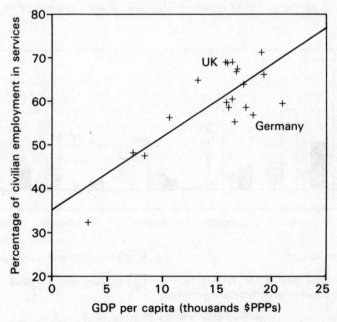

Source: OECD National Accounts, vol. I; Historical Statistics, 1960–90

Figure 16.2 Economic development and service sector employment; OECD economies (1990).

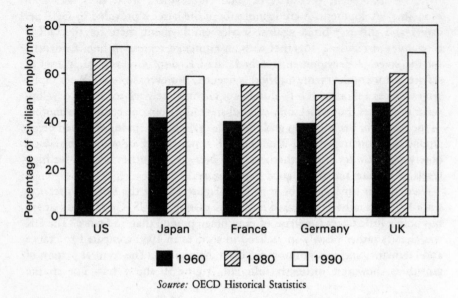

Source: OECD Historical Statistics

Figure 16.3a The growth of employment in services; five economies, 1960–90.

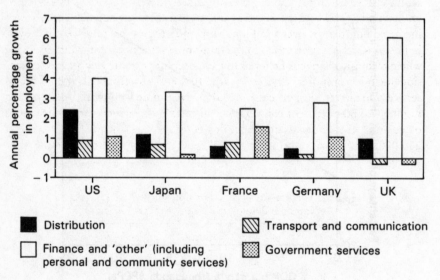

Source: OECD National Accounts, vol. II

Figure 16.3b The growth of service sectors; five economies, 1979–89.
Note: Germany 1979–88 only

pattern of growth is in the UK, with the overwhelming bulk of employment growth coming in financial, business and 'other' services, with transport and communication, and government, registering declines.

To see whether this pattern was actually unbalanced in some significant sense it is important to understand the sources of growth in service sector employment. In fact, it actually follows two quite distinct phases in the post-war period, as Table 2 reveals. In the first, up to 1973, the growth in employment was mainly in non-marketed' services (i.e. in health, education and public administration where output is not directly sold). To some extent these categories may have acted as a residual employer helping to maintain full employment, but they also reflected the epoch of the welfare state and the merit good. After 1973, and especially after 1979, the situation is effectively reversed with only restricted growth in the non-market sector.

In terms of the numbers of extra jobs generated over the 1979–90 business cycle, more than half a million were in distributive activities (and of these well over half were in hotels and catering, mainly in the boom period after 1985). Transport lost about 100,000 jobs, mostly in railways and shipping, with air transport raising the numbers it employed by about 10,000 jobs. 'Other' services increased employment by about 750,000 – numbers in public administration fell, but education workers increased somewhat and health workers increased their numbers by about 250,000; a whole range of services such as sanitary services, cultural and recreational activities all substantially increased employment. The biggest sectoral gains were in banking, finance, etc., which increased numbers by over a million. Three-quarters of this total were, however, in business services rather than in the traditional areas of banking and insurance where technical change is believed to have been important. Key areas of expansion include computer services (nearly 100,000), professional and technical services (architects, design, etc.), 150,000; even more important were growing numbers of management consultants and market researchers, and other forms of business service (in security, employment agencies and so forth) – about 250,000. Jobs in accounting and legal services also increased by more than 100,000.

Table 2 The growth of service employment (per cent per annum). Employees in employment (GB only)

	Non-marketed services[a]	Marketed services
1948–73	2.2	0.8
1973–90	1.0	1.7
1979–90	0.5	1.9

[a] Public administration, health and education
Sources: British Labour Statistics Historical Abstract 1886–1968, HMSO, 1971; Employment Gazette, Historical Supplement, no. 3, June 1992

Overall, jobs created elsewhere in the economy more than compensated for those lost in manufacturing. But structural changes of this magnitude have considerable repercussions on a regional and social level. In 1989 there were over 600,000 fewer full-time jobs for males compared to 1981,[11] a figure approximately balanced by an increase of females working full time. The increased employment could be explained by over 900,000 extra part-time jobs, two-thirds of which went to women. The quality of work on offer also must have varied enormously, with a striking contrast between pay and conditions in the banking sector compared to the rapidly growing tourism and leisure sector. On a regional level the fact that manufacturing jobs were more heavily concentrated in northern regions, while service sector growth was concentrated in the south-east and East Anglia, meant that regional differences widened considerably (Begg and Guy 1992).

The very diverse range of employment created in services over the last business cycle creates difficult problems of interpretation, especially regarding the extent to which employment will start to grow as the economy recovers from the recession of the 1990s. It is possible to categorize service activities into those which act as inputs into other activities (producer services), and those which are part of final consumer demand (consumer services); demand for either kind of service may originate from domestic or external sources.

Of the various types of growth conceptually possible, it is clear that exports of services have not been the dynamic element in the growth of service employment; indeed as Table 3 shows, the volume of (non-factor) service export growth has declined steadily over the post-war period and was remarkably stunted over the period 1979–90, and with appreciably faster growth in the imports of services. That this was not reflected in the balance of payments on services over the period was partly because of the initially much higher *level* of service exports compared to imports (so that a similar growth rate produces a higher absolute effect) and a tendency for the terms of trade in services to move in favour of the UK. Nevertheless, a remarkable upshot of these various trends was that manufacturing exports actually increased as a proportion of total exports (from 58 per cent in 1979 to 64 per cent in 1992).[12]

Table 3 UK trade: the growth of volumes of goods and services (average annual percentage growth)

	Exports of goods	*Exports of services*	*Imports of goods*	*Imports of services*
1955–73	4.5	5.1	5.4	3.6
1973–79	4.6	3.4	2.3	2.5
1979–90	3.9	0.7	5.0	3.4

Source: UK National Accounts/CSO

Of course many of the activities of the institutions comprising the City of London appear not as elements of trade in non-factor services but as part of the account in interest, profit and dividends (IPD).[13] As Figure 4 shows, the balances on both services in total and IPD, expressed as a proportion of GDP, have been declining after recording peaks in the mid-1980s. This is also true for the balance on financial services. Outside the financial sector, the position on international travel calls for comment. From a position of surplus in 1985, the balance deteriorated rapidly in the second half of the 1980s; just as the consumer boom sucked in a huge quantity of imported manufactures, it also created a surge in foreign travel (mainly on holidays). Nor has the current recession improved matters – 1991 saw the deficit remain at close to 1 or 2 per cent of GDP. On the travel export side, although business travel grew steadily, the demand by overseas visitors for UK holidays was largely stagnant (NEDO 1992).

Thus it is largely to domestic sources that one must look if the growth in marketed services is to be explained. Evidently, the consumer boom played an important role after 1985, especially in distribution, hotels and catering and in recreational services. Deregulation of financial activities was also important. Here, care must be taken to distinguish between the temporary and permanent impetus given by a relaxation of borrowing constraints on the personal sector. Many jobs may have resulted from the once-and-for-all movement from lower to higher debt–income ratios – they will not all be required to service higher levels of debt *per se*.

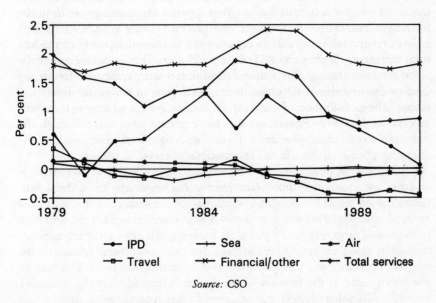

Source: CSO

Figure 16.4 Service balances as a percentage of GDP, 1979–91.

However, much more important has been the growth in producer services. As Barker and Forsell have revealed by comparing the 1979 and 1984 UK 'input–output' tables, there was a rapid increase in the inputs of business services required per unit of output across a broad range of industries, including manufacturing (Barker and Forsell 1992; see also Mayes below, Chapter 17). While some may see this as a move towards a more 'information intensive' economy, the size of the effect in the UK may also point to a more idiosyncratic preference for sourcing via the market.

The extent to which the growth of services over the 1980s was domestically driven makes the prospects for a similar growth of employment during a recovery in the 1990s very much an open question. Prospects for enhanced penetration of external markets with exported services may not be as great as commonly supposed, even with the creation of a unified market in Europe (in financial services, some of the relevant ideas are discussed in Chapter 10 above). At the same time there is ample evidence of uneven development. The explosive growth of producer services in the south-east worsened the regional problem not least by making corporate relocation there more attractive and consequently stiffening a hierarchical regional structure.

GLOBALIZATION AND TECHNICAL CHANGE

A changing international division of labour has been the essential accompaniment of industrialization from its beginnings in the eighteenth century, and capturing the possibilities of technological change provides the fundamental motive driving the accumulation activities through which change occurs in the location of production. Increasingly, this process is being articulated through truly international firms, able to organize the functional activities of production, marketing, finance and R&D on a world scale. The 'globalization' of the world economy through international firms in this sense is the term frequently used to describe this latest phase in the developing international division of labour. The globalization of world capital markets is a key adjunct to the whole process. In the case of Britain and Europe, economic integration through the European Community provides a further and significant dimension to the changing place of Britain in the international division of labour.

In this phase of development, international investment flows and strategic alliances are increasingly important phenomena, especially from the 1980s. Globalization might be thought to diminish the importance of the individual national economy. This would be a mistake for several reasons. First, although transnational firms may have a global reach, demand is often more fragmented, frequently along national lines. Second, national institutions remain of the utmost importance and may play a key role in location decisions. This may be particularly true in the location of the higher value-added, more innovative activities. Dunning (1993) has suggested that government, despite the

358

increasing non-interventionist stance, may actually have increased its influence in this area.

The substantial acceleration in the pace of foreign direct investment activities, including acquisitions and mergers across national frontiers, has been accompanied by just as spectacular growth in a variety of forms of industrial extra-market linkage – joint ventures, cooperative research agreements, cross-licensing and so forth. These alliances are seen to be especially important in developing generic technologies such as information technology and biotechnology. Many alliances can be thought of as extending the technological reach of transnational firms (Hagedoorn and Schakenrad 1991).

The 1950s and 1960s, the so-called 'golden age' of accumulation in the capitalist world, witnessed relatively quiescent international competition. This was based upon a considerable technological gap between the US and the rest of the world and active technological competition between the US and the Soviet Union. Low wages and low productivity elsewhere meant that price competition arising from external sources was not a fundamental feature for many US producers. In this context, economic integration in Europe and the build-up of the Japanese economy could be viewed in a benign fashion from an American perspective – as the growth of important markets. International investment was largely one way – from the US to Europe, Japan and the Third World – and in the decade from 1971 to 1980, the US still provided about half the flow of outward FDI from the economies of the OECD (OECD 1992).

According to Mowery and Rosenberg (1989) the effects of the heavy concentration of the US R&D efforts in defence and space activities – a build-up heavily contingent upon the Cold War – may have changed considerably between the 1960s and the present. These mainly concerned the extent of 'spillover' between military and space and civilian technologies. Thus, although the development of the jet engine had tremendous possibilities for civilian aircraft, military developments became less and less appropriate as military performance requirements increasingly became dominated by the demands of supersonic travel. Other examples from microelectronics and communication satellites point to an increasing divergence in performance demands. Moreover, the whole direction of spillover seems to be shifting in a number of key technologies. Most of these problems operate (on a much smaller scale) in the UK, where differences in organizational culture (even within firms) are also seen as significant barriers to effective interaction between military and civilian research (Smith and Smith 1992). Slowly then, the appropriateness of US technological capacities began to change.

At the same time the model of competitiveness, based on the 'American system' of manufacture (mass production, dedicated and inflexible capital equipment, and heavy use of unskilled labour) was increasingly being challenged, especially in areas such as the motor car, where inflexibility in the face of challenges imposed by successive oil shocks had left its mark.

The situation began to be transformed in the course of the 1970s and 1980s with the growing technological capacity of firms in Germany and Japan and elsewhere, utilizing alternative models of competitiveness. By the 1980s the newly industrializing countries were also increasing their exports of technically relatively advanced products. Extracting rents from technical change and innovation became much more central to the strategies of US corporations, and increasingly Japanese and European corporations. Rapid penetration of some-times quite fragmented markets relied to a greater extent upon the ability of firms to coordinate resources across national boundaries with FDI as a key vehicle. In the later 1980s and especially after 1985 the growth of FDI has indeed been remarkable, with the total flow generated by the OECD growing by over 31 per cent per annum between 1983 and 1989. By the end of the decade outward flows represented about 5 per cent of OECD exports (OECD 1992). Compared with earlier periods there has been considerable structural change in the direction of these flows, with the US becoming a major host country for investment from Europe and Japan. By 1988, the stock of FDI in the US held by EC and Japanese companies was considerable – at $194 billion and $53.4 billion, respectively. This contrasted with US assets in the EC and Japan of $131 billion and $18 billion, respectively. By contrast, Japanese stocks in the EC are considerably more modest – totalling somewhat over $12 billion; the reverse stock (EC in Japan) was, however, reported as being only $1.7 billion. Despite the extensive coverage given to manufacturing industry, it is services which have tended to predominate in the explosion of FDI, largely for reasons of tradability as discussed above. According to the UNCTC, services were accounting for 55–60 per cent of flows by the end of the 1980s (UNCTC 1991).

The UK has played a major part in this story. Table 4 shows the large share of the UK in both inward and outward investment in the OECD in the late 1980s. This is not perhaps so surprising as Britain has always played a key part in the internationalization of production. For inward investors, the well-developed market for corporate control is obviously a significant factor, as is the placid attitude of the British government to the issues raised, the UK's low labour costs and the English language. On the other hand, the sheer magni-tude of UK investment overseas raises important questions about the commit-ment of British management to the UK (see, for example, Keep and Mayhew 1993[14]). During the 1980s, the numbers of acquisitions of US businesses comfortably outstripped those made by Canadian, German or Japanese firms (OECD 1992). Evidence presented by Williams et al. (1990) suggested that no more than 40 per cent of the turnover of the top twenty UK-owned engineering companies is now generated within the UK.

It is clear from the evidence discussed that, despite the prominence given to it, Japanese inward investment into the US or EC is small compared to EC–US flows, and it is largely in areas outside manufacturing in distribution and finance – distribution activities, for example, have always bulked large in

Table 4 Shares of FDI flows, 1985–9 (percentage of total OECD flows)

	1985 to 1987	1988 and 1989
Outward investment		
US	25.3	16.9
Japan[b]	16.2	27.6
EC[a]	50.1	47.6
of which		
UK	23.4	20.6
Germany	9.4	8.7
France[b]	6.5	10.8
Inward investment		
US	59.3	51.4
Japan[b]	1.2	– 0.6
EC[a]	37.3	45.8
of which		
UK	15.0	18.0
Germany	2.2	2.9
France[b]	5.7	6.6

[a] Excludes Denmark, Greece, Ireland and Portugal; inclusive of intra-EC flows
[b] Excludes reinvested earnings
Source: OECD (1992)

Japanese strategy for market penetration (Williamson 1990). Prevailing impressions to the contrary may have something to do with the feverish pitch of Japanese FDI in 1988 and 1989, as well as the impact of Japanese production methods on indigenous economies, not to mention just a hint of xenophobia in the literature. The timing of the surge in Japanese investment into the EC makes it clear that there was a perceived need to be in position prior to the creation of the single market at the end of 1992, although investment in Europe was a logical next step following the creation of considerable local supply capacity in the US.

As far as Japanese manufacturing investment in the EC is concerned, the UK share seems to have been the largest (Yamawaki 1993). However, the sectoral composition of this investment varied across countries, with the UK being a favoured location for electronic and electrical equipment and (along with Spain) for transportation equipment. The debate on the nature of this Japanese inward investment on the UK economy and its longer-term implications for performance is far from complete, and still further from being conclusive. The line taken by NEDO was consistently in favour of the openness of economies to inward investment as this best stimulates indigenous capacities (see, for example, Ricketts, Chapter 10 above, and Eltis *et al.* 1992). From the other side of the fence it has been suggested that in (for example) motor-car production, the advantages of Japanese production methods are largely mythical, or at least severely overstated, and involve rather simple methods of work intensification. In particular, the famous Japanese system of sub-contracting is seen as a means by which large firms exploit smaller firms which have lower profit rates and lower wages (Williams *et al.* 1992). The sub-contractor also acts as a buffer allowing the larger firm to maintain more stable employment. On the other hand, rather similar wage differences across firm sizes are found in many countries (Odagiri 1992).

Economic theory has proposed a number of models designed to explain the growth of transnational production, quite apart from the obvious need to locate to avoid barriers to trade. The 'internalization' hypothesis for example maintains that high transaction costs in many arm's-length markets favour common governance and ownership structures. For a variety of reasons, trans-actions costs are rather higher where 'knowledge intensive' production is involved, and so transnational activity will tend to be involved with technically more advanced, innovative activity. On the other hand, R&D activity appears to be the last and least likely of managerial functions to become inter-nationalized, although the pharmaceutical industry does appear to be an important exception. The inference form this is that the spatial location of international production will tend to follow that of the corporate hierarchy (Hymer 1979). However, in Britain there is evidence that foreign firms contribute significantly to innovation (Pavitt and Patel 1990).

INDUSTRIAL POLICY AS AN AGENT OF CHANGE

Policy represents the final agent of change to be discussed, one just as hotly disputed as deindustrialization and globalization. It is not the intention here to discuss the whole gamut of economic policy but to concentrate upon the role of a subset of policies specifically aimed at stimulating technical change, innovation and competitiveness of industry. The macro climate and the formu-lation of policy at the macro level inevitably sets the agenda for this subset. For the 1990s the overriding macro legacy in Britain is the dilemma posed by 'the twin deficits' in both the government's budget and in the balance of payments, both of which seem to be structural (i.e. not wholly cyclical) in nature.

Two paths out of the dilemma present themselves: the orthodox route of curbing public borrowing and hoping that this will stimulate the private sector (by, for example, lowering the long-term rate of interest and permitting tax cuts). It is of course possible that a more integrated European and global market may provide a more powerful stimulus to recovery, but the portents are not all good for the UK in this regard.[15] An alternative, more dynamic, path would be to focus on the competitiveness of UK industry and attempt to generate sufficient export-investment-led growth to transform the balance of payments position and allow for sufficiently rapid growth to begin to reduce unemployment. Essential to this particular approach would be an industrial strategy targeted at investment and innovation – the twin pillars of industrial competitiveness. An obvious advantage would be that the policy would be directly addressing one of the major problems inherited from the previous decade – a desperate shortage of capacity in the tradable sector of the economy. Enhanced profitability in that sector would then serve as a platform for an improvement in the public finances. Given this starting point the following discussion will be restricted to policy intended to promote competitiveness rather than those intended to ameliorate the impact of structural change (which will include much regional policy, for example, where the aim is frequently to redistribute income and relocate production according to a political agenda). For present purposes we may think of industrial policy as the subset of economic policy intended to promote industrial competitiveness by the use of measures intended to influence micro-markets. It therefore will include competition policy, technology and innovation policy, and measures to stimulate investment in both physical and intangible assets.

As European integration proceeds it seems inevitable that more emphasis will be placed on industrial policy as constraints on monetary and fiscal policies (imposed through the Maastricht Treaty) begin to bite. At the same time, however, integration is imposing constraints on industrial policy, as well as raising issues about the appropriate location of policy-making – at local, regional, national or Community level. The EC is determined, for example, to curb the use of direct cash aids to industry, applying Articles 92 and 93. More general disillusion with subsidies has been reported (Lehner and Meiklejohn 1991), and this may help the Commission in its objectives. At the present time the UK has a relatively low level of state aid for manufacturing (comparable as a proportion of manufacturing GDP with Germany and significantly less than France or Italy (Commission of the European Communities 1991)). The increasing importance of European competition policy will also tend to curb some 'restructuring' policies aimed at declining industries and ailing firms. A process of substitution can of course be expected as new policy instruments are designed and evaluated, and it can be anticipated that technology-cum-innovation policy will increasingly loom large within industrial policy.

Stated baldly, using industrial policy approach to achieve macro objectives, sounds attractive but the difficulties are clearly enormous. The arguments against an interventionist strategy are powerful and well organized. In theoretical terms, the vision of the economy that has guided the development of policy in Britain has been that of the universal efficacy of the market rather than the idea of competition. So much is clear from the basic approach to privatization, where it is ownership that is important. If, however, it is accepted that the functioning of an economy can best be grasped in terms of systems of interlocking markets then the starting point for an interventionist strategy is the idea of market failure. Typical market failure arguments for intervention include public goods and externalities (R&D, training, education, industrial standards, for example), increasing returns, the development of infrastructure, market-power considerations, and the taking on of riskier investment projects, especially in the field of high technology.

But market failure alone is not a sufficient justification for intervention because it then has to be proved that matters will be improved, i.e. government failure may be just as likely as market failure and this is the favoured position of what might be termed the sophisticated non-interventionist. Sources of government failure include imperfect information, simple 'myopia', the divorce between those who benefit and those who pay, and the 'capture' of regulatory agencies by bureaucracies and/or special interests.

The non-interventionist argument is perhaps more compelling in the UK because of the widespread belief that industrial policy has failed in a real sense. Policy towards high technology is exemplary in this respect. The important work by Ergas (1987) suggested that, hitherto, technology policy in Britain could best be described as 'mission oriented', i.e. as focusing on radical innovation which is intended to achieve aims of national importance. Projects such as Concorde and the AGR reactor are usually summed up as hugely expensive failures (Henderson 1977; see also Sharp and Walker, Chapter 18 below) and they almost certainly crowded out other innovatory paths. Despite impressions to the contrary these kind of projects are not yet dead, even in the non-defence private sector: BT, for example, continues to rely on System X at the instigation of Oftel and the nuclear industry is still heavily subsidized (Ergas 1993). These missions are all heavily centralized in terms of decision-making and tend to involve only a few key players. France has also pursued a mission-oriented technology policy but with apparently a greater degree of success, based on superior administrative capacity and less radical innovation – a good example being the high speed train (TGV) which was essentially based on 'stretching' and adapting existing technologies. But failures also are apparent in areas such as VCRs and computing.

The technology policy of Germany and Sweden, on the other hand, is classified by Ergas as being 'diffusion oriented', characterized by the decentralization of objectives within regions and sectors, and with an emphasis on public good provision – education, collaborative research and product standardization. As Sharp and Walker note below (Chapter 18), this involves considerably greater state assistance to small and medium-sized enterprises. In competitiveness terms, the result is flexible networks of small firms, especially where systems manufacture is important, i.e. in much of engineering. Competition is important but so are 'extra-market' institutions. Where the German system may be weaker is in the system's capability for adjustment – out of traditional areas of specialization and into newer (and possibly faster-growing ones). Figure 5 shows the dynamic evolution of G7 export shares between 1979 and 1990 for Germany, France, the UK and Japan according to a simple classification of industries based on the OECD sectoral databank. Although the categories are very crude, the figure does illustrate the rather rigid character of the European pattern of specialization compared to Japan, which has successfully shifted the pattern of specialization into 'knowledge-intensive industries' (e.g. in electronics). This might be taken as evidence that the decentralized diffusion-oriented strategy of Germany lacks the strategic and developmental capacity of the Japanese system, and is partly constrained by sectoral interests.

Nevertheless, the conceptualization of German technology policy by Ergas does bear an affinity with the growing literature on a model of competitiveness known as 'flexible specialization' and based on classic examples in the Baden-Württemberg district of Germany and Emilia Romagna in Italy (Piore and Sable 1984; Cowling 1990). According to this literature, the competitive performance of flexible specialization is demonstrably superior to the American system based on massed production. Streeck has argued that the former system is crucially dependent upon a well-developed social dimension to the economy and is threatened in principle by the Single Market, which he sees as essentially an exercise in deregulation. Public goods bulk large in the functional requirements of the model and he stresses in particular the requirement of 'redundant capacities' on the part of the workforce, chiefly in non-specific, high-level skills. Investment in these may be difficult to justify on an individual project basis but are essential for the flexibility required by the workforce. Consequently, regulation creating these capacities can actually improve competitiveness, not in the static sense but in a dynamic, structural sense (Mayes *et al.* 1993).

Agglomeration economies of the sort described by Alfred Marshall many years ago are an essential aspect of the geographical clusters characterizing the model of flexible specialization. The question particularly relevant for UK performance is whether they are likely to disappear in a process of internalization which would follow merger and rationalization – a process only too easy given the capital market and corporate governance forms discussed in Chapters 11 and 12 above. The thought experiment of substituting an independent owner-managed firm within an industrial district with a 'quasi' firm operating within a multi-divisional corporation suggests that the answer may be yes. With capital control coming from the centre, participation in cooperative ventures will be more difficult, and longer-term investment projects will not be easy to justify to top management. In this sense, internal structures within the multi-divisional form tend to mimic the 'outside control' discussed by Prevezer and Morris above (Chapters 11 and 12, respectively). The growing dependence of the regions of the UK upon branch plants is a related phenomenon.

Outside technology policy, other attempts at industrial policy in the UK are also tainted. Static economies of scale have in the past featured strongly in restructuring exercises. This owes much to the widely-held view throughout Europe in the 1960s that national fragmentation of markets in Europe meant that the size of indigenous firms was inadequate for competition with the US giants. This resulted in considerable laxity in the UK and elsewhere with regard to merger policy and a legacy for Europe of 'national champions', each close

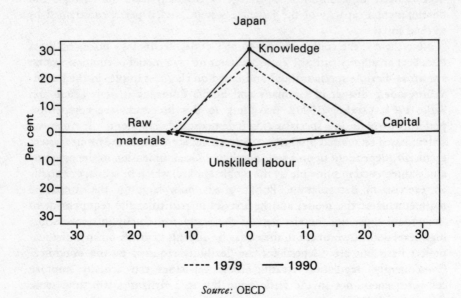

Japan

Source: OECD

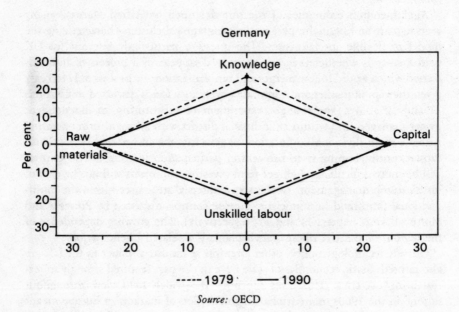

Germany

Source: OECD

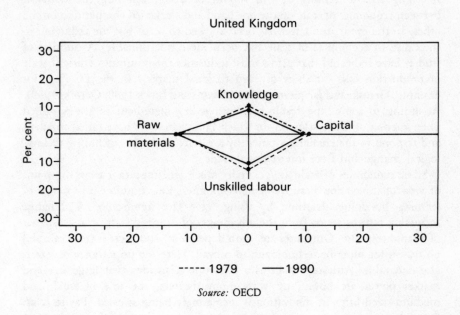

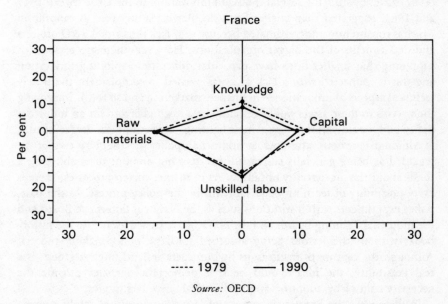

Figure 16.5 G7 export shares: Japan, United Kingdom, Germany and France.

to the ear of government and partly protected through domestic policies. Assessing the desirability of this should be about assessing the trade-off between economies of scale on the one hand and weakened competition on the other. In the event, the latter has been allowed to occur but the reduction in costs due to economies of scale has been more questionable. A number of studies have indicated that across most industries the minimum efficient scale of production falls far short of even national markets in the EC (see, for example, Geroski and Jacquemin 1985; Adams and Brock 1988; Geroski 1989). According to some, the result has been a key ingredient in the so-called phenomenon of 'Euro-sclerosis' in which European firms have failed to adapt and respond to the challenges posed by a variety of shocks, including techno-logical change and freer international trade.[16]

Static economies of scale are generally much less important from the point of view of innovation than dynamic economies, i.e. cumulative processes of learning by doing, learning by using, etc. The significance of dynamic increasing returns stems from the advantages of an early start or at least that of a rapid response. Outcomes are 'path dependent' and there is (for example) no reason for superior technologies to prevail. Here the importance of size is also debatable. Although there is a Schumpeterian idea that large size and market power are bound up with innovativeness, the role of small and medium-sized firms in innovation is increasingly being stressed. Pavitt *et al*. (1987) have, by studying several thousand innovations in the UK between 1945 and 1983, suggested that smaller firms do play a leading role in innovation which is consistently underestimated because they lack the formal R&D projects and departments of the bigger organizations. However, there are reasons for supposing that smaller firms have particular difficulties exploiting innovation and this is connected with a lack of assets needed to complement the purely technical aspects of innovation – in finance, marketing and so forth. Improving their access to these assets would certainly be a justifiable aim for an industrial policy and would certainly assist in enhancing competition for larger firms.

Although previous attempts at industrial policy in the UK cannot be regarded as being generally successful this does not amount to establishing a thesis about the inevitability of failure. As in market-driven processes, there is every possibility of learning behaviour within the policy process. In the past, policy experiments with institutions such as the National Enterprise Board and the Industrial Training Boards and the NEDC have passed away into the history books without the lessons being absorbed into the policy-making process. Although the capture of institutions by bureaucracies and interest groups is a real possibility, the idea should be that democratic agencies provide the necessary control by adopting appropriate evaluative techniques.

In these ways the Popperian concept of 'social engineering' might provide a guideline for the development of policies in which smallish experiments can be constantly evaluated. Even this, however, presupposes the existence of a strategic capacity with a genuine democratic input. The disappearance of such capacity may be one of the significant legacies of recent economic history. Precise consideration of instruments is beyond the scope of this chapter, but after a period of neglect there is considerable ammunition for the challenge presenting itself for industrial policy.

CONCLUSION

Change is endemic in today's world. Trying to summarize its nature through concepts such as deindustrialization and globalization can present only partial, distorting and ultimately ephemeral characterizations. Nevertheless, they are useful aids precisely because the emphasis is on *processes* of change and therefore can be used to counter more orthodox 'equilibrium' approaches to economic thought. By illustrating a few of these ways of characterizing economic change it is hoped that some idea has been gleaned of how the UK fits into the evolving international political economy.

In many cases the issues are unresolved, especially regarding the ultimate impact of increased European integration and the effect of the massive gross flows of international investment that have been both entering and leaving the country. However, whatever one's stance on these issues, the economic legacy of the more recent past is one that will impose a great challenge for Britain's tradable sector. Increasingly, rather than the reverse, this will require enhanced competitiveness from manufacturing industry. More cost-cutting, productivity-enhancing investment seems unlikely to be adequate, and ways must be found to find investment strategies which expand capacity. As Driver shows in Chapter 7 above, this will require greater risk-taking. In addition it will require an industrial strategy, for many of the problems have a structural dimension, especially in terms of corporate governance and capital market issues, public good provision and the need to bolster the competitive process by encouraging the smaller firms to challenge the giants.

NOTES

1 See, for example, Gershuny and Miles (1983).
2 Nevertheless, attempts have recently been made to assess educational 'outputs' in terms of success rates in nationally comparable exams. In principle these could be used to generate productivity measures. Critics have suggested that the nature of the input should be taken into account so that it is 'value-added', that is being assessed.
3 In fact, measures of productivity growth need to be taken with at least a grain of salt. There is considerable variety in the methods adopted by statisticians in different countries as to how output in services is to be measured. Although physical measures are common in transport, frequent use is made elsewhere of deflated value series, in which case the quality of the output measure is heavily dependent upon the deflator adopted – too general a deflator (or an inappropriate one) can, as we see below, be seriously misleading. In other cases, employment itself is used as an indicator, in which case any measure of productivity is essentially circular.

Sometimes arbitrary assumptions are made regarding the growth of productivity. As a curio-sum, the CSO assumes a positive rate of advance for a doctor in the private sector but a zero rate for one in the NHS! (NEDO 1990.)

4 Excluding capital formation in each case.
5 Literally, to have one's heart on the left and one's wallet on the right.
6 The CSO's output measure for the UK rose by 2.1 per cent per annum over the period 1979–90, while the number of employees (GB only) rose by 2.8 per cent per annum.
7 For evidence on this point, see Summers (1985).
8 According to the *New Earnings Survey* (London: HMSO), median weekly earnings for a male manual worker in 1993 were £207.10 in distribution, £272.60 in transport and communication and £235.50 in banking, etc.
9 See, for example, Gatsios and Seabright (1989). Davis and Smales (1989) describe the principles behind the ERM strategy as that of the 'driving licence ', i.e. you can drive in a particular country provided that you abide by host-country rules. Although *institutions* cannot be prevented from operating on this basis, *products* can, and in practice this could represent a formidable barrier to market entry.
10 Note that this may make the analysis of foreign trade in services through standard export data misleading, since exports (as in the UK) are usually seen as deriving from the country of location (Petersen and Barras 1987).
11 Data from the *Census of Employment*, 1981 and 1989.
12 Also important for this result was the declining significance of North Sea oil exports.
13 It is used to be possible to trace the net impact of the City's main institutions through a specially constructed table in the CSO's balance of payments 'Pink Book'. With the net balance deteriorating rather rapidly after 1986 (ironically the year of the 'Big Bang') mainly because of the position of the insurance industry it disappeared from view with the 1991 edition.
14 They quote the example of Pilkingtons, which although widely regarded as a UK company, in 1990 employed only about 21.6 per cent of its workforce in the UK and more recently removed its headquarters to to Brussels; they show that many other UK-owned firms are following similar strategies.
15 Studies of the likely impact of 1992 on UK industry based on the identification of '1992 sensitive sectors' have tended to the conclusion that parts of British industry will lose out in the competitive struggle (cf. Mayes *et al*. 1993).
16 Although the disease is often thought of in terms of unemployment and the labour market, it is not at all clear that the cause rather than the symptom is to be found there.

REFERENCES

Ackerlof, G. (1970) 'The market for "lemons": quality uncertainty and the market mechanism', *Quarterly Journal of Economics*, vol. 84, pp. 488–500.
Adams, W. and Brock, J. (1988) 'The bigness mystique and the merger policy debate: an international perspective', *Northwestern Journal of International Law and Business*, vol. 9, pp. 1–48.
Barker, T. S. and Forsell, O. (1992) 'Manufacturing, services, and structural change', in C. Driver and P. Dunne (eds), *Structural Change in the UK Economy*, Cambridge: Cambridge University Press, pp. 14–44.
Baumol, W. (1967) 'The macroeconomics of unbalanced growth: the anatomy of urban crisis', *American Economic Review*, vol. LVII, pp. 415–26.

Begg, I. and Guy, N. (1992) 'The changing regional structure', in C. Driver and P. Dunne (eds), *Structural Change in the UK Economy*, Cambridge: Cambridge University Press, pp. 45-78.

Commission of the European Communities (1991) *Fourth Periodic Report on the Social and Economic Situation anal Development of the Regions*, Luxembourg: Office of Official Publications of the European Community.

Cowling, K. (1990) 'A new industrial strategy: preparing Europe for the turn of the century', *International Journal of Industrial Organizaion*, vol. 8, pp. 165-83.

Davis, E. and Smales, C. (1989) *1992: Myths and Realities*, London: Centre for Business Strategy, London Business School.

Dunning, J. (1993) *The Globalization of Business*, London: Routledge.

Eltis, W., Fraser, D. and Ricketts, M. (1992) 'The lessons for Britain from the superior performance of Germany and Japan', *National Westminster Bank Quarterly Review*, February, pp. 2-23.

Ergas, H. (1987) 'Does technology policy matter?', in B. R. Guile and H. Brooks (eds), *Technology and Global Industry*, Washington, DC: National Academy Press, pp. 191-245.

Ergas, H. (1993) 'Europe's policy for high technology: has anything been learnt?', Paris: OECD.

Gatsios, K. and Seabright, P. (1989) 'Regulation in the European Community', *Oxford Review of Economic Policy*, vol. 5, no. 2, Summer, pp. 37-60.

Geroski, P. (1989) 'European industrial policy and industrial policy in Europe', *Oxford Review of Economic Policy*, vol. 5, no. 2, Summer, pp. 20-36.

Geroski, P. and Jacquemin, A. (1985) 'Industrial change, barriers to mobility, and European industrial policy', *Economic Policy*, no. 1, November.

Gershuny, J. and Miles, I. (1983) *The New Service Economy: The Transformation of Employment in Industrial Societies*, London: Frances Pinter.

Hagedoorn, J. and Schakenrad, J. (1993) 'Strategic technology partnering and international corporate strategies' in K. Hughes (ed.), *European Competiveness*, Cambridge: Cambridge University Press, pp. 60-87.

Henderson, P. D. (1977) 'Two British errors: their probable size and some possible lessons', *Oxford Economic Papers*, vol. 29, no. 2, pp. 159-205.

Hoeckmann, B. M. (1993) 'New issues in the Uruguay Round and beyond: an assessment', *Economic Journal*, vol. 103, no. 421, November, pp. 1528-39.

Hymer, S. (1979) *The Multinational Corporation: A Radical Approach*, Cambridge: Cambridge University Press.

Keep, E. and Mayhew, K. (1993) 'UK training policy – assumption and reality', Paper presented to the CEPR conference 'Training and the Skills Gaps', Birkbeck College, April.

Kierkowski, H. (1987) 'Recent advances in international trade theory: a selective survey', *Oxford Review of Economic Policy*, vol. 3, no. 1, Spring, pp. 1-20.

Lehner, S. and Meiklejohn, R. (1991) 'Fair competition in the internal market: community state aids policy', *European Economy*, no. 48, pp. 7-114.

Mayes, D., Hager, W., Knight, A. and Streeck, W. (1993) *Public Interest and Market Pressures: Problems Posed by Europe 1992*, Basingstoke: Macmillan.

Mowery, D. C. and Rosenberg, N. (1989) *Technology and the Pursuit of Economic Growth*, Cambridge: Cambridge University Press.

NEDO (1990) *Memorandum by Director-General*, 'The challenge of ERM entry', London: NEDO.

NEDO (1992) *UK Tourism: Competing for Growth*, Report of the Working Party on Competitiveness in Tourism and Leisure London: NEDO.

Odagiri, H. (1992) *Growth Through Competition, Competition Through Growth*, Oxford: Oxford University Press.

OECD (1992) *Technology and the Economy: The Key Relationships*, Paris: OECD.

Pavitt, K. and Patel, P. (1990) 'Large firms in the production of the world's technology: an important case of non-globalization', *Journal of International Business Studies*, vol. I, pp. 1–21.

Pavitt, K., Robson, M. and Townsend, J. (1987) 'The size distribution of innovating firms in the UK: 1945–1983', *The Journal of Industrial Economics*, vol. 35, no. 3, March, pp. 297–316.

Petersen, J. and Barras, R. (1987) 'Measuring international competitiveness in services', *Services Industries Journal*, vol. 7, no. 1, pp. 131–42.

Piore, M. and Sabel, C. F. (1984) *The Second Industrial Divide*, New York: Basic Books.

Rowthorn, R. E. and Wells, J. (1987) *Deindustrialisation and Foreign Trade*, Cambridge: Cambridge University Press.

Smith, A. D. (1989) 'New measures of service sector outputs', *National Institute Economic and Social Review*, no. 128, May, pp. 75–88.

Smith, R. P. and Smith, D. (1992) 'Corporate strategy, corporate culture and conversion: adjustment in the defence industry', *Business Strategy Review*, vol. 3, no. 2, Summer.

Summers, R. (1985) 'Services in the international economy', in R. P. Inman (ed.), *Managing the Service Economy: Prospects and Problems*, Cambridge: Cambridge University Press, pp. 27–48.

UNCTC (1991) *World Investment Report 1991. The Triad in Foreign Direct Investment*, New York: United Nations.

Wells, J. (1989) 'Uneven development and de-industrialisation in the UK since 1979', in F. Green (ed.), *The Restructuring of the UK Economy*, Hemel Hempstead: Harvester Wheatsheaf, pp. 25–57.

Williams, K. *et al.* (1992) 'Against lean production', *Economy and Society*, vol. 21, no. 3, August, pp. 321–54.

Williams, K., Williams, J. and Haslam, C. (1990) 'The hollowing out of British manufacturing and its implications for policy', *Economy and Society*, vol. 19, no. 4, 4 November, pp. 456–90.

Williamson, P. J. (1990) 'Winning the export war: British, Japanese, and West German exporters' strategy compared', *British Journal of Management*, vol. I, pp. 215–30.

Yamawaki, H. (1993) 'Location decisions of Japanese multinationals', in K. Hughes (ed.), *European Competitiveness*, Cambridge: Cambridge University Press, pp. 11–28.

17

DOES MANUFACTURING MATTER[1]

David Mayes with Soterios Soteri

For over a hundred years concern has been expressed about the relative decline of the UK as a manufacturing country. Initially it was apprehension about others catching up and large market shares being eroded. Since the Second World War, however, the worry has been that the UK has slipped steadily down the league table of OECD countries in terms of GDP per head and now lies near the bottom. Manufacturing represented the key to successful industrialization and it is clear that it has placed a central role in recent success stories like that of Japan. For a sustained period UK manufacturing lost share in world markets and within the domestic economy. The period from the early 1970s to the early 1980s was one of the most striking declines, with the balance of trade in manufactured goods moving into deficit for the first time in 1983. The concern was then expressed that while some decline was to be expected that manufacturing in the UK had moved to such a low level that it did not have the capacity to respond. That argument lost some credence in the second half of the 1980s when manufacturing again improved. The productivity gap with many of the UK's competitors was reduced; domestic and world market shares stabilized. The more recent recession and the difficulty in obtaining recovery has brought the old arguments back again and poses the question 'Does manufacturing play an especially important role in the process of growth and should economic policy place more effort on it to ensure a faster and more sustainable recovery?'

Some of the debate at the popular level is little more than a gut reaction that manufacturing is the keystone to a developed society. Some is due to the fact that manufacturing industry has a very strong and effective lobby from its established position in society. However, some of it is based on clear economic arguments; take the contribution of Rowthorn and others to the recent conference organized by the Policy Studies Institute.[2] In the wider debate many of the issues are confused, conflating remarks about capacity, productivity, export market shares and shares of activity with arguments about the sources of growth and constraints upon the rate of growth. In this paper we try to cut through some of them and consider the importance of manufacturing in the economy.

It is a trivial truth that manufacturing matters while at current relative prices there are plenty of willing purchasers of manufactured goods. The question addressed in this article is whether it is important how much of that demand for manufactures is met from UK sources. There seem to be three general lines of argument which have been pursued. The first is that if manufacturing is low in relative importance then, since the UK is an open economy, it is relatively difficult for other sectors to generate the foreign exchange necessary to pay for the desired net imports of manufactures. In these circumstances the balance of payments acts as a brake on economic growth. The second line of argument is that because of its inherently faster rate of growth of productivity, particularly at the high-technology end of the spectrum, an emphasis on manufacturing allows the economy to grow faster. The third argument is largely distributional; namely, that a decline in manufacturing would have wide knock-on effects on other firms and on employment.

According to this view, manufacturing has a relatively larger impact on other economic activity compared with those industries which can substitute for it both directly, as in the case of North Sea oil where output per head is much higher and hence employment lower, and indirectly, for services, because manufacturing involves a larger range of inputs from infrastructure and other ancillary services.

However, to some extent these arguments confuse two major issues. The first is whether the structure of the economy affects the long-run rate of growth; and the second whether the transition costs which are incurred in moving from one structure to another are acceptable. It is yet a further question whether there is any sensible form of intervention which can help achieve both the desirable structure and an acceptable transition path to it, as in the longer run one can expect continuing changes in structure as technologies, known reserves of resources and tastes change. We propose to deal with these questions in turn.

The exposition by Bacon and Eltis (1976) shows that there are several related ways of viewing the question of the importance to the economy of some key sector or sectors. The basic contention of all these approaches is that some forms of economic activity are essential to the process of investment and growth and without them other activities cannot be sustained. There is some dispute over what should be in the essential category and what in the remainder. Bacon and Eltis themselves opt for 'marketed' and 'non-marketed' outputs as the distinction, although they used 'industrial' and 'non-industrial' in their original 1974 *Sunday Times* article and Eltis (1975) used 'tradeable/non-tradeable'. The preference for 'marketed' is in part simply that it is the broadest of the various categories. It allows for construction and retail distribution to be included within the definition. Non-marketed output is composed largely of public sector services provided free of charge or at prices well below cost.

However, even this broad description provides us with difficulties, as it treats investment as relating to physical capital. One might wish to include those activities which relate to investment in human capital as well. Writers such as Prais (1990) have emphasized that it is the low level of skills and standards of the UK workforce that is a major cause of the lack of competitiveness and lower productivity of UK industry.

Choosing manufacturing, or even engineering, as the core area is clearly at the other end of the spectrum. All the other definitions of what constitutes the core embrace manufacturing. Thus while there may be agreement that manufacturing matters, there is little chance of agreeing that *only* manufacturing matters.

The Bacon and Eltis analysis shows that having a 'non-marketed' sector which is 'too large' results in heavy pressures on the economy as the demands of all the sectors on the marketed sector cannot be met, which exacerbates the problems of inflation and labour market disputes. Furthermore, the authors emphasize how the problems were made even worse by the shift from marketed to non-marketed output which occurred during the 1960s and early 1970s.

Since non-marketed outputs stem primarily from the public sector, the 'blame' for the relative decline would clearly appear to lie with successive governments. However, it is not immediately clear how much the drift towards non-marketed output has been the result of deliberate policy and how much a reaction to the poor performance of the marketed sector. The share of non-marketed output rose in the early 1980s not because that was the aim of government – it was quite clearly the opposite – but because in a recession the rise in unemployment automatically entails a switch to government provision instead of productive employment, a result which has been repeated in the last few years.

This article illustrates that, while there are clear substitutes for manufacturing, there are limitations to the extent to which they can substitute, particularly in the short run. Second, we suggest that the substitution process itself poses further problems because it is easier to shift out of some activities than it is to move into others; hence, in the interim, the problem of overall balance as set out by Bacon and Eltis is exacerbated. Third, since some of the need to substitute came from a temporary shift towards North Sea oil and gas production the exaggeration of pressures on other industries from coincident disinflationary policy has made the long-run problems for manufacturing appear worse. Fourth, the decline of services in the recent recession suggests that it may no longer be possible to rely on them to offset the difficulties faced by manufacturing, in the way that has been possible in the past. However, the article concludes that this may not be as unfortunate as it appears because it has drawn greater attention to the fundamental problems which underlie the competitiveness of UK industry, such as skills, management, investment and the process of innovation.

THE BALANCE OF PAYMENTS

In the 1950s and 1960s, before the floating of the exchange rate, the balance of payments was viewed as a constraint on economic growth because of the size of the UK's marginal propensity to import. Attempts at faster rates of growth resulted in import surges, balance of payments difficulties and ultimately contributed to the reversal of economic policy, creating the 'stop–go' cycles and a slower overall rate of growth.

The structure of the UK economy was such that, with a large population relative to natural resources, it needed to import food, energy and raw materials and pay for these by exporting other products, principally manufactures. However, in a world of increasing specialization and diversity with rising incomes and technological advance, an increase in both imports and exports of goods and services was to be expected (see, for example, Moore 1986). This expansion was aided by the progressive fall in trade barriers.

Thus to keep the system relatively balanced the UK needed to expand exports at a rate fast enough to match the increasing demand for imports. Indeed, in some cases (Beckerman 1962) the argument was put the other way round; namely, that exports lead to growth of the economy as a whole. Hence the crucial factor in growth would be to generate the exports necessary. During that period there was rather more emphasis on the capacity constraints facing UK industry than on competitiveness and on the inability to sell. Nevertheless, with a fixed exchange rate, severe limitations were placed on the ability of competitiveness to adjust in the short run. Therefore a large portion of balance of payments adjustment needed to take place through demand, given the system of economic management applied.

Further exports needed to come from some source and manufacturing, covering well over half the existing exports, was the obvious candidate. Of course, it is natural to examine the other side of the problem and also review whether all imports are 'necessary'. The same conclusion would still apply – that the imports for which the UK could most readily substitute would tend to be dominated by manufactures.

Several parts of that picture are no longer so true. For a while the UK has had a completely changed need to import energy with the discovery and exploitation of North Sea oil and consequently a further good source of net exports. Second, the need to import food has changed substantially with the high levels of subsidy under the Common Agricultural Policy. Third, further sources of foreign exchange have been steadily developed both through the provision of services and from earnings from investment overseas. Last, some of the constraints on the system were removed through the floating of the exchange rate and the abolition of exchange controls. It is arguable that the constraints on the exchange rate during the period of 'shadowing' and actual membership of the Exchange Rate Mechanism (ERM) of the European

Monetary System reintroduced some of the 'stop–go' pressures on the economy, helping to encourage the last business cycle.

It is therefore legitimate to ask whether the constraint to growth through the poor performance of manufacturing industry still exists. Just that question was posed on 17 July 1984 when the House of Lords Committee on Overseas Trade was set up 'to consider the causes and implications of the deficit in the United Kingdom's balance of trade in manufactures; and to make recommendations' (House of Lords 1985: 5).

With a floating exchange rate it should be possible to achieve such relative prices as will automatically remove any balance of payments constraint. However, the balance of trade is not the only influence on the exchange rate – indeed, many would argue that it is not even the most important influence (see Brooks *et al.* 1986, for example). If other concerns of economic policy lead to a different exchange rate, then large trade deficits can emerge. The House of Lords debate, which resulted in the setting up of the Committee, noted on the one hand a rapidly increasing deficit on trade in manufactures and on the other a high level of unemployment. It was argued, foremost by Lord Ezra, that it was the poor performance of manufacturing industry which was the key to explaining the problem. The brake on growth through the balance of payments thus occurred not so much through the deficit as such as through the exchange rate. Manufacturing industry mattered because it could not compete adequately at the exchange rate which prevailed at the time.

Until it can compete effectively, manufacturing industry will still act as a brake on growth. The main strand in the argument is that this inability to compete effectively is a long-run problem, and the short-run pressures of the early 1980s served to highlight it. It looked for a while in the second half of the 1980s that the very considerable restructuring that had been taking place in industry might have changed competitive performance and led to a more flexible, innovative and competitive industry, that was no longer hamstrung by the difficulties of the past. The recession of the last few years has, however, led to the same worries about the long run being raised again.

Let us therefore examine some of the statistical background to these assertions as they provide a common basis for all of the arguments about whether manufacturing matters and, indeed, for the wider discussion of manufacturing in Britain.

The decline in manufacturing industry

A common approach to assessing whether manufacturing matters has been to point to the way in which the industry has declined in the UK, particularly in recent years (Matthews and Bowen 1987, for example). Indeed, this was the topic of a conference at the National Institute on 'De-industrialisation' in 1978 (Blackaby 1979). It can be seen from Figure 1 that the share of manufacturing in GDP fell sharply between the early 1970s and the mid-1980s. Before and

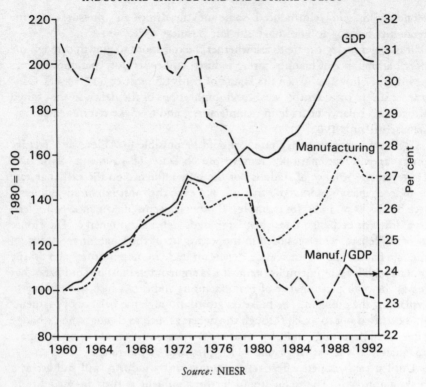

Source: NIESR

Figure 17.1 UK manufacturing (net output) and GDP, 1960–92.

after that period manufacturing growth has tracked the rest of the economy much more closely. This is revealed more starkly in balance of payments terms by comparison with domestic demand (Figure 2). While the rapid fall in the export–import ratio slowed for a time after 1973, the balance of trade in manufactures fell from a surplus of £5.5 billion in 1980 to a deficit of £17.3 billion in 1989. This type of experience is not unique to the UK. Most advanced countries have seen the ratio of manufacturing to total output fall since 1960–70 (Table 1) but the UK stands out in seeing manufacturing output also decline in absolute terms. It was only in the last part of 1987 that manufacturing output regained the level it had in 1979, although that in turn was below the level of 1973. Since then the picture has changed, manufacturing shares have ceased their general fall. Although the deficit continued to widen in the 1980s, it has since been sharply reduced, although not eliminated. However, in a major recession such a turn-round is to be expected as domestic demand falls more than foreign demand. The difficult question is whether, as the economy recovers, so the deficit will widen again, as suggested by recent evidence, with a deficit of £7.6 billion in 1992.

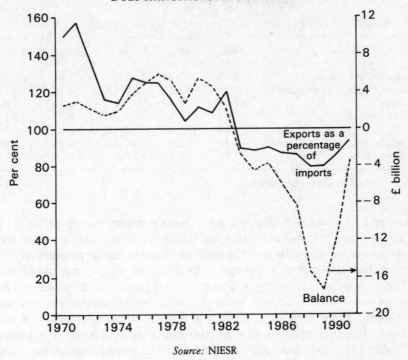

Source: NIESR

Figure 17.2 Balance of trade in manufactured goods, 1970–91.

Table 1 Value-added in manufacturing as a percentage of GDP in advanced industrial countries

Year	US	Japan	Germany	France	UK	Italy
1960	28.3	33.9	40.3	29.1	32.1	28.6
1971	24.9	35.2	37.0	28.5	27.4	28.4
1979	23.0	29.3	33.8	27.0	25.8	30.6
1983	20.6	29.0	31.1	22.5	20.4	24.7
1985	20.1	29.5	31.7	22.0	20.7	24.2
1987	19.3	28.5	31.4	21.4	19.8	23.3
1989	19.7	28.9	31.1	21.3	20.7	23.4
1990	19.6	28.9	30.8	21.1	19.9	22.2

Source: OECD Economic Outlook, Historical Statistics

Explaining why manufacturing has declined, particularly in balance of payments terms, is complex. The simplest approach is to observe what has risen while manufacturing has fallen (Table 2). In 1963, when the UK was running a small balance of payments surplus on current account, that surplus was entirely of manufacturing and interest, profits and dividends, with the lion's

Table 2 UK current account surpluses and deficits as a percentage of GDP

	1963	1973	1985	1988	1991
Manufactured goods	6.95	2.26	−1.22	− 3.81	− 0.72
Interest, profit and dividends	1.46	2.02	0.83	1.10	0.10
Services	− 0.15	1.04	2.17	1.10	0.96
Other invisibles	− 0.45	− 0.67	−1.01	− 0.88	− 0.27
Fuels	−1.25	−1.44	2.11	0.38	− 0.01
Food, beverages and tobacco	− 4.89	− 2.97	−1.21	−1.13	− 0.80
Other visibles	− 2.10	−1.75	− 0.77	− 0.79	− 0.54

Source: CSO, *UK Balance of Payments*

share going to manufacturing; all the remaining sectors were in deficit. Ten years later, in 1973, manufacturing was still in substantial surplus, while the surplus on interest, profits and dividends had risen to similar proportions and services had also moved into surplus. By 1985 the picture was completely different, with manufacturing in deficit, interest, profits and dividends still in surplus and services markedly stronger. North Sea oil output was near its maximum, hence fuels were exerting a strongly positive influence on the balance of trade compared with their traditional deficit. However, production fell after 1987 and since 1988 the effect on the overall balance has been negligible.

Nearly ten years on again the picture has changed yet a third time (Table 2, last column). No sector is in substantial deficit or surplus. All sectors of visible trade show a deficit, albeit a negligible one for fuels, partly resulting from special factors, while the rest of the account is in slight surplus.

It was the massive turnaround in the oil balance, accompanied by the improvements in invisibles, that kept the account in overall surplus until 1986, since when it has been in deficit even at the lowest part of the recession. The major impact of the rise in oil prices and the availability of North Sea oil fell on the exchange rate, which rose by 20 per cent between 1978 and 1980. Given that during the same period relative labour costs were also rising, there was a fall in the price competitiveness of UK manufacturing industry of over 50 per cent (see above, Figure 4.4, Chapter 4). It is not surprising that exports declined, imports rose rapidly and output and employment fell markedly in the face of such a change. Since then the position has improved significantly with competitiveness rising up until 1987, although falling back more recently. Relative productivity has improved throughout and, although some of the more recent worsening (up till 1991) had been due to the exchange rate, relative labour costs were still the main cause of the decline.

Clearly it would be inappropriate to 'blame' all that early rise in the exchange rate on oil, as other changes took place during the period; not least the change in the fiscal and monetary stance following the election of the

Conservative government in 1979. Inflation control, through tight money-supply restraint, was part of the core of their policy. The Bank of England, in its evidence to the House of Lords Committee (vol. II, p. 111), suggested that not more than a quarter of the exchange-rate change was due to oil. In a separate analysis for the Committee, Oxford Economic Forecasting also suggested that around half the decline in manufacturing trade over the period 1977–84 was accounted for by oil (p. 39). The other half was accounted for by 'longer-term trends': a continuation of the fall in manufacturing performance which had been evident throughout the period since the war – land, indeed, throughout the century if periods of wartime and increasing protection were excluded.

Thus to the extent that other sectors rose, the decline in manufacturing was not important, as other sources of foreign-exchange earnings were substituted for it. This picture is overlaid by any short-run policy effects, particularly in deflating the economy and by the very substantial outflows of capital that occurred after the freeing of foreign exchange from controls in 1979. Without that capital outflow, the exchange rate would probably have been higher still. This process of substitution of depleting foreign exchange-earning assets (oil) by long-run assets (overseas direct and portfolio investment) clearly made a lot of sense and helps ensure the long-run strength of the economy. It eased the impact on manufacturing through the exchange rate. However, it is also argued that a greater benefit would have been derived from direct investment of the oil revenues in UK industries.

There was a drawn-out controversy over whether the rise in oil meant that the decline in manufacturing was inevitable, stemming from work by Gregory (1976) in Australia and followed by Forsyth and Kay (1980) in the UK. Since the balance of trade is also affected by incomes at home and abroad as well as by competitiveness through the exchange rate, it would have been possible to maintain the balance of trade in manufactures, as is suggested by the Bank of England in their evidence to the Lords Committee (vol. II, pp. 108–9).

It is, however, this last point that forms the basis of the first of the questions posed in the introduction. Does the manufacturing deficit lead to a brake on overall growth through the balance of payments? In one respect the answer is no, as the exchange rate will tend to equilibrate the market, in this case by falling, which will help increase competitiveness. However, when these circumstances are combined with a disinflationary monetary policy which has much of its effect through the exchange rate, the net result is indeed a slowdown in the general rate of economic growth, aided by the high interest rates. If the exchange rate cannot fall, because it is within the ERM for example, then the deficit will restrict growth as it did before the collapse of the Bretton Woods system.

Such a deflationary outcome is part of the problem of transition following an external shock, like the discovery and development of oil resources, or cyclical adjustment, rather than a long-run problem; provided that there is not a whole series of other factors leading to decline in manufacturing performance or, indeed, any other component of the balance of payments.

The worry of the House of Lords Committee was that there existed just such a series of factors which would lead to continuing declines in the competitive performance of manufacturing industry. They suggested at least nine such factors,[3] without specifying their relative importance:

1 a lack of investment;
2 the lack of 'a sense of national purpose' to advance the industrial success of the country;
3 weak links between the various groups in society;
4 the lack of a long-term perspective when looking at industrial development, and a tendency to concentrate on short-run gains;
5 a relatively weak education and training system which was not well directed towards providing the skills that industries need, either in the quantities or to the standards required;
6 the lack of a coherent industrial policy;
7 a weaker involvement of financial institutions in the successful development of industrial enterprises than in competitor economies;
8 the existence, in other countries, of more effective barriers to trade;
9 better operating practices in foreign companies.

It would be a major task to debate whether these views are well founded. However, they do reflect the concern that it is these underlying factors which are the important issues and that they apply to the whole of industry and not just manufacturing. The main issue of consequence for the present article is the conclusion that other parts of the economy would be unable to substitute fully for the relative decline in manufacturing (pp. 42–3): 'the Committee believe that manufacturing is vital to the prosperity of the country and that services, important as they are, are no substitute for manufacturing because they are heavily dependent upon it and only 20 per cent are tradeable overseas'.

The experience since the Committee met casts some doubt on their conclusions as manufacturing has held its share of GDP. Nevertheless, most of the same points were made at the recent PSI conference (see note 2).

However, a further argument has been made, namely that some of the manufacturing 'base' (or core) has been eroded and hence sustained recovery is not possible because the capacity to do so no longer exists. A deep recession results in the closure of factories not just a temporary slowing of utilization. In these circumstances some of the assets represent substantial sunk costs which cannot be transferred to other production on closure. This even applies to human knowledge and skills, some of which will be firm or plant specific. This scrapped structure has often been built up over a very long period of time and an equivalent stock cannot readily be created by new investment in the short run.

Can other sectors substitute for manufacturing?

The House of Lords Committee based their rather negative view of the future on three items of evidence placed before them:

1 Value-added in manufacturing exports is some three times higher than in services. A 1 per cent fall in exports of manufactures requires a 3 per cent rise in exports of services to compensate. (This is based mainly on evidence from the British Overseas Trade Board.)
2 Exports of services are unlikely to be able to grow fast enough to compensate for the decline in manufacturing (based primarily on evidence from the British Invisible Exports Council).
3 Around a fifth of services output is sold to manufacturing and hence would decline *pari passu* with the decline in manufacturing.

Their view was thus very clearly that a decline in manufacturing was unlikely to be matched by a rise in other contributions to the balance of payments and hence this would slow the rate of growth of the economy. The validity of this view is dependent upon their prior conclusion that UK manufacturing was likely to show persistent falls in relative competitiveness, which would not be fully offset by improvements in price competitiveness through the exchange rate.

There are two effective routes of challenge to this hypothesis. The first is to refute the view that manufacturing in the UK is likely to decline further in relative competitiveness. The second is to refute the idea that other sectors could not substitute for it. It is the second of these which is our main concern in this article in dealing with the question of 'does manufacturing matter?', because the lack of adequate substitutes would imply that it did. If, however, manufacturing can recover and is recovering adequately anyway, then this implies that there is no need for special concern about manufacturing and hence it does not 'matter' in that sense but, of course, on the other hand the mere fact that it is recovering shows that it does 'matter'!

Certainly other sectors appear to have substituted successfully for manufacturing at the margin. If it were possible to show that the high levels of unemployment in the early 1980s were purely a transitional phenomenon and that a combination of the continuing recovery of manufacturing and the development of other industries were to continue, then a sustainable future of high employment with a lower share for manufacturing is possible. Part of the problem depends on how the experience of the last few years is interpreted. Is the recession an unfortunate interruption to a process of sustainable faster growth or was the rapid growth of the second half of the 1980s the unusual behaviour?

The recession certainly has a very different complexion from its predecessors, with a firm recession in services and a focus on the south-east of England rather than the traditional focus on manufacturing and construction, with the emphasis on investment goods. All one can say at this point is that no major forecaster is suggesting that the problem of unemployment can be eliminated over the next few years. Therefore if it is a transition, it is a very long and an unpleasant one for those who are unemployed, and counterfactual evidence would need to be produced of what unemployment would have been.

The role of manufacturing in exports is clear from Table 3. In 1991 manufactures provided over a third of the UK's current account credits, over two-and-a-half times as big a contribution as was made by the entire sum of services and over ten times as great as the contribution by oil. Only interest, profits and dividends (IPD) were anything like the same size, at 35 per cent of the total. The importance of the last figure is that a major contribution thus comes from the capital account and, indeed, in part from previous investment decisions which may have involved relocation of UK manufacturing overseas. Thus concentration on goods and services alone is too narrow. It is also important to realize that these figures are gross. There is an import content for exports

Table 3 The structure of the balance of payments, 1991

	Current account credits	
	£ billion	*Per cent*
Export of goods		
Total	103.4	47.1
of which:		
Food, beverages and tobacco	7.7	3.5
Basic materials	2.0	0.9
Oil	6.8	3.1
Other mineral fuels and lubricants	0.4	0.2
Manufactures:	84.8	38.6
Semi	29.2	13.3
Finished	55.6	25.3
Other	1.8	0.8
Export of services		
Total	31.7	14.4
of which:		
General government	0.4	0.2
Private sector and public corporation:		
Sea transport	3.7	1.7
Civil aviation	3.9	1.8
Travel	7.2	3.3
Financial and other services	16.5	4.6
Interest, profits and dividends	77.7	35.4
Transfers	6.8	3.1
Total credits	219.6	100.0

Source: CSO, *UK Balance of Payments*

of goods and services so their net contribution to the balance of payments is likely to be lower, particularly for manufactures – a point worthy of further study. It is thus clearly a considerable task for any other productive sector to substitute for a decline in earnings from manufacturing. This process of structural shift in itself presents difficulties.

The structure of exports at this level of aggregation is fairly similar to that in the mid-1980s (Mayes 1987b). IPD and to a lesser extent manufacturing have increased in importance while oil and services have fallen in share.

Mayes (1986, 1987a) argued that there were clear asymmetries in the process of change which meant that downturns were easier to achieve than upturns and hence were longer lasting. This argument is closely related to what has been described as 'hysteresis' (see Blanchard and Summers 1986, for example). The argument runs that physical capital can be scrapped readily, but new investment requires a substantial time lag for ordering, construction and so on. Furthermore, the quality of human capital is eroded by unemployment, and sustained retraining in new jobs is necessary before effective re-absorption into the labour force is possible. Third, it is much easier to leave a market than enter it: there are considerable difficulties in building up trading relationships and such relationships, once broken, are even more difficult to re-establish, as credibility is lost. A similar argument applies to R&D. A company builds up R&D capital through a period of sustained effort, much of which may be embodied in the staff concerned: once an R&D team has broken up it is much more difficult to re-create.

The policy implication of this view is clearly to attempt to reduce the impact of economic cycles where possible. However, this clashes with the long-run objective of changing general business behaviour where, unless there is a severe jolt, there is a considerable incentive for firms to continue in a relatively inefficient manner over a sustained period of time (Grinyer *et al*. 1987; Mayes 1986). In either case, manufacturing clearly matters. The question at issue here is whether permitting a short-run decline has longer-run consequences. The counterexample usually advanced is that of Norway, where there were deliberate subsidies to maintain manufacturing output over the transitional period of North Sea oil. As a result, unemployment has been that much lower. However, inflation has also been high, reflecting the expectation of the future and the increased pressure on resources.

The House of Lords Committee was clearly of the view that this 'short-run' decline had major implications for long-run growth. Hence manufacturing 'matters' in the short run and in this view it would be mistaken to allow manufacturing to decline too far in that short-run period, as the time taken for recovery is considerably longer than that for decline. Exactly the same arguments have been put forward during the recent recession with the implication that there is a ratchet effect. Each time there is a shakeout, there is a smaller range of plants and industries on which to base the subsequent recovery. A higher rate of investment may then be required for the recovery. Given the decline in a wide range of mechanical engineering much of that investment now relies on imports.

MANUFACTURING AS A SOURCE OF GROWTH

Perhaps the most well-known promotion of the relative importance of manufacturing industry comes from Lord Kaldor's (1966) inaugural lecture, in which he picked up the Verdoorn (1949) observation that high rates of output growth are associated with high rates of productivity growth. He noted the high correlation between output growth in manufacturing and output for the economy as a whole. Putting these together, it appeared that a faster rate of growth of output as a whole could be obtained from putting more resources, principally labour, into the manufacturing sector. This argument, among others, led to the introduction of the Selective Employment Tax, both to encourage productivity growth in general and to encourage labour to be shifted into manufacturing.

The well-known exchange between Kaldor and Rowthorn in 1975 (Rowthorn 1975a, 1975b; Kaldor 1975) and the updating by McCombie in 1981 cast doubt on the validity of some of Kaldor's original results. The question remains whether any effective change in the structure of the economy can be achieved by altering the nature of inputs in the economy (for example, the supply of skilled engineers). Not surprisingly, Kaldor (1975) puts the emphasis on demand, but this issue is still crucial at the present time in terms of the debate about the appropriate means of economic management. Kaldor's view, on reflection in 1975, was that subsequent evidence had indicated that it was a lack of international competitiveness rather than a shortage of labour which was the main factor explaining the UK's slower growth rate – a theme followed by many, including the House of Lords' *Report on Overseas Trade* (House of Lords 1985).

Bacon and Eltis (1976) emphasize the importance of the lack of investment in 1965–74 in preventing the desired expansion, and similar views have been expressed about later periods. They conclude that 'hence employment in Britain has suffered from technical progress instead of gaining from it' (p. 20). The ratio of non-marketed output to marketed output rose from 41.5 per cent in 1961 to 62 per cent in 1975. This placed pressure on market sector investment, on the labour market with rapid inflation and on the balance of payments, which deteriorated.

One of the main reasons for looking to manufacturing rather than to other parts of the economy as an engine of growth has been that it can provide higher levels of productivity and higher rates of productivity increase. We have already noted that this is not true compared with the oil industry. Indeed, the problem has been that the labour 'released' by the switch to the oil industry has not been re-absorbed elsewhere in the economy. If we look at estimates made of value-added per worker in manufacturing and various services sectors (Table 4),

Table 4 Value-added per worker, 1991[a,b] (£ sterling)

	GDP per head	GDP per full-time equivalent
All industries and services	19,387	21,887
Manufacturing	20,505	21,267
Distribution, hotels, repairs and catering	13,392	16,300
Transport and communication	20,615	21,418
Banking, finance and insurance[b]	28,562	30.795

a. Self-employed treated as full-time; part-time treated as half full-time. Denominator is employees in employment plus self-employed

b. As stated in note (3) in the text, value-added in the banking, finance and insurance industry and other services is subject to special factors. Thus measures of value-added per worker will also be subject to these same factors and consequently need special care in interpretation

Source: CSO; Department of Employment and Northern Ireland Employment Statistics notice

even allowing for the great difficulty of measuring productivity in service industries as illustrated by Smith (1985) for example, we can see that while distribution, hotels, repairs and catering did have a level of labour productivity considerably lower than that of manufacturing in 1991, communications and banking, finance and insurance had productivity levels around a third higher. Indeed, if we consider growth rates in productivity over the period 1971–91, those in manufacturing were only a little in excess of the economy as a whole. This is illustrated in Table 5. It is the period since 1979 when the difference has been so striking.

Output grew fastest in banking, finance and insurance followed by communications, while it actually declined in manufacturing over 1973–9. However, output per full-time equivalent worker, a measure of labour productivity, has risen fastest in communications, 3.5 per cent, and manufacturing, 2.25 per cent, for the period as a whole. When it comes to the last period, 1980–91, the picture is markedly different, with manufacturing productivity rising at 4.5 per cent per annum compared with 2 per cent for the economy as a whole, and 1.25 per cent for banking, finance and insurance, and 4.25 per cent for communications. (The consequences for employment are, of course, different, with an overall rise in 1980–91 of only about 0.25 per cent per annum but a 2.25 per cent annual fall in manufacturing, while banking, finance and insurance rose by 4.5 per cent per annum. Indeed, if maintaining a high level of employment were the principal objective, the view of what industries mattered might be considerably different as a smaller rise in output in a low productivity industry is needed to offset a fall in a high productivity areas. (The 1980–91 figures are chosen to give end-points at similar phases of the economic cycle.)

Productivity growth in manufacturing, or indeed a wider definition of industry, is an insufficient requirement for ensuring a faster rate of economic

Table 5 Trend growth for output per worker, output and employment (per cent)

	1971–91	1973–9	1973–91	1980–91
Index of output per full-time equivalent worker				
All industries and services	1.92	1.42	1.67	2.04
Manufacturing	2.19	0.66	2.66	4.46
Distribution, hotels, repairs and catering	0.89	– 0.46	0.77	2.20
Transport and communications	3.45	1.79	3.07	4.28
Banking, finance and insurance	1.29	2.34	1.56	1.30
Index of output at constant factor cost				
All industries and services	1.99	1.42	1.65	2.12
Manufacturing	0.63	– 0.67	0.08	1.35
Distribution, hotels, repairs and catering	1.77	0.22	1.42	2.80
Transport and communications	2.59	1.44	2.19	2.67
Banking, finance and insurance	5.31	4.45	5.32	5.96
Index of all employees including self-employed				
All industries and services	0.31	0.20	0.19	0.30
Manufacturing	−1.62	−1.17	−1.73	− 2.28
Distribution, hotels, repairs and catering	1.07	0.82	0.87	0.86
Transport and communications	− 0.64	− 0.34	− 0.58	− 0.83
Banking, finance and insurance	4.01	2.10	3.75	4.60

Sources: CSO, *National Income and Expenditure*; Department of Employment and Northern Ireland Employment Statistics notice

growth, as is clear from Bacon and Eltis's (1976) analysis of the period 1965–74 when output per man-hour in manufacturing actually increased by 4 per cent per annum. What they show is the simultaneous shift from manufacturing into services, particularly non-marketed government services. Thus the productivity gain in manufacturing did not result in an increase in the resources drawn into manufacturing and hence further gains. Quite the reverse, as resources were transferred to lower productivity areas. These shifts are more than would have been expected on demographic grounds. Furthermore, subsequent work such as National Economic Development Office (NEDO) (1985, 1987) suggested that the extra funds had not gone into a successful building-up of the stock of human capital through education and training. The prime importance of this source of growth has been emphasized by Sig Prais and his colleagues at NIESR (see Prais 1990).

In the same way that there appears to have been a ratchet effect downwards in employment in manufacturing during each recession (see Kilpatrick and Naisbitt 1984, for example), there was a ratchet upwards in each economic cycle for health and education. Thus employment lost to manufacturing during the recession was not regained in the subsequent upturn, while employment gained in the public sector during a recession in part as a countercyclical policy was not released to the private sector during the recovery.

What we see, therefore, are two effects, both leading to lower rates of growth: the one a structural shift away from marketed output, and the other the failure to put sufficient resources into the future in physical capital (technology) through research and development (R&D), and human capital (skills) through education and training.

In NEDO (1984) it was argued that there is a clear link between the amount of effort on R&D and export competitiveness (see also Mayes 1986). Thus an economy which underinvested in knowledge-intensive industries would actually lose out in the overall process of economic growth. This has resulted in the suggestion that resources should therefore be encouraged towards the high-technology industries. This view is one applied not just to the UK but more

Table 6 Shares in total value-added of goods, market services and non-market services (1980–4 averages, per cent)

	Goods[a]	Market services[b]	Non-market services[c]
Canada	38	42	20
United States	35	53	13
Japan	43	47	10
Australia	39	58	NA
New Zealand	41	46	13
Austria	44	41	15
Belgium	36	49	15
Denmark	34	43	24
Finland	36	37	27
France	41	45	14
Germany	45	41	14
Greece	48	42	10
Italy	46	40	14
Luxembourg	39	48	13
Netherlands	39	47	15
Norway	46	40	14
Portugal	48	41	12
Spain	47	43	10
Sweden	39	36	26
Turkey	53	39	8
United Kingdom	42	42	18
Mean	43	44	15
Standard deviation	5	5	4

a. Goods defined as: agriculture, forestry and fishing; mining and quarrying; manufacturing; electricity, gas and water; construction
b. Market services defined as: wholesale; retail; hotels, etc.; transport and communications; finance; real estate business; community; social; personal
c. Non-market services defined as: government services; private non-profit services
Source: Blades (1987)

widely to the whole of the European Community by the European Commission. There are also indications that the competitive structure of UK trade has been moving towards capital-intensive and away from knowledge-intensive types of production. The importance of manufacturing as a vehicle for technical progress is emphasized by Greenhalgh and Gregory (1991).

After 1984 NEDO examined these issues in more detail, looking at comparative efforts on innovation among some thirty industries in the main OECD countries. Two themes emerged. The first is that it is not the high R&D industries *per se* where the greatest gains occur but rather those where the UK has a strong relative R&D effort. Thus one should not conclude necessarily that the best result would be achieved by concentration on high R&D industries – nor indeed by consequence, that the best performance comes from concentrating on manufacturing and certain sectors within it. The second theme is that the differences in R&D effort between industries are much more important in explaining export performance than the variations in R&D effort within industries.

There are no particularly good grounds for suggesting that the structure of the UK economy at the aggregate level in its split between goods, market services and non-market services was particularly different from that of the other OECD countries in the early 1980s, with the possible exception of non-market services which are somewhat above average (Table 6). What one can see is that the UK has an unusually large emphasis on banking, finance and

Table 7 United Kingdom share of world trade in manufactures

Year	Per cent
1964	14.2
1969	11.2
1974	9.3
1979	8.7
1980	8.3
1981	7.7
1982	8.0
1983	7.8
1984	7.8
1985	7.8
1986	8.0
1987	8.2
1988	8.0
1989	8.2
1990	8.3
1991	8.2

Source: Monthly Review of External Trade Statistics

insurance (and energy, fuel and power), and an unusually low proportion of value-added in other services.[4]

The implications of this structure for growth depend upon the split of these services between the internationally marketable and those which are largely domestic in nature. Additionally, while the UK's loss of market share in manufacturing over the past thirty years may have been very considerable (Table 7), the loss of share in world trade in services was (according to the British Invisible Exports Council) even faster (House of Lords 1985: 366).

A disaggregated view

Considerable richness is lost by treating manufacturing as an aggregate. In particular it covers up the fact that, despite the difficulties of the past few years, some parts of manufacturing industry have done well. Trying to look at growth rates over a number of years also covers up the fact that manufacturing industry has picked up more recently. This is aided by the improvement in the exchange rate and should continue.

In balance of payments terms (OTS basis), while manufacturing declined by over £23 billion between 1978 and 1989 (Table 8), the chemical industry actually improved and other transport equipment increased its favourable contribution by some £2 billion. Over three-quarters of the decline was accounted for by just three industry groups: motor vehicles; machinery; and clothing and textiles. Between 1989 and 1991 the first two categories recovered markedly, contributing over two-thirds of the reversal in fortunes, machinery actually returning to the black. However, textiles and clothing remained unchanged in the face of the general improvement, implying a further major worsening in relative performance.

However, crude balances are not particularly good indicators. Export performance and import penetration are more informative indicators. Mayes (1987b) shows that while import penetration rose in all categories between 1978 and 1986, export performance also improved in other transport equipment, metal manufacturing, chemicals, man-made fibres, office equipment and data-processing equipment, and leather and leather goods; and these between them resulted in a 1 per cent improvement in export performance for manufacturing as a whole over the period. There are thus considerable strengths (and, indeed, weaknesses) in various parts of manufacturing industry.

DISTRIBUTIONAL ARGUMENTS

We have noted earlier that, in direct terms, manufacturing productivity varies between industries. Furthermore, oil and some of the more rapidly rising service industries such as communications and banking, finance and insurance have considerably higher average levels of labour productivity. Hence the transfer of resources to those sectors actually results in an increase in the rate of growth

Table 8 Disaggregated balance of trade

	1970	1974	1978	1982	1985	1989	1991
Non-manufacturing	− 3420	− 8605	− 8302	− 2048	−1484	− 9270	− 8069
Food beverages and tobacco	−1513	− 2647	− 3150	− 3234	− 4299	− 4874	− 4577
Basic materials	−1165	− 2093	− 2716	− 2637	− 3313	− 4142	− 3052
Fuels	− 742	− 3865	− 2435	3823	6128	− 254	− 438
Semi-manufacturing	290	− 362	527	− 35	−1414	− 5310	− 2136
Chemicals	244	593	1447	1945	2512	1912	2811
Textiles	151	64	− 235	− 749	−1342	−1566	−1391
Iron and steel	119	−178	8	−105	123	85	381
Non-ferrous metals	− 259	− 324	− 309	− 251	− 526	−1100	− 582
Metal manufactures	166	189	440	414	114	− 922	− 340
Precious stones and silver	− 64	−153	− 270	136	− 247	95	− 24
Other (mainly wood and paper related)	− 67	− 558	− 554	−1425	− 2051	− 3814	− 2991
Finished manufacturing	1964	1983	3124	232	− 4399	−14259	− 3908
Machinery	1042	1253	2892	2080	− 369	− 3701	145
Road vehicles	700	728	273	−1386	− 2891	− 6933	−1622
Other transport	78	173	47	931	972	1638	1991
Clothing and footwear	−13	− 238	− 402	−1014	−1436	− 2844	− 3062
Scientific instruments and photographic equipment	55	36	10	0	43	− 65	175
Other miscellaneous	101	30	303	− 373	− 717	− 2355	−1494
By category:[a]							
Consumer goods	354	− 283	−1480	− 4793	− 6737	−11780	− 6907
Intermediate goods	765	1222	2478	2773	1978	− 2962	− 467
Capital goods[b]	776	890	2129	1446	− 542	−1167	1489

a. Less erratics
b. Based on the United Nations broad economic categories analysis
Source: Monthly Review of External Statistics

and probably also in the prospects for growth. However, with relatively slowly rising demand and surplus labour, such a transfer exacerbates the unemployment problem. Of course, the opposite result occurs if the resources are transferred to lower productivity areas like distribution or hotels and catering. While this may reduce economic growth, it could lower unemployment.

The interesting question, however, lies in the feedback effects. If it is the case that there is far more input from ancillary industries associated with manufacturing, then a decline in the manufacturing industry may have a more than proportionate effect than the consequent rise in employment elsewhere, even though the direct impact may be larger. The social consequences may be different as well if the job losses are concentrated in regions with already high unemployment and the job gains spread widely over the country. Thus one might have objectives for some sort of balanced growth and not just for specialization.

Relatively little work has been done on this interlinkage. Driver (1984) examined the interdependence of the manufacturing and services sectors within the economy. He noted first of all that the effects of an increase in final demand for manufacturing did not have a proportionately greater effect than an increase in demand for other industries, either directly on its own output or indirectly on the output of other industries – as calculated through the 1979 input–output tables. (This is, of course, subject to all the normal objections of using past average rather than future marginal coefficients in input–output analysis.)

Using the 1984 input–output tables Greenhalgh and Gregory (1991) suggest that the demand for services generated by the demand for manufacturing is clearly greater than the other way round, implying a higher feedthrough into the rest of the economy. Some of this greater feedthrough reflects a change between the 1979 and 1984 economy as shown by the input–output tables (Barker and Forsell 1992). Services increased more than the dramatic fall in manufacturing and some producer services appear to play a more important role as suppliers to manufacturing than they did five years earlier, possibly partly a result of the trend towards outsourcing. It is noticeable that the increase in demand comes not from final demand but from other industries right across the board. However, one should note that input–output analysis of this form does not capture investment needs of industries properly and therefore gives only a short-run picture of interdependence.

This would appear to imply that, while manufacturing might matter a great deal to the regional economy, the implications for the country as a whole from the sectoral shifts are less important. The rise in demand for business services more than compensated for the decline in manufacturing. Experience from the recent recession might bring this into question as the regional pattern has been reversed, reducing rather than accentuating disparities.

SOME CONCLUDING REMARKS

It seems, on a very crude basis, that the UK could operate satisfactorily both in terms of the level of output and its rate of growth at a range of levels of manufacturing activity around its current level, as this is the experience of other advanced countries. However, these are remarks at the margin. A continuation of the progressive decline of the importance of manufacturing since the war at the same rates seems unlikely, as other industries cannot continue to expand to fill the gap at a commensurate rate. Agriculture has been buoyed up artificially through the Common Agricultural Policy. While the winding-down of that policy may be slow, it seems unlikely that it will be further strengthened. North Sea oil is a once-and-for-all gain. While other resource discoveries or, indeed, technological advances which could have a major effect are possible, they are almost by definition not predictable. Trade liberalization has also affected the pattern, with a surge in both exports and imports of manufactures as a result of membership of the European Community now extended to a wider range of goods and services by the 'completion' of the internal market. Trade barriers are now much lower but still substantial, particularly on areas outside manufacturing which will be covered, in part at any rate, for the first time in the GATT Round in Geneva if it succeeds.

All this indicates that manufacturing does matter and that, indeed, its importance in the economy may increase over the next few years. It does not, however, imply that special measures are called for to assist manufacturing rather than other industries, except to aid the process of transition from one structure to another as there are asymmetries in the process of change. The current government policy is very much one of trying to create the 'climate' in which change dictated by the 'market' can take place. However, many rigidities remain, some of which are inherent (in time lags, for example), and some of which are specific to the UK (such as the system and standards of education and vocational training). It is these, and other fundamental causes, which have contributed to the decline of manufacturing and the slower rate of growth of the UK in the past, which 'matter', rather than manufacturing *per se*. As those problems are corrected, the economy as a whole is likely to improve its performance and manufacturing along with it. In these circumstances of favourable growth it is unlikely that people will find much meaning in the question, 'does manufacturing matter?'![5]

NOTES

1 An earlier version of this paper was published in the *National Institute Economic Review* in November 1987. Anand Dawar helped in assembling the original tables and figures. This new version was produced at the request of the ESRC Industrial Economics Study Group for a meeting on 14 May 1993. Original material is reproduced with permission.
2 'The future of UK industrial competitiveness', 23–4 March 1993.
3 'At least' because there is no single list of factors and the discussion is very wide-ranging, covering many facets of competitiveness which could be singled out in their own right, such as the quantity and nature of R&D.
4 In the UK, expenditure on financial services is not deducted from the output of individual sectors in deriving value-added. Instead, a global adjustment is made. The rapid growth of this negative 'adjustment for financial services' between 1975 and 1985 may be part of the reason for the fall in output in other services and may affect the comparisons.
5 In discussion of the paper Paul Stoneman has suggested that relatively little divides those who argue that 'manufacturing matters' from the remainder who argue not that manufacturing does not matter but that it has no special role in the economy. Many of the latter view the decline in manufacturing as a symptom of the wider problems of the economy while the former regard it as a cause. However, this is to a considerable extent a circular process as poor performance in manufacturing contributes to that poor general performance.

REFERENCES

Bacon, R. and Eltis, W. (1974) 'Budget message for Mr Healey: get more people into factories', *Sunday Times*, 10 November.

Bacon, R. and Eltis, W. (1976) *Britain's Economic Problem: Too Few Producers*, 2nd edition, Basingstoke: Macmillan.

Barker, T. and Forsell, O. (1992) 'Manufacturing, services and structural change, 1979–1984, in C. Driver and P. Dunne (eds), *Structural Change in the UK Economy*, Cambridge: Cambridge University Press, Ch. 2.

Beckerman, W. (1962) 'Projecting Europe's growth', *Economic Journal*, vol. 72, December.

Blackaby, F. (ed.) (1979) *De-industrialisation*, London: Heinemann.

Blades, D. (1987) 'Goods and services in OECD countries', *OECD Economic Studies*, Spring.

Blanchard, O. J. and Summers, L. H. (1986) 'Hysteresis and the European unemployment problem', *NBER Macroeconomic Annual 1986*, Cambridge, MA: MIT Press.

British Industrial Performance, 4th edition, NEDO, October 1987.

Brooks, S., Cuthbertson, K. and Mayes, D. G. (1986) *The Exchange Rate Environment*, London: Croom Helm.

Driver, C. (1984) 'Employment income, services and the input–output structure', NEDO Economic Working Paper, no. 13.

Driver, C. and Dunne, P. (1992) *Structural Change in the UK Economy*, Cambridge: Cambridge University Press.

Eltis, W. A. (1975) 'How public sector growth causes balance of payments deficits', *International Currency Review*, vol. 7, no. 1 (January–February).

Forsyth, P. J. and Kay, J. A. (1980) 'The economic implications of North Sea oil revenues', *Fiscal Studies*, vol. 1, no. 3, pp. 1–28.

Greenhalgh, C. and Gregory, M. (1991) 'Why manufacturing matters: directions for industrial policy', in R. Dore *et al.*, *Improving Britain's Industrial Performance*, London: Employment Institute, pp. 14–23.

Gregory, K. (1976) 'Some implications of the growth of the mineral sector', *Australian Journal of Agricultural Economics*.

Grinyer, P., Mayes, D. G. and McKiernan, P. (1987) *Sharpbenders: Unleashing Corporate Potential*, Oxford: Basil Blackwell.

House of Lords (1985) *Report from the Select Committee on Overseas Trade*, HL 238 I–III, London: HMSO.

Kaldor, N. (1966) *Causes of the Slow Rate of Growth of the United Kingdom*, Cambridge: Cambridge University Press.

Kaldor, N. (1975) 'Economic growth and the Verdoorn Law – a comment on Mr Rowthorn's article', *Economic Journal*, vol. 85, pp. 891–6.

Kilpatrick, A. and Naisbitt, B. (1984) 'A disaggregate analysis of the slowdown in productivity growth in UK manufacturing industry in the 1970s', NEDO Economic Working Paper, no. 12.

McCombie, J. S. L. (1981) 'What still remains of Kaldor's Laws?', *Economic Journal*, vol. 91, pp. 206–16.

Matthews R. C. O. and Bowen, A. (1987) 'Keynesian and other explanations of post-war macroeconomic trends', paper presented at the conference on 'Keynes' *General Theory* after fifty years', NEDO, September.

Mayes, D. G. (1986) 'Change', Discussion Paper, no. 31, New Zealand Institute of Economic Research.

Mayes, D. G. (1987a) 'Asymmetries of change in economic behaviour', Vite-Bulletin, no. 8.1, Tilburg University, Spring.

Mayes, D. G. (1987b) 'Does manufacturing matter?', *Natoinal Institute Economic Review*, November, pp. 47–58.

Moore, L. (1986) *The Growth and Structure of International Trade since the Second World War*, Hemel Hempstead: Wheatsheaf.

Murfin, A. (1987) 'Service industries in the UK economy: background data', mimeo., NEDO.

NEDO (1984) 'Trade patterns and industrial change', memorandum by the Director General.

NEDO (1985) *Competence and Competition*, London: NEDO Books.

NEDO (1987) *Challenge to Complacency*, London: NEDO Books.

Prais, S. J. (1990) *Productivity Education and Training: Britain and other Countries Compared*, London: NIESR.

Rowthorn, R. (1975a) 'What remains of Kaldor's Law?', *Economic Journal*, vol. 85, pp. 10–19.

Rowthorn, R. (1975b) 'A reply to Kaldor's comment', *Economic Journal*, vol. 85, pp. 897–901.

Smith, A. D. (1985) *Productivity in the Distributive Trades: A Camparison of Britain, America and Germany*, Cambridge: Cambridge University Press.

Verdoorn, P. J. (1949) 'Fattori che regolano lo sviluppo della produttivita del lavoro', *L'Industria*.

18

THATCHERISM AND TECHNICAL ADVANCE – REFORM WITHOUT PROGRESS?[1]

Margaret Sharp and William Walker

INTRODUCTION

Britain is a medium-sized industrial nation with a secondary, if occasionally still significant, role in contemporary economic and political affairs. To the foreign observer, this may be a statement of the obvious. But it is not a description that many British people find easy to accept.

In the first half of this century, decline was to some degree masked by the military defeat of the principal European rival, Germany, and by the economic misery experienced by the United States and other industrial nations during the Great Depression. The weakness of Britain's international position really struck home in the 1950s and 1960s, politically through the inability to hold the Empire together and economically through the persistent failure to match the growth rates of other OECD countries.

In the post-war era, the 1960s and 1980s stand out as the periods in which the most determined and coherent efforts were made to halt the decline. However, the approaches taken could hardly have been more different.

During the 1960s, the guiding assumption, whether under Conservative or Labour governments, was that the market economy could no longer be left to its own devices. The state had to intervene to improve industrial management and to redress the inequities of income and opportunity that were seen as inherent to the capitalist system.

In stark contrast, the guiding assumption in the 1980s was that the market economy *must* be left to its own devices, and that Britain's economic deficiencies had stemmed in large part from the state's creeping protection of individuals, firms and sectional interests. Hence the privatization of state monopolies, the attack on trade unionism, the shift away from direct taxation, and a whole range of measures and inducements that came to be known as 'Thatcherism'. Although it is associated particularly with the government presided over by Mrs Thatcher from 1979–90, as a philosophy it has dominated the successor administration of John Major as much as the earlier period. Indeed, ironically it has sometimes emerged in its starkest and most

397

uncompromising guise under the Major administration, as, for example, in the privatization of British Rail or the run down of the coal industry.

It is tempting to conclude that this sharp change in economic philosophy (1979 marked the discontinuity) was a rational response to technical change – the shift from large-scale 'Fordist' manufacture to the more fluid, decentralized style of industrial organization brought about by the revolution in information technology.[2] While there may be some truth in this, Thatcherism was shaped with an eye more to the past than the future – it was a reaction to yesterday's failings rather than prescience of what lay around the corner. Moreover, it rested on the Hayekian notion that a liberal market economy always provides a superior foundation for economic advance and for political order and morality. It was thus from the outset a political as well as an economic doctrine.

If truth be told, until recently[3] the Conservatives have shown remarkably little interest in technical change, or concern for Britain's position in the technological pecking order. In part, this is the natural consequence of its *laissez-faire* policies. How technology was used and produced was the responsibility of private enterprise and not, outside defence, of the state. The Department of Trade and Industry became fond of saying that it was 'technology neutral', meaning it had neither the right nor the desire to indicate preferences or back them with funds.

Moreover, with the important exception of nuclear weaponry and nuclear power, advanced technology has been ascribed little symbolic or cultural value, as the reluctance to join European space ventures demonstrated. The Thatcher government's deepest belief was that the individual energies released by emancipation from past constraints would drive economic modernization – that technical and other forms of advance would follow, and not precede, the revolution in social attitudes and behaviour. This contrasted with the 1960s when there way an almost obsessive concern with technology as the harbinger of the good life (Harold Wilson's 'white heat of the technological revolution'), and as a symbol of Britain's ability to remain a Great Power.

The Thatcher government's comparative unconcern with technical change, and its impact on economic performance, are important themes in this chapter. While the indicators of output and productivity growth present an extremely mixed (even confused) picture, we shall see that Britain's innovative performance continued to deteriorate relative to its major competitors. Whatever the conclusion, one is struck by the Thatcher government's economic daring, or foolhardiness, depending on how one sees it. Here was a medium-sized industrial nation liberalizing its markets from a position of industrial weakness, and during a technological revolution in which it played only a minor part. The mid-nineteenth century policies of *laissez-faire* and free trade were fine when Britain was the undisputed industrial leader. To apply them in the 1980s was decidedly risky.

THE HISTORICAL LEGACY

Britain's early industrial development and rise to global economic supremacy still cast their shadows over the contemporary scene. What is astonishing in retrospect is the length of time during which Britain maintained industrial leadership – 1760 and 1880 are often cited as its beginning and end, although Britain was still the largest trading nation in 1914 – and the extent of that leadership. In comparison, the period of US supremacy (1920–70?) seems more fleeting and circumscribed.

The backward glance is more than nostalgia. Particularly in the 1980s, there developed within the Conservative Party a fascination with the culture and economic philosophy of the Victorian period, when *laissez-faire* policies and industrial power reached their zenith – the one, it was inferred, arising from the other. There was similar fascination in the (idealized) workings of the US economy which, almost alone, was seen to maintain the Victorian tradition of self-help and economic liberalism.

Study of the nineteenth century also helps reveal certain characteristics of the British economy and society which seem to have endured the upheavals and policy reversals of this century. Everything has changed, and yet nothing has changed. It is therefore worth drawing out, if all too briefly, a few themes from the earlier period of British economic history, while indicating their relevance to the present context.

The individual entrepreneur

A notable feature of the First Industrial Revolution is the association of innovations with names: Tull and the seed drill, Hargreaves and the spinning-jenny, Watt and the steam-engine, Telford and road-building, Stephenson and the steam locomotive, Brunel and railways and steamships – the list is endless, and not just confined to Britain. At this stage in technological development, it was possible for the individual entrepreneur to command the range of theoretical and practical knowledge required to produce the most sophisticated innovations of the day.

This individualistic nature of management and innovation fitted well with the economic liberalism of the age, which in turn had strong social and political roots, not least in the Protestant emancipation from church and state. Landes, Hobsbawm and various other historians, however, have argued that Britain was, as a result, ill-adapted to the more institutionalized, systematic, science-based form of technological activity that underpinned the Second Industrial Revolution.[4] The institutional reforms begun in Britain in the second half of the nineteenth century and carried through into the twentieth century can, in this respect, be seen as attempts to change into a different set of clothing, but one that never quite seemed to fit with the social values and structures that had evolved in the previous century. The reforms of the 1980s amounted to the abandonment of this attempt in the face of repeated economic failure. Instead, they tried to replicate the social relationships that apparently served Britain so well in the earlier age.

The role of dissenters

One of the constant themes of British economic history is that the industrial innovators of the eighteenth and nineteenth centuries were outsiders to the social elite, and very often religious dissenters or non-conformists. With the occasional exception of financiers, very few came from the established middle classes. Indeed, a phenomenon much remarked upon by social historians is the speed with which entrepreneurs and their offspring were 'captured' by the aristocracy with its anti-industrial values, while continuing to enjoy the rent from accumulated commercial assets.[5] Two institutions stand out as perpetuating this tradition: the public schools and Oxbridge with their emphasis on character-building and non-technical curricula; and the monarchy which, although long deprived of executive authority, has continued to give security and legitimacy to aristocratic interests and values.

Despite Britain's long experience of industrialization, pre-industrial values have therefore survived surprisingly intact in the upper reaches of society, their tentacles always reaching out for new captives. In this context it is fascinating that the Thatcher government was pre-eminently a government of dissenters and outsiders. Mrs Thatcher herself and many of her advisers and political supporters come from non-conformist working or lower-middle-class backgrounds, or were in other ways outsiders to the established order. Indeed, her greatest scorn was reserved, not for Socialists, but for traditional Conservatives (the 'Wets') within her own party with their seemingly disingenuous attachment to both aristocratic values and egalitarianism. It also helps to explain her alienation from the traditional 'establishment' of academics, churchmen, the BBC and senior men of affairs.

However, the Thatcherites are dissenters with a difference. Unlike the nineteenth century northern variety with their strong links with engineering and manufacturing, their backgrounds and careers had chiefly been in service industries such as retailing, property and finance in the south of England. They also lacked their predecessors' strong belief in progress through education.

Educational backwardness

Education has long been a central issue in British performance. Our early industrialization did not rely on mass education. Until the late nineteenth century (perhaps even later), there was no education 'system' in Britain. In contrast to Germany, Japan and even the United States, where organized education was the prelude and springboard for industrial advance, in Britain education was disorganized and lacked any strong association with the aims of economic development.

Until the mid-nineteenth century, education in Britain was carried out by an unregulated patchwork of churches, voluntary organizations, and by some ancient foundations (e.g. Oxford and Cambridge) which had little connection with the industrial world. The principal source of technical education was the apprenticeship system, where emphasis was on 'learning by doing', which was appropriate at that time.

Primary education for most children in Britain came in the 1870s when an element of literacy was becoming essential. Compulsory secondary education had to wait until 1944! The reform of the public schools in the 1850s and 1860s did nothing for the bulk of the population. It was intended to turn the children of the expanding middle class into 'Christian, English gentlemen', which meant studying the classics, and gave little or no place to scientific and technical subjects. These subjects only became part of the general curriculum with the later expansion of the grammar schools and 'red-brick' universities of northern England (Scotland had embraced technical education at an earlier date, partly as a result of being more open to continental influence).

Economic historians are now agreed that this failure to establish an adequate education system was an important cause of Britain's difficulty in adjusting to late nineteenth- and twentieth-century industrial requirements. Despite various attempts at reform this century, and the considerable expansion of education after 1945, the scene is still one of relative neglect. For some reason, education has never been as central to notions of social and economic progress in Britain as it has in other industrial nations. Indeed, the attempt in the 1980s to bring new vitality to the economy was accompanied by the impoverishment, as well as reform, of the already backward education system.

Internationalism

British economic expansion in the nineteenth century was an international phenomenon. The Imperial trading system hinged on the export of finance, technology and manufactured goods, and the import of raw materials and food – what has been referred to as a 'vertical' division of labour.[6] While Britain's geopolitical ascendancy depended ultimately on technological and military (especially naval) superiority, three other aspects are worth noting.

First, Britain's strength was linked to the opening up of new territories in North America, Australasia and Africa, and their colonization by successive waves of British and other European emigrants. This created a mass market for manufactured goods and the source of the widening variety of raw materials used in production. It was predominantly an extra-European movement, causing the British economy to become less and less integrated with its continental neighbours.

Second, the formation of a dynamic capital market, based on the City of London, played a central part in British economic expansion. In addition to supporting trade and industry, it provided the investment capital for much infrastructural development (especially railways) in the United States and elsewhere. This in turn led to Britain becoming the centre of international finance, and created a complicated socio-economic dynamic whereby the interests of the City of London and its social elite (and of supporting sterling and maintaining a strong position in international financial markets), often conflicted with the interests of productive industry.

Third, in the nineteenth century Britain became the hub of an elaborate raw material, food and energy trading system. But while manufacturing was largely carried out within national frontiers, resource trading (coal being the exception) was strongly multinational from the outset. As such, the enterprises that developed around it were less affected by the decline of the national economy, shifting their ground to take advantage of other nations' and regions' economic advance. To this day, resource trading is one of Britains strongest specializations, with firms like BP and Shell (oil/gas), Unilever (food) and RTZ (minerals) remaining among the largest of their kind in the world.

One of the results of these developments has been a growing sense of apartness between manufacturing and those sections of the economy dealing with financial and material flows (which should now be extended to include retailing). While the former has declined, the latter has flourished; and while the former has remained occupationally unpopular among the educated elite, the latter has provided its principal source of new employment and income, including unearned income. This in part explains the country's intellectual orientation.

> Surely part of the explanation of the conservative approach to the application of science and technology – at the upper levels of the educational system, in particular – is that the tasks the dominant class has chosen to face, whether in the City money markets or in Whitehall, have been adequately dealt with by the use of what Balogh referred to as the 'crossword puzzle mind'.[7]

The brutality of British industrialization

Although highly successful in global terms, the changes that accompanied the industrial revolution in Britain were traumatic for large sections of the population. The enclosures which drove people off the land, the terrible conditions in factories, mines and cities, the effects of pollution, the lack of any economic safety net – all engendered a deep ambivalence about the benefits of industrialization.

These social pains of industrialization had a costly legacy. They led to the growth of a particularly distrustful, adversarial form of trade unionism, and eventually to the formation of a mass political movement embodied in the Labour Party; to the gradual increase in state regulation of health and safety, hours of work, and the use of child and female labour; and to the notion of industrialization being tarnished in popular and middle-class culture.

Efforts to arrest decline were thus accompanied by equal and even more persistent efforts to find more humane forms of economic organization. This duality in policy is evident well into the post-1945 period, the concern over social conditions having been given added weight by the hardships of the 1930s. It was decisively overturned in the 1980s. Central to Thatcherism was the affirmation that the general social benefit from unfettered capitalism far outweighed any detriment, and that nothing would be achieved by the state intervening to soften its effects. By meddling, the state had, it was argued, both stifled the economy and prevented the poor from bettering themselves.

THE STATE AND TECHNICAL ADVANCE, PRE-1979

By and large, the state in Britain has not acted as a catalyst to industrial and technological development. Between the mid-eighteenth and last quarter of the nineteenth centuries, its economic role was largely confined to regulatory functions (financial markets, property law, etc.) and to the advancement and military protection of foreign trade. The next hundred years brought a rising tide of state intervention in the economy, but it was often hesitant, usually resisted, and seldom as determined and forthright as in other countries. Moreover, it tended to be reactive, not proactive. Contrast this with France, where the state has generally seen itself as a creator of new modes of production and as an entrepreneur in its own right.

The two world wars and the Cold War were especially important in bringing a more active stance on technical change. They gave legitimacy to state sponsorship of technological and industrial development and they brought the first direct funding of R&D; the establishment of government R&D laboratories; the use of procurement as an instrument for creating new production capabilities; and the use of industrial planning in energy and other areas. In general, the new products and processes emerging from wartime activity gave credence to the notion that the state could usefully play a part in accelerating the development and diffusion of new technologies.

Continuing military demands on industry had the added effect of creating industrial sectors that were predominantly under the wing of the state. Britain's leading role in the defence of north-west Europe and its adherence to nuclear weapons meant that substantial state resources were committed to the nuclear, aerospace, shipbuilding and electronics industries. Britain has been second only to the United States in its per capita commitments to defence R&D, and since military technologies (or quasi-military technologies like nuclear energy) were assumed to represent *the* technological frontier, the state often took upon itself the role of prime mover.

The 1960s, and particularly the period 1964-9 when the Labour Party was in power, were the apogee of state intervention in the economy, and of belief in its restorative effects.[8] The following features of government policy in this period are worth noting:

(i) *Rationalist optimism.* The Keynesian macroeconomic management practised at this time, the adoption of indicative planning, and the use of various interventionist measures to restructure industry and induce technical advance can all be seen as part of the same rationalist approach. The future was considered sufficiently predictable, the analytical techniques available and the industrial system malleable, to allow the state to play a central role in control.

(ii) *Partnership.* Industrial progress was seen as best achieved through partnership between government, the trade unions and industrial management, as manifested in the National Economic Development Council (NEDC). Consensus between these parties would, it was hoped, bring greater control over incomes, agreement on industrial strategy and an end to the traditionally adversarial style of management and trade unions.

(iii) *Expansion of education.* Education was seen as holding the key to true equality (equality of opportunity) as well as being necessary to support economic and technical advance and to self-fulfilment. The reform of primary and secondary education to encourage more open, child-centred learning, was accompanied by a major expansion of higher education in the universities and polytechnics. This was to be the age of opportunity for all.

(iv) *Emphasis on manufacturing.* The Labour Party was traditionally the party of the industrial north. This, and the increasingly grave balance of payments problems, gave manufacturing, and especially the engineering industries, pride of place in economic policy-making. Efforts were made to bolster existing capabilities through import substitution and export promotion, and to stem the drift of employment from manufacturing to other sectors via a selective employment tax which hit the service industries harder than others.

(v) *Emphasis on technology.* Industrial decline was attributed particularly to the failure to develop and apply new technology. Britain's good record in scientific discovery and invention was not translated into innovation, nor were new products or new manufacturing processes rapidly taken up by industry. Efforts were made to increase the return on scientific research, and to hasten the application of new process technologies such as NC machine tools via investment grants, demonstration projects and a host of other measures.

(vi) *Scale economies.* Enlarging enterprises through arranged marriages, ostensibly to give them greater opportunities for reaping economies of scale was regarded as a key to higher productive efficiency. Fragmentation was viewed as a source of weakness. Thus the government, through the Industrial Reorganisation Corporation, supported the wave of mergers across the engineering industries which created 'national champions' such as GEC in electrical and

404

electronic engineering, British Leyland in motor vehicles, ICL in computers and Alfred Herbert in machine tools.

The retreat from these policies began in the 1970s. The oil crises and stag-flation of that period brought disillusion with Keynesian policies of macro-economic management, and greatly eroded belief in the government's powers of omniscience. In spite of perceptions to the contrary, the industrial strategy of the 1970s, with its panoply of sector working parties and tripartitism, was predicated on an economic philosophy which suggested that there were, for Britain, no winners, but a huge backlog of missed opportunities across the industrial board. The basic problem was diagnosed as being that Britain was producing products that were frequently ten years out of date on machines that were twenty years out of date.[9] The solution required a wholesale upgrading of quality, attention to detail and the pursuit of high value-added oppor-tunities. Selective grants were available to encourage re-equipment on a sector-by-sector basis, big was no longer necessarily beautiful and increasingly inter-national competitiveness became the key success indicator.

Old habits, however, died hard. When Rolls Royce, and subsequently British Leyland, ran into difficulties, they were bailed out by the state which sub-sequently became the largest shareholder. The National Enterprise Board (NEB), set up in 1975 to catalyse new technologies, was rapidly turned instead into a rest home for 'lame ducks'. And major decisions of the 1960s – parti-cularly Concorde and the programme to build a succession of nuclear power stations based on the advanced gas-cooled reactor (AGR) – continued to drain scarce technological resources to 'big projects' rather than dispersing them more generally across industries.[10] Despite all the efforts to revive economic fortunes, the domestic economy did not prosper, international trade shares continued their decline, and many interventionist policies came to be regarded as failures.

More than anything else, the discontinuities brought about by the oil crises shook industrial confidence. Manufacturing investment slumped, unemploy-ment rose, but so too did inflation. Struggling to control inflation, govern-ments gradually allowed the maintenance of full employment to slip from the top of the politico-economic agenda. The ultimate humiliation came in 1976 when, faced by rising public sector and balance of payments deficits, the government had to call upon the International Monetary Fund for help. Hence-forth, pride of place was given to the reduction of inflation and public borrowing. The former was achieved mainly through the administration of a tough incomes policy run in conjunction with the trade unions – the so-called Social Charter. The *quid pro quo* was a succession of labour laws which considerably strengthened the role of the trade union movement – indeed, one cabinet minister subsequently described the Social Charter as a matter of 'all take and no give'.[11] When successive rounds of the incomes policy hit increasing opposition from rank-and-file members, the spirit of cooperation rapidly caved in, culminating, in the autumn of 1978, in a succession of inflationary wage claims and a wave of public sector strikes which were dubbed the Winter of Discontent. For many this was the last straw in a decade of vacillation during which the power of the trade unions had grown to excess and that of managers was too severely curtailed.

In part, Thatcherism was therefore a response, and a naturally opportunist response, to perceived failure. This goes some way towards explaining the three main prongs of government economic policy in the 1980s:

1 the retreat from industrial intervention, and the return to a *laissez-faire* approach to industrial issues;
2 the use of monetary instruments – the control of the money supply, public sector borrowing, interest rates – as the foundation of a macroeconomic policy whose main task was to control inflation;
3 the reining-in of trade union power with the introduction of successive legislation gradually constraining their influence and marking an end to any attempt at tripartite consensus.

But Thatcherism also marked the end of the long period during which successive British governments had seen it as their responsibility to help strengthen technological capabilities. The Thatcher government largely disavowed this responsibility, partly out of belief that industry should look after its own affairs, and partly because it displayed little understanding of the importance of technological capabilities or of the means by which they are acquired. Its approach to economic regeneration paid surprisingly little attention to the costly and painstaking accumulation of technological resources which has been so much a feature of Germany's and Japan's economic success.

THE RECORD OF THATCHERISM

In Britain, as elsewhere, economic performance across the last fifteen years has varied. The 1980s began with the worst recession since the 1930s. The combination of high inflation, a monetary squeeze and a strong petro-currency pound brought exceptionally high unemployment and a significant loss of industrial output. This was followed by a period of strong recovery, with falling inflation and a rapid growth of output and productivity, especially within manufacturing. As Figure 4, Chapter 4, shows, manufacturing productivity increased faster during the 1980s than in her major competitors, and this trend has persisted into the early 1990s, through the deep recession which followed the Lawson boom.

Whether the 1980s were a real step forward for the British economy is hard to judge. Some attribute the depth of the 1989–92 recession to the Treasury's financial mismanagement in the second half of the 1980s. Others claim that it is just the latest manifestation of Britain's long-standing economic malaise. While the productivity gains must be applauded, a brief look at what happened over the past fifteen years to the structure of the British economy and its trading performance, to the allocation of surplus income, and to levels of innovative activity, inclines us to the latter view.

Changing industrial structures

A marked feature of the last fifteen years has been the fall in share of output contributed by manufacturing industry (see Figure 1, Chapter 17). Such shifts have occurred in all advanced economies but have been particularly marked in Britain. The high growth of labour productivity in manufacturing means that the drop in employment has been even sharper – from well over one-quarter of total employment in 1979 to approximately one-fifth in the early 1990s. The overall share of industrial production (agriculture, energy, manufacturing, construction) did not fall as steeply, mainly because of the rise in the contribution of North Sea oil and gas.

The corollary to this drop in manufacturing has been the growth of the service sector and, particularly, until the recession of the early 1990s, the growth of output and employment in banking, finance and insurance, and of employment in distribution, retailing and hotels. Changing shares of output have been matched by investment, with fixed capital formation in the service sector exceeding that in manufacturing. Indeed manufacturing investment in the 1980s in real terms was below that of the 1970s (see Table 2, Chapter 7), supporting the view that much of the productivity increase in manufacturing has been due to labour shedding, the scrapping of inefficient plant and improvements to working practices rather than to improvements in plant and machinery.[12] In other words, technological change played a relatively unimportant part in boosting manufacturing productivity, the dominant role being played by cutbacks in labour, and by improvements in the effectiveness with which capital and labour were being managed.

Looking at it from a longer-term perspective, the shift to services in the 1980s added a further twist to the political and economic marginalization of manufacturing in Britain. The growth of the financial sector resulted in the City acquiring even greater influence over economic behaviour and policy formation.

Foreign trade

Somewhat similar trends emerge in relation to foreign trade. Britain's share of world exports has held steady throughout the period (see Table 7, Chapter 17), but this has not prevented a serious deterioration in the current account which, with a peak deficit of over 4 per cent of GDP in 1989, was still in deficit at the height of the recession in 1991 (see Figure 4, Chapter 3). Some of this has been caused by a weakening of the oil price and a reduction of the surplus on invisibles. But the main culprit has been the growth of manufactured imports which, between the cyclical peaks of 1979 and 1990 grew from 14 per cent of GDP to 17 per cent, against a small fall in exports (from 16 per cent to 15 per cent).

The Thatcher view was that the trade deficit would diminish as final demand was reduced in 1988–90 by high interest rates, and that, in any case, the deficit was accounted for by rising imports of investment goods. Certainly industrial capacity has been insufficient to cope with sharp upturns in growth as happened in 1987–8. This suggests that the abilities of British manufacturers to compete with foreign producers have weakened, and there is an increasing range of products, particularly capital goods, for which there is no longer any British supplier.

British manufacturing has also come increasingly to depend on the activities of foreign multinational companies. As Chapter 16 shows, during the 1980s, direct foreign investment into the UK grew substantially, with Britain retaining its status as the favourite location of US, and now Japanese, investment in the European Community. In a number of vital sectors foreign firms now predominate: Ford, GM, Peugeot and now Nissan, Toyota and BMW in automobiles; IBM, DEC and Fujitsu (ICL) in computers; Matsushita, Sony and Hitachi in consumer electronics; Intel, Texas Instruments and NEC in semiconductors. Indeed, the encouragement of import substitution via foreign investment has arguably become the central industrial policy response to the trade deficit. But it also means that in important sectors there is no major British-owned company still operating. For example, with the exception of defence electronics, there is now no major British-owned company operating in the electronics sector. These companies are also increasingly important contributors to exports.

Inward investment has nevertheless been outflanked for most of the decade by outward investment in both scale and growth. The pattern of outward investment was different. Much foreign investment into Britain has been in manufacturing, while British investment overseas has been heavily oriented towards the service industries (hotels, retail, air transport, insurance, publishing, etc.). The United States, and not Europe, has been its favoured location. Also worth noting is the huge growth of outward portfolio investment, indicating that a significant part of savings in the UK were being channelled abroad.

These trends point towards a worrying structural dynamic. Internationally, Britain's comparative advantage resides increasingly in the service sector. However, Britain may be falling into the trap whereby the overseas income generated by the service sector is being outweighed by that sector's propensity to suck in imports of manufactured goods as it becomes more capital-intensive. In other words, a dynamic service sector requires a dynamic manufacturing sector if serious trade imbalances are to be avoided. Certainly, during the 1980s the income growth that the expansion of the service economy was itself generating, created demand for consumer durables and other goods that the manufacturing sector could not meet.

Table 1 Distribution of UK manufacturing productivity growth, 1979–89[a]

	1989 (*relative to 1979 = 100*)
Manufacturing sector output	
Output	112.2
Employment	74.0
Productivity[b]	151.6
Manufacturing compared to all business	
Manufacturing/business prices[c]	95.0
Business/manufacturing productivity[d]	84.1
Manufacturing income	
Real income[e]	104.3
Real profits[f]	143.9
Real wage income[g]	94.5
Real wages per head[h]	127.8
Real profits per unit of capital[i]	127.7
Use of manufacturing profits	
Investment[j]	112.8
Real dividends[k]	173.2
Real share prices[l]	224.8

a *Sources:* Table 4.2 from J. Michie (ed.), *The Economic Legacy 1979–92*, Academic Press, London. Sources cited are as follows: CSO, *UK National Accounts 1991*, Tables 1.7, 2.1, 2.4, 13.7, 17.1, plus 1979 data from CSO; *OECD Labour Force Statistics*, UK Tables III, IV; *IMF Financial Statistics*; CSO *Business Monitor P5*, no. 21, Table 2 and no. 14.

b Manufacturing real value-added per person employed.

c Manufacturing value-added deflator divided by business sector (GDP less dwellings, public administration, health and education) deflator.

d Business-sector total factor productivity divided by manufacturing total factor productivity (with labour and capital stock inputs weighted by 1979 income shares).

e Manufacturing output divided by ratio of consumer prices to manufacturing prices, i.e. purchasing power (in terms of consumer goods) of manufacturing incomes.

f Manufacturing gross profits (including excess of self-employment incomes over average wage) deflated by consumer prices.

g Manufacturing income from employment, adjusted for self-employment, deflated by consumer prices.

h Real-wage income divided by manufacturing employment.

i Real profits divided by manufacturing (gross) capital stock.

j Gross fixed capital formation including assets leased by manufacturers.

k Estimated from dividends in accounts of manufacturing companies operating mainly in the UK, deflated by consumer prices.

l Industrial share prices deflated by consumer prices.

The allocation of profits

This conclusion is reinforced if we look at what happened to the profits generated by industrial and commercial enterprises. Table l indicates that while manufacturing income as a whole rose between 1979 and 1989 by only 4.3 per cent, profits rose ten times faster, by 44 per cent. However, the proportion of those profits reinvested in productive capacity was relatively small – over the whole period manufacturing investment (including leased assets) rose by 12.8 per cent, whereas dividend distributions increased by 73.2 per cent. As the recently published *R&D Scoreboard* noted, British companies are content to invest, on aggregate, 1.55 per cent of sales revenue and 19.7 per cent of profits on R&D. The equivalent numbers for the world's largest 200 companies are 4.59 and 94.3 per cent.[13] Whereas the Thatcherites, on gaining office, had argued that, once profits were restored, industry would invest in plant and equipment and R&D, the record does not bear this out. On the contrary, increased profits went to increased dividends which in turn help to inflate share prices and feed the speculative boom of the later 1980s. Figure 1, based on OECD data, shows indeed that for the period 1979–88 Britain experienced one of the fastest rates of growth in profits and, next to the US, the lowest increase in manufacturing investment.

This phenomenon was further encouraged by the government's macro-economic policies over much of this period. The persistence of high real interest rates, maintained in part to support the value of sterling, forced firms to seek higher short-term profits. The traditional dependence on stock-market finance has also, all too often, resulted in investment and R&D being viewed as 'consumption' rather than 'wealth-creating' activities. To quote Ingham:

> One paradoxical ... feature of the contrast between stock market and bank finance economies is that the former have lower levels of overall capital investment, generate less external finance and exhibit lower growth rates, but also declare company profits which are significantly higher than those in the latter.[14]

This was well demonstrated in the 1988/89 joint GEC–Siemens takeover of Plessey. International comparison showed GEC and Plessey to have been consistently more profitable than their competitors but to have equally consistently slipped down the international league table of electronics companies measured by size and market share.[15] A further twist is added by the ease of corporate takeover in Britain (as in the United States). High profits and dividends have been sought in order to maintain stock ratings but the relatively open market in corporate assets has encouraged British firms to give growth by acquisition a higher priority than organic growth. As a result the 1980s saw the triumph in Britain of management by financial criteria. It was the age of the financial conglomerate (Hanson Trust, BAT, even GEC) managing disparate assets as distinct profit centres. While encouraging cost-cutting and thus

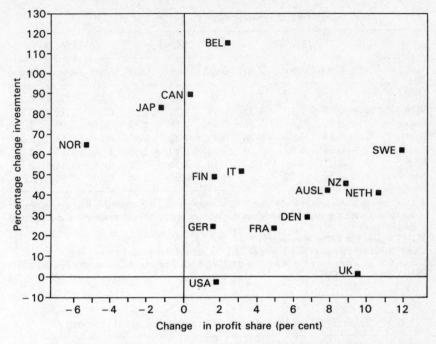

Source: J. Michie (ed.), *The Economic Legacy*, London: Academic Press, Figure 4.3, p. 86.

Figure 18.1 Manufacturing investment and profits in OECD countries, 1979–88.

productivity growth, such firms seldom show concern for the longer-term processes of technological accumulation and organic (i.e. internally generated) output growth.

Levels of innovative activity

By international standards, British expenditure on R&D as a proportion of output remains quite high (Table 2). But if defence and other government R&D is excluded it looks more modest, having now fallen well below US and Japanese rates of spending and below the European average. Most significantly, the growth of R&D expenditure, both as a whole and that financed by industry, has not matched that of other industrial nations, despite showing some signs of recovery since the mid-1970s. Table 3 gives the sectoral breakdown of R&D expenditures for the period 1985–91 in current prices. This shows how much the overall increase in industrial R&D is boosted by the very much higher rates of R&D growth in chemicals and pharmaceuticals. It emphasizes, yet again, the relatively poor performance overall when it comes to investing in longer-term assets and skills and, as we have seen, contrasts with the very fast rate of growth in profits and dividends.

411

Table 2 R&D expenditures as a percentage of GDP

	1976–80			1981–5			1986–90		
	Govt	*Indust.*	*Total*[a]	*Govt*	*Indust.*	*Total*[a]	*Govt*	*Indust.*	*Total*[a]
UK[b]	1.30	0.80	2.10	1.10	1.00	2.30	0.85	1.12	2.25
West Germany	0.99	1.18	2.23	0.99	1.52	2.54	0.98	1.79	2.83
France	0.91	0.75	1.76	1.14	0.88	2.12	1.16	0.97	2.28
Italy	0.35	0.38	0.76	0.49	0.45	0.97	0.64	0.53	1.23
Sweden[b]	0.84	0.96	1.70	1.01	1.50	2.58	1.10	1.73	2.93
USA	1.21	1.04	2.30	1.30	1.34	2.70	1.38	1.41	2.85
Japan[c]	0.50	1.20	1,85	0.52	1.66	2.34	0.49	2.05	2.71

a There are small amounts of R&D finance from other sources, e.g. charitable foundations, hence the total is normally slightly more than the straight aggregation of government and industry combinations.
b 1975 figures *not* 1976–80 average.
c OECD estimates: figures relate only to R&D in natural science and engineering.
Source: OECD. Taken from Table 2.6.7 in the 1992 Annual Review of Government Funded R&D. HMSO, for Cabinet Office

Table 3 Sectoral breakdown of R&D spending, 1985–91 (£m)

	1985	1991	Annual increase (%)
Chemicals	942	1,886	12.3
Mechanical engineering	263	310	2.8
Electronics	1,759	2,180	3.6
Other electrical engineering	126	102	– 3.5
Motor vehicles	372	525	5.9
Aerospace	818	1,121	5.4
All manufacturing	4,673	6,644	6.0
Manufacturing without chemicals	3,731	4,758	4.0

Source: SPRU R&D database

Analyses of British innovative output by Pavitt and Patel among others are even less encouraging. Although one has to beware of time-lags in the patenting data, Table 4 shows that Britain's share of patenting of new inventions in the United States has fallen, while that of other European nations has risen. Table 5, which gives the numbers of patents filed there by major British and German firms, shows the relative and absolute decline of British inventiveness even more plainly. The depressing feature of these figures is the continuing decline of the British share even in a period, such as 1986–90, when the economy was growing faster than most others.

Table 4 Shares of west European patenting in the US, 1963–90

	1963–8	1969–74	1975–80	1981–5	1986–90
West Germany	34.21	36.37	38.60	41.56	41.35
France	13.62	14.46	14.46	14.70	15.20
United Kingdom	25.15	21.36	17.93	15.66	14.94
Switzerland	8.78	8.58	9.00	8.05	7.08
Italy	4.34	4.85	4.98	5.50	6.36
Netherlands	4.74	4.43	4.45	4.68	4.88
Sweden	5.31	5.25	5.70	5.03	4.61
Belgium	1.65	1.94	1.78	1.62	1.65
Finland	0.25	0.47	0.72	1.04	1.37
Denmark	0.94	1.09	1.04	0.99	1.00
Spain	0.42	0.49	0.57	0.42	0.65
Norway	0.51	0.54	0.64	0.56	0.63
Ireland	0.06	0.13	0.11	0.16	0.25
Portugal	0.03	0.04	0.02	0.03	0.03
Total	100.00	100.00	100.00	100.00	100.00

Source: SPRU/OTAF database

Table 5 Patenting in US by UK and West German large firms in chemical, electronic and mechanical engineering sectors

	1969–74	1981–6	Change (%)
UK	3,955	2,474	– 37
West Germany	10,297	12,631	+ 23

Source: P. Patel and K. Pavitt, 'A comparison of technological activities in FR Germany and the UK', *National Westminster Review*, May 1989

Conclusions on the record of the 1980s

Technical progress in Britain under Thatcherism therefore appears to have related more to the use of new technology (viz. productivity improvements) than to its development. Process change has taken precedence over product innovation. The priority given to cost-reduction and higher profits has led firms to shed labour and modernize working practices, and to seek growth by trading in assets rather than by creating new technological capabilities. The abandonment of Inmos, the pioneer of the transputer, was symptomatic of industry's growing aversion to technologies with great potential but high risks. In so far as new manufacturing capabilities have been established in Britain since 1979, they have mainly been the result of Japanese and US multinational investment.

413

There are two notable exceptions. One is in the chemical and pharmaceutical industries where investment in new technology has stayed high. Indeed, the pharmaceutical industry is Britain's major success story with four firms, Glaxo, Smith Kline Beecham, ICI (now Zeneca) and Wellcome now amongst the top twenty firms in the industry. Interestingly it is an industry where production skills *per se* count for little, the crucial parts of 'value-added' being in drug discovery (research) and in marketing, both areas where Britain has some comparative advantage.

The other exception is the defence sector. During the first half of the 1980s, British expenditure on defence R&D increased rapidly, and then tailed off slowly as the budget was squeezed. Britain ranks second only to the United States in the proportion of technological resources allocated to defence purposes. A consequence of such heavy channelling of resources, in a market where international competition is lessened by the political constraints on arms exports by Germany and Japan, is that defence production now constitutes the area of engineering in which Britain's greatest competitive advantage resided. However, the international market is now so diminished that export opportunities are very limited.

Various studies have suggested that these high levels of defence expenditure have been among the most significant causes of decline in Britain's engineering industries. The high spending levels have encouraged management to operate in the relatively safe haven of protected markets, and absorbed a large proportion of Britain's limited high-technology resources.[16] For much of the 1980s, 'optimization' of positions in defence markets was also a central strategy of GEC, British Aerospace and several other British high-technology firms who then had difficulty in adapting to the new conditions when the climate changed so completely with the collapse of the old Soviet empire towards the end of the 1980s.

Looking back, therefore, over the record of the last fifteen years, two factors stand out. First, the growing share of services, particularly financial services, enhanced the economic power and influence of the City. The incentive structure thereby established, with its emphasis on realizing short-term gains, has had a pervasive influence over risk-taking and vitiated against investments with long-term and uncertain payoffs, precisely those involving the use and exploitation of new technologies. Second, within the manufacturing sector, much of the new investment and output growth has occurred as a result of foreign investment in the UK. Productivity growth in British-owned companies has been largely achieved through labour-shedding and better management of existing resources, and has not been accompanied by an expansion of innovative capacities.

THE STATE AND TECHNICAL ADVANCE IN THE 1980s

Technical change also ranked low on the Thatcher government's list of concerns in the 1980s. While other nations focused increasing attention and resources on technology as they tried to stay in the international race, Britain stood out in the 1980s for its comparative disregard of these issues. This is evident in the government's reduction of its own expenditure on R&D, and its reluctance to match the growth of spending on scientific research experienced in France, Germany and other advanced countries.[17] Moreover, while these competitors tend to increase R&D expenditures in periods of recession in order to create new markets, British firms are more reluctant to make such investments.[18]

Since 1979 there have been three distinct phases in the Conservative government's policies in this area. Up to 1984, and roughly coinciding with Mrs Thatcher's first administration, policies in support of innovation were not so different from those of previous administrations. Sir Keith Joseph, Secretary of State for Trade and Industry from 1979–81, while railing against all forms of industrial support, found himself perforce supporting the state-owned steel, shipbuilding and car industries to an unprecedented degree through the recession of 1980–1. His successor, Patrick Jenkin, determined to give priority to supporting new rather than old industries. He created the post of Minister of Information Technology and via its incumbent, Kenneth Baker, launched the Alvey Project which was one of the most ambitious programmes of support for high technology ever seen in Britain. Aimed at promoting pre-competitive R&D in electronics, the programme was very successful at developing collaboration between industry and the higher education sector but found that often the necessary interface with corporate R&D was lacking, creating barriers to technology transfer and further exploitation.[19]

A distinct change of course came in the mid–1980s and reflected two sets of priorities. One was the insistent pressure to limit public expenditures. The other was the increasing strength of the non-interventionist, deregulatory wing of the Conservative Party, which had received a fillip from the unexpected popularity of the privatisation of British Telecom. From 1984 onwards, efforts were made to bring innovation policy, and the general handling of state-industry relations, into line with neo-liberal orthodoxy. They led in time to the MoD's procurement reforms, the Department of Trade and Industry's 1988 Enterprise Initiative, and the various Education Reform Acts. The advent of the Major administration seemed likely to herald yet another change of course, and there has indeed been talk from ministers of the importance of manufacturing industry. But for all the talk, action has been limited and the general trend of policy, as noted earlier, has remained *laissez-faire*, with privatization, 'market testing' and purchaser/provider splits extending to most areas of the public service.

This shift in policy is central to understanding the change that took place under Thatcherism. The first five years represented, as we have said, little departure from the stance of previous governments. Broadly speaking the starting point for British (and other) governments in formulating industrial policy was a set of observations about industry's international performance, backed up by analyses identifying areas of strength and weaknesses at both aggregate and sectoral levels. These formed the basis upon which policy measures were formulated – the state acted like a doctor, making diagnoses and specifying regimens and medicaments. And, like a good doctor, it did not follow the Darwinian principle of survival of the fittest, but preferred to see the sick returned to health alongside the fit.

The free market, enterprise and value for money

It is this concept of the pragmatic 'doctor state' which was so thoroughly rejected after 1984. In its place has been put a far more doctrinaire approach which was built deductively upon the Holy Trinity of the 'free market', 'enterprise' and 'value for money'.

The free market came to be seen as the natural, most efficient, stable yet dynamic regulator of economic activity. By intervening in the market earlier governments, both Labour and Conservative, had, in the eyes of these new evangelists, committed a number of cardinal sins; they had wrongly assumed that their judgement and knowledge were superior to those of firms active in the marketplace; their interventions had disturbed market mechanisms and diminished perceptions of risk by providing a safety net for erring companies; and they had encouraged too cosy and corporatist a relationship between industry and the state.

The Thatcher concept of *enterprise* was even more idiosyncratic. To start with, it denoted a broad cultural movement. In the words of the DTI's 1988 White Paper, 'The key to continued economic success lies in the further encouragement of the enterprise of our people'.[20] It was a romantic vision of the natural condition to which 'our people' should return after the years in the wilderness. At the same time, enterprise was highly individualistic. The principal actors are individuals and individual firms – notably small firms – whose separate and competitive activities from the market. But the entrepreneur was not necessarily, or even primarily, a creative force generating or exploiting new scientific and technical knowledge – the essential qualification was that the entrepreneur should operate a new or expanding business, whether it be a sweatshop, a software house or a property company.

Value for money, for its part, provided the central key to action in areas where the state has been unable to shift the locus of activity into the private sector. It has served the twin objectives of improving public sector performance and reducing public expenditure. The implicit, and even explicit, assumption was that the public sector was by definition parasitic and wasteful of resources, while the private sector was efficient, productive and virtuous. Wherever possible, therefore, public services were subcontracted out to private sector concerns, and decisions devolved to the firm level. Ironically, where this proved impossible and government retained responsibility for allocation decisions – in areas such as basic research, education and training – its search for value for money has led instead to increasing centralization and *dirigisme*. In education, for example, we have seen the national curriculum imposed on schools, combined with encouragement to opt out, all of which serve to diminish the role of the local education authority and enhance central control. Interestingly, although the Major government of the 1990s rejected the fervour of the Thatcher commitment, its adherence to the goals has proved even more tenacious – indeed much of the full implementation of the Thatcher doctrines were left for this era. In education the national curriculum as been followed by the attempted introduction of compulsory testing and the publication of league tables; the purchaser/provider split has been extended from areas such as health, to social services and the research councils, and the concept of 'market testing' for public services has become commonplace in many areas, including government laboratories, and now threatens even the higher ranks of the civil service.

Implications for policy

What effect did this idolization of 'the market', 'enterprise' and 'value for money' have on policy? Although changes were often less dramatic than the rhetoric led us to believe, all departments concerned with science and technology have found themselves implementing major reforms according to these three principles.

(i) *R&D support*. The three principles were applied rigorously to the support of both basic and applied research. As far as basic research was concerned, the Thatcher regime from the start treated the academic world as a prime example of the parasitical tendencies of the public sector. Budgets were tightly controlled, barely rising over the decade to meet general inflation, let alone adequately to recompense for the increasingly capital-intensive nature of all fields of scientific research; emphasis was put on 'relevance' with industrialists being imported onto research councils and university courts to advise on industrial needs while the search for 'value for money' led to increasingly complex exercises in accountability in an area where, by its nature, much of the pay-off was long term, uncertain and non-quantifiable. This approach culminated in the 1993 White Paper on Science and Technology[21] introduced by John Major's new Minister for Science, William Waldegrave, which rearranges the responsibilities of the Research Councils, puts more business people on their boards and gives them all new, industrially-oriented mission statements.

It is significant that the White Paper signally failed to address the major failings in innovation on the part of industry, reflecting the fact that Waldegrave's remit extended only to the academic research base, leaving the DTI with its traditional responsibilities for industrial innovation and the Ministry of Defence (MoD) still dominant in defence-related research interests. The failure to address industrial innovation was, however, symptomatic of the way policy had been developing. From the mid-1980s

417

onwards, the Conservatives had progressively withdrawn funding from 'near market' R&D on the grounds that this was industry's responsibility, sanctioning only spending on pre-competitive R&D through its joint LINK programme with the Research Councils (see below), and via the European collaborative programmes – not, it must be said, from any great enthusiasm, but more in the interest of gaining Britain's *juste retour* and avoiding responsibility for thinking strategically about the direction in which technologies and industries should develop.[22] The result, as Table 6 shows clearly, is that the DTI's contribution to funding R&D fell sharply and by the end of the decade amounted in real terms to only half its earlier commitment. Given a similar pattern in other spending departments as the 'near market' doctrine was carried through, it is not so surprising to find Britain alone among OECD countries in registering a sharp fall in government support for civilian R&D.

(ii) *Enterprise.* The 1988 *Enterprise Initiative* therefore had the effect of reducing government support for industry as a whole. Enterprise was promoted, however, through continued support for small and medium-sized businesses (SMEs), which were regarded by the Thatcher government as the stormtroopers of its enterprise initiative with, on the one hand, a range of special grants, loans and consultancy schemes available through the DTI and, on the other, substantial tax concessions available through the Business Expansion Scheme Indeed, it is estimated that the proportion of those employed in plants employing less than 100 people increased from 17–18 per cent in the 1970s to 25 per cent by 1989.[23] It is estimated that the total value of the various SME promotion schemes amounted to some £510 million in 1988/9. Table 7 indicates how this £510 million is distributed between various heads and compares those expenditures with equivalent expenditures in West Germany. What is notable about this comparison is first, that, in spite of a deliberate policy to target the SME sector, overall UK government support as a percentage of GDP is less than half that of West Germany. Second, that whereas 20 per cent of the (substantially larger) West German expenditures go to promote R&D, only 2 per cent of UK expenditures do so.

Table 6 Government expenditure on R&D in real terms, 1982–3–1992–3

	£ million (1991 prices)			
	1982–3	*1985–6*	*1988–9*	*1992–3*
Total	5,492.9	5,858.7	5,193.9	4,997.1
of which DTI	443.3	504.2	362.5	204.2

Source: Annual Review of Government Funded R&D, Cabinet Office, HMSO, 1992

Table 7 Support for small and medium-sized enterprises in the UK and West Germany, 1988–9

Type of support	UK		West Germany	
	£ million	per cent	£ million	per cent
Special regional assistance	108.5	21.2	167.1	9.1
Research and development, technology	10.0	2.0	375.2	20.3
Loans, grants and guarantees	3.8	0.7	1,093.4	59.3
Start-up assistance	199.0	39.0	61.7	3.3
Training	110.0	21.5	81.5	4.4
Information and consultancy	77.9	15.3	64.7	3.5
Other	1.6	0.3	0.3	–
Total support	510.8	100.0	1,843.9	100.0
Total support as percentage of GDP	–	0.10	–	0.25
SME activity as percentage of GDP	–	32.2	–	46.0

Source: G. Bannock and H. Albach, (eds), *Small Business in Europe: Britain, Germany and the European Commission*, Anglo-Germany Foundation, London, 1991.

Even though the proportion of SMEs in Britain has increased fast, the figure is still well below comparable figures for West Germany and Japan where approximately 50 per cent of the workforce work in plants with less than 100 employees. Dynamic small firms are part of the Japanese export success story – and indeed are also seen as success stories in countries such as West Germany and Italy where they have established niche capabilities in areas such as machine tools, clothing, knitwear and furniture. The absence of their equivalent in Britain is painfully obvious. For example, a recent study of the employment of scientists and engineers in British manufacturing industry found that from a sample of 700 firms in all size ranges, only 50 per cent undertook any R&D, and 50 per cent of these did not employ a graduate scientist on R&D work. Confronted by recession and aggressive competition from, amongst others, foreign firms, too many British companies cut out R&D altogether and resorted to the low price, low cost, low productivity route to competitiveness even though there was clear evidence that those that chose the alternative high productivity (and high R&D) route outperformed their competitors over the longer run.[24]

(iii) *Public procurement.* The 1970s saw the proliferation of schemes which linked public procurement with attempts to upgrade product capabilities and design and to establish production capabilities in infant industries. With the notable exception of defence, such schemes have now been abandoned and in general the user, whether public or private, was seen as having no special responsibility to assist the development of the supply-side. Privatization, which has often been accompanied by deregulation and the explicit injunction to the utilities to seek the lowest cost source of supply, whether it be British or foreign, has already had a major impact in the transport, telecommunication and energy sectors. This is aptly illustrated by the situation in the coal industry where the knock-on effects of the privatization of electricity has been to destroy the market for British-mined coal (in favour of, on the one hand, gas and, on the other, cheaper imported coal). What remains of the British coal industry is scheduled for privatization in 1994–5, with cost pressures favouring the extension of the lower cost open-cast rather than deep-mined coal. The demise of the deep-mined coal industry puts in jeopardy the future of the British mining equipment industry which had benefited over the years from a close and mutually beneficial 'maker-user' relationship with the nationalized coal industry and helped to contribute to its impressive productivity record.[25]

A further extension of privatization has been the introduction of compulsory competitive tendering for many government and local authority services. While this has destroyed many cosy relationships and shaken up sleepy bureaucracies, it has also added to the cost-cutting, low wage/low productivity syndrome noted above. R&D departments have been axed – from British Telecom down to horticultural departments – in the search for short-term cost savings. While many of the nationalized industries may have overspent on R&D, it has yet to be seen whether their private successors will provide adequately. Current indications suggest that, along with the majority of firms in British industry, they will give higher priority to dividends than to R&D.

Contradictions and evasions

Neo-liberal doctrine therefore provided a clear guide to action in a number of areas. In other respects, however, it has provided the government with a poor framework for dealing with the problems of innovation, and resulted in a policy approach which was riddled with inconsistencies and evasions. Not that some good did not come from the changes – many of the interventionist policies of the 1960s and 1970s were heavy-handed and distorting, and it is appropriate that those receiving public funds should have to justify their activities. Nevertheless, despite its fondness in identifying itself with the forces of progress, Thatcherism, if anything, reinforced the historic prejudice in British society against industrial activity, and against the learning of new technical skills and the establishment of new technological capabilities. This was done by down-playing the importance of manufacturing; by the implicit favour shown to service industries; and by the endorsement of the culture of short-term profit-making.

Moreover, while it may bring immediate gains in productivity, short-termism is ultimately destructive of technological development, for this is always a long-term activity involving the deferral of immediate gains in the interest of future benefits. By setting its imprimatur on the financial approaches that have dominated the management of both public and private affairs, the Conservative governments of the 1980s and early 1990s have encouraged withdrawal from, rather than a deeper engagement in, high-technology manufacturing. Equally important, the government has, in its rhetoric and actions, displayed a lack of understanding of the conditions for success in late twentieth-century industrial capitalism. A number of examples serve to illustrate this point.

Writing about the innovation policies of the 1960s and 1970s, Henry Ergas categorized Britain, along with France and the US as having 'mission-oriented' technology policies, in contrast to the German or Swedish systems which were 'diffusion oriented', with emphasis on widespread use and take-up of new technologies, as distinct from the spearheading of one or two major projects such as Concorde or nuclear power.[26] Today, as we have seen, this style of policy no longer dominates the British scene. But nor does Britain today qualify to be counted among Ergas's 'diffusion-oriented countries'. Ergas highlights in particular two aspects of the infrastructure required for this approach. One is the decentralization of institutional support, the other the broad base and high level of skills and education. In both, Britain's capabilities have, if anything, deteriorated in the 1980s. Scientific research has suffered from a series of cutbacks and reorganizations which have centralized yet further decision-taking. The education service has been subject to a perpetual squeeze on expenditure driven by the belief that major strides in efficiency could be achieved.

(i) The failures of educational reform

The failures of educational reform, particularly in the early and mid-1980s, present perhaps the starkest indictment of the Thatcher approach. Advanced industrial activity is increasingly witnessing the abandonment of previous distinctions between skilled, semi-skilled and unskilled labour. For modern economies to operate effectively, everyone requires skills. For Britain, which has traditionally been backward in education and skill training, raising the levels of achievement right across the population is therefore the major challenge for any government. Successive Conservative administrations have failed to meet it. Instead, they have been obsessed with the financing of education – with achieving value for money and limiting the jurisdiction of local authorities – disregarding the longer term implications of decisions.

At an early stage in the first Thatcher government, Sir Keith Joseph declared that Britain could 'not afford' to invest in education until the economy had been strengthened, seemingly blind to the evidence that Britain's repeated failures in education – the generally poor levels of achievement at 16, the low staying-on rate after 16 and, above all, the lack of any systematic education or training for the majority leaving at 16 – underlay the perennial weakness in the economy. What Britain needed more than anything else in the 1980s was wholesale reform which inspired in young people a thirst for learning and self-improvement.

Instead, we saw a series of half-hearted reforms whose aim was primarily to contain public expenditure and make education more 'efficient', and to bring the teaching profession to heel. It is significant that the proportion of GDP that Britain devotes to education has dropped from 5 per cent in the early 1980s to 4 per cent today. There was a distinct element in the Conservative Party which seemed to hanker after the re-establishment in the state sector of the elitist grammar schools for the top 20 per cent of intellects, modelled on these public schools – hence the establishment of City Technology Colleges, the encouragement given to schools to 'opt-out' of the locally controlled education systems and, perhaps above all, the obstinate refusal to listen to advice and reform the narrow A level curriculum for those 25 per cent staying on at school after the age of 16.

The educational problem for Britain is not, however, the top 20 per cent who perform well in any school, but the bottom 80 per cent which Britain has traditionally neglected. While the new national curricula may help raise standards, it will fall on stony ground unless the mass education system is properly resourced. Above all, little will be achieved until the proportion staying on in education or undertaking systematic training after the age of 16 is substantially improved.

There are some signs that this may at last be happening, but as much thanks to recession as to government action. Even in 1989, as many as 51 per cent of 16-year-olds old went straight from school into employment, with fewer than 4 per cent of these continuing in part-time education.[27] Equally, the proportion of those aged 17 staying on in full-time education rose dramatically from 33 per cent in 1987/8 to 55 per cent in 1992/3.[28] Part of this is undoubtedly accounted for by the lack of jobs – indeed the proportion of 17-year-olds in part-time education fell from 18.2 per cent in 1987/8 to 11.3 per cent in 1992/3 as unemployment amongst this age group increased. The trend will have been further boosted by the withdrawal in 1988 of employment benefit from those under 18 which effectively requires all 16- and 17-year-olds to enrol in the youth training programme if they are to draw any state assistance. Nevertheless, all would agree that it is far better for this age group to be involved in some rather than no training, and the very marked increase in education by young people in the last few years is the most hopeful sign for the economy. How far the trend remains once the recession is over still has to be seen; the experience of the early 1980s indicates that there is something of a ratchet effect – once participation in education and training is boosted in this way, it does not fall back commensurately.

(ii) Training

One may conclude, therefore, that the age participation rate has improved *in spite of* rather than because of Thatcherism. The same may also be true of employers where, belatedly, the training message may be getting through.

A 1989 survey found that there had been a substantial increase in the amount of training offered to those in employment since the early 1980s.[29] Considerable variation exists from company to company and, as with R&D, those who took training seriously and integrated it into 'human resource management' tended to outperform others.[30] Again, however, these developments have taken place against a backdrop of government muddle and indecision, and with the goalposts constantly being shifted. The Youth Training Scheme, established in the early 1980s, was the *ad hoc* response to fast rising youth unemployment. It became a highly centralized and extended activity under the Manpower Services Commission which was then, in 1988, switched overnight to become the Training Agency. Finally in 1990 its responsibilities were privatized and decentralized and taken over by locally-based TECs – Training and Enterprise Commissions – part-funded by central government but organized and run by local industrialists. Although mirroring the favourite Thatcher panaceas – bringing industrialists in to run the show – and plagued by the usual disease of poor funding and arbitrary decisions, the TECs have at last provided Britain with a network of training organizations which are responsive to local needs and local conditions. Indeed it has led one commentator to remark, 'Behind a smokescreen of rhetoric alleging that the new policies were borrowed from the United States, Britain has in fact been moving fast toward a German-style training system'.[31]

(*iii*) *Corporatism and corporations*

In spite of its preference for private sector management, Thatcherism has been somewhat schizophrenic towards large firms. As we have seen, individuals, small firms and competition rather than corporatism and cooperation, provided the ingredients of the ideal capitalist world conjured up in the Thatcher government's statements on economic development. Corporatism in particular has been vilified, and collective, institutionalized activity, especially in large firms, plays little part in its vision.

> The ability of the economy to change and adapt was hampered by the combination of corporatism and powerful unions. Corporatism limited competition and the birth of new firms, whilst, at the same time, encouraging protectionism and restrictions designed to help existing firms.[32]

Yet the revolutionary changes in industrial organization pioneered in Japan have depended on close cooperation at all levels – between workers working in project teams on the shopfloor, between departments, within firms, between firms and their suppliers, and between firms and government. The hierarchical command structure characteristic of industrial management in the UK and USA, and the huge disparities in income levels within firms, have been superseded in the Japanese case by an emphasis on collective decision-making, and on a flatter income distribution. The Thatcher emphasis on individualism, and its tacit acceptance of widening income disparities, have thus gone against the grain of developments in industrial organization in other parts of the world. Indeed, even in the US, bringing a new collective ethos to industrial activity was the central recommendation in a recent authoritative study of industrial decline.[33] The main institutional form in most industrial sectors today is the large firm, which is becoming more dominant as a result of the recent wave of takeovers and mergers in Britain and Europe. As Pavitt, Prais and others have demonstrated, it is their failure, particularly in the engineering sector, that lies at the heart of Britain's post-war industrial decline.[34]

The Thatcher instinct was, as always, to trust the market. If industry is sufficiently profitable and is exposed to competition, it will have both the means and the incentive to adapt and prosper. If large firms still fail, then so be it – the sanctity of the market defines the boundaries of responsibility. Likewise, its attitude towards mergers has been to interfere only where issues of competition were at stake – hence the hands-off approach to the El Fayed bid for Harrods, the Ford bid for Jaguar, even the Hanson bid for ICI. Its interference in 1986 in the GEC bid for Plessey was conditioned mainly by MoD fears of the effect on competition for defence contracts. Once they were laid rest by the putative opening of the European armaments market, it gave its blessing to GEC's and Siemens' joint take-over choosing to turn its back on the potentially serious consequences for Britain's ability to sustain its own advanced electronics capabilities.[35]

The problem for Britain is that there are no strong institutional mechanisms for dealing with aberrant large firms. The banks and financial institutions in Britain have traditionally maintained a distance from industrial management; and if a firm does underperform, profitability always being the indicator, the usual solution is to encourage its takeover, or the rationalization of its assets to shed the less successful parts. There is no equivalent to the German Supervisory Board, where a firm's performance is monitored and managerial changes can be forced to bring improvements. The different ways in which the troubles facing Volkswagen and British Leyland were dealt with are, in this respect, revealing. In the former case, the starting assumption was that the company's core activities should remain intact, and should be reformed from the inside. In the latter case, the company has been progressively dismantled through sell-offs and takeovers. Even the jewels in the crown – Jaguar and now Rover – were allowed to fall into foreign hands.

(iv) Nationalism versus internationalism

Finally, there are the contradictions in the international stance. Thatcherism was pre-eminently about *national* revival. Its strong nationalistic streak is as evident in its approach towards innovation as in any other aspect of economic policy. It has applauded, but has been innately suspicious of, the EC's commitment to competition, and has left the Community in no doubt that it disapproves of its softness towards corporatism.

In the field of civilian technology Britain is now very much the follower rather than the leader in Europe, partly through its attachment to *laissez-faire* policies, partly through industrial weakness, and partly through the Conservative instinctive mistrust of things European. The reality is that Britain is now locked into European technological cooperation, and that, for British high-technology firms, as for many others, Europe provides the only means of achieving the requisite scale of innovative activity. Thus Esprit, Race and Eureka in electronics, and Airbus and the European Space Agency in aerospace, are the primary contexts within which British firms, and especially large firms, pursue their technological objectives. The British government has played a minimal – and at times obstructionist – role in these developments. The lead has come instead from industries and governments in France, Germany, Italy and (in electronics) the Netherlands, as well as from the European Commission itself. Britain has ceded its leadership in civil aerospace to France (although Rolls-Royce remains the pre-eminent aero-engine manufacturer); is a reluctant participant in the European space programme; and is not involved in the large semiconductor programmes (Jessi etc.). In electronics generally no British firms have joined with Siemens, Thomson, Philips, Olivetti in trying to mobilize resources to respond to the technological challenge coming from US and Japanese firms. Instead, many British firms have been prey to takeover – or, strictly speaking, acquisition – by their foreign competitors leaving very few British-owned companies operating in front-line technological activities in electronics. Only in defence has Britain taken the lead in creating a more integrated European Market.[36]

The technological legacy of Thatcherism

What conclusions then can be drawn about the technological legacy of Thatcherism? In the first part of this article we highlighted the daring – or the foolhardiness – of Britain liberalizing its markets from a position of industrial weakness. Is it too early to come to conclusions?

Looking back on the last decade, it seems increasingly likely that historians will identify this as the period when Britain disengaged itself from high-technology manufacture, or at least from the *development* of advanced technology. With the possible exceptions of the chemical, pharmaceutical and aerospace industries, Britain under Thatcherism became a technological follower rather than a leader.

This has not, however, been true of the service sector. In financial services, retailing, property, hotels and other areas, Britain has been one of the leading actors and innovators on the international scene, even if the recession has blunted its current impact. There is little doubt that Thatcher policies helped the astonishing (and ultimately unsustainable) growth of the service sector. Its macroeconomic policies, with deregulation in both banking and foreign-exchange controls, encouraged consumption, travel and leisure services, while the deregulation of telecommunications thrust the City of London into the forefront of innovation and experimentation. Nor were the service sectors inhibited by the inherent skill shortages of the British economy. Their relatively monopolistic position – and relative success in a world of relative decline – enabled the City in particular to pre-empt some of the brightest products of the schooling system, and since their skills do not rely upon the acquisition of any systematic knowledge base, to train them adequately on the job.

The problem with this scenario – with the progressive withdrawal from a lead position in manufacturing and increasing specialization in the service sector – has become all too apparent in the early 1990s. It has meant that, as time goes by, most of the capital equipment required has had to be purchased from abroad, or at best from foreign companies located in Britain. As a result the expansion of investment required does not have the multiplier effect on domestic manufacture – with knock-on effects to strengthen Britain's manufacturing base in these sectors. On the contrary, as the chronic trade deficit reveals, the manufacturing sector is now quite unable to stem the flow of imports feeding any expansion of domestic consumption and service activities. These service activities, the bubble having burst, are now generating insufficient foreign income to keep the trade account in balance. Without very substantial foreign investment in manufacturing it is not easy to see how this structural imbalance can be put to rights.

Taking the long view, therefore, it would seem that Britain has not succeeded through the long years of Thatcherism in constructing, or reconstructing, an innovation system which can support technical advance or sustain its position among the international pacesetters. The reasons are as much social and institutional as they are economic. While there has been an attempt to bring new energy to the economy, one is forced to conclude that the *laissez-faire* policies have diminished, rather than strengthened the ability to withstand foreign technological competition. It is, for example, symptomatic that the Waldegrave white paper,[37] having correctly identified the crucial issue as the link between science and technology and economic performance, should, in spite of ample evidence of the failure of the business community to invest adequately in R&D and technological performance, concentrate its attention on measures which enhance the role of the business community in the allocation of funds to basic research. This evasion of the central problem reflects, yet again, the unwillingness of the British political establishment to face up to its own failures. Without a more substantial effort to change Britain's economic priorities and political culture, we shall go on shuffling the same cards – rearranging the institutional deckchairs – while Britain's relative economic decline continues unabated.

NOTES

1 An earlier version of this chapter appeared in *The Political Quarterly*, vol. 62, nos 2 and 3, April and July 1991, as a two-part article under the titles, respectively, of *The Historical Background* and *The Thatcher Legacy*. We are grateful to the editors of the *Political Quarterly* and its publishers, Blackwell, for permission to publish this amended version.

2 B. Jessop, *Thatcherism: The British Road to Post-Fordism?* Papers in Politics and Government, University of Essex, 1989.

3 Since the 1992 election, John Major has appointed William Waldegrave as a Minister of Cabinet Rank (Chancellor of the Duchy of Lancaster) with responsibility for science (as well as consumer affairs), and under his auspices a wide-ranging review of science and technology has been published as the white paper, *Realising Our Potential: A Strategy for Science, Engineering, and Technology* (Cmnd 2250, HMSO, London). Michael Heseltine, as President of the Board of Trade, has also given priority to innovation, albeit with sharply reduced budgets.

4 See D. S. Landes, *The Unbound Prometheus: Technological Change and Industrial Development in Western Europe from 1750 to the Present*, Cambridge University Press, Cambridge, 1969; and E. J. Hobsbawm, *Industry and Empire: An Economic History of Britain since 1750*, Weidenfeld, London, 1968.

5 This thesis is expounded at some length in S. Weiner, *English Culture and the Decline of the Industrial Spirit*, Cambridge University Press, Cambridge, 1981. Reprinted by Penguin, 1985.

6 See the argument in Chapter 2 of M. Sharp and C. Shepherd, *Managing Change in British Industry*, International Labour Office, Geneva, 1987. (No. 5 in their series Employment, Adjustment and Industrialisation.)

7 From G. Ingham, *Capitalism Divided? The City and Industry in British Social Development*, Macmillan, London, 1984.

8 See Chapter 6 in M. Sharp and G. Shepherd, op. cit. note 6, above. See also P. Mottershead's chapter on industrial policy in F. Blackaby (ed.), *British Economic Policy 1960–74*, Cambridge University Press, Cambridge 1978.

9 See David Stout, 'De-industrialisation and industrial policy', Chapter 8, in F. Blackaby (ed.), op. cit. note 8, above.

10 P. D. Henderson, 'Two British errors: their probable size and some possible lessons', *Oxford Economic Papers*, July 1977, pp. 159–205.

11 The phrase was used by Joel Barnett, who had been Chief Secretary to the Treasury during the period of the Social Contract, in the television series 'The writing on the wall', produced by Channel 4 in the early 1980s.

12 R. Layard and S. Nickell, 'The Thatcher miracle', Centre for Economic Policy Research, Discussion Paper No. 315, 1989.

13 *The 1993 UK R&D Scoreboard, Company Reporting Limited*, 68 Dundas Street, Edinburgh EH3 6QZ.

14 G. Ingham, *Capitalism Divided? The City and Industry in British Social Development*, Macmillan, London, 1984, p. 72.

15 'The GEC–Siemens bid for Plessey: the wider European issues', Kevin Morgan, Bernard Harbor, Mike Hobday, Nick von Tunzelmann and William Walker. PICT Working Paper No. 2, SPRU, University of Sussex.

16 See M. Kaldor, M. Sharp and W. Walker, 'Industrial competitiveness and Britain's defence', *Lloyds Bank Review*, October 1986.

17 J. Irvine, B. Martin and P. Isard, *Investing in the future*, Edward Elgar, Aldershot, 1990. Government funding of R&D fell from 0.72 per cent GDP in 1981 to 0.5 per cent GDP in 1990 according to OECD sources. Although a number of other OECD

countries experienced slight falls, this 30 per cent reduction is greater than for any other industrialized country. (Turkey fell faster!)

18 The DTI's R&D scoreboard shows that for the year 1991/2, a recession year, R&D spending increased by 6 per cent whereas for the top 200 international firms it increased by 8 per cent. British firms are content to invest an aggregate 1.55 per cent of sales revenue and 19.7 per cent of profits in R&D whereas the equivalent numbers for the world's largest 200 companies are 4.59 per cent of sales and 94.3 per cent of profits.

19 K. Guy, L. Georghiou, P. Quintas, H. Cameron, M. Hobday and T. Ray, *Evaluation of the Alvey Programme for Advanced Information Technology*, HMSO, London, 1991.

20 Department of Trade and Industry White Paper, *DTI – The Department for Enterprise*, Cmnd 278, HMSO, January 1988.

21 *Realising Our Potential: A Strategy for Science, Engineering and Technology*, Cmnd 2250.

22 The Treasury also insists that the cost of European programmes are borne by their 'sponsor' departments within the overall public expenditure limits set. The result is a total loss of 'additionality' from the EC expenditures which is wholly contrary to the spirit of EC initiatives which conceives them as supplementary to existing national expenditures. It is ironic, given the emphasis by the Treasury on additionality to be achieved on its own spending under such schemes as SFI, that it should so firmly snuff out any possibility of such gain from the European programmes. See House of Commons Select Committee on Education, Science and the Arts, Session 1990–1. First Report *Science Policy and the European Dimension*, HMSO, London, December 1990.

23 Alan Hughes, 'Big business, small business and the enterprise culture', Chapter 13 in J. Michie, *The Economic Legacy 1979–1992*, Academic Press, London, 1992, p. 306.

24 D. Bosworth and R. Wilson, University of Warwick, *The Role of Scientists and Engineers in Technology Change*, ESRC Innovation Update Series, June 1993.

25 John Surrey and Mike Parker, *Unequal Treatment: British Policies for Coal and Nuclear Power, 1979–1992*, December 1992, SPRU, Brighton (SPRU Special Report).

26 H. Ergas, 'The importance of technology policy', in P. Dasgupta and P. Stoneman (eds), *Economic Policy and Technological Performance*, Cambridge University Press, Cambridge, 1987.

27 DES Statistical Bulletin 9/90. Educational anal Economic Activity of Young People Aged 16–18 in England 1975–89. July 1990.

28 'Participation in Education by 16–18 year olds in England, 1979–80 to 1992–3', June 1993.

29 The Training Agency, *Training in Britain: A Study of Funding, Activity and Attitudes, Main Report*, HMSO. London, 1989.

30 The Training Agency, op. cit., note 29, above.

31 Judith Marquand, 'Human resources and human ingenuity', in C. Crouch and D. Marquand (eds), *Ethics and Markets: Co-operation and Competition in Capitalist Economics. Political Quarterly, Special Book Issue*, Blackwell, Oxford, Autumn 1993.

32 DTI, 1988 White Paper, p. 1.

33 M. L. Dertouzous, R. K. Lester and R. M. Solow, *Made in America: Regaining the Competitive Edge*, MIT Press, Cambridge, MA, 1989.

34 P. Patel and K. Pavitt, 'The international distribution of technological activities', *Oxford Review of Economic Policy No. 4*, 1988. S. Prais, 'Qualified manpower in

engineering: Britain and other industrially advanced countries', *National Institute Economic Review*, February 1988, pp. 76–83.

35 Morgan *et al.*, op. cit., note 15, above.

36 W. Walker and P. Gummett, 'Britain and the European armaments market', *International Affairs*, Summer 1989.

37 *Realizing Our Potential*, op. cit., note 3, above.

INDEX

suppliers, relations with 102–3, 186
Sweden: industrial policy in 364, 421;
  investment fund system in 139–40;
  labour market in 303; patents in 413;
  R&D in 412
Switzerland 210, 211, 413

takeovers and mergers 222, 224–37,
  410, 424
taxation: incentive structure and 274,
  298–9; investment promotion and
  139–40; public services and 349–50;
  short-termism and 250;
  takeovers/mergers and 228, 233
teamwork 185–6
Tebbit, Norman 314
technological balance of payments 114
technology: economic growth and 5;
  'gap' hypothesis of 84–7, 145–6;
  globalization and 358–62;
  government policy on 364–5,
  403–26; historical development of
  399–403; innovation and 101–4;
  (measures of 104–14); international
  trade and 40, 69–72, 77–9, 84–7;
  investment and 131; nature of 6
tendering, competitive 420
Thatcher, Margaret 13, 15, 17, 23, 397
total factor productivity 38–9
trade, international 6, 407–8; balance
  of see balance of payments;
  competitiveness of manufacturing
  exports and 57–63; composition of
  51–4; demand in 79, 91–4; EC and
  53–4, 394; economic growth and
  40–9, 51–4; innovation and 69–72,
  78–9, 85, 144–8; (model of 149–53);
  inter-industry variation in 81–4;
  manufacturing sector 40–1, 51–2,
  57–73, 76–95, 356, 376, 378–80,
  384–5; performance in 76–95, 356;
  service sector 40–1, 53, 352, 356–7,
  384
Trade and Industry, Department of,
  (DTI) 11, 22, 398, 418, 419
trade unions: pay settlements and 16,
  302, 405–6; regulation of 13, 274
Trades Union Congress (TUC):
  economic policies and 13, 16, 18;
  Labour Party and 11, 16, 18; NEDC
  and 14
training see education and training

Training Commission 322–3
Training and Enterprise Councils (TECs)
  22, 323, 324–30, 331, 335, 423
transaction costs 195
transfer of technology 103
transport 3, 355
travel 357
Treasury 1
tripartism (corporatism) 1, 2, 23, 423–4

unemployment: 138, 278–9, 282–3;
  benefit system and 274; inflation and
  269–71; long-term 293; market
  clearing theory and 268–9; wages and
  268–9, 272, 273, 291–2
unions see trade unions
United States of America: capacity
  utilization index in 121, 122;
  corporate capital structure in 194,
  202–7; corporate control in 219,
  253–4; corporate takeovers/mergers
  in 229–31; education and training in
  122–4, 165; financial sector in 208,
  211; foreign investment by 359–60,
  361; GDP levels in, 32, 33, 34;
  growth accounting exercise on 37–8;
  industrial policy in 421; inflation in
  280; interest rates in 180;
  international trade and 48; (high-tech
  share of 71–2); investment in 118,
  129, 137, 181; labour costs in 58;
  labour market in 276–8;
  manufacturing sector in 379; patents
  in 113; profits in 177; R&D in
  106–8, 111–12, 146, 359, 412;
  return on capital in 178; service sector
  in 348, 354; technology in 114, 359;
  unemployment in 279; wage
  bargaining in 303
universities 123–4, 165

vocational training see education and
  training
voluntarism 21, 24, 308, 309–10

wages 128; bargaining for 276, 282,
  294; (decentralization of 292, 301–
  4); costs of 4, 58–63, 87, 281–2,
  288–91; distributional issues and
  298–301; inflation and 281, 288–98;
  minimum 274, 275; policies on
  15–16, 294, 405; productivity and

438